PRIVILEGE AND PROFIT

A Business Family in Eighteenth-Century France

PRIVILEGE
AND PROFIT

A Business Family in
Eighteenth-Century France

P. W. BAMFORD

UNIVERSITY OF PENNSYLVANIA PRESS

Philadelphia

To William S. Haas and Robert Gale Woolbert

FRONTISPIECE: Portrait of Pierre Babaud de la Chaussade. From a portrait hanging in the Administrative Offices of the Forges de Guérigny, published in A. Massé, *Monographies nivernaises: Canton de Pougues* (Nevers, 1912).

Library of Congress Cataloging in Publication Data

Bamford, Paul W. (Paul Walden), 1921–
  Privilege and profit.

  Bibliography: p.
  Includes index.
  1. Iron industry and trade—France—History—18th century. 2. Industrialists—France—Biography.
3. Babaud de La Chaussade, Pierre, 1702–1792. I. Title.
HD9522.5.B36   1988   338.7'6691'0944   88-26127
ISBN 0-8122-8135-7

Contents

Preface

This book was begun as a short study of Pierre Babaud de la Chaussade, merchant-ironmaster, purveyor of timber, anchors, and irons to the navy of France in the eighteenth century. Chaussade the businessman remains the focus of the book. But the effort to understand his affairs obliges us to enlarge the focus. The sources that survive allow us to give attention to persons associated with him and to see their collaboration as a long-term family business venture and a highly privileged enterprise. Like his father and elder brother, Chaussade was a lifelong timber merchant. Chapters 1 to 3 of the book therefore deal with phases of the family's contracts, its privileges, and its notable financial successes in the timber business in the period from 1720 to c. 1740. Those were vital decades of family history, an important "capital accumulation" phase, and an apprenticeship of decisive importance for the young Pierre Babaud de la Chaussade. They enable us to understand Chaussade's intricate involvement in a series of partnerships with his elder brother, Jean Babaud; his father-in-law, Jacques Masson; his sister-in-law, Marie Boesnier (Babaud-Masson); and a long succession of surrogates.

Chaussade's own historical distinction as a businessman derives principally from his management of forges and his manufacture of anchors, irons, and steel for the French navy and colonies. But as an examination of the interrelated phases of his business career reveals, his importance rests on family foundations: a long family apprenticeship and a considerable measure of family capital. Family members had interests in forest exploitation and in leasing and operating forges at least as early as the 1720s, and from the 1730s onward Chaussade shared in an apparent series of family decisions to commit a large proportion of additional funds to metallurgical enterprises, including the purchase of the anchor forges at Cosne. That action showed the Babauds to be in accord with their partner Jacques Masson, who had been buying seigneuries and other forge-related real estate, especially in the Nivernais, for decades, obviously persuaded that those were promising investments.

Ultimately Chaussade was the family member who benefited most from that long preparation. It was he who contributed most to the development of the metallurgical business that other family members initiated. He was the one who wrestled with the varied and intricate problems of iron and steel production, marketing, transport, and the management of labor. He and Marie Babaud-Masson both endured from the early 1740s onward the severe fluctuations in the navy's demand for metal products. But after Marie withdrew from the business, he alone undertook to adapt the family's methods to meet the major problems that characterized the business of selling anchors and irons to the navy. He was the one who undertook the concurrent expansion and diversification of the business, who sought to develop new commercial and colonial markets to offset the effects of the navy's erratic demand. And it was he who was nearly ruined by the navy's practice, consequent on the shortage of funds, of offering contractors the choice between accepting promises of partial payment in the form of annuities paying very low interest over a long span of years, or receiving no payment at all.

Chapters 4 through 8 deal with these matters. They reveal much about the relationship of government to the business milieu in eighteenth-century France. Government strongly supported some privileged businesses, including these family enterprises. It even helped to finance private business enterprises and could be moved to confer a wide range of special privileges on individual entrepreneurs or firms. But the government also kept in force a morass of obsolete taxes and controls and created new ones, including impediments to transport that not only restricted but in many cases throttled the development of large-scale commerce. Any industrial enterprise designed to produce for commercial markets located at a considerable distance from production sites was destined, in eighteenth-century France, to encounter severe economic and bureaucratic impediments to the transit of merchandise. This book recounts Chaussade's struggle with these problems, describing his entry into the commercial-colonial irons market on a large scale and his fight to survive and prosper in the French commercial manufacturing milieu. Our evidence shows that he may have been a major supplier of iron and steel to certain markets in central France in relatively close proximity to his manufactures in the Nivernais, such as Paris (accessible via the canal of Briare); but he lost the struggle to become a major seller of French-produced iron and steel in other French commercial markets, notably the potentially very large maritime market at the Atlantic-Biscay ports. Even his alternative efforts to export to French colonies faded with the approach of the American War (Chapter 8).

Notwithstanding his commercial failures, Chaussade remained active as a leading government contractor in the iron and steel industry in France. In the last two decades of his business career, he was not only a manufacturer but also a merchant-middleman, subcontracting a large amount of work to other French manufacturers. In the seventies he himself imported large quantities of iron and steel from abroad. Furthermore, he supplied a wide range of other materiel to the state, including vast quantities of timber for its arsenals. He must at that time have been the navy's largest, as well as its most senior, contractor. He was trusted, a close associate of Minister of Marine Sartine in the period of the American War (1776–1781). He was recognized as an able and wealthy merchant-manufacturer, a distinguished landed nobleman-industrialist described by the minister of marine as "unique in the realm" (Chapter 9). Chaussade sold his forges to the king and "retired" in 1781, and in the years that followed used his wealth, status, and leisure to continue to promote the family's aristocratic connections and prestige. He arranged suitable marriages and provided rich dowries for his granddaughters by his first marriage; his only son to reach adulthood died before Chaussade's retirement, and the daughters and granddaughters were thus the hope of the family. In "retirement" he pursued the long-standing family interest in the purchase and management of land, especially seigneurial properties. His enthusiasm and intellectual energies, surpassing his physical limitations as a chairbound octogenarian, even led him to take advantage of some prime investment opportunities occasioned by the French Revolution. He was busy purchasing confiscated church properties on the very eve of his death in 1792 (Chapter 10).

The complex affairs of Chaussade and his associates generated abundant records. Both business and personal affairs left nests of notarial minutes and files, and the family's government contracts generated long runs of correspondence and related series of papers that are scattered in the files of in-letter and out-letter series of public archives over a timespan of almost sixty years. There are no account books, and no private (family) records have been available, but the papers that were accessible have helped to fill that gap.

In preparing this study, I have incurred a host of obligations to archivists and *bibliothécaires,* members of that remarkable guild that makes a profession of helping, among other things, the conduct of research. Many must go unnamed, though their help and counsel were often important.

Some archivists gave me continual help over many years, notably the late Olivier de Prat, Georges Bourgin, and Meurgy de Tupigny; during more than a quarter of a century, Thérèse La Tour and Etienne Taillemite helped on this and other projects. Professor and Madame Bertrand Gille (archivists both) gave encouragement at an early stage of the work, allowing me to make notes on M. Gille's student *inventaire* of the archives of Guérigny and on a paper he wrote on the Forges de la Chaussade in his student days at the Ecole des Chartes; the archive he inventoried is now incorporated in the holdings of the Archives Départementales de la Nièvre at Nevers. Michel Antoine in person and Jean Colnat in person and in correspondence helped with references, counsel, and interpretations of their own writings (published and unpublished) on Lorraine, eastern France, and other subjects. Mirelle Forget (Toulon), Geneviève Beauchesne (Lorient and Rochefort), and Marie Descubes of the latter port all helped on this and other projects in extraordinary ways: all of them typed and sent extracts or entire texts of selected documents—heroic effort in pre–Xerox days! After her "retirement," Mlle. Beauchesne graciously set aside her own research work while I was at Lorient and for several days worked with me sifting papers in the Lorient port archive and library.

In the Archives Départementales de la Nièvre, at an early stage of the work, Bernard de Gaulejac gave immense encouragement and help, loading my table in the (then) crowded old archive with dossiers, bundles, and boxes of documents. Years afterward his successor, Mlle. Chabrolin, was also helpful, even taking the trouble to organize for me a tour, guided by regional experts, to nearby Guérigny, the hub of Chaussade's local holdings. The librarian at the Bibliothèque Municipal at Nantes, archivists at the Archives Départementales (Loire-atlantique), and two bibliothécaires at Cosne—first the late Mme. Yon d'Alligny, then Mlle. M. Guibal, her successor, all helped forward the work. At many other archives and libraries, documents were made available by *déplacement;* at port archives and at the Archives Nationales with its *Minuterie centrale,* and at the Bibliothèque Nationale in Paris, the services left little to be desired. I want to express appreciation for the encouragement and help of the late Professor André Reussner of the *Ecole de Guerre Navale* and that of a succession of the *chefs* and other helpful persons in the *Service historique de la Marine Nationale* of France for assistance in the use of the navy's archives and libraries, in Paris and at the ports. In addition, Ulane Bonnel, Guy Thuillier, Gérard Martin, Jean Babaud, "Louis Aurenche", M. et Mme. de la Lezardière, and a long-time personal friend Marcel Bernard, all helped to lighten, guide, or forward the work in much greater measure I suspect than they realized.

In this country many colleagues and friends have helped over a long period of years. Initially Shepard B. Clough interested the writer in economic and business history; he in many ways, and T. S. Ashton during a summer visiting professorship at Columbia University, both watered the seeds of this Chaussade project. Garrett Mattingly, Leo Gershoy, and Beatrice Hyslop all helped with introductions to many scholars in France. Later, at Ohio State University, colleagues Walter Dorn, Warner Woodring, Robert Bremner, Paul Varg, Morton Borden, and over in Economics Dave Harrison and Bob Gallman, gave support and counsel not forgotten; OSU awarded the Howald Faculty Fellowship to support research on the project, and that same year the Research Center in Entrepreneurial History at Harvard also gave financial aid at the behest of Arthur H. Cole whose enthusiasm produced a subsequent published commentary on the project. Over the years many friends have helped in a variety of ways, among them R. G. Albion, John F. Bosher, Herman Freudenberger, John R. Harris, R. R. Palmer, Harold Parker, Fritz Redlich, Herbert H. Rowen, Joseph Shulim, Warren C. Scoville, Frank Spooner, Frank Trout, A. M. Wilson, and David Young. At the University of Minnesota colleagues Theodore Blegen, John Bowditch, Louis Degryse, Phil Jordan, Edwin Layton, Armand Renaud, Jacob Schmookler, D. H. Willson, and graduate students Robert Carey Adams, Glenn J. Ames, Neil Betten, Janis Cers, Joseph Fisher, Thadd Hall, and Jonathan Webster helped in a variety of ways. At a late stage of the work Louis Degryse, Harold Parker and Martha Vogeler gave the entire manuscript close readings, and helped make improvements.

Since 1973 financial assistance for the enterprise has been granted by the College of Liberal Arts and Graduate School of the University of Minnesota in the form of several quarter and sabbatical leaves, and several travel grants; the research was also assisted by fellowship grants from the American Council of Learned Societies and the Bush Foundation. The writer wants to express sincere appreciation for all their assistance.

Most of all of course I am beholden to my dear wife who helped continually, sanctioned all the research travels, persisted in her support, and made it possible to bring this "Chaussade enterprise" to publication.

PWB

Introduction: State and Family

State Policy and Privileges

Many historical circumstances deterred economic development and created problems for business in France in the old regime.[1] This introduction will describe some of these inhibiting conditions and effects. A second section will consider the careers and mentality of a family of entrepreneurs who responded to those conditions by waging systematic campaigns for privilege, defined as "the granting of exclusive rights or immunities to selected individuals or groups." Their relations with the state, and the interplay of their own and other business interests, underscore the importance of privilege to the success or failure of a firm. Furthermore, their enterprises reveal some significant strengths and weaknesses of industrial and commercial development in early modern France.

One broadly inhibitive factor for the French economy of the old regime was the foreign policy of the state. At least until the American Revolution, it was dominated by the territorial designs and dynastic aims of the monarchs and their ministers. Those aims were essentially political, not economic. State activity in foreign affairs was subordinated to the political objectives of the Bourbon dynasty on the continent of Europe. Louis XIV clearly indicated the pre-eminence of such political aims in his own thinking when he remarked in 1668 that "if the English . . . would be content to be the greatest merchants in Europe, and allow me, for my share, all I can conquer in a just war, nothing would be as convenient as for us to cooperate." Foreign economic policy, when it could be said to have existed at all, was usually employed simply as a political or dynastic tool. Measures in support of French commerce and shipping, such as Colbert's levies on foreign shipping in French ports (*droit de frêt*), were readily compromised by exemptions granted to individual powers in the interest of political gains. Major treaties of the period from 1660 to 1783 bear witness to French willingness to sacrifice economic interests at the peace table in favor of dynastic or territorial advantages on the continent of Europe.

A fundamental aim of every state is to ensure its own survival as a political entity, and circumstances often dictate the primacy of political objectives. But as the most powerful state in Europe after 1648, France faced no serious external threat to its security. Hence its pursuit of political objectives in the period can be considered simply the choice of French monarchs and their ministers. French business firms had to contend with political governors who voluntarily sacrificed the welfare of the business community to other purposes in foreign affairs. This orientation contrasted markedly with the economic and imperial objectives dominating the actions of the English and Dutch.

A second condition affecting French business enterprise and economic development was the reliance on war as the medium of foreign policy. The frequency of international struggle in the period has moved some historians to refer to the period as the Second Hundred Years War. Between 1635 and 1815 France was at war roughly three-fifths of the time. Those struggles, with the expenditures that they involved, were probably more burdensome to France than to any one of its enemies. This is not to say that France spent a larger proportion of national income in those wars than did its enemies. But a comparison of French and, for example, English financial administration would show that Bourbon France was less capable of meeting those expenditures, in addition to other government disbursements, and of liquidating the ensuing debts, because the French economy was burdened to a much greater extent with unreformed and probably unreformable privilege and fiscal anarchy.

Furthermore, French war efforts were primarily military in character, with sea action distinctly secondary and almost invariably unsuccessful. Hence the maritime branch of French economic life, though it largely supported the sea wars, languished with discontinuous opportunity and suffered heavily time after time without receiving compensatory benefits. Britain's maritime economy, on the contrary, prospered even in wartime in trade, in foreign markets, and in colonial enterprise beneath the cloak of British naval supremacy. It can be added that France's primary tool of war—the army—conferred no economic advantages comparable to those conferred on England by the British navy. Indeed, though the age is not usually supposed to have suffered the burdens of "total war," there were times when French (and foreign) armies seriously interrupted normal economic life or crushed by their presence and operations economic activity in frontier provinces and in neighboring cities and states.

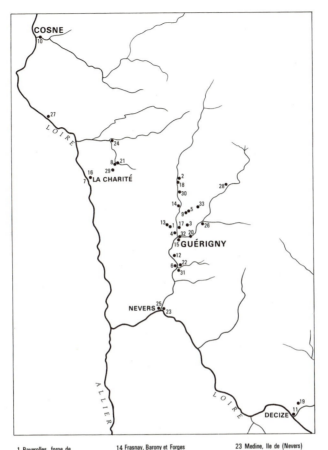

1 Baverolles, forge de
2 Beaumont la Ferriere
  Beauregard (see La Vache)
3 Biez, Fief de
4 Bizy, Chateau, Haut fourneau
  et forges de
  Blaterie, Domaines de (see La Vache)
5 Chamilly
6 Chantemerle, Fourneau, forges
7 Charité (see La Charité)
  Chatre, domaine (see La Chatre)
8 Clavières, Forges de (see La Charité)
9 Colombiers, Chateau de
10 Cosne, Forges et fineries
11 Decize De Dampierre, forge de
  (see La Charité)
12 Demeurs, Forges de
13 Dinon, Forges de (Bizy)

14 Frasnay, Barony et Forges
  Freliniere, Forge de (see Guérigny)
  Gondelins (see Guérigny)
  Grandemaison, Forge de
  (see La Vache and Ravaux)
  Greux (see Demeurs)
  Grossoeuvre (see La Vache)
15 Guérigny, Chateau, Forges et Village
16 La Charité, Prieure de
17 La Chatre, Domaine de
18 La Douée (Doue) Fourneau et forges de
19 La Machine, Mines de charbon de terre
20 La Poelonnerie
  Marteauneuf, Beauregard
  (see Ravaux/Raveau)
21 La Vache, w/ domaines de Blaterie,
22 Le Greux (Demeurs)
  Machine (see La Machine)
  Marcy (see Poiseaux)
  Marteauneuf (see La Vache)

23 Medine, Ile de (Nevers)
  Miquard Forge de
  (see La Charité)
  Mouchy (see La Vache)
24 Narcy
25 Nevers
  Ouvrault (see Demeurs)
  Poelonnerie
  (see La Poelonnerie)
26 Poiseaux
27 Pouilly
28 Premery
29 Raveau/Ravaux Richerand
  (see Demeurs)
30 Saint Aubin
31 Urzy-Demeurs
  Sauvage, Haut Fourneau
  (see Saint-Aubin)
  Toreau (see La Vache)
32 Villemenant-Marcy,
  Barony with chateau and forges
33 Vingeux, Etang and Forge
  (see Frasnay)

Map of Guérigny–Cosne region

In summary, it can be said that the subordination of economic interests to the achievement of political aims in foreign affairs, and the frequency and peculiarly burdensome character of French participation in the wars of the period, exercised a generally depressing effect on French economic life and business enterprise.

In the conduct of internal economic affairs, the Bourbon state was motivated by similarly dynastic aims, with similar effects on business conditions. The mercantilism that Schmoller described as a system of state-making found its fullest European expression in Colbert's program of economic development, a program intended primarily to increase the power and glory of the Bourbon monarchy. In the early years of Colbert's administration, a fairly clear conception of the interdependence of dynastic interests and long-term economic development influenced state action in economic matters. By the 1680s, however, Louis XIV's aggressive preoccupations had reduced the Colbert program to a series of expedients, the essential purpose of which was economic exploitation—the raising of revenue for dynastic warfare. In the last decades of the Great Reign, French businessmen felt the impact of multiplied royal devices—monopolies, exclusive privileges, new taxes, and sales of offices on an unprecedented scale—intended to steer economic energies into fields of enterprise of short-term utility, and to channel wealth into the coffers of the king. Mercantilist encouragements to business were neglected; the regulatory features of state policy exacted the last sou in taxes to support royal policies that were damaging and exhausting many branches of trade and industry. The unresponsiveness of the Grand Monarch to economic interests was nowhere more forcefully demonstrated than in religious policy. Culminating in the notorious Revocation of 1685, that policy was unshaken by the exodus of population, technical skills, and business capital that its demand for religious conformity entrained.

These features of seventeenth-century policy remained in force, with further discouragements, down to the end of the old regime. Diplomacy remained almost entirely political in its motives and objectives. Ministers of finance faced ever greater financial pressure. They were continually forced to compromise schemes of long-term economic development by accepting expedients to produce immediate funds. Indeed, the institutional maladies usually associated with the old Bourbon monarchy—laxity of executive controls, incompetence and venality of officials, and extremes of financial confusion and pressure—were peculiarly characteristic of their administrations. Confusion and contradictions in economic policy destroyed the continuity of state action in economic affairs. If luxury industries were encouraged, basic industries—woolen textiles, tanning, soap making, lumbering, shipbuilding and shipping, iron—were

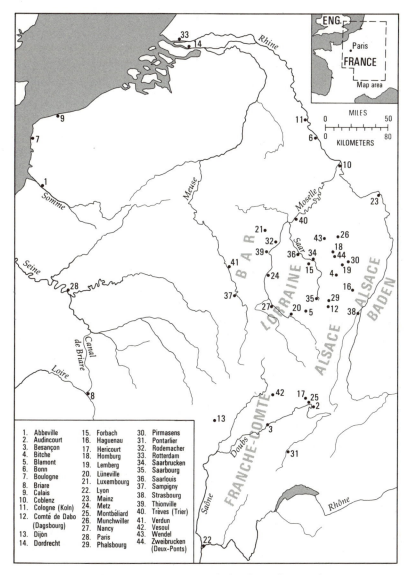

1.	Abbeville	15.	Forbach	30.	Pirmasens
2.	Audincourt	16.	Haguenau	31.	Pontarlier
3.	Besançon	17.	Hericourt	32.	Rodemacher
4.	Bitche	18.	Homburg	33.	Rotterdam
5.	Blamont	19.	Lemberg	34.	Saarbrucken
6.	Bonn	20.	Lüneville	35.	Saarbourg
7.	Boulogne	21.	Luxembourg	36.	Saarlouis
8.	Briare	22.	Lyon	37.	Sampigny
9.	Calais	23.	Mainz	38.	Strasbourg
10.	Coblenz	24.	Metz	39.	Thionville
11.	Cologne (Koln)	25.	Montbéliard	40.	Trèves (Trier)
12.	Comté de Dabo	26.	Munchwiller	41.	Verdun
	(Dagsbourg)	27.	Nancy	42.	Vesoul
13.	Dijòn	28.	Paris	43.	Wendel
14.	Dordrecht	29.	Phalsbourg	44.	Zweibrucken
					(Deux-Ponts)

Lorraine, Alsace and Franche-Comté-Montbéliard. Timber Exploitation Sites and River Shipment Routes.

laden with regulations, inspections, taxes, and fines. The multiplication of laws and taxes brought "all the horrors which can make a profession disgusting, cause work to be hated, and stifle industry." Immoderate taxes, badly conceived, cost more to collect than they returned to the treasury. Confiscatory taxation damaged many industries and destroyed others. Magistrates of the Parlement of Provence had reason to mourn in the 1760s that "if anyone today should make a record of all the national manufacturers which have been destroyed within the past hundred years, he would be terrified by the prodigious number of corpses produced by the blows of finance."[2]

Such conditions could by themselves have given rise to widespread circumspection and caution in the conduct of businessmen. But at least one other phase of government action reinforced the tendencies toward business conservatism: the system of privilege.

Privilege was, of course, peculiar neither to France nor to the eighteenth century, yet it can be contended that the French businessman then, and perhaps since, has faced it in peculiarly entrenched and damaging forms.

In the old regime businessmen had to contend, first, with a privileged class of nobility; second, with individuals or groups who had obtained, one way or another, the right to perform acts forbidden to others or the release from certain obligations. The varied and extensive rights and prerogatives of these two groups included a complex range of advantages in social, legal, governmental, and economic affairs. Those who possessed such privileges were able to engage in business enterprise under especially favorable terms that could seriously damage the interests of the business community at large.[3]

It must be emphasized that privilege is not necessarily an evil in itself. The awarding of certain types of favors and advantages to a limited number of people may be a practical way of advancing economic development and the welfare of the general population. But such privileges can become damaging when granted too frequently and without due regard for national economic interests, or when retained long after the disappearance of the conditions that called them forth. And these were precisely the circumstances in which privilege operated in eighteenth-century France. There was a numerous, long-established, and often self-serving nobility, and a very large number of individuals and groups who had obtained and sought to preserve economic privilege by legal and extralegal means. Some groups or families held for decades, or even for centuries, exclusive rights that were a drain on the society's economic energies and an obstacle to successful business enterprise. Clearly, privileges might encourage those who possessed them, but they also discouraged many who did not. Possessors of privilege could excel in business competition; indeed, they could forestall or even destroy competition. Skill and application, or individual efficiency and merit, on the part of unprivileged businessmen could seldom match the economic advantages and power that privilege conferred. The French business community at large, including certain vested corporate interests, bitterly criticized and sought to limit grants of privilege by the state in the eighteenth century, and such criticism did reduce the number of such grants. Yet the privileged nobility became ever more numerous and influential in France during the last century of the old regime.

Privilege reinforced the tendencies toward business conservatism created by other political, social, and economic conditions. The French businessman knew that the monarchy would not protect his interests consistently; he had reason to fear the irresponsibility, fiscal exactions, and corruption of officialdom. In the routine of their daily affairs, businesspeople saw and suffered from the artificial preferments that others more influential than they enjoyed at the hands of the state. The response to these circumstances could take any one of several forms, depending on the individual businessman's capacities and state of mind. Owners of the small firm with limited resources, fearful of taxation and concerned for their survival, were apt to make security and the continuation of routine their first concerns. An entrepreneur of means could become a passive investor. He might choose to invest in an office, retire from active business, and enjoy the immunities, dignities, and ease that the sinecure conferred. Such inclinations were certainly common in the French business community. But France had its venturesome entrepreneurs as well. Some were willing to accept the uncertainties and risks of expansion in their own and new fields of endeavor by traditional or novel means. Individuals of such stamp might also buy an office in the conviction that the privileges of office minimized some of the risks of doing business, and with the knowledge that the dignities of a high office could be an entrée to fruitful associations and opportunities for profit higher up on the socioeconomic scale. The social status that a purchased office conferred was highly important, and even essential for success, in some fields of enterprise in the old regime.

These features of French business life had contradictory effects. They inhibited and they encouraged business enterprise. But conservatism and caution were probably the more common reactions, especially on the part of small business owners, who were apt to become bitter, dissatisfied, and desirous of reform at the expense of the privileged. On the other hand, the very existence of privilege, which was accessible to the well-to-do of the Third Estate under certain circumstances, encouraged the more resolute to strike out and seek privileged status for themselves.

One avenue that such business firms might follow was government contracting. In associating themselves with the state in a service capacity, they could avoid some of the uncertainties encountered in commerce and industry. State contracts afforded not only privileges, but also a partial cushion against government graft and corruption—and at times opportunities for them. It is with representatives of this group—resolute seekers after preferment and privilege through government contracts—that this book is concerned. As will be seen, this family became the beneficiary of very significant privileges; family members spent a good part of their business and professional lives and fortunes, and an immense amount of their business imagination, talent, and energy, in seeking ever greater privileges. Yet they never reached the top of the ladder of preferment, for their progress was blocked by the privileges of others.

Family Purposes and Profits

What qualities of the businessmen and the single businesswoman who were the leaders of this family—their ages, religion, social condition, property holdings, and government connections—help to explain their status, their privileges, and the character and success of their business operations?

The eldest member of the group was probably Jacques Masson of Geneva. Near him in age were the half-brothers Jacques Boesnier-Duportal of Saumur and Daniel Duportal of Rotterdam. Jean Babaud of Bellac, a fourth member of the group, may have been a few years younger; he brought his still younger brother, Pierre Babaud (de la Chaussade), into the business, at first as a junior partner. As *fournisseurs* of timber for the navy, the Babauds were following the vocation of their father, Pierre Babaud de Beaupré. Jean Babaud's young widow, Marie (*née* Boesnier), played a significant, albeit carefully supervised, role in the business after the successive deaths of her husbands.

All these individuals descended from Protestant ancestors who had experienced the repressive religious policies of Louis XIV. Each generation and branch of these families made its own decision in matters of religion. Family groups did not necessarily act with unanimity, and of course individuals behaved differently in the face of the prevailing religious repression, by which they were all affected in varying degree. Some, like the Babauds of Bellac, were apparently moved to abandon their traditional beliefs and become converts to the orthodox Catholic faith. We cannot be certain whether they were classifiable, using the terminology of the time, as "old" or "new" Catholics: that is, whether they converted before or after 1685. Others, such as the Boesnier-Duportals, were divided and apparently became scattered: the elder brother, Jacques Boesnier-Duportal,

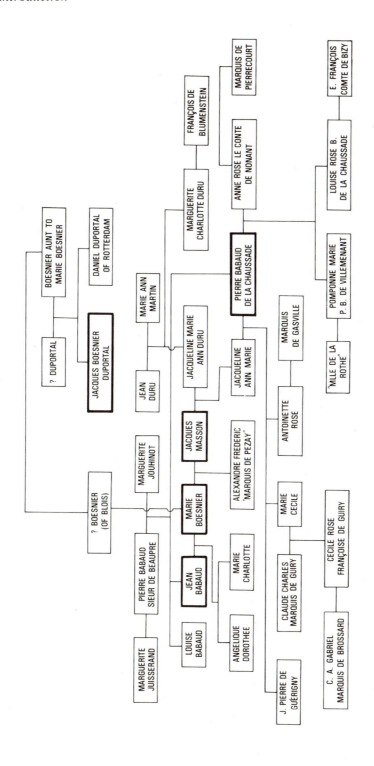

became a "new Catholic"; his younger brother, Daniel, settled in Rotterdam, where he may have remained an adherent of Protestantism or become a Catholic as well. Jacques Masson's Protestant ancestors also chose to emigrate from France, to Geneva; but Masson himself apparently decided to return to France, abandon the Protestant faith, and accept the prescribed Catholicism. He and the Boesniers were, according to Herbert Lüthy, new Catholics.[4] All these entrepreneurs, in any case, were ex-Protestants.

These people, and many of their ancestors, must have asked themselves how they could hope to do business, much less prosper, if they adhered to the Protestant faith in the realm of Louis XIV. Catholic aristocrats of robe and sword were the real governors of France. Its king was advised, and sometimes led, by the members of the First and Second Estates, who formed a powerful bureaucracy and a highly privileged Catholic aristocracy, the *de facto* fount of law and privilege in the state.

The government of France expected subjects of the king to accept the religion of the king, a prerequisite of the most elementary kind for the acquisition of privilege. Some privileges were granted by the authorities to reward persons who were or who became converts to Catholicism. Conversely, subjects who did not accept the *Religion Catholique, Apostolique et Romain* were subject to extreme disabilities. For example, the civil registers of the state were maintained by Catholic clergy. Hence all marriages, births, and deaths in France required the services of a priest and the sanction of the Catholic Church to be recognized as legal—for Protestants an obstacle with far-reaching consequences. Lüthy refers to that problem in asserting that "from 1685 to 1787 French Protestants lived . . . in illegality."[5]

Conversion to Catholicism solved these problems. It conferred membership in the majority, eliminated "outsider" status, and enabled the ambitious to rise socially or to enter government service. Thus, for example, the best-known entrepreneur of this family, Pierre Babaud de la Chaussade, had to present documents certifying his Catholicity in order to purchase the office of *secrétaire du roi* that conferred his noble status.

But conversion apparently did not annihilate Protestant connections. The act did, of course, separate the convert from overtly obstinate "heretics," but it effectively joined him or her to a very large, far-flung, and disparate society of ex-Protestants, "new Catholics," nominal Catholics, and others in whose eyes the false or ambiguous situation of many members of the group tended "to efface confessional frontiers" (to use Lüthy's phrase), and even made for religious indifference within the fraternity.[6] The timing or circumstances of conversion made little difference. Parents, grandparents, or even more distant relatives may have made the formal conversion choice, in obedience to the wishes of the king, or in response to threats of penalties or force, or both. Ambiguities in convert or ex-Protestant status cloaked or disguised, but did not remove, the fraternal bonds among ancestral Protestants. Those bonds were especially important in international business. Both Protestants and ex-Protestants "belonged" by reason of membership in a family, to a group, or as Lüthy said to a network (*reseau*) of Protestant connections.[7] The act of becoming a convert to Catholicism did not put such connections beyond reach regardless of the time or circumstances attending the establishment of membership in the prescribed Catholic Church. Business opportunities afforded by association with Protestant or other ex-Protestant business groups, inside or outside France, could still accrue to the convert. Ex-Protestants, such as the members of the Bellac branch of the Babaud clan clearly benefited from their bi-partisan status. Although their legal status as Catholics was indispensable in their business with state agencies, it was doubtless useful to have at least limited acceptance in the Protestant network as well.

Beyond Catholicity, noble status itself probably contributed most to the capacity of a commoner and ex-Protestant, or anyone else, to acquire privileges. Thus it was important that every major partner in the family business was ennobled: Masson by the duke of Lorraine in 1736; the Babaud brothers by purchase; and Marie Boesnier[-Babaud-Masson] through her marriages. The status conferred privileges and, as a concommitant, facilitated and reinforced sociopolitical contacts with the governing elite in France that had value far beyond the well-known tax advantages of *noblesse*. Chaussade lived long enough to cultivate more fully than others in the family the potentialities of nobility. Ultimately he purchased such status for his son and, using dowries, arranged marriages for his daughters with well-established members of the nobility, thereby effectively establishing his own family status. Significantly, at the wedding of Chaussade's daughter Marie Cécile (1756) to the Chevalier Marquis de Guiry, the guest list included no fewer than three of the king's ministers of state: D'Argenson (war), Machault (marine), and Rouillé (formerly marine and future secretary of state for foreign affairs). Clearly, as early as 1756, Pierre Babaud de la Chaussade could be said to have arrived.

Another road to status and privilege was the purchase of landed property. The business family studied here made a practice of purchasing properties that were capable of conferring seigneurial powers. Such properties had both honorific and economic usefulness. The military aspects of feudalism had, of course, passed away by the eighteenth century, but seigneurial properties could link the owner as a vassal, with welcome ties and nominal obligations, to some of the most distinguished persons in the region where the seigneury lay. Ownership of a seigneury could confer powers and prerogatives, and on some properties a high degree of judicial authority, even some police powers, over the populace of the estate. In short, our ex-Protestant noble entrepreneurs enjoyed privileges, regional recognition, the distinction of being seigneurial lords; such status and connections could provide influence with royal intendants (principal regional representatives of the crown), and much *de facto* power over the local populace, in the province where their estates and dependent enterprises lay.

Armed with Catholicism, noble status, and their seigneurial estates, these businessmen pursued still another source of privilege: they systematically sought contracts to supply merchandise to the armed forces of the king. They became defense contractors. Among government contractors there was a hierarchy, some being more privileged or advantaged than others because they rendered services deemed more important to the government; some were more experienced, reliable, better-known, and better-connected than others. Defense contractors ranked especially high. Like officers in the armed forces, contractors rendered highly valued services to the crown, albeit with less attendant personal risk and less honor and *gloire*. There could be rich remuneration for the contractor, yet he ran a serious economic risk because of the extreme fluctuations in the armed forces' needs for supplies and the possibility of long delays before payment. Hence the contractor faced the danger of being overwhelmed by creditors. These risks might be seen as justifying the defense contractors' status in the realms of commerce and industry. Only financiers ranked above them in opportunities for privilege and profit.

All this authority, prestige, and privilege was enhanced considerably for our business people by the fact that the great forge they came to own and operate at Cosne was (at their behest) dignified by the ministry of marine as the premier producer of large anchors for the royal navy. Accordingly, that particular industrial establishment was given the privilege and title of Forge Royale. That status identified the Forge, and by association its dependencies and owner-operators, as importantly connected to the service of the king; and when the partners built another great forge at Cosne, it and the anchors it produced were similarly privileged, as were the great forges that they also owned or later built at Guérigny and Villemenant. All of them, producing great anchors for the royal navy, were considered collectively to be the Forges Royales.

The members of this family channeled much of their business energy and entrepreneurial talent, and not a little of their credit and financial capital, into efforts to acquire privilege. A considerable part of this study is concerned with identifying and analyzing these efforts. Though deriving from Protestant families with modest resources, they managed to transform themselves into privileged Catholic nobility, proprietors of huge seigneurial estates with vast dependent woodlands and forests. Chaussade, the leader of the family for more than half a century, became a highly privileged supplier of timber and masts, anchors, irons, and steel for the navy, and owner-operator of a firm that was certainly one of the largest business conglomerates in France. The family, and after their pattern Chaussade, conducted business in the knowledge that the acquisition of privileges was absolutely essential to success. But Chaussade was to learn that even a high degree of privilege and status did not guarantee the success of large-scale manufacturing enterprises in eighteenth-century France.

I. A Family in the Timber Business

CHAPTER 1.

A Family of Entrepreneurs: Jacques Masson, the Babauds, Marie Boesnier, and Duportal of Saumur

Jacques Masson

The Protestant parents of Jacques Masson were living in Geneva when Jacques was born, perhaps in 1693. Masson belonged to the group known as "new Catholics."[1] He was drawn to France during the War of the Spanish Succession (1701–1713), and was at Lunéville in Lorraine at the end of the war, serving as agent of the banker and government contractor Antoine Paris. They were occupied with the exploitation of the forest of Commentry, which Antoine was then in process of acquiring from the duke of Lorraine. These early connections with Antoine Paris and the business of forest and estate management in or near eastern France were continued by Masson through much of the remainder of his life and were the roots of his later partnership with the brothers Babaud for timber exploitations in Lorraine.

Many details of Masson's early life and rise to wealth and power remain obscure. We have some indications of his status in 1719, when he married Jacqueline Marie Duru. Their marriage contract shows that Masson was then living in bourgeois circumstances, apparently an employee of the Paris brothers.[2] His new father-in-law, Jean Duru, was a merchant goldsmith and jeweller. A notarial act of 1721 refers to Jacques Masson as "entrepreneur général des ascinages"; he was involved in the speculations associated with the Law affair,[3] and later claimed that their failure had cost him a fortune, including eleven houses at Havre-de-Grâce, stockpiles of "copper, lead, furniture and other movables, and even the greater part of my books, which were dear to me," all disposed of in order to discharge obligations to creditors. Masson made these assertions in 1729 when his "credit rating" was low. Both he and his secretary-clerk, Barrault, were then in prison on suspicion of fraud.[4]

But Masson was not discredited. Nor was he disqualified for high office in the French ministry of finance by the accusations or by his short-term imprisonment in Lorraine or even by his failure to pay anguished creditors for years after they had won court judgments against him. These blemishes on his record did not stop the rise of his business fortunes.

The Paris Brothers, Leopold of Lorraine, and Jacques Masson

Masson's emergence from obscurity and attainment of wealth and power in Lorraine and later in France grew out of his ties with the Paris brothers, bankers and entrepreneurs who were among the most powerful financiers in France at the time. They prospered as grain speculators, government contractors, bankers, and *munitionnaires* to the armed forces of France. They showed themselves to be imaginative, capable of locating, creating, and exploiting profit possibilities in a wide variety of enterprises, especially in state-connected operations. Masson dealt particularly with Antoine Paris, *trésorier des finances du dauphiné*, eldest of the brothers. After Antoine's death in 1733, Masson had dealings with the other two, Joseph Paris-Duverney (d. 1770), *directeur des finances*, and Jean Paris de Montmartel (d. 1776), marquis de Brunoy and *garde du Trésor*. Transactions between Masson and each of these men are recorded in the archives of French notaries from at least as early as 1713; Masson served continually, if not continuously, as an *homme d'affaires* associated with the Paris brothers until his death in 1741.[5]

Through the twenties and thirties, the Paris brothers prospered mightily. Critics of John Law's innovative fiscal schemes, they had the temerity (or foresight) to express their reservations in writing. Though exiled to their estates in Law's time, they were vindicated and recalled when the Law scheme collapsed; indeed, the Paris brothers presided over the liquidation of the system and in the process came to exercise great influence in the French ministry of finance, only to suffer exile again, temporarily, for their criticism of Cardinal de Fleury.[6] But they staged a powerful comeback during the War of the Polish Succession (1733–1735). In the forties, according to one commentator, "the financial operations of the War of the Austrian Succession were entirely in the hands of the Paris brothers, Paris-Duverney in the capacity of *munitionnaire général,* Paris-Montmartel providing funds as *garde du Trésor royal.*"[7]

Duke Leopold of Lorraine was moved to consult the Paris brothers in the 1720s about getting the finances of Lorraine in order. He had earlier borrowed large sums from them and still owed them 400,000 livres (de France) in 1728; and he had sold them several major properties. According to Masson, it was in relation to some of the forest properties that the Paris brothers had bought from Leopold that Masson was sent by Antoine Paris as his agent to the ducal court in 1723.[8]

In a self-justifying *mémoire* written in 1729, Masson described his arrival at Leopold's court in 1723, carrying a letter of introduction from Antoine Paris in which

> Monsieur Paris . . . begged the Duke to receive at Court a friend who had his confidence, and the authority to act as his surrogate in making any arrangement desired by His Highness regarding the forest of Commerci, which had been sold to the Sieur Paris some years before.

The forest was duly exchanged for other wooded land. Masson had accepted the commission "simply to please Monsieur Paris." Until June 1724, "the feeble talents God gave me for business afforded me nothing but the satisfaction of working secretly for those whom chance or merit placed in the service of princes or their ministers." This surprising admission—that Masson had had a role as agent of Antoine Paris while in residence at the ducal court—seems unlikely to have inspired trust or quieted the suspicions of his accusers. The statement was part of Masson's later (1729) denial of the more serious charge, that he had personally misappropriated several millions from the ducal treasury in the period 1724–1728. He was at pains to deny not only those charges, but also that his intimate collaboration with the Paris brothers had extended into the period 1724–1729.[9]

In 1724, with or without the collaboration of the Paris brothers, Masson "formed an association with the *fermiers généraux* [of the Duchy of Lorraine] and a certain Roussel and his associates."[10] Together they drew up and presented to Leopold proposals for fiscal reform designed to deal with the ongoing fiscal crisis (essentially the debts) of Lorraine. Evaluating their general proposal, Leopold decided to consult the Paris brothers. They quickly responded with a refinancing proposal of their own. These proposals, and others too, perhaps, Leopold seriously considered, but he accepted none at the time. Ultimately he did use some of the procedures they recommended. But he wanted to bring about reform on his own and without the self-serving features of the plans offered by outside advisor-financiers. Ironically, in trying to implement his "independent" policy, as he called it, to which he clung with some uncertainty from

1724 until his death in 1729, Leopold came increasingly to depend on Jacques Masson as counsellor and aide. With Masson's encouragement, he repeatedly rejected proposals of further loans.

In May 1926 Leopold elevated Masson to a newly created post as director-general of the *Régie des Fonds Affectées aux Payements des Dettes de l'Etat.*[11] A bit later Masson was also named to the duke's *Conseil des Finances,* the established fiscal body that continued to function independently of the *Régie.* At about that time Masson became a naturalized subject of the duke and thereby a legal insider.[12] As director of the *Régie,* Masson controlled an agency of the government of Lorraine empowered to receive and disburse certain revenues of the duchy, including the product of the administration of waters, forests, and domains.[13] Both the *contrôleur général des finances* and the *Chambre des Comptes de Lorraine* were ordered to transmit immediately to Masson detailed and certified *états* and inventories of every kind related to the debts and revenues of the state; henceforth copies of all such papers were routinely to be sent to the director.[14]

Nominally the director-designate of the *Régie* was to function under the "authority and inspection" of three commissioners from the ducal council, who were designated by name.[15] Precisely how these three inspectors should carry out the key function they were assigned was not indicated. As a practical matter, it could not have been easy for them to monitor Masson, who enjoyed wide powers and the entire confidence of Leopold. To bring the director to order was bound to be difficult even if they acted in unison, with much hard work and regardless of cost to themselves. In the circumstances, it was not practicable for the three to inspect the operations of a director of a diversified and complex agency when, as will be seen, he did not want their surveillance and was so uncooperative and careless as not to keep any register, journal, or other systematic record of receipts and expenditures for almost three years. The three commissioner-inspectors were obliged to allow Masson to administer the *Régie* as he pleased, in a slipshod, chaotic fashion; yet legally the fiscal anarchy that ensued was their collective responsibility.

In those three years Masson became Leopold's most influential advisor on financial affairs. Leopold has been called many things—profligate in his early years, and in later life incompetent, irresponsible, and senile. In the final analysis, he allowed the fiscal administration to slip out of his hands. The details and subtleties of Masson's rapidly increased influence with the old duke would make a study in themselves. His influence stemmed in considerable measure from his ability to bring about substantial increases in state revenues. Leopold would not (he said) sanction any expedient that increased taxes on the people, or any new loans in view of extortionate rates of interest they involved. He was, however, apparently willing to try almost anything else. Masson's operations produced large increases in ducal revenue, especially by accelerating forest exploitations and sales from ducal domains, but also by other expedients. He was able to persuade Leopold that he was the best hope for liquidating state debts.[16]

In the spring of 1728, Leopold sought a new and detailed assessment of the condition of the duchy's finances. Accordingly, Masson concocted a new plan for reform. Leopold had high hopes for it, it seems, but before putting it into effect, he again approached the ubiquitous Paris brothers, seeking their counsel and approval (he still owed them 400,000 livres). Antoine Paris had an estate at Sampigny, in the Barrois, and just happened to be visiting at Lunéville when he learned of Masson's new plan. He consented, when asked, to give Leopold his counsel but indicated that he needed to know about it in detail. Accordingly, Leopold instructed Masson to go to Sampigny to see both Antoine Paris and his brother Jean, his former (and perhaps his current) employers and collaborators.[17]

The Paris brothers advised against a central feature of Masson's plan, the imposition of a new *capitation,* yet they admitted that some such impost seemed inevitable unless the ducal treasury were strengthened by outside help of considerable magnitude, such as "only the Paris brothers could provide," to use Masson's phrase.[18] Antoine Paris urged Leopold to borrow a large additional sum and said that he personally wanted to see the Paris brothers supply it: Antoine and Masson were reportedly working to persuade the younger Paris to consent to the loan. On 7 October Masson wrote to assure Leopold that he could count on receiving the first installment of the loan (300,000 livres) in the first three months of 1729 in order to pay off the first of the urgent debts.

Leopold hesitated for some time.[19] Finally, in February 1729, he issued an *ordonnance* dealing with the administration of finances.[20] Comprising twenty-three articles designed "to clear the accounts," it condemned many existing abuses, some of them obviously Masson's work. Article 20, for example, required that all *trésoriers, receveurs,* and other accountants maintain a register or journal in which they "will write, immediately and without leaving any blank spaces, their receipts and expenditures . . . in order that . . . one can know at all times, in an instant, the exact state of their accounts." A "double-entry" system was prescribed; all receipts were to be entered in words and letters in the text "and without figures."[21] The *ordonnance* further decreed that the director-general was henceforth to assist the *contrôleur général;* apparently these two were no longer to keep two independent, separate sets of books. Nevertheless, Masson, as the director-general-designate of the combined system, apparently still had the soveregn's confidence.

But disaster struck at the end of March 1729, when, after a short illness, Leopold died. Masson's position at court was transformed. As he himself told it:

> On the twenty-seventh of March, fifteen minutes after the death
> of His Highness, M. de Coussey, Secretary of State *de service,*
> came and sealed my papers, which were locked in a cabinet to
> allow me to use the rest of my apartment. At the same time an
> officer and four gendarmes of the Bodyguard of His Highness
> were ordered to keep me under visual surveillance night and day,
> not allowing me to write or speak to anyone. The Sieur Barrault,
> my secretary, was arrested with me, and many sentinels were
> posted at the doors of my house to keep me isolated.[22]

This account suggests that Masson was held under house arrest. In fact, he appears (perhaps later) to have been imprisoned in the Tours de Notre Dame de Nancy. *Mémoires* written in his defense emanated from that prison, and the orders for his arrest decreed that he be conducted "under good and sure guard . . . to the Tours de Notre Dame de Nancy, where he will be handed over to the resident concierge of said prison."[23]

Other accounts state specifically that Masson was taken to prison. In the days that followed, four councillors of state and Her Grace the *Regente* were named to examine Masson's papers, "to discover what was done with the millions that had passed through my hands." Between twenty-five and thirty sessions were held. According to Masson, the results of the inquiry were "not favorable to the suspicions" of his accusers. He was able to account for outlays of "many millions," but some serious questions and accusations remained to be answered:

1. That in four years of fiscal management, Masson kept no registers of receipts and expenditures; that he had confounded Leopold's affairs with the private business of the prince of Craon (Leopold's father-in-law); that Masson himself owed "very great sums" to the state; and that "his whole establishment [the *Régie*] was in a state of disorder and extreme confusion";

2. "That this disorder, and my loyalty to persons to whom His Highness [Leopold] was known to refuse nothing [referring to Craon and others who had transferred large sums abroad], rendered me

violently suspect"; that Masson was "the organ and instrument of many of the causes of the exhaustion of the treasury of S.A.R."; and that much of the revenue designated for the retirement of debt, deriving from sales of forest cuts, profits from the mint, and other other sources, was inexplicably diverted to other, unknown uses;

3. That Masson had persuaded the late duke to negotiate new leases on lands in order to obtain revenue "*par anticipation* and without observing the formalities"; that he "profited unduly and through intermediaries" from the losses sustained by the issuance and transmission of notes, and from the negotiation of treasury notes, drafts, and receipts; that he profited personally from the sales of hereditary offices and by secret agreements; that he paid off personal obligations with state funds and acquired holdings far in excess of his personal resources; and that he owed Duke Leopold 546,141 livres; and

4. Finally, that Masson's contracts with the Sieur [Jean?] Babaud for the exploitation of wood from the forests of Lorraine, and his share of the profits of the conversion and sale of such wood to France for the French navy, were "incompatible with the functions of the offices with which the late duke honoured him."

Masson summarized the charges with understatement: "It was concluded from these varied accusations that there is reason to presume that I am guilty of embezzlement." [24]

Masson insisted that during his five years in office he had sought only to liquidate the debts of the prince of Lorraine, although much evidence pointed to greater indebtedness and fewer assets at the end than at the beginning of his program of retiring debts. [25] His personal obligation to Leopold amounted only to 277,127 livres, he said. [26] Concerning the charge that his bookkeeping "method" was scandalous, he admitted that he "had not kept either a register or detailed statements" of accounts. A daily or running account, he said with more emphasis than clarity or persuasiveness, was hardly necessary when "the proof of one part can serve as a basis for estimation of the other." As for the discount rate, about which there was also complaint, Masson claimed that Leopold had been happy when "the Sieur Masson received 900,000 livres in cash from transfers of 1,000,000"; a 10 percent discount was not excessive, he insisted, especially when "the Sieur Masson could find no such sum of cash in the hands of a Lorrainer" and therefore had to deal with foreigners (perhaps the Paris brothers). In fact, said Masson, the 7,500,000 in transfers actually produced the sum of 7,230,994 in cash—a discount rate of less than 5 percent![27] Concluding this phase of his defense with confidence, Masson said: "I have proved . . . that the discounts, interest, fees, and costs that are the inevitable consequence of converting paper into silver are the unique cause for the shortage of around 300,000 livres, which are in deficit."[28]

Masson readily admitted his close liaison with the duke's father-in-law, the prince of Craon: "I am delighted to have occasion to declare that I will remain, all of my life, a zealous servant of his Illustrious House." Conceding that he had a half-interest in the lease of the prince's lands, he denied any conflict of interest, since he had entered into those arrangements before assuming the responsibilities of office in Lorraine. Never had he sacrificed the interests of the duke of Lorraine in order to increase the revenues of the prince of Craon—if it turned out that way, it was certainly not by his intent.[29]

Masson admitted that he had purchased a one-third interest in the *Fermes Générales de Lorraine* at a price of 250,000 livres: such sums "are not so difficult to come by as is supposed by persons who ignore the resources of those who understand business." He insisted hotly that he could readily make such an investment, that it was not of great magnitude in the light of the wealth that he had earlier possessed, which at one time (he said) had enabled him "to advance as much as a million livres, and to have 450,000 clear, before the consequences of the revolution of 1720 [Law's failure] imposed the cruel necessity of sacrificing everything."[30] A few investment holdings offered no grounds for suspecting him of a breach of trust. Far from spending lavishly, he had even omitted to develop a property he possessed in the French province of Nivernais (his Guérigny holdings) "lest I be accused of extraordinary expenditures."[31] (The evidence shows that Masson did in fact take steps to develop his Guérigny holdings—not by improving the forges, but by buying forest land and rights from neighboring seigneurs.)

Masson also pointed out that in the exercise of his functions, he had incurred very substantial personal costs. During the five years of his tenure in Lorraine, he had kept a house in Paris, from which his absence had been very prejudicial, and had been obliged by "indispensable necessity" also to maintain households at Lunéville and Nancy. It was also just and fair, he said, that he should have recovered the costs involved in maintaining his various offices and staffs, including those of the *Régie* itself, and his travel expenses for the five years he had been "uniquely occupied with the affairs of the prince."[32]

Leopold himself contributed significantly to the sorry financial state of his realm, not only by his employment of Masson, but by three decades of expenditures that consistently exceeded the state's revenues. He spent on foreign policy, on extravagant state ceremonies, and on enormous gifts to family and favorites. In Lorraine, as elsewhere at the time, some of the *grands seigneurs* in the top echelon of the state administration were, to employ the phrase of another, "too great to do anything but collect the emoluments" of the posts they held; thus, for example, the comte de Carlingford, appointed *surintendant des finances, chef des conseils,* and *gouverneur de Nancy* was for fifteen years a costly figurehead whose duties were performed by an *intendant des finances*.[33] The prince of Craon, another of the *grands,* certainly played a role as a recipient of extravagant favors. Indeed, a number of distinguished noblemen, and some more humble persons as well, were included among the recipients of orders "payable to bearer" in a curious list that indicated the totals of the sums they received: [34]

M. le Prince de Guise	550,000
M. le Prince de Sixheim	76,000
M. le Prince de Craon	628,250
Samuel Levi "Juif"	296,600
M. de Spada	256,300
M. le Marquis de Stainville	118,616
M. le Marquis de Bassompierre	118,614

It was extraordinary to have such large sums on drafts drawn "to bearer"; and there was other evidence of "disorder and confusion" in the treasury accounts: gifts, payments to persons "incognito," the creation of multiple offices, double-employment, and sales or pretended sales of tenures and lands.

Masson not only failed to refute all the charges made against him, but did not even try to answer them in any thoroughgoing fashion in his *mémoires.* If he was, in strict legal terms, in the clear, it was only because of his close associations with the duke: the inspector-commissioners appointed in 1726 to oversee the operation of the *Régie* were shackled. Masson did some very questionable things under the umbrella of their nominal surveillance, ostensibly for the purpose of increasing state revenue to produce liquidity and to pay off state debts. As director-general, he had the power to favor friends and collaborators by granting, selling, changing, or exchanging land and forest leases, tenures and rights, prerogatives and privileges of many kinds. His vast powers, and the complete absence of regular, systematic accounting, created an ideal milieu for Masson.

The confident tone of Masson's defense suggests that he thought he was away free, but he was at least in part deceived; he knew Leopold, but not François of Lorraine, Leopold's successor. Leopold's *largesse*—the lands and tenures, rights and privileges he had prodigally given or allowed to be given or sold—was so extensive as to bring the ruling house and the economy of the duchy itself close to ruin. Neither the councillors nor François III himself could tolerate that. Even before François arrived to take up residence in Lorraine, the undoing of the doings of Leopold was begun.[35] For this purpose the Council appointed in August 1729 the first of a series of commissions to implement a decree that annulled all alienations of domains accomplished since 1697. The commissioners were ordered to proceed with the greatest secrecy. Ambulatory inspectors located and visited lands that had been alienated. Claims and rights were evaluated, with the holders presumably compensated if justified, but no less certainly relieved of them by forfeit if that was the will of the Council and prince.[36]

Similar commissions were empowered to examine the rights and liberties, privileges, and letters patent of nobility abundantly dispersed by Leopold. Some of these were annulled. Additional study of notarial records and the archives of Lorraine might throw more light on the effect of these decrees on the affairs of Jacques Masson. He had acquired forges and other properties and held them privately or indirectly (that is, with partners). He used notarial secrecy to mask some significant operations, but powerful partners could also afford safety, as with his share of a new lease on the great forge of Moyeuvre, held from his ally the prince of Craon.[37] Some of Masson's privileges, however—for example, the letters patent of nobility that he said were conferred on him—were swept away in the reaction.[38] More serious for him, perhaps, were claims from erstwhile collaborators who had paid him fees for his favors but who were forced by the commissions to forfeit grants or arrangements he made in their behalf, and who returned to Masson seeking reimbursement or alternative compensation.

Leopold's death and the reaction that followed it inaugurated new phases both in Masson's personal history and in the history of Lorraine itself. For the time being, Masson's official role in the government of the duchy ended. His imprisonment was apparently brief. He still had his powerful friends, the brothers Paris among them. And he also had some significant properties in the Nivernais, where at least part of the profits of timber operations were converted into real estate holdings. The Nivernais was Masson's favored haven. In Masson's name, a Parisian lawyer named Joseph Antoine Mogot in 1720 purchased a seigneury near Nevers for 95,500 livres—perhaps Guérigny. In September 1721 the same lawyer contracted another obligation at Nevers for Masson, borrowing 37,500 livres, which was used to make a payment on the property purchased earlier.[39] By then Masson's landholdings in the region included several seigneuries and forges. In January 1724 we see him buying woodland exploitation and other seigneurial rights on 95 *arpents* (an *arpent* was approximately one acre) of land near Guérigny[40] and the following May another 281 *arpents* of woodland rights and a stand of six- to twelve-year-old trees.[41] Masson was looking to the future, building real estate holdings, gathering parcels and the forest fuel sources needed to support forge or foundry operations on the properties he already held near Nevers. This was the obscure origin of the far-flung industrial establishment later built on Masson foundations by the Babauds, especially by the young Pierre Babaud after he had married Masson's daughter, Jacqueline.

After 1729 Masson's activity in Lorraine and adjacent Rhineland regions was connected closely with the execution of the forest exploitation contracts he had granted to his partners (hence to himself) during his tenure as director-general of the *Régie*. Complaints about such conflicts of interest apparently lost validity once Masson was relieved of his administrative powers. Although the new duke and his associates must have wanted to cancel Masson's contracts, they did not do so. The enterprise was already under way; legal complications and costs would ensue from cancellation. Potentially far-reaching international complications and pressures might also result. Moreover, the contracts promised to produce revenue that was desperately needed for the duchy. This portion of Masson's interests in Lorraine thus survived the death of Leopold and the subsequent crisis.

The Babauds and the Boesniers

In these forest exploitations Masson's partners were Jean Babaud of Bellac (a tiny town near Limoges) and Jacques Boesnier Duportal of Saumur. It was a family operation—a fact of great influence and importance. The relationships were very intricate (see genealogical chart). All the partners were related by blood or by marriage. Masson and the Babauds were somehow connected through the Duru family. Documents relating to Jean Babaud's marriage with Marie Boesnier (1728) reveal that Jacques Boesnier Duportal was Marie's cousin. That explains why Jean Babaud's widowed mother consented to serve as *caution* for all the partners, including Duportal, when they were seeking advances of funds from the navy to help finance their timber operations.[42] Marie Boesnier, from

Blois, was described as daughter of a "very rich merchant" of that town. The family character of the business was further underscored by the fact that Jacques Boesnier Duportal had been the business partner of Pierre Babaud, Senior, Sieur de Beaupré (henceforth referred to as Pierre Babaud I) and also of Jean Babaud. Jacques's younger brother Daniel also aided the business. He was in the timber business at Rotterdam in the Netherlands, one of the principal cities to which the partners sent their rafts of timber, just as Daniel himself was a principal customer. Later, around 1732, Jacques Boesnier Duportal was suddenly forced to withdraw from the partnership, apparently because of poor health (he died before October 1733). Young Pierre Babaud (later to be known as Babaud de la Chaussade) was then taken into the business as a junior partner; presently he married Masson's daughter Jacqueline, and was made a full partner in the business, thereby in effect taking the place of the late J. B. Duportal among the senior partners.

Jean Babaud learned the timber business from his father, Pierre Babaud I. Father and son (and apparently Duportal as well) had worked together logging trees from the forests of central France, cutting and buying timber and other forest products for sale to both commercial buyers and the French navy. By the mid-1720s Pierre Babaud I had retired from the business. Hence it was Jean Babaud who negotiated the contracts with the French navy to purchase trees taken from the forests of Lorraine. Masson, of course, was the partner most responsible for getting the initial contract for cutting timber in Duke Leopold's forests. Masson also negotiated contracts with the prince of Craon and other proprietors disposed to sell trees. Ultimately trees belonging to dozens of private woodland and forest owners were acquired for cutting purposes, at first in the duchy of Lorraine, later in Montbéliard (for Toulon), and also in Alsace and various principalities on the Meuse and in the Rhinelands and states of the Empire.[43]

As a partner in the enterprise, Masson was very active. One of his important contributions resulted from his powers as director-general of the *Régie.* In that post Masson had *de facto* control over the administration of waters and forests in Lorraine. His charge was to increase the ordinary and extraordinary income deriving from forest exploitations in Duke Leopold's domains, in part by increasing the volume of timber cut there. Accordingly, he was given special authority to deal with the administrators of waters and forests, who could be expected to resist his plans.[44] To guarantee that the "will of the prince" (and Masson's purposes) would prevail over the opposition from such conservation-minded and "routine-ridden" bureaucrats, the duke explicitly decreed that the orders of the director-designate "will be executed without delay" by the *commissaires généreaux reformateurs* and all other officers of the water and forest administration. Ducal officials who experienced difficulties or required assistance in the execution of the director-general's orders were instructed to address the *Régie* itself. Masson was a *de facto grand maître des eaux et des forêts,* to whom all forestry officials had "direct access" and the duty of obedience, and from whose decisions there was no appeal.[45]

Under these circumstances Masson's services in facilitating forest exploitation would have been worth 10,000 livres a year, and then some, to the partnership. After Leopold died and Masson was relieved of his helpful powers and functions, his partners may have thought about modifying the terms of the partnership. But they needed only to be patient. Comparable authority in Lorraine would again be given to Jacques Masson when the principality was controlled by France in 1736 and he was accorded by the French *contrôleur général* wide powers in the management of its affairs.

Meanwhile, in other principalities (especially in Montbéliard), Masson did them excellent service in rationalizing the expansion of their holdings and interests through acquisitions in the wood fuel (charcoal) iron industry. The degree of their confidence in, or at least their continued dependence on, him is suggested by their decision, with the coming of the War of the Polish Succession, to constitute him as the agent (*procureur*) for Jean Babaud in Paris for all matters related to their joint fulfillment of the naval contracts.[46]

Family Affairs After the Marriage

In 1732 Masson's wife, Jacqueline Marie Anne Duru, died. Her death had pervasive consequences for Masson. The usual inventory after death placed a modest valuation of 10,485 livres on the furnishings they held in common; the remainder of the property of the ménage (*non-commun*) had to be divided into the Masson and Duru shares. That potentially difficult operation was made much easier by the willingness of the father of the deceased to recognize his granddaughter, Demoiselle Jacqueline Anne Marie, aged twelve, daughter of the deceased, as heir of the entire Duru share.[47] Thenceforth, daughter Jacqueline figured prominently in much that Masson did.

Indeed, less than two years afterward, she was one of the principals in another major family event. Doubtless after long and careful calculation in Masson and Babaud family councils, Jacqueline and Pierre Babaud were betrothed. Whatever the importance of such decisions for the individuals, the main consideration was certainly the long-term interest, especially the business interests, of the families. The marriage implied that a decision had been made to join the Masson and Babaud families with an important and practically indissoluble bond—one that both families probably hoped would concentrate and strengthen family and business alike. High aspiration was surely present, because these were ambitious and energetic people. The bridegroom, Jean Babaud's younger brother Pierre, had for some years assisted in the family timber business and had recently become a full partner in the families' forest exploitation enterprise. Jacqueline was then fourteen, Pierre twenty-eight years of age.

This linking of the families with new bonds provided the occasion for a significant gathering of many members of the clans with a selection of benevolent dignitaries and friends. Such occasions enhanced the prestige and stature of the families concerned, and even their business prospects. For the modern historian, this particular gathering was important because the actual marriage contract in the notarial archives lists (as such documents commonly did) the names of the persons in attendance. Family relationships otherwise unknown were thereby revealed, and suggestions (precious to the historian) were made as to the socioeconomic connections, status, and stature of the principal families and individuals involved.

Much *éclat* was no doubt given to this Masson-Babaud union by the presence of the king's minister of marine: "*Très Haut et Très Puissant* Monseigneur Jean Fréderic Phelipeaux Chevalier Comte de Maurepas, *Conseiller, Ministre, et Commandeur dans des Ordres du Roy.*" In the records of the occasion Maurepas was named "friend" (*amy*); and a faithful friend he was, perhaps especially to Jean Babaud, but also to the groom. The three were near-contemporaries, long and closely associated with the navy; two of them—Maurepas (1701–1781) and Chaussade (1706–1792)—were very long-lived.[48]

Property was, of course, an important consideration when marriages were arranged. First there was the determination of how the property of the newly wedded pair would be held, whether *commun* or *non-commun*, or some combination of those methods; then there was the matter of the dowry. In this case the property of the newlyweds was to be held *en commun*, conforming to the *coutume de Paris*. Jacqueline's dowry comprised a very substantial congeries of properties, plus cash. Included were the land and seigneury of Guérigny and Masson's portion "of one-third of the *concession des Marais du Bas-Languedoc.*"[49]

The dowry contract reveals something of Masson's taste and capacity for intrigue, speculation, and high finance, and the consequent complexity of his affairs. The dowry itself went far beyond generosity, and other notarial acts indicate that it was simply one of many excuses for (real or fictitious) transfers of Masson's assets to the couple. In the process Masson managed to withdraw his equity from the partnership for timber exploitation and transform himself from a creditor and possessor of very substantial holdings into a debtor with obligations that largely exceeded his assets.

Transfers of Masson's properties were already taking place in March and April 1733, a year before the marriage; in later months many others took place through *lettres de change* drawn on Paris, Nancy, Frankfurt, and Bonn bankers by both Chaussade and Masson.[50] Masson seemed to be (but was not) moving toward retirement from the partnership in timber exploitation with the Babauds. Some of his transfers were substantial; some were very small indeed.[51] Certain payments were made by Chaussade to "liberate the Sieur Masson from his personal creditors." At least one of Masson's creditors, a certain Sieur le Fort of Paris, agreed to forget 1,000 livres of the interest due to him from Masson if Chaussade would pay off Masson's obligation, which he did.[52] Chaussade also paid off Masson's obligation to J. Fuleman et Cie., incurred long before and confirmed by a *sentence du Consulat de Paris* which had condemned Masson to pay Fuleman some 800 livres.[53]

Not only was the entire amount of Masson's equity in the timber exploitation partnership eventually paid over to the Babaud brothers; at least as early as February 1736 Masson was engaged in borrowing from them. He had borrowed 21,527 livres by February 1736, an obligation he formally recognized as a debt due to be repaid (presumably from his estate) "by preference."[54] But such debts did not prevent Masson from acquiring land at Guérigny, transferred to him in payment of a debt of 6,000 livres (owed to him by a church chapter at Nevers) by "the venerable and discrete person, P. B. du Bouche." That same day Masson "borrowed" an additional 30,000 livres from Jean Babaud at 5 percent, for which he pledged the seigneury of Guérigny (already pledged as part of Jacqueline's dowry) as security.[55] Masson also "pilfered" from the dowry in another way, and added further legal complications, by selling off the Languedoc reclamation and canal concession that he had promised to Jacqueline and Chaussade as part of her dowry.[56]

Still another fiscal device for drawing Masson's assets from the partnership was the joint purchase of an office by Jean Babaud and himself (through a person by the name of Nicholas Mathieu).[57] The office in question was that of *receveur général des finances de Lorraine et Barrois*, purchased at a price of 300,000 livres "*monnoye de France*"(!), plus a bit more as the cost of "*reception.*" Jean Babaud agreed to pay half of the total. Mathieu was to hold the place and receive certain emoluments and allowances, with the provision (art. 7) that it was "permissible" for the Sieur Babaud, his widow, or other heirs to appoint the Sieur Babaud de la Chaussade to hold and exercise the rights conferred by the office. This office was created, very helpfully, by an edict of the king of Poland, nominal successor to Duke François III of Lorraine, on 25 September 1737.[58]

The Death of Jean Babaud

These intricate arrangements were made when Jean Babaud was in the last stages of his long-drawn-out, immobilizing mortal illness, about four months before his death from the malady whose symptoms he himself had described years before as those of a "severe cold"—perhaps tuberculosis.[59] Plagued with health problems from as early as 1732 or 1733, Jean Babaud continued to direct the partners' timber exploitations from his headquarters at Bitche in Lorraine, traveling as he could, but with ever-decreasing frequency over the years. He made his home at the fortress town of Bitche, where he apparently had many friends. When he traveled to nearby Nancy on business, he several times lodged with his friend, banker, and creditor, Dominique Antoine. As his health deteriorated, he came gradually to depend more on aides or surrogates, and on his partners.

Jacques Masson was the partner most largely depended on for handling the group's affairs in Paris, as attested by the *procuration* he received from Jean Babaud in late 1733.[60] But Masson also traveled on occasion to Lorraine and to other Rhineland territories to conduct negotiations with forest owners; dealings with princely owners seems to have been his particular speciality. Masson carried much of the responsibility for organizing and initiating the partners' Montbéliard exploitations, which involved opening the Doubs River as a waterway for shipments of timber traveling the Saône-Rhône route toward Marseille and Toulon.

The younger Pierre Babaud was employed in a wide variety of tasks, dealing with small landowners, loggers, navy inspectors, and raftsmen. Superintending field operations, he oversaw cuts in Lorraine and worked with the Duportals on river shipments, *passeports,* and toll payments. He also made visits to the Netherlands—imperative after Duportal's demise. Dordrecht and Rotterdam were termini for the timber shipped down the rivers Rhine, Moselle, and Meuse and embarkation ports for the partners' shipments to France. It was with good reason that Pierre Babaud de la Chaussade's name appeared as a full partner in the enterprise when new contracts and terms were negotiated with the navy in 1733.

In that year Jacques Boesnier Duportal and the other partners agreed on terms that allowed Duportal to take his entire equity and retire from the business.[61] His place and responsibilities in the partnership were partly assumed by Masson and Chaussade. In a new family partnership set up after Duportal's demise in 1733, Jean Babaud held 50 percent, Pierre Babaud 30 percent, and Jacques Masson the other 20 percent of the shares. At that time (1733) the total monetary value of Babaud's half-share was calculated as 315,477 livres.[62] These new arrangements provided for a close-knit family operation. But they were destined, for a variety of reasons, to be wrenched by much stress and strain.

After Duportal retired, both Pierre Babaud and Jacques Masson began to play much more obvious roles. It was a difficult time for the partners. Duportal was a senior with long experience in the business; up to that point the partners had depended heavily on him and used the services of his brother, Daniel Duportal of Rotterdam. Furthermore, international war and consequent military movements and tensions in eastern France and the Rhine River basin complicated the exploitations taking place and soon upset routine entirely. The crisis (and then the War) of the Polish Succession were upon them. Jean Babaud's physical condition was deteriorating, and Masson, for his part, was after 1736 to be tied up by commitments in the French ministry of finance and therefore no longer able to concern himself with forest exploitations in the field. Supervision of the timber exploitation enterprise devolved increasingly on the youngest and least experienced of the partners, Pierre Babaud, and on surrogates or substitutes for the partners to whom certain responsibilities had to be delegated, among them men with such names as Mangin, Baudry, Le Tessier, and Prieur.

Timber-cutting operations and shipments of timber were complicated by the movements of personnel and changes of domicile resulting from the pressures and confusion of war. As the pressures mounted and the partners' workload increased, their accounts and some of their administrative methods were disclosed, as early as 1736, to have been slipshod. The partners resolved to start new registers and a different system of accounts on 1 January 1737, hoping that these changes would clarify the status of their respective shares. At the outset (1736) the new accounts were to show Jean Babaud with an equity of 255,476 livres and Pierre Babaud with 60,000 livres.[63] By then all of Duportal's claims on the partnership had been paid off; Masson was regularly withdrawing his equity from the accounts almost as soon as it accumulated, although he remained a partner.

But it was also in 1736 that Masson was designated "to work under the orders of *Monsieur le Contrôleur Général* with the affairs of Lorraine." His new responsibilities obliged him to maintain establishments at both Versailles and Paris, thus (he persistently complained) pushing his expenses far above the level of spending his government salary allowed.[64] Masson could and did claim that he needed continually to liquidate his equity in the partnership to meet personal expenses. But of course his influence on the affairs of his partners remained great. They had many ties; it was in this period that Jean Babaud consented to purchase for 150,000 livres a half-share of the office of *receveur général des finances de Lorraine et Barrois* with which Masson was surreptitiously connected.

Moreover, Masson and the Babauds were joint owners of much property, many seigneuries and forges, and extensive woodland exploitation rights at Guérigny, Cosne, and elsewhere. Masson was the initiator of this enterprise, at least in the decade of the thirties. He had led the Babauds to the Nivernais, had invested continually in Nivernais properties for at least fifteen years. As a family they committed themselves by the midthirties to acquiring and reviving a scattered group of forges for anchor manufacture. In December 1735 one member of the family, in a *mémoire* to the ministry of marine, trumpeted the family's motives and achievment in developing (i.e., acquiring) an industrial complex, including dependent properties, on the upper Loire:

> The Sieur Jean Babaud with the Sieurs Masson and Babaud de la
> Chaussade are the sole proprietors of the forges and . . . [the]
> mill at Cosne. A single family has made this acquisition, with a
> single purpose in view: to perfect the manufacture of anchors,
> and to merit the protection of Your Lordship by attachment to
> the service of the navy.[65]

They planned to concentrate anchor production at Cosne and Guérigny; other irons could be produced or bought elsewhere. The "protection" they sought was, of course, special privilege—and exclusive contracts with the navy.

Death was painfully slow in coming to Jean Babaud. But he could not sell out to his partners and retire, as he would have liked to do; they did not have the means to buy his 50 percent interest in their enterprises. Had he insisted on withdrawing his capital, he would certainly have terminated the business. He chose instead to leave his capital committed. His gradual deterioration gave him time to plan for his family, to arrange an orderly transition in the control of their mutual affairs. The transition he planned called for the use of a surrogate to manage his share and to act in the interest of his wife, Marie, and their children after his death. This plan was actually an adaptation and extension of the methods increasingly employed by all the partners in managing their growing portfolios and far-flung affairs.

On 8 December 1738, in view of his ever-worsening physical condition, Jean Babaud, jointly with Masson, gave a procuration to Jean's trusted *commis*, Pierre François Goossens, to take both their places in the administration of the society when Jean could no longer continue.[66] In effect, Goossens' prominence in the business dated from that time; Jean Babaud died less than one week afterward, and the partnership was known for about one year thereafter (February 1739 to May 1740) as "Widow Babaud and Company."[67] Several other partial reorganizations took place in the two years that followed, redividing or rearranging responsibility for various operations.[68] But Goossens remained associated with the business, first with the partnership, then with Marie Boesnier, and finally with Chaussade alone, through almost two decades.

An important development in the history of the partnership came in the summer of 1739, following Jean Babaud's death, when Masson and Chaussade obtained an "emergency" contract with the navy to supply a variety of naval stores from "the north," meaning stores brought from the Netherlands or the Baltic. Goossens was also to be associated with the execution of those contracts, which will be discussed in detail below.[69]

Marie Boesnier

Marie Boesnier, though highly intelligent, had no evident role in these business affairs, except to lend her name for a short time to the new society set up immediately after her husband's death. She and Jean Babaud had had two children, Marie Charlotte and Angelique Dorothée; it was Jean Babaud's apparent wish that his daughters' interest in his estate, and in the timber and iron enterprises, would be preserved and monitored by Marie Boesnier. About Marie's determination, competence in business matters, and personality we know little; but she certainly had her children's interests in mind. One is tempted to attribute such qualities as business acumen and independent spirit to her or to imagine that she was encouraged over the years by her ailing spouse to perform business chores, to work with him, even to travel for him and learn the business. One might suppose that she was influenced—as indeed she may have been—by some of her relatives to play an active role herself in the management of the business. Whatever her inclinations, she was probably legally incapable of doing much beyond accepting the prearranged plan, allowing her late husband's selected representative, Pierre Goossens, to act for her.

In the view of Jacques Masson, himself a widower since 1732, this arrangement was not ideal. Marie was young and apparently attractive; she might be disposed to remarry, and complications could ensue if she married outside the family. To prevent that, Masson himself married her in December 1739. Another likely motive for Masson's action was his need for money. Perhaps he was a gambler; certainly he was extravagant.[70] Marie agreed, surprisingly, to community of property in the marriage, thus giving Masson a great deal of control over at least part of her inheritance. (It seems unlikely, given Jean Babaud's careful preparations, that her daughters' portions were accessible to Masson, or even to Marie Boesnier herself, in consequence of this second marriage.)

Masson was a remarkable manipulator. His public image and the record of his affairs, though blemished and shabby even in terms of the ethics of his own age, were not a serious impediment to him. He had powerful friends, not least of them the Paris brothers. He held key posts at high levels of government, lived at Versailles, met and dealt socially and professionally with the governing elite. His cash flow was enormous; he was continually liquidating assets and accumulating debts. Even his family obligations seem to have been unpaid. The impressive dowry he promised to his daughter and her husband was never delivered—or if given, it was taken back; the real estate holdings he promised her were either sold to her husband or ceded to others. In 1739 Masson's equity in the partnership, then known as "Widow Babaud and Company," was nonexistent; he owed his partners 51,722 livres, having withdrawn no less than 162,000 livres since the last accounting and division.[71] Masson's debt to his son-in-law alone at about that time was calculated by Chaussade at 196,484 livres.[72] Apparently Masson wanted it that way; his arrangements left him with little cash and few "accessible" (discoverable) assets to pay off debts. The absence of assets was discovered, with incredulity even in the family and with disbelief and dark suspicions among creditors outside after Masson's sudden death on 11 June 1741.[73] Years of litigation followed. Curiously, exactly one week before his death, Masson purchased the barony, lands, and seigneury of Frasnay for 155,000 livres, and in doing so handed over to the seller, in the presence of the notary, 55,000 livres of the purchase price in specie—"Louis d'argent et monnoye ayant cours." No wonder creditors found it hard to believe (after his death) that Jacques Masson was a pauper.[74]

The intrafamily phases of the legal struggle that followed Masson's death were played out over more than a decade between Pierre Babaud de la Chaussade and Marie Boesnier. As a start, both she (or her attorneys) and Chaussade ordered separate inventories of the Masson estate. Both inventories revealed that Masson, entrepreneur and banker, *premier commis du contrôleur général des Finances de France,* a man who bought real estate with cash, was a pauper—worse, was deeply in debt. Hopes of collection seemed so bleak that creditors outside the family formed a company to coordinate their efforts.[75]

Settlement of Masson's estate was enormously complicated by the many overlapping and contradictory claims put forward by outside creditors and male and female offspring by successive spouses. The foremost problem was the paucity of assets. One special complication as far as the family was concerned was the fact that his new wife had borne a son by him only one month before his demise. Thus Masson's only son was born penniless. Marie Boesnier Babaud-Masson, twice widowed and left with minor chidren by each husband, acting no doubt with advice from her attorneys, and perhaps from Chaussade, sought help from the crown in early July 1741: "The widow of the Sieur Masson, *Premier Commis de M. le Contrôleur Général,* begs His Majesty to grant a pension to his son, aged only two months, to whom he has left nothing whatever."[76] The king consented to grant a pension of 800 livres a year to Masson's infant son, named Alexandre Frédéric Jacques Masson; he would later be known as the Marquis de Pezay. His godfather was Maurepas, minister of marine.

Relations between Chaussade and Marie Boesnier and their respective attorneys immediately after Masson's death must have been extraordinarily complex. She was still quite young and, of course, inexperienced in business; all parties to the complex affair must have been distraught, confused, and uncertain. Each of Masson's children had a claim on part of the estate, and Marie Boesnier must often have consulted with the attorneys about their interests as well as her own. Chaussade for his part knew intimately many of the properties in question; he could estimate present and potential values, and his overall view would have enabled him to plan. He was free to act, and did. He and Marie must have known each other well, and she was evidently willing to accept his initiative. Hence, five months after Masson's death, on Chaussade's advice (and that of attorneys), Marie issued two documents, one renouncing her share—there being insufficient to pay creditors—and naming "the *Sieur Masson mineur,* sole heir," and the other issuing an "*abandon général* of all assets to the Sieur de la Chaussade" for the payment of creditors. Earlier, six weeks after Masson's death, Chaussade had obtained cancellation of the long-term (thirteen-year) contract he and his two later partners had had with the navy, and in its place obtained a new contract in his name alone, without any advances paid, calling simply for payment when acceptable timber was delivered.[77] Chaussade thereby tightened his control over the business, showed the Boesnier attorneys and the Masson creditors his strength, and eliminated any possibility that Marie Boesnier or her late husbands' surrogates (or creditors) could unilaterally decide to operate independently.

The attorneys and creditors were slow in coming around. The boy-heir was too young—given the high infant mortality rates of that age—to justify firm legal plans. They must also have had some reservations about Chaussade, but were reassured when he renounced, on his wife's behalf, their claim to any share of her father's estate.[78]

Chaussade undertook to pay off the creditors and, within the limits of the available assets, satisfied them within the year that followed. To assist in accomplishing that task, Chaussade received from the widow Masson the sum of 24,500 livres; it must have cost him a good deal more than that to settle Masson's debts.[79]

Chaussade would certainly have faced an impossible task had he been called on to follow Jean Babaud's wishes and immediately pay over to Marie Boesnier the entire value of Jean's share in the equity from the partnership, amounting at the time of his death to about 350,000 livres.[80] To pay out so large an equity might have been a possibility if the rate of profit and expansion enjoyed by the partners in the 1730s had continued in the 1740s. As the following chapters show, it did not, for a variety of reasons.

Secrétaire du Roi au Grand Collège

Two other events of the forties were of great importance to the family, and especially to Chaussade. The first was Chaussade's purchase of a government office in 1743; the second, the death of his wife, Jacqueline, in 1744, which apparently resulted in a significant struggle with Marie Boesnier.

To purchase the very prestigious office of *secrétaire du roi au Grand Collège,*[81] Chaussade saw fit to borrow 100,000 livres at 5 percent interest.[82] The purchaser of such an office was required to present his birth certificate, another document attesting to his conformity to the "Religion

Catholique, Apostolique et Romaine," and several letters of recommendation, all of which Chaussade did, thus creating a nice nest egg for the historian.[83] In later years, the syndics of the *Compagnie des Secrétaires du Roi* were obliged by the royal treasury to collect additional sums by special assessment from the holders of this office. Thus Chaussade was asked to pay an additional 40,000 livres in 1770,[84] and he had difficulty raising 30,000 in cash to pay the assessment at that time.[85]

Why did Chaussade buy this office? Where human motives are concerned, answers are bound to be complex and fraught with uncertainties. The purchase was obviously an investment and not the result of any excess of liquidity in his accounts—he had to borrow to buy it. The purchase was also very much a privileged act. Some historians have judged acquisition of such an office to be evidence of "unenterprising conduct," a disposition to relax or retire, or a willingness to pay a high price for noble status. Regarding the last motive, we might note that Chaussade had earlier received through inheritance a share of a minor office that conferred a lower level of *noblesse*.[86] Chaussade relished the prestige and privileges (including nobility) this office conferred. But he had no intention of abandoning business—in 1743 he had almost fifty years of business life ahead of him. We should note also that the "salary" attaching to such an office constituted an infinitesimal return on funds. Since Chaussade borrowed the entire purchase price and most if not all the funds to pay later assessments, his purchase amounted to the use of private credit to support the royal treasury, a loan of borrowed funds to the crown, though of course with the expectation of receiving some returns on his investment. Far from being evidence of retirement, his purchase was *de facto* the purchase of *noblesse* and perquisites; it was an act of enterprise. He aimed to acquire greater favor and acceptance among aristocratic government officials, to rise in the hierarchy of the social and business communities, and thus to improve his bargaining position as a government contractor.

Furthermore, significant judicial and tax advantages were enjoyed by incumbents of the office of *secrétaire du roi au Grand Collège*. The office conferred judicial rights, and Chaussade was continually involved in litigation. The office conferred personal exemption from various sales and consumption taxes, such as the *gabelle* (salt tax), from *la marque de fers,* certain *péages, octrois des villes,* and *logement des gens de guerre.* (See glossary.) For a man of wealth and property, having seigneuries and forest, a man who traveled much, who had frequent cause to deal with landed proprietors and officials who were noblemen, *noblesse* and the privileges of the office were of very real socioeconomic worth—quite inseparable from the pleasures associated with leaving the Third Estate and rising into the Second. Chaussade seems to have felt those pleasures even before the act conferring the office was signed and sealed. In March 1743 he wrote to one of his subordinates: "I have purchased a charge as *Secrétaire du roi* in the *Grand Collège*. The following are the titles you henceforth will give me in all your [correspondence and notarial] acts." There followed Chaussade's own detailed list of his titles and dignities.[87]

The year after his purchase of this office, Chaussade's wife died.[88] This event complicated his relationship with Marie Boesnier. Jacqueline's death gave Masson's son by his second wife (the infant Alexandre Frédéric Jacques Masson) certain claims. Marie Boesnier took matters into the courts in 1745. Eventually, in 1755, Chaussade was moved to establish an annuity of 1,200 livres *per annum* on the "terre de Guérigny," 1,000 for "the Sieur Masson" (Boesnier's son) and 200 livres for the Dame Marie herself.[89] That was Chaussade's last act in his successful campaign to acquire clear claims and complete control of the erstwhile family business.

A Family Enterprise, 1728–1756

Over the quarter-century from 1728 to 1755, all three of the original partners passed from the scene. One withdrew from the business for unknown reasons but soon afterward died; two were removed—one after a long illness, the other unexpectedly—by death. Pierre Babaud de la Chaussade, a younger brother of one original partner and the son-in-law of another, was by 1752 the sole surviving member of the group still involved in the family business. Chaussade cannot be considered heir to the assets of the firm. Though the partnership had prospered in that first decade from 1728 to 1738, with a big and growing business in timber and wood products, as well as sales to the navy, the assets Chaussade could accumulate as a junior partner were relatively small. Little of the substantial profit made by the partnership reached him. Moreover, when Duportal withdrew, he and his brother in the Netherlands had to be paid off. By far the largest share (50 percent) of the residual assets then belonged to the hard-working senior partner, Jean Babaud. It was his intention that those assets would remain committed to the business even after his death, and for a number of years his widow and her children, through surrogates, continued to participate, leaving their equity in the business. Jacques Masson contributed importantly, as we have seen, to the business and its profits, but he was a veritable sponge as far as the assets and profits of the firm were concerned, withdrawing his entire 20 percent share, borrowing from his partners far beyond that, and leaving a legacy of debt that seemed to dilapidate the assets of the others. After a series of setbacks and continual friction and litigation with Chaussade over the years, Marie Boesnier also withdrew her share of the assets. By 1755 she had sold all her residual interest in the business to Chaussade, receiving cash and annuities in payment.

It was Chaussade, the most junior partner, who began the decade of the fifties by buying the last fraction of the forge and foundry properties from Marie Boesnier Babaud Masson in 1752 and settling annuities on her and on Masson's son in 1755. Thus, significantly, the entrepreneur Pierre Babaud de la Chaussade did not receive their shares as a legacy. He acquired their assets by purchase. He bought them out. How could the junior partner generate the funds to buy out all the others? The chapters that follow will try to answer that question.

CHAPTER 2

The Development of the Family Timber Business, 1728–1738

The Origins of the Business

In 1728 the partners Jacques Boesnier-Duportal of Saumur and Jean Babaud of Bellac were known in their home towns as timber merchants of modest means. Jean Babaud's background included some years of shipping timber down the Rhine, as attested by contemporary comments of the toll keepers at Bonn.[1] He was the son of a timber merchant and provincial office holder and had probably worked for some years as helper in his father's prosperous timber business. Duportal, on the other hand, had first been a merchant of wines and spirits, probably involved in the export trade. By 1728 he had been associated with Jean Babaud for at least seven or eight years in cutting and selling timber in the *généralité* of Poitiers around Saumur, at St. Maixent, Niort, and Parthenay. Near the last-named place the two had joined with a third man as lessees of a forge belonging to the duke of Mazarin. Much of the timber they sold was cut under contract for the navy, but they may have been able to use some of the trimmings and refuse from their logging and lumbering operations to help fuel their forges.[2] Jacques Masson was one of their business connections in eastern France, as Masson himself affirmed in his *mémoire* of 1728.[3]

When these partners agreed to undertake exploitations in the forests of the duke of Lorraine, they were taking on a job of extraordinary magnitude and difficulty. The amount of timber they promised to extract and deliver, the physical distance involved, and the time required for making deliveries compounded the difficulties of the enterprise. Their principal problem at the time was one of financing. The contract they signed with the navy in 1728 required them to deliver between 150,000 and 300,000 cubic feet of timber a year for five years—more timber per year than

Babaud and Duportal had delivered in the entire seven- or eight-year term of one of their largest earlier enterprises.[4] Major transportation problems included the need to use international waterways and the inevitable delays incurred in passing dozens of toll stations and frontiers. Many months were required for timber trees to be purchased, cut, brought to the rivers, gathered into rafts, and shipped downstream to the Netherlands, there to be embarked and shipped by sea to French naval arsenals at Brest and Rochefort. At the arsenal the load would be disembarked and inspected before being "received." Even after reception, delays of weeks or months might normally occur before entrepreneurs actually received payment. Thus the funds of the entrepreneurs would routinely be tied up for several years. Forest proprietors often wanted payment when their trees were cut or removed from the land; loggers, carters, *flotteurs,* and attendants at toll or duty stations along the roads and rivers had to be paid with minimum delay or none at all, as did the shipowners, especially non-French ones.

In November 1733 Maurepas, the French minister of marine, wrote to the *contrôleur général des finances* to explain the difficulties being experienced by the partners in negotiating letters of exchange, ordinarily drawn on Paris to pay local labor. These troubles, he reported, had obliged the Sieur Babaud "to use the *Carosse de Strasbourg* to transmit in specie the sums necessary for his exploitations, and for this purpose he has need of an order to the director of the *fermes* [tax office] at Chalons to allow passage of up to 60,000 livres per month in specie that he will address to the Sieur Croiquot, his correspondent at Strasbourg."[5] Babaud and Duportal claimed that they simply did not possess the capital reserves and credit needed to finance the operation.

Hence the navy had agreed, in the contract of 1728, to give the partners a large loan in the form of an advance payment for timber to be delivered. The advance, in the amount of 100,000 livres, was very large indeed, considering that an average daily wage for an able-bodied laborer at the time was often under one livre. Repayment of the advance would be made by deductions from payments due to the entrepreneurs for timber they delivered, and the navy consented that such deductions were to be made "only from [payments due] for *fournitures* of the last year of the five-year contract."[6] A loan of that magnitude from the crown called for a credit rating of the borrowers. Hence the intendants and *subdélégués* of certain provinces were asked to determine whether the entrepreneurs' assets, and those of their *cautions,* amounted to 100,000 livres in value. The intendants at Poitiers and Limoges and their assistants undertook a serious assessment of the real estate, credit, and general business reputation of Jean Babaud and his partner (and *caution*) Jacques Duportal. They concluded that the aggregate holdings of Babaud and his various *cautions* (among them his mother, Jacques Duportal, and the latter's wife and father-in-law) were sufficient, though without a great deal to spare, as security for the advance.[7] The loan (or advance) was allowed. But the *subdélégués* of Bellac and other localities were ordered not to allow any of the property of Babaud's mother or brother-in-law (Sieur Galicher), or other *cautions* to be sold until the full terms of the entire contract were fulfilled.[8]

The forests of Lorraine and Alsace produced an abundance of oak and fir growing at sites accessible to the northward-flowing Rhine, Saar, Meuse, and Moselle rivers. Those rivers formed a network of transit that could carry large quantities of timber from the remote forests of Lorraine and from Alsace and other Rhineland localities northward to the great riverports of the Netherlands that had access to the sea, Dordrecht and Rotterdam. But there were problems involved in using this downriver network. At various points on the rivers, municipalities, principalities, kingdoms, and even empires held sway, controlling one or both banks and the traffic on the river; in wartime they might close the passage to some shipments and keep it open for others, often collecting tolls in the process. In 1700 there were said to be twenty-nine French and foreign toll stations on the Rhine between Strasbourg and the United Provinces, and half a dozen more between the Dutch frontier and Dordrecht.[9] Each toll raised transit costs and reduced proportionately the value of commodities descending from sources upstream. Thus the owners of the oak and fir forests of the upper reaches of the rivers suffered the economic anguish of having the market for their timber restricted by the riverain collectors downstream. Normally they could not get their product into the hands of the buyers of the naval powers unless Dutch merchants, controlling the mouths of the rivers, served as middlemen. Hence the plans of our entrepreneurs were probably watched with real interest by forest proprietors in need of a market for their trees.

The preliminary stages of the exploitations in Alsace and Lorraine saw navy officials dispatching letters with copies of the contract to French ports, even to Le Havre and to the *Compagnie des Indes,* announcing the availability of timber for government constructions. A letter to M. de Creil at Metz asked his cooperation in facilitating the work of the entrepreneurs.[10] The ports reported that curved timber and "principal members" were the pressing need.[11]

The Pursuit of Privilege, Expansion, and Quality Control

One of Jean Babaud's first concerns, judging from the correspondence, was with the tolls that were levied on the partners' timber as it passed downriver to the Netherlands.[12] His objective was to obtain the most favorable treatment for their shipments, and ideally to pay no more than the Dutch paid on timber descending the Rhine. To this end he complained that the tolls levied on their shipments were arbitrary, and that others were receiving more favorable treatment. From Bonn, in the Electorate of Cologne, the count of Pletenberg responded via the French ministry of foreign affairs that, on the contrary, the *douanes* (tariffs) at Bonn were levied "without distinction of person or nation."[13] If that was the practice at Bonn, it was apparently otherwise along the considerable stretch of the Rhine controlled by Cologne. The French minister of marine encouraged Babaud to let him know if he had "solid reasons" to respond to the count's claim.[14] More than a year of exchanges ensued and the ministry of foreign affairs exerted its pressure before the Elector of Cologne agreed to order that "in the future the *flottes* of the Sieur Babaud would be taxed on the same basis as the ordinary *flottes* of the Dutch."[15]

This was exactly the privilege Babaud sought. It was advantageous because not only the navy's timber, but any other wood shipped to the Netherlands by the entrepreneurs, even for their private account, would pay minimum tolls. In practice this advantage was augmented by the fact that the huge *flottes* of timber descending the river ordinarily included a mélange of wood of varied quality with different destinations: trunks destined for France, other wood of lower quality that was (or would be) sawn into timber and plank, and a third component, presumably of lesser value, that would be sold in the Netherlands. The entrepreneurs could thus confound their own interests with those of the navy, and pay lower tolls even in their private traffic. At times this confusion of royal and private interests moved the owners of toll stations to complain. M. le Prince de Talmond complained in 1732 that Babaud's *flottes* passing the station at Sarrelouis included "wood other than that described in the *passeport* of the king . . . for your personal account." The prince demanded that Babaud pay the duty that was due to his *fermier* (a certain Maillefer) and threatened legal action if he did not. The French minister of marine asked Babaud "to report" what he did about this.[16]

Babaud also had troubles in his effort to extract "equal treatment" from the Elector of Trier. There too the minister of marine promised to bring the weight of the French state to bear if Babaud could provide proof, as he apparently did, that the tolls demanded of him were higher than those paid by others: "if we get the proof, [we] will make them do us justice."[17] As late as April 1731, the minister was still seeking for Babaud's shipments the same treatment that Dutch shipments received.[18]

Babaud had other problems as well. The inspectors sent by the navy to mark trees judged to be suitable and accessible in Lorraine and Alsace quickly sent negative reports to the ministry about the quality of the timber trees they found (or were shown). They reported many common-place but serious faults, such as timber afflicted with frost-crack or heart-shake. An extraordinary number of trees were reported to be rotted at the heart, a defect suggesting overage. The large size of the timber produced also suggested that very old stands of oak were being designated for the loggers. These reports were a matter of serious concern to the minister. "It is to be hoped," he wrote, "that they will not have the same defects. . . . It is important that I know for certain what help we can draw from Lorraine because, if it will not amount to much, I will have to be more restrictive about allowing [non-navy] cuts of timber in France."[19]

The minister's concerns were probably intensified by his own inexperience. Maurepas was conscientious and hard-working. When Babaud proposed to widen the geographic area in which trees were sought, Maurepas immediately approved expansion of Babaud's exploitation from the forests of the duke of Lorraine to private forests in Lorraine and royal and private forests in eastern France within portage of the major rivers. When reports of poor quality persisted, the apprehensive minister ordered dispatch of a trial shipment of 4,000 cubic feet as a sample of the wood that was "attacked by the defects." The pieces in the lot were to be numbered, given the mark of the royal navy (fleur-de-lis and anchor), and delivered—half of them to Rochefort, the rest to Brest.[20] In the late summer and fall of 1729, fears were developing, especially in the minister's mind, that the whole Lorraine project might fail. He repeatedly spoke of a need to increase the geographic extent of the cuts and reminded subordinates of the need to "use all means to recover the advances the Sieur Babaud has received."[21]

During 1729 relations steadily worsened between Babaud and the navy's principal representative in Lorraine, the Sieur Francy. He seems to have played on the minister's fears and created a variety of problems for Babaud, who probably had more reason than anyone for concern. From the first there had been delays in getting operations started. Deep snows in Lorraine in January 1729 had all but paralyzed the work of the inspectors seeking out suitable trees. After the cutting began, more friction developed because of the geographic expansion of the cuts and the consequent delays in the work of the inspectors, who were supposed to examine, approve, and then number each piece after felling and record the number of pieces that went into the water. Records were also supposed to be kept of the pieces that composed each *flotte*. Babaud added to the complexity of the inspectors' work, possibly through carelessness but probably intentionally; he knew that he would have more freedom to do as he pleased if the inspectors were busy elsewhere. He and the inspectors criticized each other continually. Writing to Babaud, the minister expressed anger:

> I have found great contradiction between what you [i.e., Francy and Babaud] write. . . . You abuse my patience, tire me with your quibbling. . . . You [Babaud] hide from him everything you are doing and continually change the project so that no one could possibly know what you are up to or comply with the rules of the service. If you do not reconcile your differences, I will be obliged to send to Lorraine one of the bondsmen (*cautions*) of your contract. He will see that you keep the king's officers informed of all the procedures required for marking, cutting, debarking, and squaring trunks, and for their provisional acceptance and transport by land and by water, and that you are not permitted to omit conforming to the rules to which you agreed in your contract.[22]

A few days later he wrote to Babaud again, saying that Francy had informed him of an exchange with Babaud on 27 August:

> When you were asked what pieces composed the trains, you replied that only your *flotteur* knew that, and that if you could sell the others in Holland, you would send only a dozen pieces to Rochefort, and none to Brest. I am astonished at such speech. I find it highly extraordinary that you think the rules do not apply to you. I tell you now that if you fail to conform to the procedures . . . I will regard it as a breach of contract and move immediately to seize the properties put up as your security and proceed to their sale to obtain restitution of the advances you have received.[23]

One issue in the quarrel between Francy and Babaud concerned the best method of processing timber trees. Francy had experience, apparently, in supervising exploitations in France; he had technical expertise and a post in the naval service that made him an influential counsellor to the minister. He consistently maintained that trees should be processed in Lorraine, in the forests or on the riverbanks, as was customary in France. The minister, who did not know or understand the alternatives at the out-set, initially (and for some months) agreed with Francy. Babaud preferred the alternative method: floating entire trunks downriver to be quarried or sawn in the Netherlands. Francy and the minister agreed, first, that de-fects in the timber could be discovered more easily after the trunk was quarried or sawn and, second, "that there is reason to fear" that Dutch sawmills, operating without navy supervision, would not properly con-trol the thickness of the timber and plank they produced, "which happens very commonly. . . . It is better that the sawing be done by hand in Lorraine. The Sieur Babaud can still include in *flottes* the plank [he makes] from the defective trees for sale in Holland." [24]

Jean Babaud must have found such comments discouraging. He knew that the work of Dutch sawmills was efficient and reliable, and certainly preferable to handsawing timber near the cutting site. He contended that virtually every tree considered by the navy inspectors fit to be marked for cutting was also fit to be skidded out of the forest, hauled to the rivers, and rafted to Holland. Furthermore, Babaud was doubtless aware that downriver passage was cheaper for logs than for wood that was already sawn, since the toll stations generally levied heavier tolls on the latter. [25]

To his credit, the young minister consulted people who knew more about Dutch sawmills than he and Francy. Near the end of 1729, Maurepas became persuaded that Babaud knew what he was about and that Francy, though perhaps going "by the book," was wrong to insist on handsawing logs in Lorraine, mistaken about Dutch sawmills, and mis-taken also in his persistent opposition to Babaud's work. Maurepas wrote to Francy telling him that he had learned on excellent authority that the wind-driven sawmills of Holland could, after all, be depended upon. He also told Francy that the Sieur Babaud was arranging the details of a new routine and was to use his own method henceforth. Furthermore, wrote Maurepas, "I have chosen you with the Sieur Morineau to go to [the province of] Champagne to mark 6,500 trees. . . . The Sieur de Ruis Embito will remain in Lorraine . . . to oversee the felling of trees and rough-hewing of trunks for downriver shipment *entière*"—that is, un-sawn, as Babaud wished. [26] Thus Francy was relieved and transferred, but not before he was ordered to visit the pieces Babaud had gathered on the banks of the Saar to be sent to Holland for sawing that spring. [27] A year afterward the Sieur de Ruis Embito was ordered to conform entirely to Babaud's wishes in this matter: all trees, even trunks selected for the use of the navy, could be sent to Holland to be sawn.[28]

But Babaud and his partners did not send all their wood to Holland for sawing. Many considerations led them to divide the work. Abundant low-cost labor could be had in certain parts of Lorraine. Cheap and efficient water-powered sawmills operated there within easy reach of some felling sites and tended to offset some of the advantage to be gained by floating whole logs to Rotterdam or Dort.[29]

Naval Timber and Bois d'Hollande

The timber most sought by the navy included a variety of special shapes, curved timbers and knees (*courbes*) particularly, some of them occurring rarely in nature. Other pieces sought were distinguished principally by their large size: for example, the oak keel pieces 50 or 60 feet long and 28 to 30 or more inches thick. Many comparatively ordinary naval timbers were 30 to 35 feet long and 20 to 25 inches thick. One monster of the navy's timber assortment was the *cabestan mêche*, a piece of oak that might be 40 inches square and 18 to 20 feet long. A *cabestan mêche* of 160 cubic feet would be worth 385 livres on delivery at Brest, a skilled laborer's salary for a year.[30] Most of the timber that Babaud shipped from Lorraine for the navy contained between 30 and 35 cubic feet.[31]

The system of rafts and *flottes* by which this naval timber was transported to the Netherlands encouraged, and even required, the inclusion of considerable quantities of non-naval wood in the raft. The high-value pieces (or the logs from which such pieces would be cut) were mixed with many other pieces, mostly oak but also much fir, beside the riverbanks to form rafts of various sizes, depending on local conditions, the amount of timber at hand, and especially water depth and custom. Rafts were customarily descended on the Saar, Moselle, and Rhine to Coblenz, the juncture of the rivers. Coblenz was, in effect, the marshaling point where great numbers of logs or rafts of logs and other pieces were gathered. The *cadre* was formed by gathering many unsquared logs, including fir and others that float well, and joining them together. To form a *flotte*, fir and other large quarried pieces were gathered; with holes bored into the ends of each, they could be linked and joined end-to-end. These trunks formed a border or rampart that was three trees high on all sides of the *flotte*, in effect, a box 1,000 to 1,200 feet long and 140 to 150 feet wide. Sawn pieces and, ordinarily, many rows of timber were piled on each other within the enclosure as cargo. Even merchandise could be embarked, as in a boat. The mass of the *flotte* sank with the weight of its cargo, but to a maximum depth of six feet.[32]

Pieces destined for the navy, especially the curved timber cut from live oak, were extremely heavy and dense. *Flottes* constructed exclusively from such naval wood would barely have surfaced, even without cargo. Hence the claim that it was "absolutely necessary" to include other pieces, especially overaged ones, that had been rejected by the field inspectors as being of no value for naval constructions. This wood was abandoned to the entrepreneur as far as the navy was concerned, although he presumably made arrangements with the proprietor of the forest or the local populace or workers before undertaking removal. Pieces of this secondary material, left unnumbered, found places alongside the numbered pieces of interest to the navy. Great quantities of it were cut and sent downriver to Holland. Among the varied components of this *bois d'Hollande* were pieces Babaud described as "*Wagenholz, Pfeifolholz,* and other grossly quarried wood, floating by themselves, that supported the pieces of naval timber scattered among them."[33]

All this was apparently little understood in the ministry of marine when Babaud and his partners began their exploitation in Lorraine. In France, naval exploitations usually took out what was useful for the navy and little more. Hence questions were raised about the great quantities of non-naval wood being sent down to Dort (Dordrecht). Babaud himself prepared a substantial *mémoire* in 1732 describing the nature of this wood and his private traffic in wood products from the forests of Lorraine and Alsace: "a necessary by-product of his contract with the navy."[34]

As to what proportion of the cuts and shipments were for the navy, and how much was Babaud's own private traffic, Babaud himself gave some hint. In the spring of 1732 he had 114,000 cubic feet of timber piled on the banks of the Saar, provisionally approved by the navy for shipment; with that timber he planned to combine 5,000 pieces of *Wagenholz* and make the whole lot into a single *grande flotte* at Coblenz, to be sent down to Dort. There, he said, the *flotte* would be broken up. The 114,000 cubic feet for the navy would soon afterward be shipped by sea to Brest and Rochefort. The larger pieces of *Wagenholz,* twelve feet in length, were to be sent to Saardam, "where they will be sawn into *planches à rouant* [Rouen?] . . . for the Paris market, for parquet flooring, wainscotting, paneling, or other furniture and finishing lumber." He promised to produce certificates later in the year proving this as their destination. The remaining *Wagenholz* pieces, six feet long, were destined to be cut into staves for barrels and shipped to La Rochelle and Bordeaux.[35]

As early as February 1732, the minister was aware that the overall *value* of Babaud's private trade largely exceeded the value of the wood he delivered for the navy's use.[36] This was repeatedly confirmed. Much more difficult to determine was the proportion of the *volume* attributable to his trade. The proportions were obviously variable, differing with phases of the exploitation, and from one *flotte* to the next. The best indication was provided by the entrepreneurs in 1737 when making a new agreement related to the distribution of income and profits among themselves. Their figures gave a valuation of 45,000 livres to the material descended for the navy, and 211,468 livres to the miscellaneous wood products sent to (and sold in) Holland for their private account in 1737.[37]

Wartime Complications

Representatives of the French monarchy at various vantage points aided Babaud and his partners in descending their timber on the "international" waters of the rivers. For example, the navy maintained an agent in the southern Netherlands who functioned at both Dort and Rotterdam. Thus the minister of marine in early July 1732 notified the Sieur Potin, agent at Rotterdam, that "the Sieur Schaaf of Coblenz, *flotteur du Rhin*," and Babaud's designated *flotteur* for 1731–1732, was bringing down a shipment destined for Daniel Duportal of Rotterdam. Schaaf was paid half his fee in advance and the rest after the timber reached Brest and Rochefort.[38]

The *flottage* of timber became more complex in wartime, requiring even more active correspondence and cooperation from the navy. Thus in April 1734 the tensions and troop movements associated with the War of the Polish Succession were seriously affecting operations on the upper Rhine; Babaud and his partners found it necessary "to borrow the name 'Sieurs Antoine et Terwen'" for their ongoing operations in the *générali-tés* of Metz and Strasbourg and in some neighboring forests situated in the territory of the Empire. For the *flottage* of their wood on the Moselle our entrepreneurs "employed some subjects of the Elector of Trier and other princes of the Empire." In the spring of 1734, these German employees were on the point of abandoning their work because their families and worldly goods were being threatened by troops, especially by French troops moving into their country as well as into Lorraine. In these circumstances the ministry of marine sought energetically, and apparently

successfully, "to procure for these persons whom the Sieur Babaud is obliged to employ the *passeports* and protection of which they have need."
He advised one of the *intendants* of the region that "it is important to His
Majesty's service that the *flottage* of this wood is made promptly and
without interruption."[39] About eighteen months later, flottage was apparently entirely interrupted. War threatened. Hence the order went
out: "It is necessary that you stop marking and felling operations in the
Empire in order not to arouse new suspicions among persons seeking to
discover if the wood being cut is for France." All operations by naval officials were ordered halted until further notice.[40]

Babaud and his partners also enjoyed aid from the navy when their
timber was shipped from Dort and Rotterdam to France. Their timber
contract allowed them ten sous per cubic foot to cover the cost of shipment by sea. Such payment, in ordinary circumstances, was sufficient to
ensure that ample numbers of Dutch or other commercial ships would be
available for the work. Dutch bottoms were principally used, their freight
rates being reportedly low, but French shippers, and on rare occasions
even English ones, might be hired.[41] For the larger timbers, those 50 or 60
feet long, vessels specializing in the timber traffic or very large vessels
must have been required, since only they were apt to be equipped with
hull doors (*sabords*) and oversized hatches. At times it may have been
difficult for the captains of timber carriers to find return cargo.

Some combination of adverse circumstances apparently led Babaud in
June 1732 to claim that he "will not find in [all] Holland enough ships to
transport the 100,000 cubic feet of wood due to arrive from Lorraine at
the beginning of July, and the 200,000 of this year's cut due to arrive
in the fall"—an exaggerated plea intended to obtain the loan of several
of the navy's cargo carriers (*gabarres*) to help with the work. Babaud
offered to pay the navy eight sous per cubic foot if the *gabarres* could be
used.[42] He was granted the use of the carriers on the terms he proposed
but was urged to use them energetically, "with extreme diligence," and
warned that "if they employ more than two months in their navigation
[i.e., Brest-Dort-Brest], the expense of salaries and victuals for their crews
will be charged to him."[43] Each *gabarre* could carry an estimated 4,000
cubic feet of timber, indicating that about twenty-five cargoes would be
required for the timber on hand in July, and seventy-five cargoes for the
1732 season.

When shipments arrived at port, the captain of the carrier (if non-
French) might insist on immediate payment, an incidental disadvantage
of using foreign carriers and an added advantage of using the navy-owned

ships. Babaud and his partners had correspondents with multiple responsibilities at both Brest (Sieur Salomon) and Rochefort (Sieur Masson). They assisted in the examination of bills of lading and unloading, and received and paid out funds (including advances) on incoming cargoes. Thus when two Dutch *flûtes* arrived at Brest on Babaud's account in January 1731 with cargoes of timber from Lorraine, naval officials (on the minister's order) advanced 10,000 livres "to pay the freight and cost of discharging the cargo."[44]

From the very beginning of the exploitation, the quality of the deliveries from Lorraine was under fire; at the ministry it was said that "various faults were found with this wood, on which sentiment was divided."[45] We have noted the apprehensions and discouragement that attended this phase of the work. Councils of experts were convened at each port to assess the shipments arriving from this newly tapped source, to judge the qualities of certain pieces already used, and those still stored in the yards at the ports. Apparently there was agreement that the wood was "faulty" by the conventional standards used at the ports. The councils at the ports were held to be supporting the opinion that "most of the faults attributed to this wood did not affect its utility for the naval service."[46]

The one major, unacceptable fault—rot—was said to be "most manifest in pieces of large dimensions because they derived from the oldest trees." The schedule of payments used in Babaud's first contract rewarded, and thus encouraged, delivery of such large timber pieces as were reportedly available in the little-tapped forests of Lorraine. But when the councils of construction pointed this out in June 1730, the minister decreed that the ports would henceforth use the tariff of 1718 in the evaluation of Babaud's deliveries. This earlier schedule had included smaller, more modest-sized timber in the first (most highly priced) class. Babaud's reaction was to assure the naval authorities that henceforth he would "choose only young, living trees about 150 years of age."[47]

These developments apparently improved not only the acceptability of timber from Lorraine, but also the profitability of Babaud's whole operation. He was better paid for timber of smaller dimensions. He had less incentive to run risks in selecting and delivering very large, doubtful pieces; the vast mature oak stands then found in parts of Lorraine were condemned by the navy's inspectors as dangerous and "overaged," giving Babaud strong arguments to use in jousting with forest proprietors about prices. Thereby the giants of the oak forest stands of Lorraine (and Montbéliard) were left for the "private use" of the entrepreneurs as *bois d'Hollande*.

Threats to the Enterprise

Perhaps the most serious threat to this remarkable business venture developed early in its "start-up" period (1728–1731). A number of extraordinary circumstances coalesced to underscore this threat in 1731. One was the failure of the Paris banking house of Donnadieu et Chambon, which compromised the partners' credit at a time when the enterprise was still at an early stage, heavy investments of capital had been made and were continuing, and returns were still far off, since deliveries had not even begun. At that stage fiscal stability could be tipped dangerously by relatively modest setbacks, such as the failure of the bank mentioned above.

An additional complication was the fact that Babaud and M. de Ruis Embito, Francy's successor, did not get along any better than Babaud and Francy. Ruis Embito, as noted, was the navy's principal official overseeing operations in Lorraine. Friction between the two men surfaced in February 1731, when the exploitation had been under way for over two years. Thousands of trees had been cut, but nearly all the trunks and timber still lay in the forest, at the sawmills (six at Bitche), or on the riverbanks in Lorraine. Babaud was under great pressure. He must have wanted action. Everything was prepared for the downriver shipments to begin in the spring. But it was winter. Ruis Embito and the *contremaîtres* and carpenters were evidently not as active as Babaud wished. The minister had reason to write to Ruis Embito urging that his carpenters be "usefully occupied. I recommend also that you take care that they hold to good conduct. Your own is not a good example." [48] Two months later it was disclosed that Ruis Embito had caused many hundreds of planks to be sawn to the wrong dimensions, with the result that reception of Babaud's *bordages* at the naval arsenal was suspended. [49] Ruis Embito was severely reprimanded by the minister and at the same time threatened with dismissal from his post for his complaints about Babaud. Maurepas himself was persuaded that Babaud had "done nothing reprehensible":

> It is very extraordinary that the good order you yourself described in all the *ateliers* [letters of 25 January and 9 February] fell into the great disorder you describe during Babaud's seventeen-day absence to visit Versailles. . . . your other observations appear equally unfounded. They attack the personal character of the entrepreneur without giving any sort of substantial detail about his breaches of his contract. What you are doing at Bitche [headquarters of the operation] is distracting your own attention from

the needs of the service and causing trouble. I am going to get an order from the king to send you back to Rochefort. An officer charged with an important mission abroad should think only of doing a good job.[50]

For the minister of marine to write in such terms to a career service employee of the state, one of his own subordinates, can certainly be seen as an extraordinary favor to the entrepreneur concerned.

Unfortunately for Babaud, Maurepas did not (perhaps could not) carry out his threat to relieve Ruis Embito until sixteen months later.[51] Thus Babaud was still forced to deal with Ruis Embito in Lorraine when the Masson-Babaud enterprise was struck by its most serious crisis: the failure in July 1731 of Donnadieu et Chambon. The duke of Lorraine, or his *Conseil* for him, ordered seizure of 93,000 cubic feet of Babaud's timber on grounds of nonpayment for the timber cut in his forests. Maurepas had to follow suit, placing seizure orders on the same timber in the name of the king of France as surety for the 100,000-livre advance the Babaud and Company had received.[52]

In Maurepas, Babaud and his partners for many years had a firm friend and a powerful one. Maurepas wrote to the court of Lorraine, explaining the French king's seizure order and seeking "to obtain for this *fournisseur* freedom to continue to process the trees already cut and transport them to the rivers." [53] Babaud suggested, as an expedient, changing the terms of his contract, canceling the requirement that timber be delivered to the ports and inserting a clause allowing provisional reception of the timber on the banks of the rivers at a proportionately lower price; the timber could then be transported downriver as the property of His Majesty, immune to seizure by creditors.[54] Maurepas even approached Cardinal Fleury about plans to help Babaud, but without obtaining any help: the affair "was not to his taste." [55]

But Maurepas ultimately concluded that "the payment of M. le Duc de Lorraine is the first obstacle to remove." On 2 September 1731, Babaud was scheduled to leave "immediately" to visit the court of Lorraine at Lunéville to establish an exact account of the amount of his debt and obtain the release [of the timber] by means of the help I will procure for him." As the minister's disposition to cooperate became clear, the number of Babaud's creditor-claimants multiplied to include not only the duke of Lorraine, but also a Paris banker by the name of Bernard; lumbermen, carters, and *flotteurs* seeking their wages; Daniel Duportal of Rotterdam; and Dominique Antoine, banker of Nancy, among others. Settlement with the duke of Lorraine was the key to the settlement of all accounts.[56] However, the sum total of the claims was enormous, estimated by Maurepas as 83,000 livres.[57]

On 14 October 1731, Maurepas granted the 24,837 livres needed to pay the duke "for the timber destined for the service of the king, and some help beyond that, taking account of the cost of exploitation and transit."[58] But he said that he thought it "ridiculous for [Babaud] to have offered to the Council of the duke of Lorraine letters of exchange drawn on his Paris bankers even before establishing the total amount of the account, and without being certain whether I would order reimbursement, or whether I had determined the sum I would give. . . . I [nonetheless] intend to hold to the promise I made."[59] There remained the problem of Babaud's private wood, which had also been seized in Lorraine, for which payment was also sought and for which Maurepas long resisted providing transit funds. But finally he consented to try to obtain even those.

In late November Maurepas announced that he had rendered an account of the whole affair to the king. At the minister's urging, Louis XV agreed to accept title to the naval timber provisionally, and to advance all the sums due to the duke of Lorraine and all the funds needed to transport the wood, even Babaud's own, by *flottage* on the rivers to Holland and by sea to France.[60]

Describing these concessions to the banker Bernard in a letter dated 24 December 1731, Maurepas explained that the king was paying 53,000 livres to the duke of Lorraine, the sum total of Babaud's debt for the trees, and was also advancing "nearly 80,000 as the cost of descent to Holland and transport by sea to Rochefort and Brest. All these expenses deducted from the value of the navy's delivery will leave only about 40,000 for him [Babaud], supposing it arrives without accident and that there are no rejects." But he reminded Bernard that such credits would not be in Babaud's hands for some time, "because the deliveries will not be made at the ports until July or August, the shipments having not yet departed Lorraine."[61] By Maurepas's calculation, the value of the 150,000 cubic feet delivered in 1731 alone would pay off the 240,000 in "advances" Babaud and his partners had received, and render them a modest profit of 40,000 livres for their trouble. This, of course, took no account of the profit from Babaud's private traffic in the Netherlands and with buyers in France, which would enable the entrepreneurs to finance their own operations in 1732. This they did, delivering far more than 150,000 cubic feet that year.

Indeed, the partners were taking out so much timber that by June 1732 the court of Lorraine called a halt to the marking of trees for Babaud because he already had marked or cut more than sufficient numbers to complete the terms of his contract.[62] Babaud, it seems, was buying more timber from the duke of Lorraine than the latter wanted to sell and selling more to the king of France than the officials of French naval arsenals wanted to buy; and the whole operation was being guided, supported, and in large part financed by the ministry of marine.

Success did not prevent the entrepreneurs from asking for and obtaining another "advance." This new loan of 112,000 livres from the king, granted in December 1732, again without interest, was obviously a substantial help to the partners. The occasion for it seems to have been a desire to encourage and facilitate the expansion of exploitations into Alsace and other localities. Now that their exploitations were proceeding well in those eastern regions, never before tapped by the navy, they evidently deemed it desirable to take out all the timber they could without delay. The minister knew that the new loan was a boon to the partners; he meant it to be, and wrote to Babaud to underscore the point that the loan was "a particular favor, which should excite him to make every effort to finish the job quickly."[63]

Extending the scope of their operations, the partners moved to acquire trees in French-owned territories, particularly the province of Alsace and the environs of Metz and Thionville. Exploitations in French territories involved them with French laws designed to control both the cutting and the export of wood. The French *Ordonnance* of Waters and Forests (1669) obliged the owners of timber trees to sell to naval contractors, or not sell at all. That law was advantageous to Babaud and his fellow entrepreneurs in a variety of ways. Forest proprietors in eastern France were forced to deal with them; the "monopoly" clause in Babaud's contract made him the exclusive buyer of timber in the region. The infrequency of naval cutting in the region predisposed proprietors to sell their mature trees while they could, before they became overage. The most likely alternative market—selling to the Dutch—was closed to French forest proprietors by an *arrêt du conseil* of 18 August 1722 that imposed a blanket prohibition on exports of wood from France.[64]

Circumstances peculiar to exploitations in Alsace included the fact that the *ordonnance* of 1669 was only partially applied, and energetically resisted, in that province. The forests had been badly treated by both the local population and foreign merchants, including the Dutch.[65] That, with the earlier refusal of permission to the Dutch, may help to explain the determined opposition Babaud encountered at the hands of the intendant Paul de Bron of Alsace when he undertook to buy timber for export from that province. The intendant declared that permission could not be given to Babaud "without violating absolutely the *arrêt du conseil* of 1722." Available supplies of wood had become insufficient "for the *service des fortifications* and defense, for hospitals, and for the heating needs of the inhabitants of Alsace, who," he said, "are paying ten, twelve, and thirteen livres a cord for firewood." They would pay double that, he declared, if Babaud were permitted to undertake cuts.[66] Naturally the wood destined for Babaud's private traffic was the object of his vehement opposition. Maurepas proposed various expedients—restrictions on the geographic spread or the extent of the cuts, or on Babaud's private traffic—but to no avail.[67] Far from making concessions or compromising, de Bron mobilized high-ranking military men against the proposed cuts. MM. les Maréchaux de Berwick and Du Bourg declared emphatically to representatives of the navy that "they did not believe any cuts of wood should [then] be allowed, even with the proposed restrictions"; indeed, observing that dense woodlands were important for defense, they both expressed the more ominous conviction that it might be advantageous to halt certain cuts being made in the forests adjoining Alsace—in Lorraine for example.[68] (See discussion below.)

Expert military opinion is not easily contradicted by civil or naval authorities, in France or elsewhere, and it might seem that Maurepas and Babaud were beaten in the battle for Alsace that year, not only by de Bron and the marshals, but also by the *contrôleur général* and a certain Sieur Oursel. The latter was discovered to be carrying on forest exploitations in Alsace under the auspices of the *contrôleur général*. Maurepas complained that Oursel's work "renders the exploitations of the *fournisseur* for the navy very difficult, even impracticable, when he exploits in the same or nearby cantons."[69] Thus in September Maurepas appeared to retreat. Tacitly admitting defeat, he halted work for the navy in the province of Alsace: "it does not appear that we can continue exploitations in Alsace at present."[70] Writing to de Bron, he observed (surprisingly and not very convincingly) that "the fear of excessively depleting the woodlands in the present circumstances is the principal reason for stopping the cuts."[71]

Concern for forest depletion and the fate of wooded lands in Alsace was out of character for a French minister of marine. The minister's action was evidently intended as a blind. As subsequent developments proved, neither the navy nor Babaud had any intention of halting the exploitation and shipment of timber from Alsace, even in the face of war. A vast number of trees had already been felled. The plan was to use fictitious or assumed names and to employ surrogates or front-men, but in any case to continue downriver shipments for the navy as before.

The Sieurs Terwen

Jean Babaud and his partners, his brother Pierre, and Jacques Masson (Jacques Duportal having retired about this time), now found themselves embroiled in the Rhineland repercussions of the dynastic maneuvers of France, the Polish "succession" crisis, and the consequent War of the Polish Succession. These developments produced an even closer working relationship among the entrepreneurs and new ties with the *Etat Major* of the navy. Maurepas publicly canceled their contract with the navy for timber exploitations in the Rhine basin. But secretly a new contract was made with the partners, using borrowed Dutch names, such as "the Sieurs Terwen."[72] This revised contract called for delivery not merely of 750,000 cubic feet of timber, the maximum agreed upon earlier, but "all the timber that the Sieur Babaud can cut and deliver beyond that until otherwise ordered."[73] It was foreseen that in descending the river, the agents of "the Sieurs Terwen" would enjoy "protection" and "neutrality" and all the advantages usually accorded to Dutch merchants in their conduct of commerce.[74]

The need for "neutral" identity to mask French timber exploitations was short-lived because the War of the Polish Succession itself was short. It is doubtful that our entrepreneurs could have successfully worn this mask for long; but the device enabled petty principalities and states along the rivers to continue to accord to Babaud's shipments the "equal treatment" and passage they gave in peacetime. Apparently Jean Babaud himself visited Holland again in the winter of 1733/34 to arrange details for descent of the *flottes* and to consult at the Hague with M. le Marquis de Fénelon (probably the French ambassador). On returning, Babaud sent his faithful clerk, Mathieu Wegelin, to the "Imperial camp," where Wegelin obtained from the "prince of Bevern" [sic] all the *passeports* he sought, "in the name of the Sieurs Pierre Antoine and Pierre Terwen."[75]

Not all the problems were so easily ironed out. In fact, contradictions and ambiguities were underscored repeatedly. Our "Dutch" merchants were descending wood, they claimed, for commercial purposes (to avoid confiscation by the Imperials, who would seize French-owned wood, especially naval timber). But at Haguenau, for example, the French toll agent on duty declared that all wood descending the river was subject to his toll unless destined for the navy; moreover, he said, French laws forbade Dutch merchants to export any wood, and most particularly timber suitable for repairing naval vessels. He stopped the *flotte* and threatened to seize the cargo, but was explicitly forbidden to do so by the intendant de Bron.[76]

But on the highest levels of the French service, things went most smoothly for the partners' "Dutch" shipments. Maurepas was apologetic in importuning M. le Comte de Belleisle "about this detail" of *voiturage* for Babaud's wood. The comte commanded "the greater part" of the localities where Babaud's cutting operations were taking place. Belleisle was especially helpful in obtaining overland transport service for Babaud's timber.[77] Even so, there were serious delays. Writing to one naval official, Maurepas urged him to continue to try to overcome obstacles. "See that the *fournisseur* pays the carters the wages earned, and when they are discontented with reasonable payment and try to take advantage, you can support the representations of the *fournisseur* with the [authority of the] intendant and others responsible for putting a stop to such difficulties, and seeing that the service of the king is not delayed."[78] And in writing in October 1735 to the marquis de Fénelon in Holland, Maurepas urged him to "continue to protect the Sieur Babaud." The marquis certainly did that. Showing perhaps an excess of zeal when one of "Terwen's" shipments was seized by the Imperials, he suggested that the matter of the damage sustained by the partners be taken before the States General of Holland. Maurepas quickly vetoed that plan: "Act only secretly in this affair."[79]

In 1735, to give the partners "the means of completing the contracts made and to be made," Maurepas obtained from the king an additional advance: "the sum of 300,000 livres in four equal payments of 75,000 livres each: the first [to be paid] immediately, the second, third, and fourth in April, July, and October 1735, which sum will be repaid by being withheld from the last payments for shipments remaining to be made in execution of the contracts with him of 22 August 1728 and 30 October 1733."[80] This phraseology suggests that the earlier advances (100,000 and 115,000) had not yet been repaid and would be paid off as the contracts were completed. The new "advance" would tide the enterprise over the payoff period and effectively delay repayment (again without interest) until the new contract reached its final, payoff stage. This new contract called for deliveries of 600,000 cubic feet in six years, beginning 1 January 1736, at the rate of 100,000 per year, the timber to be drawn from the *généralités* of Metz and Strasbourg in the duchy of Lorraine. The contract provided further that the entrepreneurs were responsible for meeting all the extraordinary expenses the war occasioned, such as higher seaborne shipping rates and the increased costs of obtaining *passeports*, cartage, *flottage*, and so on. But all war-induced "seizures and confiscations, and deterioration of the wood by enemy action, including damage [or losses] resulting from delay in descent of the Rhine and its tributaries, sieges of strongholds, construction of bridges, or other obstructions by troops of the king or the enemy, or resulting from weather or negligence of conductors of *flottes,* will be at the charge of His Majesty."[81] It was a good contract from the standpoint of the entrepreneurs.

Opening the River Doubs

Beginning at least as early as the fall of 1733 and continuing over the next six years, Jean Babaud's health underwent spasmodic but progressive deterioration—no doubt a trying experience for this strong, apparently blunt-spoken, and obviously energetic man. At the onset of the Lorraine enterprise he had personally supervised cuts in many scattered localities, running the navy's inspectors ragged, but by the fall of 1733 he was probably criticized for his inactivity.[82] Increasingly he was obliged to abandon travel and field work and confine himself to handling the accounts and paperwork at the offices the partners kept in the town of Bitche. For about three years, beginning late in 1733, Jacques Masson seems to have assumed part of the field work burden. In that period Masson had a leading role in correspondence with Maurepas and in negotiations with forest proprietors. He was also much involved, as we will see, in the Montbéliard and Doubs navigation schemes of those years. On many occasions he is seen involved with cartage and *flottage* problems facing the partners during the Polish Succession period. As a result of that war, as we have seen, France was to acquire Lorraine and Masson was to move out and up, to high responsibility in the French ministry of finance, while keeping his ties with the partnership.

The concurrent role of the youngest partner in this period remains obscure. Perhaps he supervised the exploitations and undertook the inspection work with naval officials that Babaud had been obliged to drop. He was involved with the forges and foundries the partners held along the Loire. In general, as the youngest of the partners, Pierre probably did for his handicapped older brother, and for his new father-in-law and the partnership, whatever he was told or expected to do.

Clearly Maurepas was imaginative, flexible, and generous in finding ways to reconcile the entrepreneurs' interests and those of the navy and king. Like the entrepreneurs themselves, with whom he was obviously on friendly terms, he was energetic and determined in seeking expedients to forward the work. Masson, master of expedients himself, was the partner receiving most of the minister's letters from 1734 onward. It was Masson who was sent on special missions to Alsace and Lorraine "to profit from the opportunities" when the needs of the military would allow the transit of wood to the banks of the Saar, Moselle, and Rhine en route for Holland.[83] Masson received the special orders to furnish "immediately" extraordinary quantities of stave wood for barrels.[84] It was Masson who wrote to the minister, noting that there were still trees in the *comté* of Bitche to be logged; it was Masson who wrote to communicate his fears that "the Sieur Babaud is not in a fit state to travel to [nearby] Lunéville" to negotiate a contract. Therefore Masson went alone[85] and managed to negotiate the purchase of the stands in question from S.A.R. Madame la Duchesse de Lorraine.[86] And it was Masson, fulsome and not overmodest in reporting on the measures he took, who sought to ensure exploitation rights for the partners in the woodlands belonging to the *duché des Deux Ponts, des terres de Nassau, Blucartel,* and others in the environs, as well as those of the Palatinate, which were within reach of the rivers Blize and Nahe. Masson sought entrée to Cardinal "Shöenbornn," in whose forests, he said, "there are rare timbers for the construction of vessels."[87]

From Masson's correspondence we also learn that it was he who sought to forestall a group of Dutch merchants—presumably real ones—the Sieurs Wonderwald, who had "already purchased 8,000 of the finest trees in the *bailliage* of Lemberg belonging to the comte," and how Masson hoped to arrange to log the rich stands in the forests of Lemberg, "terres de l'Empire," belonging to the "very old and infirm" comte of "Hanau."[88] Masson could be very persuasive with such men, and Maurepas apparently provided him with a very potent letter signed by himself, comte de Maurepas, *secrétaire d'état pour la marine* to Louis XV. The very next month came the rich fruit—the count's consent: "It suffices for me to know, Monsieur, that I will be doing something agreeable to the king, and that you honor the Sieur Masson with your protection, to decide me to grant with pleasure what you ask me to do for him."[89]

When signed in 1735, this contract allowed the partners to take 10,000 trees of medium size, five to seven feet in circumference. The actual exploitation was probably managed by Pierre Babaud, since from 1736 onward Masson was, as we have seen, increasingly involved with the ministry of finance, and Jean was confined at Bitche. It must have been Pierre, or his surrogate, who saw to the logging of 5,000 of those trees by 1738. That year the prince of Hesse-Darmstadt (heir to the estates of the old count) agreed to allow them to take the second half of their allotment, and 5,000 *Wagenholz* as well, from the forests of "Pirmassens, Munchwiller, Lemberg, Eppenbron, Berenthal, and Philisbourgh, all in the *bailliage* of Lemberg, and 1,500 trees from the forest of Wimenauve [*sic*] in Alsace." This last group of 1,500 were located far up in the mountains forming the frontier of Alsace with Lorraine, in the most remote parts of the comté of Bitche, and could not for the most part be taken out.[90]

Shortly before Jean Babaud's death in December 1738, the partners were offered trees by M. le Baron Desteincallenfels (agent of the Elector Palatine) and by Madame la Duchesse des Deux Ponts, oaks in the "comté de la Petite Pierre in Alsace." In April 1739, 1,600 trees were promised that could be logged and skidded to the banks of the Saar.[91]

Jacques Masson and the brothers Babaud were also drawn to the potentialities of the forests of the comté de Montbéliard. Montbéliard was an enclave jutting into eastern France from the Swiss cantons on the east, much of it the property of the duke of Würtemberg. Over the years ordinances from the duke and his Council (1726, 1736) had sought to stop abuses in the forests of Montbéliard and to control general use because of the "rarity of wood needed for the operation of his forges."[92] Yet even in the 1730s there were still some fine forest stands in Montbéliard. The navy's inspectors found between 400,000 and 500,000 cubic feet of timber situated within easy access of the River Doubs,[93] a river (ultimately) flowing southwest and joining the long Saône-Rhône route toward the Mediterranean, to supply the ports of Toulon and Marseille. The total distance for Doubs-Saône-Rhône *flottage* almost equaled that from Alsace to Rotterdam and Dort or the Saar-Moselle-Rhine route, and there were toll stations on the Saône-Rhône route as on the Rhine. But the obstructions along the northeasterly reaches of the Doubs presented problems that were unique.

The possibility of opening the River Doubs to navigation was discussed in different terms by different entrepreneurs and examined and re-examined many times during the Spanish domination of the comté and also in the eighteenth century.[94] The failure to reopen the route to navigation can probably be explained by the lack of sustained need, rather than by the technical difficulty of the job. The opposition of dam- and mill-owners on the river was also a consideration tending to discourage those who might undertake the enterprise. In discussions relating to opening the Doubs, a significant distinction was made between opening the river for navigation and opening it merely for *flottage*. The latter, it was later admitted, could be re-established with relative ease.[95]

At first the projectors led by Masson tended, in their reports to the minister, to emphasize the difficulties involved in opening the river, whether for navigation or for *flottage*. Barthelemy de Vanolles, the intendant in whose province the jurisdiction of Montbéliard lay, did the same, until the contract with the partners was actually signed. Only then, apparently, was mention made of the fact that the Doubs was "formerly" navigable. Vanolles showed admiration and strong partisanship for Masson; literally, Vanolles was Masson's advocate.

Exactly how easy or difficult it would be to establish navigation or *flottage* no one seemed initially to know. As late as 1759, the Doubs was still considered unnavigable.[96] In 1734 Vanolles reported that the river was passable only for firewood—"lightweight and not very long"—from its northern hook as far southwest as Besançon. Rocks at certain places in the river "very much hinder" *flottage* (significantly, he did not say that rocks would prevent the passage of "large or heavy pieces of wood"), but he believed that the obstacles in that section of the river could be overcome. The opening of the stretch southward to the juncture with the Saône "will perhaps be more difficult, and costly," though he admitted that the river below Besançon had yet to be inspected.[97]

Such reports from Vanolles (and Masson) apparently elicited the suggestion in the ministry that the whole project of *flottage* be dropped and consideration be given instead to taking the naval timber out over the roads. Some private forests of Montbéliard, and in the *bailliage* of Vesoul, it was reported, were served by roads described as "très beau." But this alternative would involve other problems, according to Vanolles, not simply because of the distance involved (sixteen or seventeen "great leagues"), but also because the roads in question were used for the transport of grains and forage for the army operating in German areas. This service was said to "require more than 15,000 vehicles in the course of a year, and I fear that even this [number] will not suffice. This may lead you to decide to open the Doubs River for *flottage*."[98]

In the spring of 1735, however, the French *Conseil d'Etat* issued an *arrêt du conseil* ordering the owners of all mills and sluices on the Doubs to construct *portières* to allow navigation and the *flottage* of the king's timber.[99] Later in the spring the *Conseil* ordered a *constructeur* named Le Vasseur to go to the region and report on the problem.[100] Initially Le Vasseur had a good deal of difficulty getting in touch with Jacques Masson.[101] His reports on the *flottage* project, dated 11 April and 17 May, emphasized the problems posed by the owners of mills and dams, making little mention of natural obstacles or obstructions.[102] During the summer Le Vasseur and Masson apparently spent a considerable amount of time together, and Masson deeply impressed the intendant with his expertise. Vanolles became in effect Masson's mouthpiece.[103]

The intendant convened a panel of navigation and construction experts at Audincourt in the presence of the Sieurs Masson, Le Vasseur, and Coste, the latter being *subdélégué* de Montbéliard and Vanolles's subordinate. All was ready, but by chance, "at the moment of departure [for the river], the Sieur Coste fell dangerously ill"; to avoid delays, Vanolles said that he had no alternative but "to substitute the Sieur Masson to write up the *procès verbal*." [104] Masson completed the job in less than six weeks; his report was an impressive document, a manuscript of eighty pages and forty-nine maps in color, designed to convince the minister of the practicability of clearing the Doubs for *flottage*. This work Masson first agreed to undertake and complete for 52,278 livres; later he agreed to perform it gratis to the extent needed for his own operation (i.e., no permanent works), provided he received certain exclusive privileges for ten or twelve years. [105]

Vanolles was delighted with the report; his letter of transmittal praised Masson's "knowledge, his understanding, and his integrity." Whatever the plan for *flottage*, said Vanolles, "the most essential course of action is to charge the Sieur Masson with the work." His long letter discussed details, described certain conditions that Masson considered indispensable, and concluded with a suggestion of his own—that the trees of the *parc* of Montbéliard, partly removed by earlier cuts, be replanted as part of Masson's exploitation: "I communicated my idea to the Sieur Masson and proposed that he pay the cost. . . . He consented, in writing, on condition that it not exceed 3,000 livres." [106]

By the end of June 1736, it was calculated that 37,000 trees in Montbéliard had been marked as suitable for cutting by the navy. These trees were concentrated in the stands of several major forest owners, and scattered over many communal forests of the region: [107]

1. Forests of the comte de Montbéliard and the duke of Würtemberg — 1,336 trees
2. Forests of the communities of the *comté* — 10,662 trees
3. Forests of the *domaine de la seigneurie d'Héricour*(t?) — 866 trees
   Forests of the former's communities — 13,027 trees
   Forests of the communities of the seigneur of Blamont — 684 trees
   Forests of the communities of the seigneury of Chatelet — 1,051 trees

   (items under 3 bracketed together) — 15,628 trees

It was expected that an additional 10,000 trees would be found suitable, which would make an aggregate total of about 1 million cubic feet of naval timber.

Masson and the Babauds encountered different circumstances in dealing with each category of owner. The first was expected to present the least difficulty: the ducal succession was in question, Prince Leopold Eberhard having died leaving many children from many beds, some not legitimate. However, Arnold François, baron de Tornaco, governor of the principality of Montbéliard (for the duchy of Würtemberg) had to be dealt with.[108]

Tornaco demanded 15 livres instead of the 5 the partners expected to pay for each tree (forester fees included), and also sought to reserve the branches of the trees that were felled.[109] Both Masson and Jean Babaud dealt with the baron. The contract was signed in Babaud's name at Paris in October 1736 and included significant compromises and concessions on both sides.[110] The terms were, nevertheless, favorable to the entrepreneurs, granting them entire disposition of the trees themselves and the use of local labor for cartage at controlled (i.e., low) wages. The authority of the governor of Montbéliard was clearly at their disposal.

The following January the partners signed a fifteen-year contract with the navy for deliveries to Marseille and Toulon from Montbéliard and the regions accessible to the Doubs. The contract required (art. 18) that the usual register be kept recording the size, quality, and number of each piece of timber cut and shipped, and the *fournisseurs* were promised preference over all other *fournisseurs* in the region where cuts were made. Within eighteen months two important amendments were introduced, providing that officers at the Mediterranean ports "could not reject or hold out in entrepôt any pieces from the provisionment unless they had been so damaged or altered in shipment that they could not be usefully employed . . . and the *rebuts* cannot, under any pretext, exceed 5 percent of the provisionment."[111]

These remarkable terms virtually forced the Mediterranean ports to accept shipments from the partners regardless of the quality of the timber delivered. The process of selection was to take place in the forest or on the riverbanks, before shipment. This was even more high-handed than the practice at the Atlantic seaboard arsenals. But all the deliveries of the partners, whether from Lorraine, Alsace, Montbéliard, or other adjacent timber-producing localities, enjoyed exceptionally favorable treatment under the terms of the contracts the partners obtained. The central administration of the navy ordained it so. Complaint or criticism at the ports of destination, which was abundant, had little effect, at least in the administration of Minister Maurepas.

Some of the most outspoken opposition to the Montbéliard exploitation came from foresters, notably a certain Sieur Hatzel (or Hartzel). In late 1736 and 1737, Jean Babaud's agent reported that Hatzel had put forth arguments full of falsehoods that were "easy to destroy." Furthermore, "under the specious pretext of love of *la patrie*, [Hatzel] exposed Monsieur le Baron de Tornaco to a riot where he had need of all his resolution to dissipate the storm. . . . [Hatzel] spread abroad in Montbéliard word that the governor had sold off all the wood and was going to produce total ruin . . . , [that] the cuttings of Babaud et Cie. had not left a single tree big enough to produce a beam." [112]

Foresters described the events on the opening day of logging operations, when the partners' subcontractor Prieur arrived in the company of two naval officials and about thirty axmen. With apparent trepidation, the foresters allowed them to enter the *parc*. Ignoring the custom of leaving a certain number of trees (*balivaux*) for reseeding and ultimate reproduction of the stand, the loggers had by the second day cut nearly all the trees.[113] That was only the beginning. Subsequent logging crews of three to four hundred workers continued the process of felling and quarrying trunks; the crews and their dependents were themselves so numerous that they "caused a considerable rise in prices of foodstuffs, especially grains . . . , causing townsmen and rural folk alike to complain." By May 1739 "murmurs" were redoubled: grains were becoming scarce, prices were high; yet the prohibition on imports of grains from Burgundy and Alsace continued to be enforced with the usual rigor.[114]

Complaints from the local foresters apparently piled up on the desk of Grand Forester Stattler of Montbéliard. The severity of the grievances led him to leave the area on 11 December 1737 in quest of M. le Baron de Tornaco, in whose hands alone lay the authority to control the loggers. But Tornaco, it seems, was a difficult man to reach. Stattler was informed that Tornaco was to visit Vienna and Brussels and might therefore be absent for many months; no one was available to deal with the abuses or grievances incident to the exploitation.

"I have always dealt with these men with much courtesy," Stattler reported, "without making any gratuitous trouble for them. But when I see that they exercise too much authority to the detriment of His Serene Highness [i.e., the duke], my duty and my conscience oblige me to oppose them." He was grieved by the fact that trees in the forests of the duke of Würtemberg were being marked with the *marteau*, or stamping tool, of the king of France, and that cuts were being made everywhere, with no regard for prescribed limits, the size of the trees themselves, their age, or their condition. Furthermore, the loggers were trafficking in wood: "workers and axmen take great pieces of wood and give them to their hosts or landlords, or to their carters." He bitterly criticized the practice of allowing workers to take trimmings; those responsible for operations were keeping poor accounts, carrying off everything more than three feet in circumference, and destroying most of the remainder in the process. They refused to obey any Montbéliard official, and complaints to Tornaco seemed fruitless even when he could be reached. The communities of the region had sent two deputies to make representations at the court of the duke, but without result. Hatzel thought the situation hopeless.

Other complaints came from the *Conseil* of Montbéliard and from the proprietors of forges and mills. One forge owner claimed that Babaud's contract could not be executed without completely overturning the entire forest management system, which required that ten trees be left on each *arpent* to replant and replenish. Instead of leaving ten selected seed-trees to repopulate, as the duke's *ordonnances* decreed, the entrepreneurs took or degraded everything: "the bad trees that they left in bouquets cannot repopulate the great open spaces." Regarding the communities' oaks, one forge owner remarked that he would "prefer to have a tax of 100,000 livres imposed than to see the entrepreneurs cut all the wood the navy has marked." [115]

Returning to Montbéliard (from Paris, it turned out), Tornaco offered a sad sort of remedy. This "allotment scheme" for the whole of Montbéliard he suggested in an effort to persuade (in effect, bribe) the French navy's *fournisseurs* to limit their cuts. Each village was called on to offer a certain quantity of oaks as a free gift; those without woodlands were to give money instead. The hope was that the entrepreneurs would elect not to cut all the trees, as their contract allowed them to do. Technically, the *don gratuit* of the populace was to be considered a "gift to the prince"; but the partners were to be the beneficiaries. [116] All the judges of the region and all the communities, realizing how helpless they were, consented to this scheme. [117]

The partners' immediate response was defensive and negative; interestingly, they emphatically disclaimed complicity in devising the Tornaco scheme. And when the scheme was publicized, they denied that any restricting agreement or promise, written or verbal, had been made: "I declare to you positively that I never agreed to this," said Jean Babaud; "... I will require the strict execution of my contract." But as the signatory author of the partners' response, he quietly consented to accept the proffered *don gratuit,* in a "spirit of conciliation," while continuing to insist that "I have never renounced the condition of my contract that promises delivery of all the trees marked [and to be marked] for the navy."[118]

Records of the exploitation leave unclear the total size of the bribe that was offered and accepted, but the following table suggests that at least 4,962 trees were received from the communities alone:[119]

Of the 11,384 trees marked and delivered, the division was as follows:

Forêts de Son Altesse Serenissme	1,438
Du Bois Bourgeois (dont la coup a été achetée par S.A.S.)	1,062
Des Communautées qui ont delivrées en Don Gratuit	4,962
Des Communautées par Vente	3,922
	11,384 *arbres*

It was not until six months after accepting this gift (15 October 1738) that Babaud announced his intention to limit his cuts to 12,000 trees.[120] He remained insistent on the right to exercise his legal privilege of taking what the navy wanted. In effect, he and his partners would be content with taking the cream of the crop, the 12,000 trees already marked for felling, all of which were ridiculously undervalued.[121] Finally, the partners, with Babaud as their spokesman, acceded to the communities' wishes and halted cuts, but only temporarily, as events were to show; after Jean Babaud's death in December 1738, his partners resumed exploitations in Montbéliard, using surrogates.

The Hazards of Shipment

The first downriver shipment of timber from Montbéliard apparently did not take place until January 1739. At mid-month it was reported that fourteen *coupons*—small rafts suited to the shallow conditions of the upper rivers—had descended the Doubs to Besançon; some of the gates or sluices had been found to be in need of "retouching" (i.e., enlarging), but according to the intendant Vanolles, "there is reason to believe, Monsieur, that the *flottage* will be successful."[122]

His optimism was justified. Ten or more letters written from Lyon the following year by the navy's excellent field representative, Charron, confirm that a vast quantity of Montbéliard timber was moving south, though not without occasional accidents. On 11 February Charron reported the arrival at Lyon of "a raft and a half" of oak timber—pieces gathered up by the entrepreneurs after their *coupons* "had been destroyed and dispersed along the Saône by violent winds." Fortunately, Charron reported, he had moved the rafts downriver past the bridges for greater security; in mid-February "we are menaced by ice . . ." and cold so extreme "that the Saône was frozen above the City."[123]

Two of the fourteen mills outside the city posed a perennial problem for rafts descending the Saône to Lyon. The response to Charron's complaints was always that the mills were essential to the city and that there was no other place to put them. In 1734 Charron reported that earlier a boat had been lost close by these mills with seventy persons aboard, and another since then with six or seven persons.[124]

In the spring, when the thaw came, Charron reported the arrival of many rafts—a total of forty between May and the end of July—some "loaded with curved timber" and *sciage,* all from Montbéliard, together amounting to 100,000 cubic feet.[125] Six new rafts had arrived at Lyon by 10 August, and by mid-September rains had produced a rise in the waters of the Saône, so that Charron sent a certain Sieur Friset up into Burgundy "to construct larger rafts (*radeaux,* capable of carrying about 2,500 cubic feet) of wood from Montbéliard, to avoid the expense of descending the wood in the smaller *coupons.* It seems certain that at least 200,000 cubic feet of the partners' timber descended the Doubs, Saône, and Rhône to Toulon and Marseille in the course of 1740.[126]

There were at least thirty-two toll stations along the Rhône at which timber was subject to inspection and duty.[127] At each station the rafts— *coupons, radeaux,* and *grands radeaux*—halted for inspection. Inspectors came aboard; *passeports* were presented. The *passeports* were literally that, documents allowing naval shipments to pass, with the understanding that the king would pay a predetermined fee; sometimes, however, the king paid a reduced fee or none at all on royal navy materiel. The *passeports* exempted the *flotteurs* and their employers from the necessity of paying cash. The inspectors determined the amount due, and the raft was then allowed to proceed. There were charges of smuggling, but the naval agent Charron disparaged these: "it is impossible to pass [100 livres of iron] in fraud from Franche-Comté to Arles [as some "petty merchants" claimed had been done] . . . without the knowledge of more than thirty stations it must pass, with two or three agents at each station."[128] The scrupulous alertness of some agents and the burdensome character of the system were both pointed up when, because of low water, a raft of Montbéliard timber was made up using several extra pieces of fir. The toll station of M. le Duc de Valentinois stopped the raft for violation of the *règlement* of 20 September 1720, which allowed only two large pieces of fir per raft. The violation involved two months of delay and trial before a magistrate of Valence, who ordered confiscation of the illicit pieces and extracted from the hapless carrier a 500-livre fine.[129] Conditions of downriver traffic in France were far more restrictive and commercially difficult than those the partners encountered in shipping down the Saar, Moselle, and Rhine.

Another risk they and their subcontractors faced was the questionable quality of the timber they delivered from regions near the borders of eastern France. Inspectors at all the ports had preferences; but they also had standards of quality. And it must be admitted that the timber inspectors at all arsenals had many reservations about the quality of the timber from the forests of Lorraine.

It will be recalled that the first shipments sent to the ports from Lorraine had everywhere been judged to be mediocre or poor. By sending only the product of younger trees to the naval arsenals and classing almost everything else as *bois d'Hollande,* the partners improved the quality of the shipments to Brest, where the *rebuts* were kept to a relatively low 2.5 percent rate.[130] That rate was achieved by careful selection, shipping young, choice wood, and reducing questionable pieces to *sciage* or, sometimes, sending them to Rochefort, where no such rate was achieved.

Dislike for Lorraine timber was particularly intense at Toulon. Perhaps the oak timber standards were exceptionally high there because inspectors had at hand for comparison excellent, slow-growing Provençal and Italian oak. Whatever the case, the quality of the timber arriving at Toulon from Lorraine (and much from adjacent areas) was judged to be very poor. For example, in March 1737, 103 pieces of timber and many *bordages* of Lorraine were rejected—"because they cannot be used for [ship] constructions, and [because] afterward we will be culpable for receiving such materiel." Pieces that appeared at first sight to be sound were found to be defective when worked; construction on one vessel, one *flûte,* and two *galiotes à bombes* (bomb ketches) was abandoned because of the defects in the Lorraine timber being used. Villeblanche, the *commissaire général* at Toulon, reported that "on each of these occasions we have called in the agent of the Sieur Babaud so that he would be a witness."[131]

We can be certain that naval officials at Toulon strongly resented the clause written into Jean Babaud's Lorraine contract that prevented inspectors at Toulon from rejecting more than 5 percent of the timber delivered by Babaud (or his surrogates), regardless of quality. Identical provisions were written into the later (1739) contract of Chaussade and Masson.[132] For the partners, the risk of *rebut* (and loss) was thereby practically eliminated. The presence of such a clause in the contract, moreover, made it easier to sell shares in the partnership to surrogates or subcontractors.

It was often remarked in the documents of the 1720s and 1730s that "the rarity of construction timber in the realm obliged France to import from abroad."[133] In fact, it was not a general shortage of timber that encouraged the navy to import from abroad and led to the Lorraine, Montbéliard, and Alsace operations. The problem, particularly at the Atlantic seaboard dockyards, was a perennial shortage of selected types of timbers, and above all compass timber, curved timbers, and knees. They were hard to locate and were at all times eagerly sought both at home and abroad. But forested tracts where thick stands of trees stood close together, especially those subject to care by foresters, such as those of Lorraine, Alsace, and Montbéliard, generally produced few specimens of compass timber. Trees standing close together tend to prune each other of branches and produce longer, taller trunks, principally straight rather than curved timber and *L*-shaped knees.

At the outset of the Lorraine exploitation, in 1728, Jean Babaud and his partner Boesnier were specifically told that the navy, for budgetary as well as technical reasons, would rather receive 150,000 than 300,000 cubic feet, and needed mainly curved timber, not straight.[134] Not surprisingly, as Babaud's deliveries arrived from Lorraine, Alsace, and Montbéliard, stockpiles of straight timber grew mightily, but curved timber remained in short supply. Naval officials talked about proper "assortment," balance in the provisioning, and the need to have different sorts on hand, but straight timber continued to flow to the arsenals. In December 1735 the minister explained to Masson that "the ports at present are amply supplied (*remplis*) with wood."[135] In both 1736 and 1737 officials expressed the desire to receive only 50,000 cubic feet of timber at Brest; stave wood was overstocked. Babaud was allowed to store supplies at the arsenal "until the needs of the service require their reception," and in July 1737 he was told "not to undertake new exploitations until further orders."[136] That fall he was told to make no more deliveries to France.[137]

Yet Babaud and his partners were allowed to continue to seek out opportunities to buy standing trees and make cuts and deliveries. In October 1737 Babaud-Masson negotiations were proceeding with the "count d'Ouohenlohe" [*sic*] for the purchase of 1,200 oaks in the *comté* of Forbach, within reach of the Saar.[138] In November they were accelerating cuts in Lorraine and actually obtained from the minister permission to buy 2,500 oaks from the count of Hanau and orders to deliver the product to Holland for underwater storage at the navy's expense the following year.[139] In the first six months of 1738 Babaud exploited 296,992 cubic feet of naval timber in Alsace and the Empire, about which the minister remarked in June that "it would have been preferable to have them better assorted. Compass timber is entirely lacking at the ports, which are full of straight timber that cannot be used for lack of the curved." [140] In the same month Babaud and his partners signed a new thirteen-year contract for timber deliveries from Lorraine (to be effective 1 January 1740). In August Rochefort had an estimated eight-year supply of some types of wood on hand.[141]

The terms of the 1740 contract are interesting from several points of view. First they limit the *fournisseurs* to deliveries of 50,000 cubic feet a year, reflecting the extant oversupply, but that limit was not rigid: they could exceed it but were expected to conform to the clause specifying that only two-fifths of the annual provisionment could be in *bois longs* including *bordages* (i.e., straight timber and *sciage*); the other three-fifths had to be in *bois de gabarits*.[142] *Bois de gabarits* is, and apparently was then, a vague term.[143] It did not mean, and was not the equivalent of, *bois tors,* referring to curved or compass timber and the other special pieces that were actually in short supply. Yet Maurepas clearly thought that the contract as written required deliveries of curved timber.[144]

Mistakes could be made. Clerks were fallible; a minister might not peruse every word of every clause in every document he signed. Our quest for precision two and a half centuries after the transaction is perhaps at odds with the relations that existed between Minister Maurepas and his friends the Babauds, especially Jean Babaud, who, we suspect, was his particular friend, and who was then known to be very seriously ill. Notwithstanding the term used, it was the apparent intention of the navy to have the *fournisseurs* restrict deliveries of straight timber and increase the supply of curved. The partners found it very difficult to conform to that requirement, as will later be seen.

Jacques Masson and the two Babauds, in any case, made handsome profits buying and selling timber from the rich forests of Lorraine, Alsace, Montbéliard, and neighboring regions. The operations of the thirties made them all rich. Their contracts and successes were important not only to their immediate families and friends in varying degrees, but also to the loggers, carters, *flotteurs,* and others in their employ.

Although the navy was the intended beneficiary of their work, some naval officials and others would no doubt have maintained that the problems and costs occasioned by their forest exploitations exceeded the benefits received. Whatever the overall balance, the records reveal, as we have seen, very large-scale deliveries to the naval arsenals. Our entrepreneurs combed (some would say pillaged) the forests and delivered to the arsenals well over 2 million cubic feet of timber in their 1728–1738 operations along the borders of eastern France and the Rhinelands. A much greater volume of forest products went down the rivers to the Netherlands as their private *bois d'Hollande*.

CHAPTER 3

Deaths and Survivors: Marie Boesnier, Pierre Babaud de la Chaussade, and the Ongoing Business

The deaths of Jean Babaud and Jacques Masson in the space of two and a half years raised persistent economic problems for the family and questions about the continuation of the family businesses. Although the archives of many *notaires* used by the family have survived and are now open to public scrutiny, many details of posthumous settlements, and even some of the family's principal economic affairs of the time, are still obscure. Genealogy-minded family members (and a researcher-friend and "surrogate") have asked me, "What happened to Jean Babaud's fortune?" A far more difficult question is, what happened to Masson's?

Both men were circumspect about family affairs. Masson was positively secretive, having sought systematically during much of his life to mask his activities and hide his wealth; hence his sudden death brought special problems, as well as shock and anguish, to the family. Yet we must try to distinguish the broad outlines of the transfer of the business to the heirs, Marie Boesnier [Babaud-Masson] and Pierre Babaud de la Chaussade. The family made extensive use of surrogates, *régisseurs*, and lessees to manage different phases of the business; they also used surrogates and lawyers to handle their own tenuous and sometimes prickly partnerships. Only parts of their relationships are known to us through the fragmentary records.

Forest Exploitations

The family operations in eastern France continued. The cuts first resumed in the forests of Montbéliard and Franche-Comté, then in Lorraine and Bar and adjacent lands. Later the family also engaged in the importation of naval stores from the Low Countries and the Baltic.

Chaussade and Marie Boesnier faced serious problems in Montbéliard and Franche-Comté. The partners had run roughshod over local interests in Montbéliard, and although Jean Babaud had promised to halt the cuts there, Masson and Chaussade had afterward resumed them. Chaussade and Boesnier prudently decided to use middlemen in the work. A mémoirist (probably Chaussade himself), writing of the intended resumption of cuts, remarked late in 1741 that "the Sieur Babaud [de la Chaussade] will certainly (*immancablement*) meet unbelievable difficulties with the communities of the sequestered seigneuries [of Montbéliard], of which there are many, if he is obliged to negotiate the prices of trees individually with each community in conformity with the *arrêt du conseil* issued 27 December 1740."[1] The *arrêt* forced communities to sell timber trees judged suitable for naval use, but allowed them to negotiate with the authorized buyer (i.e., the buyer holding a naval contract) over the price. The *mémoirist* proposed another method: "All discussions and all obstacles will be removed," he said, "if it were decreed, as an interpretation of the said *arrêt,* that the price of the trees from the sequestered seigneuries will be determined by the price [paid] under the contract with the duke of Würtemberg."[2] The Würtemberg schedule of prices would allow the communities only modest increases over the prices they received on the first round of cuts and by depriving them of the power to negotiate, put them again at the mercy of the entrepreneurs.

As the original partners had done, Chaussade and Marie Boesnier sold or gave shares in their Montbéliard operations to enterprising (and evidently hard-nosed) subcontractors or surrogates who would go into the field and deal firmly with the embittered populace and, when necessary, use *arrêts du conseil* to "facilitate" the work. A letter from Intendant Vanolles to Maurepas suggests that the entrepreneurs did achieve a legal solution for their problems: "[I take it] that you are counting on this [new] *arrêt* to overcome the difficulties in the exploitation of trees occasioned by that [earlier *arrêt*] of 27 December 1740."[3]

We cannot determine when the cutting and removal of the first 12,000 trees was accomplished and additional purchasing and cutting began. But work did go on. Indeed, there was a merging of the exploitations, and of timber descending the rivers under different contracts.

As early as October 1739, a *commissaire de la marine* at Arles on the lower reaches of the Rhône reported the arrival of four rafts of oak timber from Burgundy for the provisionment of the "Sieurs Prieur and Noguier," subcontractors of the partners. About one month later three more rafts from Montbéliard arrived at Arles. *Commissaire* Gadot reported on 15 November that "tomorrow morning two large *allèges* will begin to load" the accumulated timber for shipment to Toulon.[4] Later reports came from Charron, agent of the navy at Lyon, reporting in June 1741 that the last of fourteen rafts of Montbéliard oak timber, manned by four *patrons* and fifty-six *mariniers,* had just left for Arles.[5]

By March 1742 the men arriving at Arles aboard the rafts of timber from Montbéliard carried papers in the name of another subcontractor: Antoine Louis Mangin.[6] Many rafts and boats were moving on the Rhône in the spring of 1742, bringing more timber from Montbéliard bound for Toulon. A total of 23,053 cubic feet arrived at Toulon in the month of June (but almost none during the remainder of the shipping season that year).[7] In January 1745 twenty *coupons* from Montbéliard were reported descending the Saône-Rhône toward Arles,[8] and by then still another of the partners' favorite subcontractors appears to have taken charge (or a share) of their Montbéliard-Burgundy timber exploitations: the Sieur Daniel Le Tessier.

Le Tessier apparently took over under the terms of a *marché* dated 15 March 1742 "for furnishing wood for eleven years to the ports of Toulon and Marseille from Montbéliard and other localities accessible to the Doubs."[9] In the spring and summer of 1740 between 170,000 and 200,000 cubic feet of timber arrived at Toulon from all Rhône sources.[10] Almost certainly a very considerable part—probably nearly all—came from the partners and their subcontractors, since the navy normally allowed only one major contractor to work an area, thus avoiding competition for marked trees. In a period of five months, 1,795 pieces of this timber from Montbéliard were shipped from Arles to Toulon; Le Tessier's freight bill for that period included seventeen (evidently small) vessels.[11]

Exploitations by Le Tessier in Montbéliard generally produced better-quality timber than had previously been delivered at Toulon from that source. He must have made a good profit. Previous *fournisseurs* working Montbéliard forests (Prieur and Noguier, Mangin, and also the "widow Babaud," i.e., Masson–Chaussade) had had troubles over the quality of the timber, which was judged at Toulon to be of poor quality, comparable to timber from Lorraine. A quarter, even a third, of some of their shipments was judged to be substandard. The remarkably generous system ultimately developed at the ministry of marine "in order not to ruin the *fournisseur,* who is of good faith," while ensuring that "the king would lose less," allowed the delivery of up to 10 percent substandard timber without loss. Rejects beyond the 10 percent would be the *fournisseur's* cost.[12] Le Tessier's deliveries sustained "only a 3.0 or 3.5 percent [rejection rate] despite the prejudice that had been formed concerning the quality of wood from Montbéliard."[13] Officials at Toulon were pleased to have his "intermingled" Montbéliard and Franche-Comté timber deliveries continue.

Monsieur Pomet, the naval timber inspector who worked with Le Tessier, probably deserves much of the credit for the improvement in the quality of deliveries. Pomet inspected the trees, marked those deemed suitable for cutting, and inspected them again after cutting. Earlier inspectors were supposed to follow the same procedures, but Pomet was credited with being exceptionally assiduous and careful. He apparently visited Toulon to find out precisely what defects had been found in earlier shipments.[14] It might also be noted that most of the overaged and mature timber was taken out before his time; working with younger stands, as he probably was, it was easier to keep the rejection rate low. The minister, as early as March 1741, wrote approvingly to Pomet about the care he was taking in the provisional inspection of trees after felling. By doing so, he saved the entrepreneurs much expense.[15]

Toward the end of the decade, in 1749, Pomet reported that about 27,600 oaks had been marked for cutting in the forests of the *comté* of Montbéliard alone since 1746.[16] But by 1752 the *commissaire* Faisolle de Villeblanche called the minister's attention to evidence that the forests of the Montbéliard–Franche-Comté region were approaching exhaustion. Much of the timber arriving was short or small, some so small as to be unacceptable. He saw difficulties in canceling the contract; but it was due to end in 1752 anyway. However, he urged that inspectors and markers be advised to overlook no large trees: they would be "overage" if left until the next round of cuts many years hence.[17]

The original partners must be credited with overall success in the Lorraine exploitation and with helping prepare the navy for the decade of intermittent war in the forties. But the assortment of timber they supplied was so poor that late in the thirties, notwithstanding enormous stockpiles of timber, compass timber and knees (*courbes*) were reported to be absolutely lacking. Ships could not be built with straight timber alone. Efforts were even made to use iron *courbes*. In the new timber contracts of 1738, the navy insisted that at least three-fifths of the new provisionments must be composed of curved timber.[18] The pressing need for compass and curved timber was the principal reason for the issuance of new contracts.

It was typical of the leniency of the ministry that the partners' new thirteen-year contract (signed June 1738) was not scheduled to take effect until January 1740, at which time they would begin deliveries at the rate of only 50,000 cubic feet per year. That gave the partners ample time to deliver, or otherwise dispose of, straight timber trees on which they had taken options. They were thus given eighteen months to begin to do what they should have been doing all along, and had been told for years that they should do: tailor their provisionments to satisfy the navy's actual needs.

Sometimes our entrepreneurs were specially fortunate. Babaud and Masson came suddenly (in 1738) upon an opportunity to acquire over two thousand pieces of the much-sought-after curved timber (relatively rare in the forests of Lorraine), just when the shortage was reaching a peak. Reports suggested that the timber involved was situated on a seigneury belonging to the prince-margrave of Baden Baden. The minister consented to have them deliver about 100 pieces for tests; when quality proved to be good, he accepted the proposed provisionment of 2,000 *courbes* for delivery to Brest at three livres per cubic foot—a very good price.[19] The next year the entrepreneurs, working in the forests of the prince of "Hesse-D'arnistat" [*sic*], reported another interesting and uniform stand, but this one proved less lucky for the navy, consisting of straight timber only.[20] The product of the Hesse-Darmstadt cuts could not arrive at the arsenals before 1740, at which time the new contract would be in effect, requiring 60 percent of deliveries to be *courbes*. The minister allowed them to send it, simply calling attention to the fact that the *fournisseur* "can always be required to deliver a proportionate quantity of curved timber from other localities."[21] Thus at last the minister was firmly disposed to enforce those restrictions, at least on the overall assortment of deliveries. A restriction was accordingly imposed on their cuts for the navy in the region concerned.

Another "restriction" involved the need to repay the "advances" earlier received by the entrepreneurs. By early 1740 their surrogate Mangin was reported to have completed delivery of the last shipments to fulfill the Lorraine timber contract of 1728, and had thus, according to the navy's books, paid off the advances received in that year. But over 100,000 cubic feet remained to be delivered to finish the contract of 1735.[22] In 1740 the very large advances of 1735 were being repaid—part of Chaussade and Boesnier's legacy from Jean Babaud and Jacques Masson.

At least a potential limit on the partners' enterprises came from the steps taken toward the application of French "conservation" legislation in the forests of Lorraine. The entrepreneurs' own methods had contributed to the desire to have such legislation implemented. Popular anger and outcry over damage done, the bitterness of landowners and officials, and the frustration of industry produced many written complaints. The navy itself was also an influential and self-interested "conservation lobby." The existence of forest laws (the *ordonnance* of 1669 and the *arrêt du conseil* of 1700) and the *arrêts* forbidding exports of wood from France attested to the coincidence of royal and naval desire for the production and conservation of certain types of trees as timber preserves for the navy. But serious efforts to apply that legislation were made principally in France itself. French forest law did not apply in certain French dependencies— not in Alsace or the "reunion" lands claimed by Louis XIV, and naturally not in foreign lands, such as the duchy of Lorraine. In 1737–1738, however, the succession to the duchy of Lorraine was finally settled by international arrangement on Louis XV's father-in-law, Stanislas Lesczinski, with the provision that at his death it would go to the French crown.

Steps were taken almost immediately to promulgate French forest law—or at least some laws—in the duchy of Lorraine. Various legislative measures were projected by the French ministry of finance, by the navy, and by authorities in Lorraine itself.[23] Ultimately, under the nominal auspices of the "king of Poland" (i.e., Stanislas Lesczinski) an *arrêt* was issued regulating the formalities to be observed in future cuts of wood in Lorraine and Bar.[24]

The terms of this *arrêt* allowed French naval officials henceforth to mark trees "with the arms of His Polish Majesty," thereby excluding such trees from all cuts, just as the French *arrêt du conseil* of 1700 controlled the exploitation of French forests.[25] Accordingly, a navy *commissaire* was sent in March 1740 with instructions to mark timber trees throughout the regions as naval reserve.[26] The partners were promised the same preference and facilities in the forests of Lorraine and Bar that they enjoyed in those of the realm.[27] Moreover, as long as Jacques Masson was first clerk in the office of *contrôleur général* "charged with the affairs of Lorraine," they would enjoy advantages whether the "system" of forest management in use was that of ducal Lorraine or Bourbon France. After Masson's death, however, Chaussade and Marie Boesnier were probably subject to much more restrictive controls, including rules that absolutely forbade the use of their favorite system: that of taking what they pleased.

Hence our entrepreneurs faced a "confluence" of negative circumstances. Even before Masson's death, there was evidence that the "conservationists" were ominously active in efforts to obtain the imposition of controls.[28] Considering the influence of other restrictive factors, these

were unsettling developments. The outlook for good profits was uncertain, even bleak. The partners wound down their deliveries of timber for
the navy in the first year of their new thirteen-year contract, but not their
cuts or shipments of *bois d'Hollande;* they claimed that they were "unable to furnish any timber to the Ponant [Atlantic seaboard] ports" in
1740.[29] They later asserted that the forests lacked the quantity of wood
needed to complete the provisionment for the first two years, or for the
years to come. "He [Chaussade] has up to the present bought only a
small number of oaks in the forests of Rodemalkre and others, and in
consequence it is impossible for him to fulfill the thirteen-year contract."[30]

After Jacques Masson died in 1741, as we have seen, Chaussade quickly
negotiated official cancellation of the contract of 1738 and obtained a
new contract transferring to himself most of the essential obligations and
privileges of the old. But there were differences, most of them (contrary to
his obvious hopes) advantageous for the navy. Henceforth the provisionments were to be delivered to Brest, Rochefort, and Havre "at the cost,
risk, and peril of the *fournisseur.*" This meant that Chaussade must assume entire responsibility for the quality and the safe passage of deliveries—in wartime.

The contract also offered some hope of improved quality through
Chaussade's probable intention of partly "fashioning" the timber at the
cutting sites or on the riverbanks before shipping, a procedure used, as
we have seen, with timber for Toulon, and well-calculated to disclose defects, avoid needless shipping costs, and improve quality overall.[31] Yet
Maurepas remained frankly pessimistic about Chaussade's ability to execute the contract. His doubts led him to order the navy's *commissaire* in
Lorraine, Sieur Angerant, to come to Paris: "there are many arrangements
still to be made . . . concerning the *fournitures* of timber from Lorraine
that the Sieur Babaud is once again going to undertake. . . . I need many
clarifications on this subject. It is essential that you come here and that
you bring with you all the *éstats* and *mémoires* you can on the subject."[32]
He was probably considering whether it was necessary for the navy to
maintain timber selection and inspection officials in eastern France when
the quality and assortment of Lorraine timber seemed so unpromising.

Chaussade himself probably saw his timber contract with the navy
principally as a crutch. It enabled him and his associates to continue an
active and profitable traffic in the by-products of naval exploitations.
Hence he willingly undertook to supply relatively small quantities of first-
grade, curved, and compass timber to the navy when it became available,
even at relatively high cost and risk to himself, because the contract to do
so gave him the chance to acquire and ship commercial pieces for which

ready markets existed in the Netherlands. Naturally the extent of this private traffic was different in each exploitation, and the amount and type of wood available depended on the quality of the forest stand itself, along with many other circumstances. But Chaussade needed and wanted to qualify as a buyer for the navy; the navy's timber buyer in a region enjoyed distinct advantages in his dealings with forest proprietors. In lands where French forest law was being applied, trees termed suitable for the navy could be marked as such and sold exclusively to the navy's authorized representative. Forest proprietors had to sell to the navy if they sold at all, and since the navy's buyers found it advantageous to "exploit" a region very infrequently, a forest proprietor was under pressure— indeed, was virtually forced—to sell when the buyer was on hand; unless he accepted the prices offered for his trees when they were at or near their prime, he ran the risk of being left with an overmature stand of little value when the next buyer for the navy appeared some decades later. The partners in fact wanted to make it a condition of their purchases that the overaged trees be sold very cheaply or even "abandoned" to the entrepreneurs by the proprietor.

In the early thirties, as we have seen, the partners had innumerable difficulties with the laws forbidding the exportation of wood from France.[33] To get around them they at first promised to deliver all their shipments either to naval arsenals or to French commercial markets. But over time, by means of various procedures and pretexts, and as a result of changing circumstances, they obtained a relaxation of the rules from friendly officials along with permissions (*passeports*) to export. But not all officials were friendly or cooperative. The intendant Bron of Alsace, as we have seen, was not. Acting with the regional army commander, the maréchal du Bourg, on more or less valid pretexts, Bron halted the partners' exploitation in the forest of Haguenau and seized their accumulated timber in the spring of 1738.[34] The minister of marine took a hand and carried the affair to *contrôleur général* Orry and even to the Royal Council. He soon obtained release of the partners' timber, but on condition that they never again cut oaks in forests situated "on the reverse slope of the mountains of Alsace without express permission."[35] That was not the end of it. Apparently Chaussade did obtain the "express permission" required. But he found himself in trouble again the very next year (July 1739) when a threatening letter of complaint reached him from Intendant Bron.

> I have been informed, Monsieur, that on the pretext of the permission you have obtained to purchase wood in this province for

the construction of vessels for the royal navy, you have purchased all [the wood] that you can find.

Setting aside a portion you judge to be useful to the navy
amounting to no more than a twentieth part [of your purchases],
you sell the rest to a company of Amsterdam merchants. [I am
also informed] that you have purchased from the heirs of the late
M. de Stukenstein 1,000 oaks, of which you have reserved only
63 trees for the navy, and that you have sold all the rest to this
same company [of Dutch merchants]. This could be as prejudicial to the service of the king as to the welfare of the province.

Bron demanded to know "instantly" whether these allegations were
true.[36]

Chaussade evidently continued the exploitations, avoiding dealings
with Bron when he could, buying trees either in his own name or through
intermediaries,[37] then obtaining *passeports* and organizing the downriver
transit through individual contract arrangements with his own *flotteur-
commis* and crew. All this was very complicated. A routine request for a
passeport for timber from several French and foreign sources illustrates
this complexity:

The Sieur Babaud and Company has exploited timber and must
float [it] through Alsace on the Saar next spring . . . from the
forests of S.A.S. Le Prince de Hesse-Darmstadt situated in the
comté of Hanau [*sic*] and *bailliage* of Lemberg in the territory of
the Empire, from the forests of Wimenauve [*sic*] in Alsace, and
1,400 *wagenholz* from the auction sale at Haguenau in 1740.
The Sieur Babaud and Company humbly begs Monseigneur
Bron to have the kindness to deliver a *passeport* for the wood
described above.[38]

In the later 1740s Chaussade must have been pleased to see Vanolles
assume (or resume?) the post of *intendant d'Alsace*, apparently replacing
the troublesome Bron.[39] Under Vanolles' auspices, Chaussade and one
partner (or others in their name) were still buying the product of annual
auction sales from the forest of Haguenau, and Chaussade's name appeared on one of the *passeports* of 1748 with an impressive new title:
"*entrepreneur général de la fourniture des bois pour la marine.*"[40]

Chaussade and his partners appear to have been especially interested in
seeking out timber in territory conquered and annexed by France during
and after the reign of Louis XIV.[41] Many of these territories, including

some very extensive seigneurial domains, though part of the realm of France, were actually the property of foreign princes. Separate arrangements had to be made with each prince once desirable trees were found on his property. Different procedures were used when the property was effectively subject to French law, including French forest law, and when it was not. A private contract with the proprietor might be preferable to dealing with his bailiffs, forest officers, or other surrogates. During his lifetime Masson apparently negotiated most of these contracts, sometimes dealing with the princes themselves, sometimes with their representatives.

Quite by accident, we know in some detail about the arrangements Chaussade and Masson made to acquire timber from the group of properties known as the seigneury of Rodemacher, belonging to the prince-margrave of Baden-Baden.[42] It is unclear whether the Rodemacher enterprise was initiated by the partners or the owner, Margrave Louis Georges, or his representatives. Negotiations were well advanced as early as 1739: "As regards the forest of Rodemacher," the minister of marine then wrote to his forest inspectors in the region, "I hope M. le Prince de Bade obtains the *arrêt* he seeks to put this *fournisseur* [Masson or Chaussade?] in a position to undertake the work and take out the curved timber you have found there."[43]

The partners bought the standing timber on the Rodemacher land and seigneury from the margrave for 98,000 livres. The first payment was made on 27 February 1740 (30,800 livres); the second on 2 March (67,200 livres). The following December Chaussade purchased Masson's rights under this contract (Masson liked liquidity), having the previous month bought a nine-year lease on the entire seigneury—farms, vineyards, houses, barns—in the name of one Jacques Jacquet (a resident of Rodemacher).[44] Jacquet was appointed Chaussade's resident manager (*régisseur*), with the obligation "to render annual accounting of his management and administration"[45] and to serve as *procureur général et spécial* with entire charge of the exploitation of certain woodlands of the margrave "according to the agreement at Rastatt, 30 May 1739."[46] An inventory of mid-1744 revealed that "the greater part" of the wood had been taken off the Rodemacher property, evidently by Chaussade's agent, René Duval, between 21 February 1742 and 18 June 1744. The inventory included a list of forest parcels aggregating 840 *arpents* of woodland that remained, whose value then amounted to only 45,349 livres (including 7,445 livres in firewood). It was noted that "all the wood proper for the navy and for *usage d'Hollande*" had by then been removed by Duval and Chaussade.

The Rodemacher timber exploitation and the nine-year lease on the seigneury itself are indicative of the close collaboration, even intimacy, in economic enterprise between Jacques Masson and his son-in-law. Masson was an old hand. He had decades of experience in the management of seigneurial, forest, mill, foundry, forge, and related properties. He knew how to maximize their revenues. The Rodemacher operation was thorough-going, evidently smooth, and profitable—an indication that Chaussade was receiving instruction from a master. For it was Masson, I suspect, who set up and launched the operation and then (typically) sold his rights (or share) to his son-in-law for cash. Chaussade, an apt and willing pupil, kept the Rodemacher venture going after Masson's death in 1741, and the very next year went on to buy the "Farelmeyer paper mill and its dependencies" in the City of Metz. Two years later he bought "the old chateau of Hombourg [*sic*]."[47] The Rodemacher exploitation might be seen as harbinger of Chaussade's maturity.

In the middle and later forties, Chaussade, using surrogates, was active in the region of the "Three Bishoprics" (i.e., Metz, Toul, and Verdun), cutting and shipping timber for the navy. Some of it, at least, was curved timber of good quality. He sent some 550 pieces down to Holland to await shipment to France, telling the minister that he proposed to ship them to the French port of Le Havre for the commercial market, perhaps because the pieces were of modest size. But when the navy's inspectors, sent to see them, reported the pieces to be almost identical to other *courbes* Chaussade had earlier sent to the arsenals from German Lorraine, Maurepas ordered them sent to Brest instead.[48] Less attractive was the straight timber Chaussade cut in the environs of Metz a bit later, which the minister flatly refused to have sent.[49]

It seems evident that the forties saw a great decline in the partners' naval sales of timber from eastern France and adjacent lands. This reduction reflected the minister's successive decisions to give no further encouragement to Lorraine exploitations, to oblige the entrepreneurs to deliver timber only in limited quantities, and in required assortments, at their own risk, and finally to recall the navy's inspectors from Lorraine and Alsace to the arsenals, as was apparently done.[50] The war conditions that prevailed gave further hindrance. But the traffic continued. Through the later forties, much of the provisionment sent to the navy from Lorraine and Alsace was delivered under the names of Chaussade's subcontractors or surrogates.[51]

Northern Stores

Chaussade, meanwhile, had added a new portfolio to his interests by turning actively to the import trade. He became involved in imports of northern naval stores from the Netherlands and Baltic, an area of special navy interest. The partners' timber traffic had brought them into close contact with Dutch markets, and the Netherlands trade was part of family tradition: Masson in particular had dabbled (as had the Paris brothers) in imports of northern stores, using tar and other stores as ballast or extra cargo in the ships taking the entrepreneurs' timber to French arsenals. Their sudden entry into the business of importing northern stores in 1739 probably came at Maurepas's request. The War of Jenkins's Ear broke out between Britain and Spain that year, and tensions were running high on the continent.

In July 1739 the partners agreed to supply the navy with a variety of northern stores, operating under the name of Pierre Goossens, the late Jean Babaud's principal *commis* and holder of procurations from Marie Boesnier and Masson.[52] In August the minister sent Masson a list of the navy's requirements, to be delivered "as promptly as possible" to the port of Rochefort. It included 32 large masts (24 to 27 palms), over 100 smaller masts, 3,000 pounds of copper in sheets, 30,500 pounds of lead in pigs, 1,200 pounds of tin, and 30 barrels of *fer blanc* in sheets. Initially, Maurepas estimated the value of the stores needed at Rochefort and the other ports at 600,000 livres.[53]

That was the beginning of the partners' large-scale *fournitures* from the north. Few in the French merchant community could come close to matching the partners' capital, credit, and experience in this type of enterprise.[54] The partners, as we have seen, had correspondents in Dort and Rotterdam markets in the Netherlands. They had frequent contact with Dutch shipowners, and had done business in Amsterdam. The navy would have had good reason to turn to them even had they not had close connections in the ministry.

The partner with the closest family connections in the Netherlands, Jacques Boesnier Duportal, had retired, but Marie Boesnier shared her cousin Jacques's Netherlands connections. Masson and the Babauds, for their part, had all visited the Netherlands. But before his death Jean Babaud made clear his hope that another Dutch-connected person in the firm would have a more important role after he himself became totally incapacitated or passed away; and he designated his *commis* Pierre François Goossens, member of a well-known family of Dutch merchants,[55] to aid his widow and children by assuming stewardship of company affairs. For her part the widow Babaud probably insisted that her husband's wishes be respected, and Masson consented. After Masson's death Chaussade also gave a power of attorney to P. F. Goossens. Nicolas Doyen and Gabriel Michel, a director of the Compagnie des Indes, who joined the partners,[56] evidently consented to the Goossens management. Thus Goossens as surrogate managed all the shares of all the partners in the company known at first as La Dame Veuve Babaud et Cie., and a bit later as Sr. Pierre Babaud et Cie.; he oversaw the execution of contracts with the navy, the Compagnie des Indes, and also some colonial requirements.[57]

Initially, many details of the partners' purchases of northern stores were handled by Masson. The arrangement was that their imports would be on a 5 percent commission basis. Two months after the navy listed the requirements of the port of Brest, we learn, the Netherlands correspondents of the widow Babaud (presumably Goossens and Masson) had embarked 2,100 pigs of lead aboard a Dutch ship bound for that port.[58] Although Goossens submitted estimates of prospective costs, details relating to freight and the accounts "for the expenditures made in Holland by the Brothers Terwens" (*prête-noms* or the partners' correspondents?) came to the navy through Masson's hands; Masson also handled the details relating to the purchase of 110 pieces of iron cannon in the north.[59] Within ten days after Masson's death, Chaussade had taken some of these affairs in hand. He immediately sought permission to ship 450 undersized masts to Toulon. The minister consented, but "only on condition that you guarantee that freight costs will be as low as those of the late M. Masson, and that you use the same economical methods he employed."[60]

Masson's passing clearly saddled Goossens with greater responsibility, but it also produced some characteristic Chaussade stratagems. His energies found fertile expression in various projects designed to expand the volume and variety of the partners' northern *fournitures*. For example, he proposed to ship 3,630 barrels of tar to Brest and to load all sorts of cargo to fill the "open spaces" in the holds and the between-decks spaces in ships embarking cargoes of masts. He proposed to embark common plank that had not been ordered; the minister approved, provided Chaussade did not send "too much," since the ports were already well stocked. To the port of Toulon, with the 450 small masts, Chaussade proposed to stow between decks quantities of hemp available at 28 livres the quintal, but to that the minister said no:

> That price [without freight charges] was too high, and furthermore, Toulon is already provided with all the hemp required. Nor should you send to that port any bargains that become available, neither copper, *fers-blancs*, lead, pitch, nor tar. Contracts have been let for these provisions. The port [of Toulon] is sufficiently supplied.

As regards the proposed provisionment of curved timber obtained from the Islands of the Rhine, "we must hold to the arrangements made with the late M. Masson. Nor can we accept, at the price schedule of your contract . . . the 460 pieces of construction timber from the Park de Milly [near Saumur] belonging to Mlle. de Clermont. . . . That wood was inspected last year and not judged to be of good quality for our purposes. I am sending back the *mémoires* you sent dealing with this wood."[61] Chaussade appeared to be trying to gather the loose ends left by Masson, and to explore some new opportunities. Some details (or relevant papers) apparently escaped his attention, or were unavailable to him. Probably more encouraging to him than these possibilities was the special order he received in late July 1741 for supplementary supplies of copper for Brest.[62]

On 19 August 1741 Chaussade gave his power of attorney to Goossens.[63] Soon afterward he must have left Paris for the Netherlands by one of the faster modes of passenger travel. In September the minister received a letter from him, written from Dort, reporting rises in insurance rates on cargoes destined for France because, said Chaussade, war was about to break out between Sweden and Muscovy. He asked the minister if he should buy insurance against the risks of war. Maurepas's wise response, sent hastily to Goossens (who was evidently familiar with Chaussade's whereabouts in the north), pointed out that since Dutch (i.e., neutral) ships were to be employed, Chaussade certainly needed only to insure against the risks of the sea.[64] In November 1741 the minister was pleased to learn that Chaussade's purchases from the Riga mast market were complete; the masts were already embarked and en route.[65] Chaussade proposed a new *fourniture* for the following year and sent estimates of probable costs. But his hopes were dashed; the minister responded that further purchases of masts were not then contemplated: "We will not need any more for some years."[66]

Even greater disappointment was in store. Maurepas reported "with pain" that the provisionments purchased by Chaussade and delivered in Goossens' name had many faults. The Baltic masts had "a great number of defects"; those delivered to Toulon were ill-proportioned. Sheets of red copper delivered to Brest, intended for use in heaters, were exactly half the required length. Instead of 700 livres of new copper "in rosette" and "exactly three lines thick," intended to be cut into nails and staples for use in the fabrication of gunpowder kegs, sheathing, and so on, the suppliers delivered 698 livres of used copper fragments.[67] And from Brest came complaints that as of April 1742 the port had not yet received the

27,500 *planches de Bergue* that had been ordered: "Where is this part of the provisionment?" the minister asked.[68] Two weeks later another, more insistent letter went from the minister to Chaussade: "I am counting on delivery of [at least 24,000] *planches de Bergue* by the end of next month, as you promised."[69] When 30 May came and the *planches* still had not arrived, Maurepas wrote to Chaussade to say that a Dutch ship (the *Demoiselle Anna*) had arrived at Brest from Rotterdam with a cargo of 5,924 of the larger *planches de Coperwick* for Goossens' account: "I judge these planks are supposed to be part of the 24,000 Bergen planks you are to furnish . . . but I have told M. Bigot de la Mothe [intendant at Brest] not to accept any more *planches* of this sort; the problem is not to provide the port of Brest with *planches de Coperwick,* but rather with *planches de Bergue!* "[70]

Six months later the minister still had serious concerns about Chaussade's *fourniture*. Some of the merchandise and munitions ordered for the ports had still not arrived. Maurepas wrote to Languier de Tassy, French emissary at the Hague, to obtain his help: "I have charged M. le Sr. Goossens to go to Amsterdam to purchase some munitions and merchandise needed at the ports of Brest and Rochefort."[71] Addressing Goossens (rather than Chaussade) shortly afterward, Maurepas thanked him for his *mémoire* describing masts that had been offered for purchase. But, the minister reminded him, "We have no thought of provisioning the ports with masts next year. Our only concern, as has been explained to you, is to have you deliver the fir balks (beams, *billons*) and the *planches,* whose detailed description you have," and, in addition, 200 barrels of tar for Brest, 1,000 for Toulon. He remarked that prices were "very much higher," and "the arrangements you propose for future provisioning of the ports will be out of the question if the suppliers continue to demand such prices."[72] Two months later, when several thousand unordered and unwanted pieces of stave wood were delivered to the ports, the minister, out of patience, told Chaussade: "I must tell you that it is useless for you to undertake provisionments if you do not conform exactly to the quantities, qualities, and proportions specified in the orders you received. Henceforth, every bit of the excess will be rejected when the quantities are as large as those in the recent shipment."[73]

Maurepas obviously had suspicions about some of the costs the navy was being asked to pay in connection with the commission-buying imports from the north. Maurepas wrote in the fall of 1743 to de Tassy, asking for certain details, particularly about the amount of duty levied by Dutch authorities at the ports of Holland on Dutch and foreign ships. He was promptly supplied with a *mémoire* on the subject. Whether it threw significant light on the accounts of our entrepreneurs, or was solicited in the hope that it would do so, remains unclear.[74]

The north European trade in naval materiel was both competitive and highly specialized. The shortcomings of the merchandise delivered by Chaussade and his associates were perhaps unintentional. They may have underestimated the difficulties of the trade. The Baltic mast markets in particular were fraught with pitfalls that could cost inexperienced buyers dearly. Chaussade himself traveled to the Netherlands in the summer of 1743 and again in 1744 to oversee the purchase and shipping of *four-nitures*.[75] He had proposed to deliver 49 masts of the largest sizes (20–26 palms) and 96 smaller ones (12–19 palms) at his cost and risk.[76] Unfortunately, 33 of those delivered at Brest were judged to be of poor quality. Chaussade offered naval officials a price discount of 15 percent, but the navy wanted at least 20 percent off, and probably did impose the discount.[77] This appears to have been the only mast contract Chaussade undertook to execute during the War of the Austrian Succession.

His next venture in the mast trade was made in 1749, in partnership with Gabriel Michel, a director of the Compagnie des Indes experienced in the mast traffic. Michel had been delivering northern stores to his company's arsenals for at least a decade.[78] In 1749 the navy called for bids on a new contract to provision it with Baltic stores. There were many bidders. Chaussade and Michel bid jointly on the mast contract.[79] They worked with Goossens, who apparently represented the interest of Marie Boesnier, in acquiring and executing several contracts for a variety of northern stores: copper, hemp, fir beams (*billons*) from the Black Mountains of Würtemberg, tar, pitch, and plank of certain sorts, in addition to masts and spars.[80] They were also associated with Goossens in the more important contract for masts. Masts, although a bulk commodity, involved hundreds of thousands of livres in outlay. They were on a par with ordnance and anchors as high-cost materiel; hence that contract involved greater outlay than all the other northern purchases together. Masts were scarce and perishable. They had to be acquired at second or third hand in a distant, volatile, and competitive market where the record of declining quality was paralleled by rapidly rising prices—hardly a reassuring prospect. Undeterred, the entrepreneurs agreed in 1750 to deliver a total of 886 large masts and 942 masts of medium size during the years 1751–1754. The aggregate value of the shipments would approach one million livres.[81]

The partnership to execute this formidable contract was apparently preceded by several years of acquaintance and collaboration. Masson, the Babauds, and Michel had a long-standing commercial association through the Compagnie des Indes. Moreover, Chaussade, Goossens, and Michel together provided the port of Brest with at least one cargo of masts worth some 50,000 livres the very year the new contract was signed. Two years later, when the Compagnie Général de Commerce of Copenhagen filed claims against them, it was revealed that they still had not settled all their accounts with their suppliers. The Copenhagen company claimed that they still owed 38,000 livres for masts delivered; Chaussade and associates were withholding payment because inspectors of the navy had found the cargo unacceptable on its arrival at Brest.[82]

Their difficulties with the Compagnie Général persuaded the entrepreneurs to try to develop connections of their own at the port of Riga, the principal east Baltic port of supply. Riga masts were reputedly the finest obtainable, although it was also said that their quality was deteriorating because of the retreat of the forests from the rivers and ports. Two winters were sometimes required for a great mast to reach Riga. The difficulties faced in acquiring such masts were different for buyers of different nationalities. British commercial treaties with Russia gave English merchants enormous advantages.[83] Lacking such arrangements, the French were forced to buy at second hand from merchants whose governments had negotiated privileged status.

Chaussade and his partners found that nearly the whole of the export trade in masts and other naval stores at Riga was concentrated in the hands of such British merchant houses as Wale and Fraser, Morison, Spenser, Thornton, Collins and Wale-Pierson, and Took at St. Petersburg. Masts destined for the British, Spanish, and French navies alike passed through their hands.[84] When they engaged a Copenhagen company to buy and sell for their account, as they had done in 1750, they were obliged to pay commissions to these intermediaries as well as those of the more privileged merchants at the Riga market (such as the English) from whom the Danes themselves had bought the masts.

Nor were Chaussade and his associates expert judges of the tree trunks offered for sale on the Riga market. At Riga, masts were sold in "lots" (or assortments) that usually included seven (or more) pieces, often of varied quality. The partners needed help—a master mastmaker from one of the French naval arsenals to aid in selecting the best assortments to be dispatched from Riga to the navy or to the Compagnie des Indes, for which they were also commissioned to buy. The least desirable pieces in an assortment were often resold (heavily discounted) at Riga to an Englishman named Jackson who made a business of buying such rejects and reworking them. Tricks of the trade included tamping wooden plugs into holes where rotted knots had been, using hot resin to make knots appear sound, and delivering inferior masts under the Riga name and bracking marks. The Copenhagen merchants who had served the partners as commission merchants in the earlier delivery had, knowingly or not, purchased many faulty pieces.

The partners' Baltic enterprise was much favored by a change that took place in the ministry of marine in 1749. The experienced Maurepas was dismissed by the king, reportedly at the behest of the king's mistress, Mme. Pompadour, and replaced by Antoine-Louis de Rouillé, comte de Jouy. Rouillé, called conscientious, vigilant, and honest,[85] was inexperienced in naval administration, but took as his aide a professional navy administrator, Sebastien-François-Auge le Normant de Mezy, intendant de la marine at Rochefort.[86] Under their auspices a considerable reconstruction and shipbuilding program began.

The partners asked the new minister to dispatch a mastmaker to Riga to help in timber selection, and their request was favorably received.[87] The new ministry designated a three-man technical mission to go to the Baltic. The Sieur Senac, *écrivain principale,* was much praised by the intendant because he reportedly knew both English and German and could be depended upon to maintain bourgeois appearances without *éclat* or superfluous expenditure and to develop good relations with the mast merchants.[88] Dispatched with him was a father-son team, the senior Barbé, who had had earlier experience in northern mast markets,[89] and his son, who was to follow in his professional footsteps.

The ministry reminded Senac and the Barbés that "the best masts the ports of the king have received" were delivered in 1730 by the Sieur Vallet de la Touche. The la Touche deliveries set standards by which subsequent deliveries (even in the 1750s) were judged; "all the provisionments [of masts] since then have been mediocre." Attention was called to Michel and Chaussade's claim that the masts they had supplied (almost entirely rejected at Brest in 1750) were "the best that Riga can furnish today." The new team was urged to give attention to this problem of quality and, of course, to assist with the provisionments currently being made by Michel and Chaussade. Senac was instructed to find out whether the masting trees marketed at Riga were in fact (as the partners claimed) "exposed for several winters" after felling, either at the cutting sites or en route to market; if so, it was observed, "they thereby acquire defects for which the contractors cannot be [held] responsible."[90]

The letters and *mémoires* Senac and Barbé sent back to the ministry described the Baltic market in detail, answered many questions, and generated a few others. Their reports revealed that the highly esteemed la Touche masts had been selected by two navy *commissaires* (du Vivier and

TABLE 3-1. Riga purchases, 1751

House	Inspected	Accepted	Rejected (and resold at Riga)
Wale and Fraser	873	775	98
Heidtwinekell and Newell	124	89	35

Source: Marine (Paris), B³ 509, fol. 530.

Du Bois), who screened the shipments in company with the contractor's son. Records at Riga proved that in the period from 1744 to 1751, a total of 27,668 masts and 140,325 large fir beams (*billons de sapin*) had been shipped from Riga, while the quality of provisionments "degenerated by degrees." Five or six merchants, the "bourgeois of Riga," were said to dominate the trade: even the privileged English merchants had to buy from them. According to Senac they controlled all traffic with the "highlands" (i.e., the back country). At times they bought whole forests, cuts from which they then arranged to have brought to Riga for sale in assortments—the good and the bad together. These "bourgeois," the richest merchants in the city, were described as very reliable dealers.[91]

Senac also confirmed that trunks arriving at Riga were commonly sold with their bark intact, hardly facilitating choice. Many were debarked and "fashioned" before shipment from Riga to save space and identify defects. The brakers who made up and sold the assortments were unresponsive to hints about changing the system in any detail. "Attached to their ancient rules," Senac wrote, "the brakers have not been converted."[92]

The partners' purchases of 1751 were made principally from the English firm of Wale and Fraser and the Livonian house of Heidtwinekell and Newell (Table 3-1). In Barbé's opinion, the masts he bought were "better than most, notably better than some bought for Spain." But he still apologized for their quality: "I believe that I am obliged, Monsieur, for the good of the service, to relax absolutely the extreme rigidity I have always maintained in my reception of masts; for if that is not done, it is certain that we will lack for masts; and I believe it my duty . . . to reject only those that are absolutely heated up or rotting."[93]

Michel and Company sold the *rebuts* at Riga. The first shipments to arrive at Brest were judged to be fine;[94] later cargoes were "not of the first quality," but without fundamental defects. It was reaffirmed that "no better [masts] were [sold] at Riga [this year]."[95]

The advent of the new and inexperienced minister of marine was a signal to Chaussade and his partners to try to revive some of the privileges they had enjoyed in the thirties and to bend the rules and customs of administrative practice in their favor. They had much success in reviving tactics that the veteran Maurepas had learned to proscribe. Their contract was confirmed for northern masts by Rouillé allowing them to continue as commission merchants and thus passed on to the king all the costs of the *fourniture*. That contract was in effect a reversion to a costly form of favoritism in purchasing.

Very early in the Rouillé administration (30 December 1750), Chaussade also sought to take on the responsibility of providing the navy with all the hemp it imported from the provinces of the realm and from abroad.[96] Rouillé considered the proposition but later awarded Chaussade only the right to supply the hemp imported from the north.[97] This division of the provisionment was forgotten in August 1751 when the entrepreneurs were allowed to exceed the authorized provisionment for 1751, not only for hemp, but also for pitch and tar (*bray* and *goudron*).[98] Predictably, with the ministry's "blank check" in hand, they went out and bought without regard for the navy's requirements. By the end of November, they had "largely exceeded" the total amount requested for all these types of stores; their deliveries "doubled and tripled" the requested provisionment of hemp, so that it was estimated in 1751 that the provisionment for 1753 "will not amount to much," and orders were issued to the merchant supplying hemp from French provinces to halt his deliveries.[99]

The partners' supplies continued to be uneven in quality. One shipment of Norwegian copper they sent to Brest was judged "very inferior to preceding deliveries." "Since the master founder thinks we can use it without difficulty," wrote Rouillé, "I am ordering that it be accepted, but I recommend that you instruct your correspondents to be more attentive to the choice of merchandise."[100] A later shipment of their copper was judged particularly good: "The copper from Hungary that you have had sent to Rochefort [as a trial shipment] is as good as, even better than, that from Norway."[101] In a provisionment as large as theirs, a few "shorts" were inevitable. In July 1751 fifty or sixty *planches de demi-prusse* were found at Brest to be only sixteen instead of eighteen feet in length. At Rochefort "981 plank were delivered that were only five feet long and therefore useless." But Rouillé took care of that too: "I have told them at Rochefort that they must accept them anyway," wrote the helpful minister, "but I suggest that you conform to the prescribed proportions in order not to glut the ports with useless merchandise."[102]

In 1751 Michel, Chaussade, Goossens, and company were riding high.

Literally, they saw their ships come in. Ten cargoes arrived at Brest for their account in the space of two days: the freight on those cargoes alone amounted to over 70,000 livres. Noting these arrivals in a letter to the minister, the intendant Hocquart remarked that "one can only praise the attention of these *fournisseurs* to the fulfillment of their obligations." [103] The year 1751 was the first of four good years for the partners. During each year of their contract to supply northern masts and stores, they made enormous purchases.

The only major blemish on the record was the loss of four vessels carrying "munitions for the navy" (it is not clear whether the crews were lost as well). The partners gave immediate orders for replacement of the cargoes. In fact, they need not have bothered: the cargoes "consisted of 9,000 plank and various stores with which we are abundantly provided; if there is no time to revoke the [replacement] orders, Monseigneur, you can instruct them to send these planks and irons to Rochefort or Toulon, where they may be needed." [104]

The partners kept both seaboard arsenals abundantly supplied. In September 1753 the intendant Hocquart remarked that "Brest is glutted with common plank. We have at least 200,000, enough for ten years" at the present rate of consumption. He added that Brest was also oversupplied with pitch, tar, tin plate, copper, above all with hemp, and with lead, of which the port had on hand 300,000 livres in pigs. Regarding merchandise received in July, Hocquart complained that excessive numbers of small masts had been supplied, "the largest of 23 or 24 palms . . . and those in very small numbers." A few days later, however, he was delighted to receive a shipment of additional masts, including about twenty of 23 to 26 palms. [105] A year later the entrepreneurs' purchases were still coming in. Two cargoes of masts arrived on 19 August 1754, consisting of masts of good quality and "splendid size," with two or three more cargoes (apparently the last) expected shortly, "which will give us ample supplies of this merchandise for a very long time, perhaps for thirty years." [106] Hocquart was hostile to suppliers who furnished unneeded materials in abundance and failed to deliver those in short supply. Nonetheless, Michel and Chaussade supplied another 144 great masts, 200 smaller sticks, and 10,000 *planches* in 1756. [107] Hocquart's particular concern was for the storage and preservation of this materiel. Even in 1755 he still had seven or eight hundred masts "from the north as well as France" (principally the Pyrenees), along with fir beams from the Rhineland, and more masts were en route. Ultimately, storage was arranged in the environs of Brest, up the Penfeld. [108]

Collectively the partners must be credited with supplying nearly all the northern masts and stores on hand in 1754. As individuals, they share the credit unequally because they played very different roles. As yet we have not found a notarial act that indicates what percentages of the partnership were held by Michel and Chaussade. Michel, in any case, appears to have gone to the Baltic while Chaussade remained in France. Goossens, proxy for Marie Boesnier, figured in the partnership as an active member only during the first year, 1751. In May of that year Chaussade received Goossens' *quittance*.[109] That act implied, as did the absence of his name from subsequent correspondence, that Pierre Goossens was ending his association with the partnership and had no share in the ongoing execution of the four-year contract. Indeed, the very next year Marie Boesnier herself ceded all her interest to Chaussade—her two sols (shares) of the twenty-one sol total—for the sum of 28,000 livres, and received two sols of twenty (Chaussade had the other eighteen) "for the two years 1753 and 1754 remaining."[110]

By the end of 1754, all the family business ventures had either run their course, as did the timber enterprise in Montbéliard and Franche-Comté, or had been bought up by Pierre Babaud de la Chaussade. The entire residual of the family business had finally come into his hands.

II. The New Family Business: Forged Anchors, Irons, and Steel

CHAPTER 4

The Formation of the Family Forges Royales

Great Anchors

Jacques Masson's acquisition of Guérigny in the early 1720s was the first step toward forming the industrial complex that came to be known as the Forges Royales. The seigneury and forge of Guérigny were situated on the little river Nièvre about ten kilometers northeast of the Loire. When acquired, the forge must have been very dilapidated; it was reported to be in ruins in 1728.[1] In the decade following it was rebuilt by Masson and Chaussade. By 1753 a second large forge had been built on the nearby seigneury of Villemenant, thus doubling the capacity of the establishment. Chaussade seems to have handled many details and carried responsibility for managing the forges for his father-in-law and business partner during the thirties. Ultimately Guérigny became Chaussade's provincial residence and usual place of business in the region, and hence the administrative headquarters of the Forges Royales. There Chaussade undertook to build a chateau within sight and sound of the forges, overlooking the water course from which they drew their power.

But the town of Cosne was the major anchor production center of the Forges Royales. Situated about forty miles north-northwest of Nevers (i.e., downriver), Cosne was the site of the juncture of the River Loire with a tributary, the Nohain. It offered an ideal site for machinery using water power. The waters of the Nohain ran through the town of Cosne and were dammed just before they reached the Loire, allowing a shallow lake to form. The forges were built beside the spillway; there the controlled waters of the Nohain were narrowed and made to run fast, giving the wheels their force as the waters swept past and into the Loire. The banks adjacent to the rivers provided space for storage; boats or barges could discharge cargo into storage yards and embark their downriver cargoes from warehouses at riverside. Cosne was the premier production site; Guérigny, the administrative center and secondary production site, although with the expansion of the 1750s it became nearly the equal of Cosne. Together Cosne and Guérigny became the twin capitals of Chaussade's Forges Royales.

The family partners acquired and developed at least a dozen smaller satellite forges, slitting mills, furnaces, and other facilities scattered along lesser tributaries of the Loire, all of them likewise using water-powered machinery. Their dams and sluiceways provided flows of water to activate bellows, raise the heavy ratchet and tilt hammers used in forging, and drive the rolling and slitting machinery. Water and charcoal were the principal sources of energy. Hence each manufactory was situated on a river or stream and close to woodland and forest, but also near pasture, agricultural land, and gardens, and with roads joining them. Nearly all the region's forges and mills were dependencies of seigneuries. Each of the scattered auxiliary forges had its unique congeries of dependent grinding mills and presses, houses, and cottages, huts, and other lodgings, with adjoining granaries, barns, stables, storehouses, hangars, and sheds. These nests of agro-industry included many ancient and decrepit but still useful buildings, chateau-residences for example. Thus, the chateau of Villemenant near Guérigny, though very old, was still solid. With its five-foot-thick walls, it served until about 1775 as lodging for workers and families attached to the manufactories, among them the bellowsmen, coopers, and principal clerk.[2] Other workers and the carters were housed in other premises of the seigneury or nearby. Among the dependencies of Cosne there was even a tile works, producing roofing and drainage tiles and moldings for the red-tile roofs, as well as excellent cookware. Even the obscure little seigneury of Richerand, one of the dependencies of Guérigny, made special contribution as a producer of wine, described as "not bad—it has the quality of keeping well."[3]

All these seigneuries and their dependencies were coordinated to contribute to the production of forged anchors for the navy. "Great anchors" were the most important product of this string of rural manufactories, the specialty and *raison d'être* of the Forges Royales. The anchors they produced ranged in size from grappling hooks weighing only a few pounds, fabricated at the smaller establishments, to great anchors such as the seven supplied in 1766 by Chaussade for the new ship-of-the-line *Bretagne*. Anchors for the *Bretagne* weighed from 3,200 to 8,700 livres each, with a grand total of 33,940 livres for the seven. The largest of them was probably produced at Cosne; the smaller ones, at Guérigny-Villemenant.

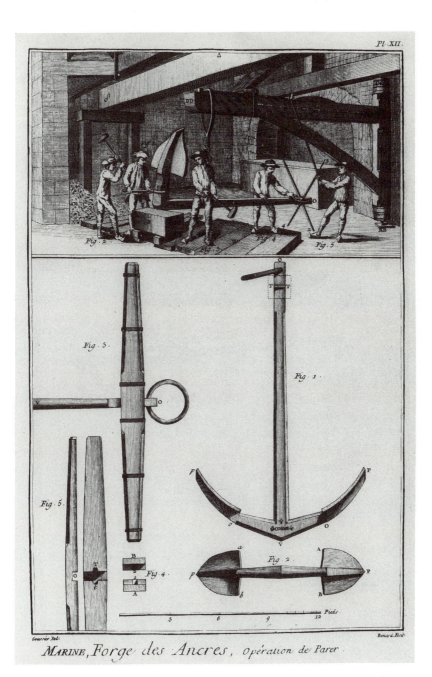

Pl. XII.

MARINE, *Forge des Ancres,* *Opération de Parer.*

From D. Diderot, *Encyclopédie, ou Dictionnaire Raisonné des sciences, des arts et des métiers* (Paris: Briasson, 1751–65, 17 vols.); Supplement à l'Encyclopédie (Amsterdam: Rey, 1776–77) (Planches), *Marine, Forge des Ancres,* Pl. XII, showing finishing (cleanup) work on a large anchor of the type produced at several of Chaussade's *Forges Royales.* The word COSNE stamped on the anchor below identifies it with these forges.

(A total of 348,700 livres of irons of various kinds were ordered and produced at the Forges Royales for that ship.)[4]

The manufacture of anchors posed many problems. Their design, form, and physical structure in relation to function were foci of attention. The physical problem of designing a heavy "hook" that would take hold of the ocean bottom, and not simply lie flat and slide, was dealt with by the device of a triangular fluke (*patte*) attached to each arm of the *T*. Special difficulties were associated with the large size anchors used for ships-of-the-line. They were among the most massive works then fabricated of iron and close to the maximum size the existing technology would allow. Before the eighteenth century, some attempts had been made to fabricate large anchors by pouring melted metal into molds, but solution of the problems associated with making large castings lay far beyond the existing technology. In that day even small cast-iron anchors proved to be very unreliable.

Officials of the navy in France were long and intensely preoccupied with the quest for bigger and better anchors for all the navy's ships. In the early 1670s, decrees from the ministry, then directed by Jean Baptiste Colbert, spelled out the precise dimensions sought, the thickness of the component parts, and the size and weight of the finished product.[5] Some inspectors at the arsenals also expressed concern over the color and brittleness of the metal, which they tested in various ways, using capstans, winches, etc. Moreover, naval officials wanted these strong anchors produced in France. The external uniformities that they were at such pains to prescribe in Colbert's *ordonnances* and through the expressed preferences of inspectors at the arsenals could be helpful, but they were not fully reliable indicators of interior quality and strength. Officials were well aware that many "variables" were involved. One group of variables was thought, in France, to be associated with the geographic origin of the iron ore, and another with the forging process employed.[6]

The source question was taken up by the French navy in the seventeenth century, and two locations in the upper reaches of the Loire valley appear to have been settled upon. At first the Nivernais was favored, but by the end of the seventeenth century, iron from the province of Berry was preferred by the navy to iron from any other part of France, especially for the manufacture of anchors.[7] The bias for Berry iron persisted strongly and was a problem with which Masson and the Babauds were obliged to contend, as will be seen. Both Guérigny and Cosne were situated north of the Loire, in the Nivernais, but they could draw on sources of iron in the Berry.

In the view of navy officials, sites for anchor production needed to be developed in close proximity to the best iron deposits and to abundant supplies of wood fuel. Thus the environs of Cosne-sur-Loire and the Nevers-Guérigny area were both pinpointed as favorable. And when Masson and his partners bought forges and seigneuries, in the Nivernais within easy reach of the iron supplies of the Berry, and ultimately obtained control of the Cosne forge itself, they proved themselves both well-informed and shrewd. They were buying favored facilities. The forges at Cosne in particular, as will be seen, were in effect a state manufactory with much associated potential for privilege; the opportunities for profit were accordingly high.

Research and Development

Experimentation in anchor production, at Cosne and elsewhere, enjoyed direct encouragement and help from the navy from Colbert's day onward. Successive ministries of marine, especially under Maurepas, sponsored mobilizations of technical, entrepreneurial, and scientific manpower. The outside talent associated with such experiments at Guérigny and Cosne included Theodore Lefevre de Chassenay, Octave Trésaguet, Daniel Bernouilli, and such well-known members of the French *Académie des Sciences* as René-Antoine Réaumur and Henri-Louis Duhamel du Monceau. The last two, eminent figures of the "technical enlightenment," addressed themselves at different times to problems of anchor design and production in papers read before the *Académie* and circulated the results of their experiments in correspondence, books, and brochures.

The navy was also in the habit of employing specialists from its own arsenals on missions of various sorts. Thus technicians were sent to anchor and iron production facilities to ensure quality and enforce strict conformity with the rules and preferences of the navy. Such salaried specialists developed extensive knowledge of metallurgy and production processes. Some of them held rank in the navy as master anchorsmiths; others were *ingénieurs du roi*. Experience with the production and (at the arsenals) the testing and repair of heavy forgings must have given these men technical skills and expertise equal to those of any country forgemaster recruited for work at Cosne or Guérigny. Their scattered reports and correspondence prove them to have been observant and alert, possessed of high intelligence as well as extraordinary technical competence.

These agents of the central administration with the mission of maintaining standards of size and quality in anchor components and other naval materiel also played an important role in the promotion of innovations. Under their surveillance, at least until the 1730s, many experiments were run and many changes in the method of anchor manufacture were tried at both Cosne and Guérigny.

Some writers identify Octave Trésaguet as the technician who, if he did not "invent," at least developed the "pyramidal bar" process of anchor construction. Trésaguet, one of the navy's *ingénieurs du roi,* was attached in 1702 to the *généralité de Moulins* by the minister of marine, Jerome Phelypeaux, comte de Pontchartrain.[8] Charged with superintending the production of anchors at Cosne, Trésaguet experimented with various methods of anchor forging, using packets of preforged bars and trying to obtain more nearly uniform quality throughout the forged anchors. It was common practice, and had been from time immemorial, for blacksmiths to unite one or more pieces of metal by heating malleable iron to a full red or white heat, then effecting a jointure by hammering them together while the metal was in a plastic or pasty condition. This was in fact the ancient art of "welding." Trésaguet and others simply applied the hand-process of the blacksmith to the mechanized manufacture of large anchors. For the two or three pieces of metal that the smith might use, Trésaguet substituted packets of forged iron bars that he welded together, layer upon layer, into "pyramids" built and maneuvered by cranes. For the forger's sledge-hammer, he substituted 800- to 1,000-pound ratchet-raised, drop-hammer machines. The welding (*corroyage*) of large pieces by this process was tried and tested by the navy over a long period.

The effort to perfect this essentially sound process occupied many men, including Trésaguet, for many years. As early as 1690 the navy's technicians involved in anchor manufacture were using the principal elements of the process at Nevers. In 1694 reference was made to the use of the "large water-powered hammer for joining together the parts of anchors" and to the manufacture of anchors "following the new method." Shortly afterward it was prescribed in a contract with a certain Sieur Grandguillaume that henceforth "all anchors must be fabricated with nothing but forged iron," with a significant and approving allusion "to those made with bars."[9] By 1700 Trésaguet had received advances from the king and a six-year contract to produce anchors using the pyramidal process.[10]

In short, the pyramidal process appears to have been developed through the work of many men, principally by master anchorsmiths from the naval arsenals, not necessarily in collaboration. The process could fairly be known as the French navy's pyramidal process. But whatever its origin or name, it did not guarantee the production of good anchors. Defective anchors continued to be produced intermittently, particularly anchors of the larger sizes. The interplay of ill-understood (or unknown) variables continually created problems, and failures recurred over a long period in the face of impatient criticism and pressure from the ministry and naval arsenals.

Finally, around 1728, the navy undertook another inventory of forges in the Nivernais and Berry, the traditional anchor-producing regions, where high-quality iron was reputed to be routinely produced. The aim was to pinpoint the forges offering advantages of site and size, either extant or potential, to serve as manufactories of the navy's largest anchors.[11] In the choice finally made, the operational economies of the Cosne location were important, but the single most important consideration was the excellence of the area's water-power resources for the operation of large forges using forge hammers of maximum size.[12] Maurepas himself visited Cosne when the site was being considered. After his visit he wrote, referring to the long-standing quest for good anchors, that anchors forged "under the great water-driven hammer" were much preferable to those "that can only be hand-forged in the arsenals of the king."[13] The next year, in 1729, the king leased the great forge at Cosne from Jean Arnaud, its owner, although it was judged not to be adequately equipped. The navy provided Arnaud with funds to enlarge buildings, and especially to build and install additional equipment.[14]

The minister's plan was to develop a major anchor production center, and of course there were many problems. The elderly Trésaguet himself was one of them. He was still involved in the manufactory at Cosne in 1730, and was still volunteering his services as late as 1737. For a variety of reasons, including advanced age and charges that this veteran had become excessively and narrowly self-interested, Trésaguet came to be considered unreliable.[15] Writing to him in April 1730, the minister's tone was urgent:

> I am expecting that this will find you at Cosne. I ask you to
> remain there [to work] assiduously and to consider, please, all
> the expenditure made to develop that manufactory and the diffi-
> culties [we have] experienced over the years. Certainly it would
> be inadvisable to allow the work to languish, considering [the
> cost of] the leases and the wages of workers, and the lack of
> anchors of many sizes at the ports.[16]

But Trésaguet was *not* at Cosne, and when he was reached at his home some distance away and persuaded to go, he remained at Cosne for only two and a half days. Afterward he offered to give written instructions by mail from his nearby estates. Maurepas was angered: "I cannot leave work of this importance in confusion, without a chief . . . if you cannot be present for the tests [of the first six anchors] . . . or at least part of them . . . I will appoint the Sieur des Longchamps to take charge alone."[17] Trésaguet finally had to be eased out. But there were other problems involving personnel and production, anchor testing, the production of smaller irons, and deliveries to the ports—complications that Maurepas can hardly have relished.

The early thirties did see, however, the production and delivery of many anchors that were judged at the arsenals to be of first quality. Writing in 1731, the navy's resident inspector at Cosne, the Sieur Tassin, observed: "The fabrication of anchors with packets of bars forged under the heavy hammer and welded entirely, or almost entirely to the heart, has now reached such a degree of perfection that we can have the long-sought confidence of safety in [anchoring] vessels at sea."[18] Tassin was a *commissaire* from the arsenals, assigned to oversee operations not only at Cosne, but also at nearby La Clavière and La Charité. His role and assiduity may be judged from the praise of a successor, who said that Tassin "oversaw [at the forges] the execution of the orders [from the ports], gave the dimensions to the entrepreneur, and [even] gave the vertical cut to the packets of pyramidal bars of which the anchors were composed."[19] With such a *commissaire* superintending the details of production, what were the roles of the anchorsmiths and the innovating entrepreneurs?

The contributions of individuals to anchor production are blurred by the importance of government-sponsored team effort. Over time, many persons worked on new designs and processes to advance this long-lived project. Their sustained efforts with the navy's help finally worked out, by trial and error, processes that could routinely produce anchors of high quality and strength and very large size.

The years from 1729 to 1735 saw the navy trying to manage its own anchor production establishment (centered at Cosne), but the experience of those years convinced Maurepas that the "enterprise" (i.e., private enterprise) method of management in anchor production was much preferable. He was persuaded that a reliable entrepreneur, or group of entrepreneurs, must be found to relieve the navy (and him) of this burden of management. That burden Masson and the Babauds invested, maneuvered and worked for many years to assume. They may even have sent young Chaussade abroad to study or investigate foreign manufacturing methods.[20]

Babaud and Company: First Contract, 1736–1754

The minister's choice of entrepreneurs was made known in 1736, when the navy agreed to pay Jean Babaud and his partners 14 sous per livre for anchors delivered to the ports at the entrepreneurs' own risk.[21] The twelve-year contract (1736–1748) specified that when orders for anchors were low, the entrepreneurs would be allowed to manufacture and deliver iron *courbes* and other irons needed at the arsenals. Thus the entrepreneurs were assured of a *de facto* monopoly for provisioning the navy with large anchors, and a regular, dependable market, it seemed, for forging from the great anchor forge at Cosne.

About the same time (1736), the minister of marine consulted the *Académie Royale des Sciences* concerning the navy's anchor problems. In response the Academy inaugurated a competition, offering a prize of 5,000 livres for the best essay submitted on the manufacture, form, or testing of anchors. Whatever the merits of the essays submitted,[22] they appear not to have gone beyond existing practice. The pyramidal bar system remained standard.

Thus in 1736 Jean Babaud and his associates entered this industry as entrepreneurs, as business managers. They were not technicians or innovators, but they had experience in the industry; at that date they had been buying up forges and forest properties along the upper Loire, especially around Nevers, for over fifteen years. They had been making those acquisitions with the knowledge that the Berry-Nivernais region had been the scene of anchor manufacture for the navy under various auspices for three-quarters of a century. Their contract of 1736 appears to have crowned a sustained series of acquisitions that had brought into their hands major components of an established industry in a region the navy had favored for decades. They also acquired control of well-developed manufacturing processes that the navy was largely responsible for developing and considered the best processes then known to European science and technology for the production of large-size forgings.

Some details of the partners' initial contract to operate the forges and other facilities at Cosne seem at first sight disadvantageous. They evidently had no choice but to become partners with Arnaud, the subcontractor who had hitherto managed the Cosne works for the navy.[23] Arnaud's partnership in this company was soon terminated at Arnaud's request, however, perhaps because he was having difficulties with creditors; he may also have been unwell.[24] The partners then agreed to buy from Arnaud the forge and other facilities at Cosne that were still under lease to the king (i.e., the navy), and in due course obtained cancellation of that lease. Concurrently they acquired by purchase all the harness, equipment, and tools used in the manufacturing and maintenance processes, much of it recently purchased by Arnaud with funds supplied by the king for refurbishment.[25] Masson and the Babauds also had the advantage of being able to use an established network of fuel and iron bar suppliers.

Finally, there was the advantage of acquiring a *de facto* monopoly. Henceforth they could expect to supply all the large anchors needed for the vessels of the navy, the Compagnie des Indes, and the French colonies—a privileged market. Their provisionments were exempt from most road and river tolls. Thus the partners escaped the economic restrictions on the expansion of facilities that limited other manufacturers. By virtue of their "defense production" contracts, they were able to expand and engage in manufacturing on a scale that would otherwise have been uneconomic and quite impracticable. (More will be said about these privileges and the negative significance of the tolls, especially in Chapter 8.)

The initial partners did not enjoy these advantages for long, because, as we have seen, two died in close succession. Jean Babaud's share of the family business was fixed on the eve of his death, by agreement among the principal partners, at 350,000 livres. That sum was scheduled to be paid to his widow, Marie Boesnier, in seven equal annual payments. Then Masson and Chaussade would be 100 percent owners of the business. But they did not—and almost certainly could not—make all seven of the 50,000 livre payments.

In fact the surviving partners did not even make the first payment, due 1 September 1739. Instead they formed a new society in 1739 in which Marie received a one-third interest; this society controlled most, perhaps all, of their contracts and enterprises of that time. But Marie Boesnier's attorneys or her surrogate, Goossens, saw to it that she received a 255,476-livre cash credit with the new society in addition to her one-third interest. Shortly afterward, Masson married Marie, and family affairs became complex. In December 1741 Marie sold a one-third interest to Chaussade, who assumed responsibility for the debts of the society and paid her 133,000 livres. At that point Chaussade may have been owner of his own and Masson's shares.[26]

The largest part of Chaussade's own wealth consisted of his share in the profits and capital of the partnership. Another, very small portion of his assets came from his share of the legacy of his parents.[27] A third part of his holdings in 1741–1743 was the product of his long-time relationship with Masson, whose only daughter he had married.[28] As late as 1742,

Chaussade was referred to as "tutor ad hoc de lad. Dme son épouse," even though she must at that date have been around twenty-two years of age. He had the "use" of her property during much of her lifetime.[29]

Because the greater part of his assets seem to have been tied up in real estate and working capital, Chaussade could claim that he could not pay off the Boesnier-Babaud share without selling property or liquidating some of their joint enterprises. Those circumstances may have helped Marie (and Goossens, her counsellor) to participate with Chaussade in a newly organized partnership in 1742. This new society was capitalized at 200,000 livres. About two-thirds of the assets consisted of "new money" from the hands of at least seven shareholders, most of them brought in from the outside.[30] Chaussade sold his share of the Cosne forges to Marie in 1743[31] and was thus dissociated entirely from the ownership of Cosne for some years.

For the next six and a half years (October 1742 to April 1749), Marie was sole owner of the Cosne forge. During this period she continued to lease Cosne to the society of associates in which she and Chaussade had a minority interest. That society assumed responsibility for the execution of the remainder of the original twelve-year contract to supply irons and anchors to the navy under the name of Daniel Le Tessier; later that contract was revised and renewed for six years (1749–1754) in the name of Antoine Louis Mangin, another surrogate.[32] Meanwhile, after a series of "bad years" at Cosne (to be described), in April 1749 Marie Boesnier sold a 50 percent interest in her Cosne establishment back to Chaussade, and in April 1752 she sold him the other half as well. By 1752 Chaussade was full owner of the Cosne forges.[33]

The rationale for using these methods was itself complex. The reason for relying on surrogates was different for different individuals and in different phases of business. Certain types of enterprise might have entrained *dérogeance* (loss of the quality of *noblesse*); a person (like Chaussade) who had acquired that social status might prefer to avoid any taint. Moreover, Chaussade was concurrently involved in a variety of far-flung ventures as shareholder, partner, *caution,* or independent owner-operator; the diversity and dispersion of his interests and holdings made reliance on administrative aides, overseers, and surrogates imperative. Chaussade and Goossens both employed resident managers, accountants, bookkeepers, and collectors to handle details. Sales, resales, and divisions of property and the formation of partnerships and companies were alternative methods of transferring assets or responsibility and raising capital. Furthermore, indirect management could mask the existence of legally binding, or potentially compromising business connections and illegal operations.

We can only guess at Chaussade's reasons for selling his interests in the Cosne establishment to Marie Boesnier, and later buying them back. Initially he certainly did not have the funds to pay off her share of the original partnership—perhaps she wanted out. When he was able to get the money, he bought the forges back. In doing so he alternately lost and regained his connection with the "great anchor" production facility so carefully developed by the navy and cherished in the family partnership as a source of privilege.

Berry Irons

The high reputation of Cosne anchors and irons, and the prestige of products from nearby La Charité-sur-Loire and the forges at Clavières, rested largely on the extensive, if not exclusive, use of irons from the province of the Berry in their operations. The irons of the Berry derived from pockets of ore mined and smelted in the region lying west and southwest of Nevers and Cosne itself and along the Loire as far as Orléans, the so-called *ligne de la Loire*.[34]

In almost the same degree that the virtues of Berry irons were extolled, the irons mined and smelted in the Nivernais were condemned, at least at the navy's arsenals, when the manufacture of anchors was involved. Thus when Tassin was sent to La Charité-sur-Loire in 1722 to oversee forge operations, his special orders instructed him explicitly to prevent the employment—under any pretext whatsoever—of pig iron from the Nivernais.[35] In 1753 the same Tassin, with over thirty years of experience as an inspector and *commissaire* behind him, still urged the exclusion of Nivernais iron from products manufactured at Guérigny and nearby Chantmerle in the Nivernais in order to eliminate "all suspicion" about the quality of the pig iron being employed.[36] It was held that irons from the Nivernais were brittle and unworkable (*aigre*), and that reputation was periodically reinforced by complaints from the ports about the irons delivered. Poor quality was frequently ascribed to the use, or suspected use, of inferior irons from the Nivernais.

Officials at the arsenals insisted that anchors for the navy be manufactured with Berry irons, and inspectors were alert to any attempt to substitute others. Chaussade could not regularly bring ores from Berry to his furnaces in the Nivernais—such bulk materials could not be transported far. Yet his forges at Guérigny and Villemenant frequently used bar iron brought in from Berry. Thus in the lease he wrote to bind one long-time *régisseur* for the Guérigny forge, Chaussade included clauses that "allowed" the lessee to buy up to 500,000 livres of pig iron a year from

Chaussade, "furnished from his furnace at La Vache in the Nivernais or from Berry, at his choice."[37] "Ordinary" irons and Berry irons were used for different products, but were never supposed to be mixed. In some manufactures destined for delivery to the French Compagnie des Indes and the colonies, or for local or regional use, adulterated or even exclusively Nivernais products could be used, since manufactures sent to those markets did not need to meet navy standards.

At first sight the obligation to bring in Berry irons for navy work might seem to have been an unmitigated disadvantage. Some evidence suggests, however, that Chaussade managed to transform this into an advantage. He alternately collaborated and competed with other owners or operators of furnaces and forges. Pierre de Guiberderie and Silvain Denis, leasees of the forges of the Priory of La Charité-sur-Loire, shared with Chaussade a contract to supply the irons needed by the navy at Brest, Rochefort, and Havre from 1744 through 1747: Chaussade was to supply half of the ports' requirements and the Charité producers the other half.[38] Those were war years, and the navy's orders for irons were accordingly large. Chaussade, apparently using pig iron or bars from Berry, supplied and shipped his half without difficulty, and in early 1745–46 went so far as to get himself reprimanded by Maurepas for maneuvers that allowed him to supply *more* than his share.[39] When new contracts were signed in 1747, Chaussade and Denis shared the Brest and Havre provisionment; but a certain Sieur Claude Le Blanc, long-time lessee of the forges of Clavières and a later *prêtenom* of Chaussade's, received the Rochefort part of the contract.[40] All these forges and *fournisseurs* were extraordinarily active in the war years of the forties, furnishing Berry irons to the navy. In 1751 Denis pulled out because he no longer held (for unexplained reasons) the lease on the furnaces and forges of the Priory of La Charité. Chaussade alone was then charged with the contract to supply Brest and Havre.[41]

Both Chaussade and Le Blanc continued for some years, sometimes sharing the same contract, to provide irons for the arsenals. In 1756, and later in 1764, this Sieur Le Blanc ("de Marnaval" at the latter date) was still lessee of the royal forges of Clavières and still had the Rochefort *fourniture*.[42] Chaussade specialized in furnishing irons to Brest (and Havre), Brest usually requiring a larger provisionment than all the other ports combined. After he repurchased the Cosne forge, Chaussade enjoyed a near monopoly of anchor production for the Atlantic seaboard arsenals for almost three decades. In all these contracts there were indications that the navy preferred the irons of Berry.

Not clear is the precise provenance, within the Berry, of the irons Chaussade used. There were many small smelters in Berry. Chaussade may well have obtained pig iron (*gueuses* or *fonte*) or forged iron bars from his sometime associates, Le Blanc of Clavières and Denis of La Charité. We know that they sent semifinished bars, and perhaps blooms (*gueuses*) with them, to be worked in Chaussade's forges in the Nivernais.[43] Yet the full network of Chaussade's suppliers of Berry irons remains obscure.

We can be certain, however, that those who sold iron to Chaussade were at some disadvantage in negotiating with him about the price of the metal. Chaussade was a privileged buyer. The minister of marine made it clear that in case of disagreement over price or refusal to sell, "the necessary orders will be given to oblige" proprietors.[44] Yet it was highly desirable to keep the good will of the producers of primary materials and that of other fabricators of components for the navy. That helps to explain why Chaussade, at least in the forties and fifties, undertook to see personally to the acquisition of irons for the forgemaster operating his forges at Guérigny.

In the one recorded dispute between Chaussade and a supplier, the navy sided with the entrepreneur. That incident occurred after Chaussade reported to the minister in July 1756, with seeming elation, that he had purchased from M. de La Belouse 3,250,000 milliers of irons, with deliveries scheduled at the rate of 50,000 milliers a month.[45] That was a very large purchase indeed, with a rapid rate of delivery. The minister must have been impressed, as Chaussade probably intended he should be; but one suspects that Chaussade particularly wanted to impress the minister with the imperative need for regularity in the payments the navy was to make to him. When La Belouse reported in April 1757 that he was engaged in litigation with Chaussade, the minister of marine (then the marquis de Moras), or perhaps Le Normant de Mezy acting for Moras, turned on La Belouse and threatened to carry the affair to the royal council "if you continue your lawsuit against Chaussade. . . . the best course appears to me to be to reach an immediate accommodation. . . . the Sieur de la Chaussade appears to me to be disposed to make all the necessary concessions."[46] Chaussade, dealing "face to face" with the minister, seems to have persuaded him to squelch both the lawsuit and La Belouse.

The Forge at Cosne

The partners' practice of delivering larger quantities of materiel than had been ordered by the navy may be relevant to Chaussade's decisions to buy and sell his interest in the forge at Cosne. In 1739–1742 the anchors and irons that the *fournisseurs* delivered to the arsenal at Brest very much

exceeded the quantities ordered and needed, and some of the merchandise delivered was also found to be faulty.[47] Masson, Marie Boesnier,
Chaussade, and perhaps other suppliers as well, outdid themselves in
such measure that only six anchors and 47,000 livres of iron were ordered in 1742 (a war period) for delivery to Brest and Rochefort in
1743.[48] The minister decreed in October 1743 that future deliveries must
conform in all particulars to the actual *états* (orders) for each port; payment for any excess would be delayed.[49] Shortly thereafter Chaussade
sold the Cosne forge to Marie Boesnier.[50]

This chronology suggests that Chaussade sold the forge in part because
the prospect for gains from future provisionments seemed bleak. The formation of the new society to lease Cosne in March 1742 had substantially reduced the Chaussade-Boesnier financial involvement not only at
Cosne, but in several other areas of naval contracting that were also becoming more difficult. Maurepas was showing a disposition to enforce
strictly the customs and rules designed to protect the navy's interest.

Clearly Chaussade had reason to anticipate short-term difficulties for
the manufactory at Cosne; and indeed, orders for anchors remained low
for some time. In April 1745 the minister reported that Brest needed only
four anchors (presumably for the year), and Rochefort none; he helpfully
noted that Toulon had ordered twelve, and he actually solicited the ports
to send in small additional orders to keep the forges going.[51] But significantly, early in 1746 *cautions* of Daniel Le Tessier, then *régisseur* of the
Cosne forge, complained that for three years Cosne had not received any
orders for large irons, apparently referring to irons other than anchors.[52]
For whatever reason, the level of activity at Cosne was kept extraordinarily low. By comparison, Chaussade's own forges were very active. At
Guérigny 87 anchors were manufactured that had not been ordered, and
having had them produced, Chaussade offered them to the navy. In May
1745 the minister informed Chaussade that they could be shipped to the
port of Brest.[53] They ranged in weight from 200 to 1,000 livres, "forged
and assembled at his estates at Guérigny and Frasnay," and apparently
using good Berry irons as the navy wished.[54] Several months later, informed that Chaussade was shipping 101 rather than 87 anchors to
Brest, the minister merely expressed the hope that the waters of the Loire
would soon rise enough to permit their descent to Nantes.[55] Even in those
years of the War of the Austrian Succession, the minister was clearly
doing Chaussade a favor in accepting those extra anchors.

Perhaps there were other considerations too. The ports had been receiving shipments of irons and anchors of poor quality in the 1740s,
some so poor that substantial numbers were rejected, notwithstanding

their having been manufactured with Berry irons. The principal cause of the defects, said the dockyard inspectors, was the use of insufficient heat in the smelting and forging processes.[56] They suggested that some features of the prevailing system of forge management encouraged poor quality. Forge managers habitually delivered carefully measured quantities of raw material to each forgemaster. Thus, 1,550 to 1,600 livres of *fonte* and about three *bannes* of charcoal (see Glossary) might be delivered to a forgemaster, who was then expected to produce at least 1,000 livres of iron with those materials. To encourage him to economize, the owner-entrepreneur often offered to pay him cash (*argent*) for wood or charcoal not consumed. But this incentive sometimes led forgemasters to shorten the processing of the metal, to the point that its quality suffered; even the best Berry raw material might be turned out as an impure, brittle, or otherwise unsatisfactory product.[57]

Similar problems could develop when fuel supplies were depleted or insufficient. Whether from the fuel shortages that affected some localities or for other reasons, including improper or adulterated raw material (suspected by some inspectors at the arsenals), irons drawn from forges on the highly esteemed *ligne de la Loire,* including Cosne and La Charité, seemed to undergo serious deterioration in quality in the forties.[58]

Whatever the case, few naval orders were given to Cosne in the middle and later 1740s. Yet we find, in the late forties, the new minister of marine, Rouillé, complaining of Cosne's failure to produce, which he said yielded serious consequences for the service.[59] It was at this point, as we have seen, when operations were at low ebb, that Chaussade repurchased a half interest in Cosne. The failure to produce, besides exerting downward pressure on the price Marie Boesnier asked, must have been very troubling to the company of entrepreneurs who had leased the forge at Cosne.

Meanwhile, Chaussade was cooperating with Rouillé. Rouillé indicated that he looked to Chaussade's forges in the Nivernais—in particular to Guérigny and Chaussade's newly acquired establishment at Villemenant—to produce the anchors that Cosne had not supplied—reportedly because it could not, but perhaps because it had not been asked to.[60] Writing to Inspector Tassin, Rouillé appeared to be explaining the use of Chaussade's facilities in the Nivernais (in lieu of those at Cosne) as a result of Tassin's own counsel: "Because you consider this arrangement, tending to relieve (*soulagé*) the forges at Cosne, [to be] suitable, I will consent to it."[61]

Obviously it was more profitable for Chaussade to produce anchors at his own home forges, Guérigny and Villemenant, than to have them forged at Cosne, where he had only a small share in the producing company that had leased that forge. In 1751 operations at the Cosne establishment were in the hand of the surrogate, Daniel Le Tessier; later, from 1753, Antoine Louis Mangin acted for the society.[62] At Guérigny all the profits from producing the irons and anchors were Chaussade's own. Officially visiting Guérigny, Tassin found no fault with the anchors being produced; and Rouillé referred to this opinion when he authorized Chaussade to continue production of ninety-one anchors "without interruption."[63] The transfer of anchor production from Cosne to Guérigny, it seems clear, had been sought by Chaussade and was requested by Tassin on his behalf.[64] Rouillé himself may have offered Tassin an opening in June 1750 by suggesting to him that some of the navy's orders might be filled at other forges because, said Rouillé, there was reason to doubt that Cosne could fulfill them.[65]

By the spring of 1751 the preferential treatment Chaussade was enjoying was so obvious that it seems to have inspired some of his competitors to pull out of the business. (There may be another explanation as well: they may have been short of fuel.) Rouillé himself was told of difficulties being experienced in leasing the royal forges of Clavières. Forge operators were naturally reluctant to renew leases when they could not be sure of getting orders to produce. Rouillé assured them that their fears were "without foundation," observing that the provisionment for Rochefort was still to be assigned and inviting prospective lessees to make their offers: "I am disposed to accord the preference to them, if they are reasonable."[66]

Significantly, in 1751 Chaussade was connected indirectly and secretly with the management of a group of furnaces and forges in Berry called Grossouvres and Sauvage. His connection was through the person of Alexandre Baudry of Nevers, with whom he was doing business at least as early as 1737. Baudry, serving as *commissaire à terrier* or *feudiste*, worked on many occasions with details of the *terriers* of Chaussade's properties around Nevers, particularly *vis-à-vis* Guérigny itself.[67] Afterward, from 1741 until about 1747, Baudry was *régisseur général* and *caissier* of a society organized to operate the Grossouvres-Sauvage furnaces and forges. As a result of his performance in that capacity, Baudry was accused of embezzlement and breach of trust, brought to trial, convicted, and condemned. But Baudry proved to be a slippery fellow with powerful friends. He arranged a separate settlement with the heirs of one of his victims at the expense of the others. He was saved from further prosecution on other charges by the financial exhaustion of his principal victims—the Everat family of La Charité and Paris, father, brother, and son,[68] who had had earlier dealings with Masson and Jean Babaud.[69] The Everats' losses in this affair were staggering: 230,000 livres plus litigation costs, as a *minimum* figure.[70]

Baudry was given refuge by Chaussade and protected from arrest and imprisonment even after he had been condemned as guilty. Chaussade gave him a post as *régisseur* of his works at Cosne and was thus able to claim, implausibly, that Baudry's services were "vital" to the production of anchors at Cosne for the navy.[71]

The Everats had a very strong case against Baudry, which they carried to the highest sovereign courts of the realm and won. But their victory was hollow. Chaussade obtained a succession of "safe-conducts" from the king, via Rouillé, by means of which Baudry avoided arrest.[72]

Learning that Baudry had been put beyond reach, the *procureur général* of Paris, Joly de Fleury, wrote a scathing letter to Rouillé condemning Baudry unequivocally and casting doubts and even ridicule on the motives of his protector, Pierre Babaud de la Chaussade. Joly de Fleury urged the minister to consider the injustice done to the Everats:

> The conduct of Baudry shows nothing less than bad faith, *in-fidelité*, abuse of confidence, and unjust withholding of the funds of another, in short a *caissier infidel.* . . . They say [i.e., Chaus-sade claims] he is director of the manufactory at Cosne. With-out him [they claim] the manufactory could not furnish for the navy. . . . in fact Baudry is neither *fournisseur* nor worker. The anchor forge belongs to M. de la Chaussade. He is the entrepre-neur and *fournisseur*. If [the safe conduct were] for himself, the pretext would be more reasonable . . . but a clerk could easily be replaced. It was not long ago that he was [replaced], as has been shown. Others could be found.

The *procureur général* found it very suspicious "that M. de la Chaussade undertakes to pay (*s'oblige d'acquitter*) all the judgments obtained against Baudry. He is his clerk. He is his man. He needs him."[73] Chaussade con-tinued to protect Baudry; in fact, Alexandre Baudry, *preposé*, was still his employee in 1764 and 1772.[74]

Whatever the details of the extraordinary relationships among Chaus-sade, Baudry, and Rouillé, so costly to the Everats and apparently bene-ficial to Chaussade and Baudry, the ties with Rouillé were obviously of importance to the development of Chaussade's business affairs. Signifi-cantly, Rouillé's tenure as minister of marine (May 1749 through July 1754) was a time of remarkable expansion and growth in Chaussade's interests and career as a businessman. Rouillé favored Chaussade and his associates with contracts that conferred *de facto* monopolies, under whose terms they purchased and imported enormous quantities of masts, spars, and other northern merchandise for the navy from the Baltic and the Netherlands on a commission basis, as we have seen. The intendant Hocquart of Brest gave an indication of the tremendous volume of their buying and commissions in the years 1751–1754 when he remarked (optimistically, as we noted earlier) that in August 1754 the port of Brest had enough masts on hand "for a very long time, perhaps thirty years."[75] Rouillé ordered the reception of virtually everything Chaussade shipped, including quantities of stores that had not been ordered from them, and much that was not wanted at all. He allowed Chaussade and his partners to run roughshod over naval management systems, to ignore the thrifty and responsible practices that his predecessor, Maurepas, had increasingly insisted upon in dealings with *fournisseurs*.

Encouragement from Rouillé and the likelihood (or promise) of privilege at his hands must have helped to persuade Chaussade to consolidate and expand his facilities in order to maximize his deliveries of all sorts of irons to the navy. Rouillé explicitly encouraged the expansion of Chaussade's plants at Guérigny, Cosne, and elsewhere on the Loire. Writing to Tassin in 1750, Rouillé expressed doubt that the Cosne forge could produce in four, or even six, years all the irons the navy was expected to require. He urged Tassin to inform Chaussade of the navy's prospective long-term needs (even though he had written earlier about the need for provisioning on a year-by-year basis) and to find out from him "how much Cosne could produce in five or six years" and what arrangements could be made to obtain the added supplies elsewhere in France in case it was possible to fabricate anchors at other forges.[76] Rouillé would thus seem to have made a considerable contribution to destroying the old prejudice that required the use of Berry irons and not others. Chaussade was already moving. At that date he had taken the first steps toward regaining control of the forges at Cosne.

Chaussade may have entertained some thought that he would get a bargain from the twice-widowed Marie Boesnier. But if the lean, problem-ridden years of the middle forties at Cosne did anything to diminish her desire to keep her funds committed in the iron industry, that was not evident in the price she and her counsellors fixed and obtained when they sold the Cosne forge back to Chaussade. In buying back the first half in April 1749, Chaussade paid fully as much as he had received when he sold out five years before.[77]

Even before he reacquired the second half of Cosne, Chaussade (with Boesnier, at least nominally) had made plans to build there "a great new forge to manufacture anchors for His Majesty's service" (as Chaussade described it). Plans called for one small and three large furnaces in the principal masonry building for the new great forge, with water channels 12 feet deep and 18 feet wide, a charcoal and coal storage barn of masonry construction beside the Loire (51 feet long and 40 feet wide), a stone granary for livestock feed (96 feet long and 36 wide), and spacious new housing for workers. These construction projects were let to Blaise Ravot, master mason and stonecutter of Cosne; the price tag was 85,000 livres.[78] No wonder Chaussade was obliged to pay substantially more when he finally reacquired the second half of Cosne in April 1752.[79]

In the three years following, Chaussade bought up the shares of the Cosne society's remaining associates at a cost of over 160,000 livres; in addition, he agreed to assume the society's debts (of over 106,000 livres) and to pay certain subcontractors, merchants, plant personnel, and external workers. The obligations he assumed were well in excess of 266,000 livres.[80] Marie Boesnier's share in the same society apparently cost him 105,000 livres.[81]

Villemenant, Richerand, and Demeurs

It was during Rouillé's tenure that Chaussade purchased the barony, land, and seigneury of Villemenant from the elderly baron de Lange; the low purchase price (48,000 livres) and the large subsequent outlays for repairs and reconstruction underscore the poor condition of this establishment when it came into Chaussade's hands. But Villemenant had special attractions for the owner of Guérigny. The ancient chateau of Villemenant and its dependencies were situated on the banks of the Nièvre quite near Guérigny.[82] For this property Chaussade planned improvements comparable (but smaller in scale) to those planned and soon afterward built some fifty miles down the Loire at Cosne. Villemenant was likewise to have a new great forge and several small furnaces for the manufacture of anchors, and housing for workers on about one-fifth the scale of Cosne. Villemenant already was (or was soon to be) the site of an important tile manufactory where roofing materials for Chaussade's properties were fabricated.[83]

In April 1750 Chaussade acquired from Louis Antoine du Creuzet a property called Richerand, in arid country; it was said in 1775, after Chaussade had owned the place for about twenty-five years, that the chateau was "not much, partly falling in ruins," with other buildings in similar state. But Richerand also had a tile works, and some solid housing.[84] In 1752 Chaussade purchased still another old property, known as Demeurs. Local tradition held that it had in earlier times been a Lutheran meeting place.[85] Later Demeurs too was described as "badly situated" and the buildings as "badly built" and needing reconstruction. But the property included forges, a tilt hammer, nailworks, toolworks, and the smelter of Chantmerle, all useful for Chaussade's growing industrial complex. He was to produce steel at Chantmerle.

About the same time Chaussade negotiated the purchase of two small forges, and their dependencies, from a certain M. de Mouchy. Earlier (1750) he had negotiated the lease of a house, land, and forested property from Bernot de Mouchy,[86] but in mid-1752 it was a question of purchasing forges, which incidentally involved him in long-drawn-out troubles with the inhabitants of nearby Raveau, as will later be seen.[87]

We know that Chaussade made at least eight purchases of forge- and furnace-connected properties in the years 1749–1752; six of these purchases were made in the month of April, perhaps because that month marked the onset of the dry season, when dropping water levels halted water-powered equipment and the transport of raw materials and irons by water.

Chaussade's outlays of funds to purchase and renovate all these properties must have been very large. Bertrand Gille reports that in 1744 Chaussade obtained two no-interest loans of 100,000 and 40,000 livres from the Compagnie des Indes, which was pressured by Maurepas to make those loans. The money was to be used to finance construction of a new great anchor forge at Cosne, destined to produce anchors for the company.[88] Those funds may have been spent in the mid-forties. Beyond that, Chaussade probably spent about 600,000 livres during the Rouillé administration. We cannot calculate the total cost of his purchases and renovations with certainty, still less determine the provenance of the funds used. But our sources provide some suggestive details. They indicate that some of Chaussade's purchases were made with loans from (or deferred payments to) the sellers, variations of contract for deed transactions in modern real estate purchases. In some instances he found the means to pay most, or all, of the purchase price in cash. He raised money by borrowing from many of his relatives, in-laws, associates, and friends; in effect his notary was his banker. The registers of the Paris notary Magnier, heavily used by Chaussade from March 1750 onward, disclose extensive borrowing in the five months from September 1752 through January 1753. Thereafter, however, the pressure was apparently relieved; the royal treasury made large payments to Chaussade and to his and Marie Boesnier's surrogates between mid-February and 7 June 1753, payments for northern stores and anchors and irons.[89] These payments to

Chaussade in the form of annuities (*constitutions*) in fact suggest the favor he enjoyed, inasmuch as the royal treasury itself—even before the Seven Years War—was hard pressed for funds.

By early 1756, all of Chaussade's forges (new and old) were in full production. The new great anchor forge at Cosne was "entirely finished" and in production by September 1751.[90] Much of the renovation and construction on his properties had also been completed. And Chaussade must have been pleased in February to have the new minister of marine, Machault d'Arnouville, send revised and increased estimates of the needs of the navy. Indeed, the size of the estimates must have shocked even Chaussade, who had foreseen large increases. The estimates for 1756–1758, reflecting the existence of major maritime war, called for deliveries of 12 million livres of anchors, *courbes,* and general irons for the aggregate needs of Brest, Rochefort, and Toulon.[91] Since Chaussade's own production did not exceed 400,000 livres of anchors per year—thus 1.2 million in three years—and 4 million livres in general irons over that three-year term, it was apparent that nearly 7 million livres of the aggregate requirements would necessarily be subcontracted or, following Chaussade's recommendation, purchased by him from other forge owners or elsewhere. Chaussade himself seems to have considered the possibility that "the Sieur de la Chaussade could . . . take possession, under an assumed name, of the holdings of two of his neighbors, and thereby make an additional million livres of iron a year." There were also other expedients that could be tried without recourse to "arbitrary power" (*l'autorité*), as Chaussade put it, meaning requisition of the product of other forges by the navy—a proceeding he saw as needed even to meet the needs of the port of Brest. Meeting requirements depended, he emphasized, "on a prompt decision on the [12 percent increase in] iron prices, and an arrangement for [the payment of] a certain, fixed sum each month during the years 1756, 1757, and 1758."[92] Whatever promises were made, regularity in payments was not a serious possibility. Yet Chaussade received very substantial (though irregular) payments from the navy even in that penurious, desperate time.[93]

Chaussade had a myriad of cares, and never more than in the decade following 1749. Provisionments from Montbéliard, Alsace, Lorraine, the Netherlands, Denmark, and the Baltic, the details of acquiring and managing at least two dozen separate properties, including a dozen seigneurial estates and dependent forges in the valley of the Loire, might seem to have occupied all his waking hours; but there are indications that he found at least a little time for leisure. For him, relaxation apparently consisted of an orderly period of work in the provinces, overseeing his forges and estates, the management of his forests and "his people," as he liked to call them. Writing from Paris on 7 September 1752, Chaussade announced, with a certain self-congratulatory assurance, that he had been in residence almost continuously at Compiègne and at Versailles since mid-June, occupied with "the service with which I am charged"; now he planned a change: "I leave this afternoon, Monsieur, with my family, to pass the autumn on my estates. May I ask, therefore, that you address your orders to me at Nevers. If I am informed of the day of your visit to the establishment at La Charité, I will have the honor of paying my respects to you there."[94]

Chaussade had arrived. The tutelage and legacies of his late father-in-law and brother and parents had been put to use. He was soon to settle with Marie Boesnier and assume full legal control of the family enterprises he already controlled in fact. In his hands the family business had become more complex, multi-leveled, and far-flung. He had no choice but to continue the practice of employing multiple surrogates, partners, aides, and *régisseurs*. Increasingly, the timber business had been passed into their hands. Chaussade himself concentrated on seeking advantages affecting the multi-faceted operations associated with the seigneury-manufactories. There too he relied heavily on surrogates, partners, and agents. He was personally most active in negotiating with the navy, in cultivating contacts on various levels of government and semiofficial agencies. But he also actively fostered and strengthened industrial and agrarian interdependence among his holdings, though he usually left the details in the hands of his experienced and loyal *régisseurs,* who functioned concurrently as industrial plant and seigneurial estate managers.

By purchasing an office as *secrétaire du Roi au Grand Collège,* Chaussade had assured his *noblesse,* but that status was further reinforced by the possession of many seigneurial properties. His social status and prestige were clearly heightened by his second marriage, in 1746, to Anne-Rose Le Conte de Nonant de Pierrecourt. His own high (and rising) social and economic status enabled him to marry the daughters of his first marriage into families high in the hierarchy of French society. Thus young Marie-Cécile[95] was wed in 1756 to Claude-Charles, Chevalier Marquis de Guiry. The guest list included, on the groom's side, the marquis d'Argenson (minister-secretary of state for war) and J.-B. de Machault (minister-secretary of state for the navy); and appearing for both sides was his intimate familiar Antoine Louis Rouillé, soon to become minister-secretary of state for foreign affairs, along with at least a score of other prominent persons, including four d'Hosiers, closely connected with the Guiry family.[96]

Chaussade provided a fine dowry for Marie-Cécile: 150,000 livres, 15,000 paid in cash on the eve of the marriage, 85,000 with interest in six months, 50,000 without interest, payable at Chaussade's own decease.

The terms of payment, however, bore the economic stamp of a man of affairs. His roots were, after all, in a family with modest (erstwhile Huguenot) connections, converts to the dignity and privileges of the orthodox Religion Catholique, Apostolique, et Romaine; his was a family risen to profit and prestige by hard work, some sharp business practices, and a successful quest for privileges that included government contracts purchased offices, and noble status. Chaussade had far-flung business associations as well as social contacts, and intimate connections with some of the king's principal ministers. And he could boast ownership of one of the great empires of industry in eighteenth-century France, the Forges Royales that would eventually bear his name.

CHAPTER 5

Procurement and Production, Transport and Payments

Fuel

In 1764 the elders of the town of Cosne-sur-Loire complained with bitterness "that the Sieur Baudry, as superintendant and manager of the forges of the Sieur de la Chaussade in the town, was buying up all the fuel in the region." In consequence, it was said, even the bakers of the town had no firewood.[1] The elders pointed to "three new foundries," as they called them, constructed by Baudry the year before, no doubt on Chaussade's orders and to his specifications. These new furnaces were said to have "consumed all the old [cured] wood available in the countryside."[2]

Hearing only murmurs at first, but later an uproar of complaint, Chaussade took steps to defend himself and his veteran *régisseur*. He contacted the intendant of Orléans to explain the situation and disparage his critics. He asked certain lay and ecclesiastical landlords of the region for expressions of opinion favorable to himself. He thought that they would suffice as a full refutation of complaints from the town. But he took the precaution of sending his own version of the circumstances to the minister of marine (then Etienne François, duc de Choiseul-Stainville), whose orders for irons his manufactories were working to satisfy, and he also arranged to have the ministry forward his report to the *contrôleur général des finances*. His defensiveness about the "new furnaces" and their extraordinary consumption of fuel suggests that he may have built them without bothering to seek permission to build. He was perhaps culpable of violating the law of 1723 that forbade the erection of new forges and furnaces—a law intended to forestall further forest depletion in France. He may also have been at pains to avoid any blemish on his reputation with the duc de Choiseul, powerful chief minister to Louis XV. Having reported that the bishops of Auxerre, Du Bellay, and De Comminge were of the opinion that the elders' complaint had been a "mistake," Chaussade then traveled to visit his forges at Cosne, in order, he said, "to judge the truth for himself."

While disparaging the complaint, Chaussade took the trouble to explain the methods used by his *régisseur* at Cosne to procure fuel. In ordinary times procurement was simple:

> Buyers and sellers of wood for two leagues [c. five miles] around [the town] customarily sell wood to my *régisseur*. He does not go to find them; they come to him to offer [to sell]. Without this outlet, not half the wood produced by the annual cuts would be sold; without this [market] the landowners and merchants would have real reason to complain. . . . I also buy wood that is brought [to Cosne] by the Loire; but I have always purchased primarily in the environs of Cosne. . . . If it were necessary to bring in all the wood consumed [at the manufactories] from distant sources via the river, the expense would exceed by more than 20 percent the value of the merchandise produced. The cord [of wood] that exceeds 10, 11, or 12 livres is too dear. I can prove that the wood I do bring by water costs me 15 to 16 livres. But I have bought it anyway, when the countryside does not furnish enough.
>
> The wood used in my slitting mills and that used by the bourgeois [of the town] is different. I need only large pieces. This is the first time that M. Baudry has had recourse to *fagots*. The 3,000 [bundles or *cordes*] that he purchased is trifling . . . [and] has raised prices in the town 2, 3, and even 4 sous . . . [but has] not created the "total dearth" that has generated so much concern.[3]

Chaussade went on to say that the twelve manufacturers of pottery (*fayance*) at Nevers consume "twenty times more than my slitting mills" and use the same wood used in the forges, and no one complains. "If the city of Cosne lacks [stove] wood, it can have it by boat in three or four days. Such wood is worthless for my slitting mills. . . . As for my manufactories, I can assure you, Monsieur, that it will be impossible to sustain them without the wood of the region [around Cosne]. I cannot fuel them by the river alone. The price of the *corde* would be a third too dear." Moreover, he observed that he had a hundred workers at Cosne on whose employment "the *bonheur* of the artisans, merchants, and bakers of the town" depended. "Thus it is clear," said Chaussade, "that I cannot do without wood from the environs of Cosne, and that the environs cannot do without the market I make."[4]

Chaussade's dependence on wood fuel (charcoal) is evidence that his methods were exactly the reverse of those used about a century earlier in the Colbert era of anchor production at Cosne, when (according to Gille) "the works employed nothing but [mineral] coal as fuel."[5] For the forging of bar iron in anchor manufacture and the conversion of bar iron into steel, charcoal was normally used in both France and England in the eighteenth century.[6] If coal alone was used, the anchors produced were of very uncertain, and therefore unacceptable, quality. The reversion to the nearly exclusive use of charcoal in anchor manufacturing in the Nivernais around 1735, and for many years following, represented a reaction against the early exclusive use of coal. Local fuel shortages were not long in developing. That problem was, of course, locally aggravated when Chaussade increased the size and number of his manufactories. As we have seen, it was to meet the needs of such new facilities that Chaussade's *régisseur*, Baudry, used extraordinary methods in purchasing fuel at Cosne in the early 1760s.

A few years later Chaussade recorded further information about management methods and the needs of the Cosne manufactories for fuel and transport: writing in October 1770 (in the third person), he described his plans:

> This month and next [i.e., October and November], the plan is to buy horses—eighty horses are needed for the service of his [Chaussade's] forges. The time is propitious, the end of the harvest season, the eve of winter when owners face the prospect of feeding draft animals through the minimum pasture season to come. . . . [These are] good months to buy good horses at good prices. Furthermore, . . . this is wood-cutting time; [Chaussade] will cut . . . in the months of November and December 15,000 additional *cordes* of wood for charcoal . . . [for Cosne. It is] indispensably necessary to prepare now. . . . [Hence, Chaussade] is going immediately to his estates.[7]

Farther up the Loire, around Guérigny and Nevers, the structure of supply and demand for fuel was similar. More wood was probably available for fuel, but there were more consumers seeking to buy. In the vicinity of Guérigny were half a dozen competing forges, furnaces, and foundries, and at nearby Nevers there were, as Chaussade emphasized, about a dozen pottery manufacturers who were heavy consumers of fuel. Furthermore, Nevers was a much larger town than Cosne, about 8,000 persons in 1750, in contrast to 3,742 in Cosne in 1752.[8] Some powerful noble families resided at Nevers, who, like the ecclesiastical lords at both towns, had to be treated with tact. At Nevers-Guérigny the buyers and sellers of wood could not be depended upon to volunteer sufficient supplies as they commonly did at Cosne and La Charité, the other major industrial towns of the region.[9]

Jacques Masson had evidently realized at an early date that fuel supplies for Guérigny were best ensured by purchasing forested lands, or woodland exploitation rights, in the region.[10] Chaussade followed Masson's example. Even tiny parcels were acquired; purchases, exchanges, and agreements to share cutting rights with small proprietors abounded in his transactions.[11] As additional forges and furnaces were acquired in the region, woodlands were also added. An inventory of Chaussade's woodland acquisition over the period 1743 – 1766 in the parish of Frasnay alone reported a total of about 320 *arpents,* and included no less than sixty-three parcels, many of them very small: thirty-two parcels of 2 *arpents* or less, about half a dozen of 1 *arpent* or less.[12] Masson and Chaussade were obviously disposed to buy land, woodland and tillable alike, in large parcels or small; even "bouquets" of trees around the countryside were purchased to ensure adequate supplies. Such acquisitions sometimes had incidental utility, bringing to hand livestock feed and, for the long term, even trees with timber-producing potential.[13]

Sometimes the parcels acquired were troublesome. Wooded tracts might be burdened by the claims of neighbors who had, or pretended to have, rights of usage. To deal with such claimants, Masson and later Chaussade employed attorneys who were specialists in seigneurial law and practice (*feudistes*); because litigation could be costly—beyond the means of the average small landowner—the mere presence of Chaussade's *feudiste* in an affair was apt to win him a speedy and favorable outcome, often by default. He had little compunction, apparently, about purchasing land with an uncertain or contested title or a dubious claim to forest usage that might entrain litigation. He could overawe, overwhelm, and prevail against nearly all claimants. Only rarely would an antagonist fight a case through repeated appeals, as did his neighbor and friend the comte de Bizy, who loved litigation (as Chaussade did, as though it were duelling) over trifles.

Rarely did an acquisition of Chaussade's entrain a legal battle as drawn out as those he had with the communal owners of the forest of Narcy. Chaussade acquired part (two-thirds) ownership of the forest and other property and claims in the vicinity; but the commune claimed "usage rights" and stubbornly sought to exercise them, even after Chaussade's attorneys had won the case against them in the courts. The commune apparently had the weight of tradition and custom on its side; Chaussade on his side had the *ordonnance* of 1669, the *maîtrise* (*royale* or *ducale*) of waters and forests at Nevers, his attorneys, and the decisions of the judges of the case. But it went on and on, from 1753 to 1781.[14]

Chaussade's preoccupation with fuel problems was perennial. Discussing in 1756 the possibility of expanding his forge production to supply the navy's needs in the forthcoming European war, he indicated that two of his forges had not operated for many years because there was not sufficient wood. The disused forges were surrounded by immense woodlands, where Chaussade (and others) had usage rights, but the woods were, he said, in a state of "total devastation" and could only be restored by establishing *maîtrises* to enforce conservation, proper management, and controlled cuts. Even under regular *maîtrise* management, he said this woodland "could not soon be restored unless M. de Moras appointed a *commissaire*" of the navy to oversee (and "enforce") restoration.[15]

"Good management," as conceived by industrial users and the service of waters and forests, allowed young trees (*taillis*) to be cut at twenty years, or even at fifteen; nearly all stands were cut at such ages if destined for industrial consumption as charcoal. A few landowners (the seigneur of La Charité, for example) regularly cut at twenty years. The product of cuts varied, of course, depending on such factors as soil conditions, weather, location, and whether or not the stand was effectively protected against depredations by man and beast. It was said that at fifteen years of age, an *arpent* of trees in good soil might produce at best 35 to 40 *cordes* of charcoal, and on the average only 30 to 35. (Although the dimensions of a *corde* varied,[16] the royal *ordonnances* prescribed firewood *cordes* 8 feet long and 4 feet high, consisting of pieces 3.5 feet long.)

In the age of charcoal iron industries, proprietors of iron manufactories everywhere were under pressure to maintain a balance between wood consumption and woodland production. By overusing or misusing available resources, they risked shortages. Shortages, though local and theoretically remediable, could easily become severe and advanced; in some areas they became so serious as to oblige industries to switch to alternative fuels or close down entirely.

Although eighteenth-century France was still relatively rich in forest resources, any abundance or shortage of fuel was bound to be a local rather than general condition. There was always a mix of local conditions affecting supply and demand, always a question of balance. Cosne was a case in point. Though located in an abundantly wooded region, the Nivernais, the town and its industries were heavy consumers of fuel. The margin between consumption and local production was narrow. Even in the 1730s some coal, the alternative fuel, was being used, and coals from St. Etienne and from Decize were being compared to determine their relative quality. In 1731–1732 Arnaud, the entrepreneur, and Tassin, the *commissaire de la marine,* obtained coal from both sources, though the proprietor of the mines near Decize made difficulties because of previous market commitments. Nonetheless, a three-year contract was arranged in 1732 for shipments from Decize to the anchor manufactory at Cosne.[17] These coal contracts were not born of imperative need. Rather, they were a by-product of the navy's general preoccupation with the need to economize wood consumption. They also showed the navy's disposition to experiment.

A few years afterward Chaussade and an associate, a man named Jars of the city of Lyon,[18] appear together as promoters of the use of coal from the mines of Saint-Rambert (near Saint-Etienne). For a time Jars and Chaussade were partners and joint-promoters of a curious scheme that threatened to break a monopoly enjoyed by coal consumers around Saint-Etienne. An association of Saint-Etienne consumers wanted to keep local coal supplies in the environs of that town for themselves. To do so they had obtained privileges (*arrêts*) from the King's Council in 1724 and 1738, forbidding shipment of local coal beyond the suburbs of the town.[19] But the Royal Council made an exception to those rules in October 1738 on behalf of a certain Sieur Baron de Vaux. De Vaux apparently drained some valuable coal pits in the region, thereby allowing coal to be delivered to the city of Saint-Etienne at about half its earlier cost. As a reward for these contributions "tending to the public weal," he obtained from the council the privilege of transporting coal from his own mines in the region to markets in Paris "and elsewhere."[20] Chaussade and Jars proposed to bring coal from the baron's mines down the Loire to the forges at Cosne. In January 1739, a shipment of 150 *voyes* was being prepared, and another of 200 *voyes* was planned for the following December.[21]

Then matters began to get out of hand. Jars apparently began dealing with mine owners who did not enjoy de Vaux's marketing privilege. The minister of marine was brought into the picture, probably by Chaussade, when Jars proposed to descend 20,000 *quintaux* of Saint-Etienne coal (not all of it from the baron's mines) to Nantes, to be stored at the Ile d'Indret pending distribution to the seaboard arsenals. This proposition was accepted by the minister of marine,[22] and navy *passeports* were issued: one to provide river clearance for the coals destined "to serve in the fabrication of anchors" (apparently at Cosne), the other for the 20,000 *quintaux* destined for the arsenals. Then, suddenly, opposition emerged in the form of a *mémoire* from the intendant of Lyon, describing for the benefit and instruction of the partners Chaussade and Jars the existence of the royal *arrêts* and the exclusive privilege of de Vaux.[23] Confusion ensued. The issue was hotly contested by Jars and de Vaux, and it came out that Jars's delivery of the 20,000 *quintaux* to the navy had been authorized by the Royal Council, which had thereby sanctioned (perhaps through forgetfulness) the breaking of the Saint-Etienne monopoly.

There was silence in the surviving navy correspondence for over two years. The affair surfaced again in the correspondence in January 1743, when the minister of marine, Maurepas, informed Chaussade emphatically that his orders for Saint-Etienne coal for his forges would not be filled, because de Vaux chose not to allow the shipments by Jars to take place. He advised Chaussade to dissociate himself from Jars, to cancel the arrangements he had made with him, and to retrieve the *passeports* issued, and suggested a possible alternative: "You can, if you wish, arrange to deal directly with M. le Baron de Vaux, who offers to deliver to Cosne the 300 *voyes de charbon* in question on the same terms as Jars."[24]

Jars was seriously compromised by de Vaux's refusal to deliver the coal, seemingly the result of a change of mind on the baron's part, for it is difficult to believe that the partners contemplated delivering his coal without his concurrence. A complicating detail was the inclusion of coal from Saint-Etienne mines other than de Vaux's. Unfortunately for Jars, he had already bought the boats needed to deliver the entire shipment. The minister suggested that Chaussade might urge Jars to try to sell his boats to de Vaux: "I believe that the baron de Vaux will consent."[25] Whatever the outcome of this fiasco, with its attendant embarrassments and costs, it seems to have soured Chaussade on dealings with de Vaux. We hear no more of the affair, nor any suggestion that Chaussade ever again seriously considered bringing coal from Saint-Etienne.

Cosne was the only one of Chaussade's manufactories situated directly on a navigable waterway that could serve as a route for coal shipments. The high transit costs involved in shipping coal from Decize, for example (from the mines by road to the Loire, then on the Loire by boat, thence by road to the manufactory) meant that none of his other facilities could be fueled principally with coal. Even at Cosne, Chaussade's choice was to make wood his principal fuel, although some coal brought down the Loire was used. We do not know in what proportion charcoal and coal were employed. Coal may have been used in some finishing processes, in reverberatory furnaces. Consumption of that sort at Cosne could not have been large in the mid-1760s, since the reverberatory facilities there were probably fineries, and not furnaces. Chaussade's 1764 rebuttal of local complaints about his heavy consumption of wood made no mention of any use of coal, the alternative "wood-saving" fuel. He admitted to building three reverberatory "fineries" (or reheat facilities), called *feux de reverbère;* "fineries" seems to be the best translation, since Chaussade referred to irons from the slitting mill passing through the *feu reverbère,*[26] which, he said, his accusers "mistakenly call furnaces (*fourneaux*)." He said nothing about using any quantity or proportion of coal to fuel these facilities. He admitted that his large slitting mill (*grande fenderie*) "consumes the greatest quantities of wood, and there is not a soul in the town who knows it better than I. Two years ago, on my return from Bordeaux, I had a small slitting mill and two heating units [*fours*] built, which rarely operate together, to make thin strap or ribbon (*feuillard mince*) and incidentally [to] procure forever for France a type of iron [steel] that before my time was drawn from Germany and Sweden." Perhaps, had he been using coal or coke, he could have blunted the charge that he was exhausting wood supplies simply by mentioning that he was using coal and not wood.[27]

Chaussade's dependence on wood fuel was, as we have seen, by choice. His predecessors and his own associates used coal; in Colbert's day only coal was used in work at Cosne. Chaussade himself was obviously persuaded in the 1730s that it might serve as a useful substitute for charcoal, to the point that he agreed to buy large deliveries of Saint-Etienne coal.

Maurepas was persuaded that it was not possible for Chaussade and Jars to do business with de Vaux, their only possible supplier of Saint-Etienne coal. [At the time, incidentally, Chaussade's involvement in family affairs led to the ownership and management of Cosne being passed to other hands.] Coal for Cosne could easily be drawn from nearby Decize, though Decize coal did not compare favorably with that from Saint-Etienne for industrial use, at least in the opinion of inspectors at the naval arsenals.[28] In fact, the coal that Chaussade used so sparingly at Cosne probably came from Decize. Coal could also have been brought down from Auvergne on the Allier and the Loire. Transport costs would be high, but could usually be passed on to the navy.[29]

But charcoal was the traditional fuel. Charcoal was the fuel most certain to produce anchors whose quality would not be questioned at the arsenals. Chaussade may have viewed as formidable the obstacle presented by the little understood and unpredictable effects of the use of coal or coke in the manufacturing process. He could have reasoned it was better to avoid those variables, and to rely instead on well-tried, predictable charcoal.

Supplies of wood fuel for forge use apparently remained abundant around Guérigny in the 1740s and long afterward.[30] Moreover, it is worth remembering that ownership and management of the forge at Cosne were out of Chaussade's hands for part of this period, making it impossible for him to experiment with new fuels. Yet France experienced scattered wood (charcoal) fuel shortages in industrialized localities and urban regions toward the end of the old regime. It was reasonable to view the possibility of a more severe shortage as a serious threat. A contemporary commentator remarked in 1780 that "the shortage of wood, which threatens nearly all the forges of the realm, has led to repeated experiments" involving the use of mineral fuel.[31] Demands on woodland resources naturally increased as industrialization advanced.

But vast forest resources remained in France. Near Blois, for example, as late as 1777, the giant forest of Russy included 6,300 *arpents* of woodland, with 4,000 *arpents* of timber trees 100 to 150 years old.[32] In the late years of the eighteenth century, under the pressure of the French Revolutionary Wars, the forges of the Nivernais employed coal "from Decize and the *département* de la Loire," while the refineries and forges at Guérigny were still using forest fuels. Indeed, as late as the last quarter of the nineteenth century (1880), the establishment at Guérigny continued to use charcoal fuel in blast furnaces (*hauts fourneaux*) and refineries to produce highly reputed "charcoal iron" (*fer du bois*).[33]

Innovation in Iron Production

Many influences affected Chaussade's decision to use a mix of charcoal and mineral fuel in different phases of the work at his metallurgical establishments in the Nivernais. Bad relations with de Vaux could only have been a precipitant. Even the high cost of transporting coal from Saint-Etienne was not prohibitive, so long as the navy, and not a commercial buyer, was the prospective customer. As one naval official observed: "No pretense of economy, or other motive, must prevail over the necessity of having good anchors."[34]

By restricting or eliminating the use of coal, a producer effectively controlled many of the uncertainties in the process of anchor production. The scientists and technologists of the old regime understood little of the chemistry of ferrous metals; even the elementary process of combustion was only beginning to be understood as a result of Lavoisier's studies. Much more mysterious was the complex chemistry of coal. Trial and error and long experience, however, revealed that in the production of anchors and certain other manufactures, high standards of uniformity in the composition and strength of the metal could be achieved. In anchor production, the specific objective was to reproduce large numbers of

forged iron components or pieces of predetermined size and uniformly
high quality. That was a demanding, difficult task. A premium was placed
on the intelligence and experience of forgemasters using well-tried char-
coal-fuel methods.

The need for routine in the management of production does not deni-
grate the businessman or his intellect, or his interest in innovation or his
disposition to test and to experiment. Chaussade in particular had such
interests, as will be seen, and he pursued them in production, and especially in connection with marketing problems. But as a businessman he
was bound to produce products of acceptable quality, to avoid rejection
by inspectors at the arsenals. Those inspectors were not interested in un-
tried production processes; they were bound by duty to be insistent on
quality, for the security of seamen and ships. *Commissaires* assigned to
the furnaces, forges, and fineries likewise aimed to achieve regularity and
quality control. They were interested in the provenance of "raw" materials and in having journals (records) kept of the fabrication process (if
only they survived!). They sought to duplicate as closely as possible materials and methods that had worked well in the past. Their function was a
conservative, not an innovative one.[35]

The possibility of innovation was virtually excluded in anchor production, but more possible in other processes. Moreover, forgemasters and
fournisseurs working for the defense establishment were apparently more
free to innovate in times of peace than of war. Thus in 1713–1738 we
find the navy itself promoting experimentation. Officials modified standards, encouraged new procedures, even expected suppliers to innovate,
and the navy itself bought or leased facilities to produce new designs.
Later, from 1740 till about 1759, predominantly a period of warfare for
France, and the period of Chaussade's management and expansion of the
family business, the intensity of demand tended to encourage the manufacture (using proven methods) of enormous quantities of regular, uniform, high-quality products to satisfy the operational needs of ships and
seamen in wartime.

Transportation and Storage

As to the total quantity of production at his manufactories, Chaussade
himself remarked in 1768:

> The Sieur de la Chaussade can prove with the *passeports* is-
> sued by the king that under [the ministries of] M. le Comte
> de Maurepas, M. Rouillé, M. de Machault, and M. de Moras,

he has never delivered to the navy less than two million [livres]
a year in anchors and irons, and there have been years when
these provisionments have been [as much as] three or four
millions.[36]

At one point early in the Seven Years War, Chaussade had orders for no
less than 8,410,000 livres of anchors and irons.[37]

The Loire, of course, was the principal highway for shipment of the
product from his own and his subcontractor's forges in the Nivernais and
elsewhere to the sea. At Cosne the problems of embarking the irons were
minimal because the forges themselves and their storage facilities were
constructed on the very banks of the river. It was otherwise at Guérigny.
There the source of power, the Nièvre, was not navigable, and Guérigny
itself was situated many miles from the Loire. Until around 1750, anchors and irons from Guérigny went by road northwest to La Charité,
where Chaussade kept a resident agent and an *entrepôt* to store them
pending their shipment downriver to Nantes. For various reasons, perhaps including the shorter overland distance from Guérigny, Chaussade
later switched the Guérigny shipments from his entrepôt at La Charité to
the larger town of Nevers.[38] However, he seems to have continued to ship
from La Charité some of the products from his other forges in the region,
for which it remained the logical riverport.

Chaussade found suitable entrepôt space at Nevers in the form of
an island called the Medine, belonging to the duc de Nivernais, ideally
situated in the town at the junction of the rivers Nièvre and Loire. Chaussade asked the duke to concede this property as a fief; he was seeking, he
said, just such a property as the Medine—no other seemed so suitable,
spacious, capable of accommodating warehouses, wagon-coach house,
stables for twenty-five horses, housing for his carters and raftsmen, and
yards for the storage of anchors and irons awaiting shipment.[39] On 1 September 1751, the duke, "considering *la qualité dud. Sieur Babeau de la
Chaussade* and desiring in this matter to give him marks of esteem and
benevolence, considering further that the establishment he proposes for
the city can only be advantageous for the service of the [king's] navy and
the town, cedes to him as a fief all the land between the two rivers." The
development of this land was to take place according to the prospectus
(plan) prepared by the ducal surveyor of waters and forests. The duke
conceded certain seigneurial dues, on condition that Chaussade pay a
"noble rent" of 70 livres *per annum* to his ducal *Chambre de Comptes* at
Nevers (founded in 1405 by Philippe of Burgundy, comte de Nevers),
and that he maintain stone levies to control flooding, leave a road eigh-

teen feet wide, build a boat landing, allow passage to those who already had concessions, and carry any contestations about affairs of the Ile de Medine to the duke's *bailliage* (regional) court for settlement.[40]

The terms of this important concession effectively underscored the duke's pretensions and his substantial regional administrative powers. The Nivernais had never been united to the crown. Granting the land to Chaussade as a fief was an act of promotion for ducal power, as was reference to the *plan* by the ducal surveyor, the "noble rent," and the referring contestations to the *bailliage de Nivernais et Donziais*.[41] Chaussade thereby became the duke's "general *concessionnaire*," empowered by his privilege to treat with holders of earlier concessions for the restriction (or extinction) of their privileges. Since many of them were *voituriers* of modest means and pretensions, most did not offer resistance.[42]

Despite the existence of this entrepôt at Nevers, the forges of Guérigny were disadvantaged compared with those at Cosne, especially where the production of anchors was concerned. Stocks of iron had to be brought from furnaces in the Berry because, as we have seen, only Berry iron was supposed to be used in the manufacture of anchors. Incoming shipments of bar iron and fuel supplies, whether wood or coal, brought by the Loire to the Medine entrepôt, then had to go many miles overland from Nevers to reach the forges at Guérigny. Finished products from Guérigny had to go back the same way, or to La Charité. Other forges owned and operated by Chaussade were even more distant from Loire transportation; but remoteness conferred on them, as it did on Guérigny, the compensatory advantage of easy access to fuel from the extensive surrounding woodland and forest. These circumstances conferred great importance on the transportation networks serving Chaussade's manufactories. He used and maintained existing roads in the environs of Guérigny and where necessary built new roads linking Nevers, the scattered manufactories, and La Charité-sur-Loire.

The Loire itself left much to be desired as a transportation artery. There were violent floods and extended periods of low water; the bed of the river changed constantly as banks of sand shifted. Indeed, "the Loire was never really a navigable stream; . . . navigation upon it was always dangerous, full of risk."[43] Navigation on the Loire was "discontinuous, the intensity of the traffic depending on the height of the water."[44] High-water problems were far more dangerous to the people of the towns and countryside than to the rivermen. It was rare for flooding to stop shipments and production, as it did very briefly at Cosne in late February 1739 and for two or three weeks (because of damage done) in June 1772.[45] For navigators, low water, not high, was the serious seasonal problem.

To deal with all sorts of transit and procurement problems, Chaussade kept correspondents or local contacts at the major riverports and at the seaboard arsenals. He also had a resident agent and receiving office at Indret, the island in the river below the city of Nantes where his anchors, irons, and timber were routinely stored pending seaboard shipment to the dockyards. Praising these scattered correspondents, Chaussade claimed (in his usual third-person style) that "the correspondents of the Sieur de la Chaussade are known in each town as good and loyal merchants; all of them will execute orders with honesty (*la plus exacte probité*)."[46]

To handle the downriver shipment of his irons, Chaussade contracted in 1744 (for example) with Peter Legrand, perhaps himself a member of that famous "Community of Merchants Frequenting the Loire." Chaussade's *marché* required Legrand to descend to Nantes all irons manufactured by Chaussade during the years 1744, 1745, 1746, and 1747 for the sum of six livres and ten sous *par millier*.[47] This appears to have been a low price. A few years later (1753) we find a report from Minister Rouillé that Chaussade's costs for shipping his anchors and irons to Nantes had risen precipitously, and, the minister remarked, "to avoid difficulties," Chaussade had been "obliged to accord an increase" in his remuneration to the river carriers "to engage them to leave with his cargoes . . . whatever the water level."[48] Still later we learn some details: that the price being paid (c. 1766) for transport from Nevers to Nantes stood at nine livres per *millier*, plus one livre and ten sous commission at Nantes, and ten sous for unloading at Indret.[49]

Low water was most apt to present transit problems on the middle and upper Loire. The difficulty of traversing the shallows of the upper river might be solved as follows: a convoy would leave Roanne on the upper river with ten boats; five of them would be left at Nevers after the entire cargo was embarked in the other five, and still further along, from Briare onward, three boats could probably carry the entire cargo.[50]

The boats employed to ship Chaussade's irons naturally varied in construction and size. An indication of size is implicit in Chaussade's report of 1770 concerning 205,000 livres of irons shipped in six riverboats from La Charité and Cosne; they evidently carried an average of about eighteen tons each.[51] Earlier, in August 1767, low water had beached a flotilla of Chaussade's boats just below Gien. Because the arsenal at Brest had a pressing need for part of that particular shipment, Chaussade decided "to buy small boats of fir construction, each capable of carrying a cargo of only 1,200 livres," so that the irons needed at the arsenal could descend without further delay.[52] The navy approved the idea, but later appears to have refused to pay the costs Chaussade incurred in executing it.[53] These craft, lightly built, were apparently used only once, being broken up on their arrival at the river mouth. Larger, better-built craft, capable of mounting masts, were also used to descend and ascend cargo.[54]

In 1752 Chaussade sought compensation because five cargoes of his irons were detained for five months at Nevers in the summer and fall of that year because of low water. He claimed the need to recompensate the carrier, who had apparently collected payment for the voyage but gone nowhere because of the low water, and he sought payment for repairs to five boats because their weak condition put the cargo of irons at extraordinary risk. These claims were seriously questioned even by Minister Rouillé.[55] More serious and embarrassing was the seizure of eighteen boats carrying Chaussade's irons after provincial customs authorities discovered that the conductor of his flotilla was trying to smuggle wines into Brittany illegally. The minister of marine washed his hands of that affair, and we can suspect that Chaussade did not employ that riverman again.[56]

Remarking on seasonal transit problems and related pressures, Chaussade himself said that "it is most important, demanding the greatest dispatch, to have the irons prepared for shipment . . . in the months of November, December, January, February, and March, which are the months of high water."[57] Elsewhere, Chaussade remarked of the Loire, "It's never navigable two months in succession"—perhaps he meant two successive months in the dry season.[58]

Low water occurred most commonly in July, August, and September and could be very serious when wartime shipbuilding or outfitting made the immediate delivery of anchors and other irons imperative. Sometimes the coincidence of emergency need and low water necessitated extensive overland shipments. Thus in 1757 thirty-eight anchors were sent overland with "the greatest possible speed" to Paris, thence down the Seine via Rouen to Le Havre.[59] Again, in 1763, a small shipment of 5,500 livres of iron sheets had to be dispatched overland in emergency circumstances to Le Havre; "to avoid the delay" of river transport, they were sent by road to Paris, "thence [presumably by river] to Rouen and to [Le] Havre."[60] For his wartime shipments in the direction of Paris, to Le Havre and other Atlantic seaboard destinations, Chaussade remarked in 1756, "'The route via the canal of Briare is preferable to that by sea via Nantes for shipping irons from the Nivernais.'"[61] But in 1768 (in peacetime), 252,000 livres of Chaussade's irons and fifteen anchors were sent to Nantes by extraordinary means "at great cost, because of the lack of water in the Loire."[62] For such shipments as these, Chaussade received extra payments to cover the greatly increased outlays that overland transport usually required.

The port of Toulon, on the Mediterranean, was the most distant and difficult arsenal for Chaussade to provision with his anchors and irons. It might be supposed that shipments destined for Toulon could best be descended to Nantes and the Indret entrepôt along with those going to Rochefort or Brest. But, surprisingly, virtually no regular shipments or even maritime contact occurred between Nantes or other Atlantic ports and the French Mediterranean coast. Indeed, it is a striking commentary on the state of the French merchant marine and French coastal traffic generally that only once in the period from 1740 to 1762 was a cargo of Chaussade's anchors dispatched by sea from Nantes en route for Toulon. On that occasion (c. 1742) the carrier touched at Cadiz, in Spain; the cargo was apparently seized by supposedly friendly Spanish authorities and never reached Toulon.[63] That wartime experience "determined M. le Comte de Maurepas henceforth to transport [Chaussade's] anchors overland to Lyon, there to be embarked on the Rhône . . . and this," wrote Chaussade in 1762, "has been the constant practice for twenty years."[64] Chaussade was willing to continue the practice, even with slightly reduced compensation. But the intendant of Rochefort, Ruis Embito, whose opinion was solicited by minister of marine Choiseul, while agreeing that Chaussade's anchors should continue to be used at Toulon, judged that "it would be easier to send the anchors via Nantes to Rochefort, from there to Bordeaux, [and] by the canal" to the Mediterranean.[65]

During those twenty years of costly overland shipments from Cosne to Toulon, several shipments were particulary memorable. In July 1758, amid the disasters of the Seven Years War, anchors were dispatched "overland from the forges at Cosne to Lyon, thence [via the Rhône and overland] to Toulon." But the minister of marine was obliged that year to inform M. le Prevost de Marchands at Lyon that the collapse of the bridge of Sevein [Sp.] (under the weight of the anchors?) had obliged Chaussade's crews "to seek an alternative route to enter the City of Lyon"; unfortunately, "when they arrived at Peter's Gate (also known as the *barrière de la Pierre*) . . . they found it too narrow to allow the passage of an anchor of 5,575 livres, with which they were charged." The minister remarked later that he had no doubt that orders had been given to enlarge that passage to accommodate the anchor in question. But he added: "I must alert you [officials at Lyon] that another anchor of very much larger size is due to arrive in the immediate future (*incessement*) at the same locality." It would be "annoying," he said, "if its shipment were delayed."[66] We do not know whether Peter's Gate at Lyon actually was widened twice in one year.

Concerning the technical details of overland shipment, Chaussade himself remarked in a 1760 letter to Daniel Charles Trudaine (1703–69, founder of the *Ecole des ponts et chaussées*) that "the transport of anchors overland from Orléans or from Tours to La Rochelle or to Bordeaux is easy, using rolling stock [*roulliers*] which do not find loads bound to the ports from Orléans or Paris. It will cost three livres and ten sous the quintal" to send irons overland by those routes.[67] In this and many other matters, Chaussade gave an impression of technical competence, of being precise and in full command of technical and commercial details with an interest in minimizing the navy's expenditure, when that could be done without cost to himself. Next to his own, he was consistently loyal to the navy's interest, especially in later life; he was probably pleased (and with good grounds) to receive the thanks of minister of marine De Boynes (Pierre Etienne, Bourgeois de Boynes) after one "low-water crisis" in which Chaussade had "neglected nothing" in his efforts to see that the much-needed shipments of irons arrived when needed: "Despite the lack of water that you suffer, both at your forges [for lack of water power] and in lack of transport because the Loire is unnavigable, you have in six weeks shipped 542,000 livres of irons, nails [*cloux*], and tools, a very great part of which has already arrived at Nantes."[68]

The Ile d'Indret, Chaussade's usual entrepôt at the mouth of the Loire, was a narrow strip now 4,800 feet long and 200 wide, described and praised as a useful naval entrepôt as early as 1692. It was then described as an islet in the river two leagues below Nantes, suitable for the storage of wood and stone, charcoal and coal, hemp, masts, iron, grains, and gunpowder destined for the Atlantic seaboard arsenals. There were said to be no navigation hazards; many carriers, and even *gabarres* of 100 tons could take on or discharge cargo concurrently. The greater part of the island was then untilled. A chateau offered some covered and enclosed storage space, including two large double-barns, a large warehouse, and an *orangerie* also stood on the island. Some of these structures then needed roof repairs. The chateau had many rooms, some in good repair "where the *gentilshommes étrangers nouveaux convertis sont fait leurs exercises.*"[69]

Except in 1751, when flood waters of the Loire inundated the place and carried off at least five or six thousand cubic feet of timber,[70] the Ile d'Indret was a safe storage place. The entrepôt was, in effect, a storage service for which the navy's *fournisseurs* paid no fees, though it saved the considerable costs that they would have incurred had each of them been obliged to buy or lease an entrepôt from landowners or private commercial interests at Nantes. In 1770 reference was made to the "Islands" of Indret—the island itself and its dependencies, including the isle called "le

Macereau"; all the buildings and facilities were, according to a 1770 account, maintained at the king's expense.[71]

The Hazards of War

The last phase of the transport of Chaussade's anchors and irons destined for the Atlantic seaboard arsenals took them by sea from Indret to the navy's dockyards or, on occasion, to Lorient, the port of the Compagnie des Indes. Navigation on the river to Nantes was generally at the entrepreneurs' risk, except for the payment of river tolls, from which the materiel destined for the king's navy was largely exempted (by *passeports*) or for which *fournisseurs* were reimbursed. But in the next stage, the risks of the voyage at sea were often assumed by the king. Such wartime risks as seizure of cargo by enemy or by privateers were invariably assumed by the crown, and occasionally also losses from great storms or shipwreck, as specified in the Chaussade-Denis contract of 1752–1757.[72]

France had laws, like England's "navigation acts," designed to encourage the use of French-flag vessels and discourage the use of foreign bottoms. The *droit de frêt*, for example, imposing a duty of fifty sous per ton on foreign ships trading in French ports, was first decreed in 1659, and might have become the palladium of French commercial navigation. Had it been enforced, Chaussade and other shippers would have been obliged to employ French-flag carriers exclusively. But it was difficult to enforce the rule even in peacetime because insufficient numbers of French commercial craft were available. Thus French buyers and sellers had little compunction about using foreign bottoms.

When French craft were available at Nantes, their owners could be obliged, under provisions of the Chaussade-Denis contract, to accept navy cargo en route to Brest and Rochefort. Thus article 4 of the contract of 1751 provided that "the *commissaire de la Marine* at Nantes will furnish, by [using his] authority [i.e., by requisition] the barks and boats needed by the *fournisseurs* or their correspondents to transport irons to the arsenals for which they are destined."[73] But Chaussade's contract also provided that "if *gabarres* or others of the king's cargo vessels are present at Nantes or in the lower river estuary, or [are] laden by His Majesty for the ports of Brest and Havre, the Sieurs de la Chaussade and Denis are free to ballast these craft with the irons they are going to send to the said ports, without paying any freight, provided no diminution of the cargo of these vessels results. The aforementioned *commissaire* will make available all facilities needed to accomplish this."[74] This attractive transport advantage was presumably available to Chaussade in both peace and war. In wartime, however, French bottoms were apt to be scarce, and coastal sealanes were perilous. Foreign bottoms were depended upon to carry naval stores to the arsenals as long as neutrals were not being seized by English cruisers. But Chaussade's irons were shipped in wartime at the king's risk, not his own. British privateers treated Dutch merchant carriers with relative leniency until about 1746 (that is, for the first two-thirds of the War of the Austrian Succession), and in the earlier period generally, the Dutch were the principal carriers of naval stores, including irons, from Nantes/Indret to Brest, Rochefort, and Havre. The British applied contraband rules during the Seven Years War (1756–1763). During the American Revolution (1776–1783), however, the "Northern Alliance" allowed the French to rely extensively on neutral carriers again. Thus in 1775–1776, before France entered the war, a haphazard group of fifteen *passeports* were issued to allow foreign shipping to load naval stores at Nantes for Brest and other arsenals without burdensome "penalties" (*droit de frêt*). Nine of the fifteen vessels named in the *passeports* happened to be Dutch, five were Swedish, and one was from Hamburg.[75] Most of them carried timber, of which Chaussade was then a principal supplier; some also carried his irons. In the summer of 1778 the minister of Marine ordered one *fournisseur* to use neutral Dutch ships as much as he could, even though (or because?) that practice maximized the chances of involving the Dutch in the war: "For your transports, you will give preference to Dutch vessels, unless the captains of that nation set their charges very much higher than those of other neutral powers."[76]

The value of a naval contract was naturally implicit in all the articles of the agreement, not merely in the prices agreed upon. The price to be paid per pound for irons of various kinds, delivered to the dockyards, was only one indication of the value of any contract to Chaussade. Prices and the agreement overall represented a compromise between the interests of the *fournisseur* and those of the navy. Chaussade's contract of 1751 offered extraordinary advantages in the terms of payment to the *fournisseur*. The privileges granted were quite comparable to those granted to the original Masson-Babaud group of entrepreneurs back in 1728 to help them finance the initial exploitation of timber from Lorraine. Article 7 of the 1751 agreement provided that Chaussade and Denis would be paid one-third of the price of each year's *fourniture* in advance, the remaining two-thirds to be paid on delivery of merchandise at the arsenal, and the advances to be repaid by the very last deliveries in the provisionment. Routine payment of the entrepreneurs was to take place in Paris on presentation of certificates of reception from the officials of the port arsenals.[77] Moreover, the contract covering deliveries in 1752–1758 conferred on

Chaussade a *de facto* monopoly. He and his partner, Denis, received the right to deliver "all the irons requested of them by the arsenals during six years." The *commissaire de la marine* at La Charité sur Loire was empowered to superintend the marketing and purchasing of Berry irons, which were to be used exclusively. Chaussade and Denis as buyers were given priority over "all other" buyers. If Berry producers or proprietors would not agree to sell at an agreed-upon price, the *commissaire* would, under article 2, "give the orders necessary to oblige them to sell."[78]

Under the favorable provisions of this contract, Chaussade and Denis for four years shipped unprecedented quantities of anchors and irons to the navy, and after Denis retired from the partnership in January 1756, Chaussade continued to supply massive quantities for at least two years more.[79] He was an energetic entrepreneur: Minister Rouillé wrote in February 1753 to the *commissaire* Tassin remarking: "It is not necessary to pressure him [Chaussade] to make shipments." But he went on to express some criticism of the Chaussade provisionments. "The principal observation I have to make to you," he said, "is to take care that the shipments this year and next [1754] do not exceed the order [*état*] given to the Sieur de la Chaussade."[80]

The *états* were careful estimates passed on to the *fournisseur* from the arsenals via the ministry; Chaussade's shipments had exceeded orders for some sizes and types of anchors, but in other categories, they fell far short. This was confirmed by the reaction of the highly competent Intendant Hocquart at the port of Toulon. Dissatisfied with the assortments of irons his arsenal received from Chaussade, Hocquart undertook to procure from Spain and Holland irons that had been ordered from Chaussade, but not furnished.[81] Friction and dissatisfaction on both sides resulted.

Circumstances beyond Chaussade's control created some of these difficulties. In order to satisfy particular needs, he had to control and coordinate the production of mine, smelter, forge and finery owners all over the Berry and Loire valley. Such owners were autonomous operators. Some were independent by nature; all had different resource, personnel, and production problems and might be inclined to resist being told by outsiders what to do, what and how much to produce. A myriad of variables affected production at the scattered forges, slitting mills, and fineries served by hundreds of men in the Berry and the Nivernais. Chaussade wrote a ten-page *mémoire* in 1756, discussing some of these problems and arguing that he would be better able to deal with some of the subcontractors if he were accorded higher prices so that he could buy more easily.[82] By the end of 1758 Chaussade seems to have satisfied the navy's

needs in all categories of merchandise in all sizes. His anchor provisionments were particularly abundant: "There is no need to furnish a single additional anchor to Brest in the course of this year," he was told in 1759.[83]

The year 1759 itself produced a series of disasters for the navy and for
France at sea and overseas, and there were also disasters for our *fournisseur*. The market for anchors and irons was wiped out; the principal
squadrons of the French fleet were defeated, captured, dispersed, or otherwise lost. Not only were the arsenals well-stocked; standing orders were
canceled. Port officials were fully aware that anchors and irons could be
salvaged from hulks, condemned vessels, or wrecks, and such anchors
could be used with extraordinary security because they had been proven
in action. To make matters worse, "at Toulon, in forges and *martinets*
established by the Sr. d'Aguillon, anchors that have suffered some altera-
tion are [being] repaired," and some people were saying it would be desirable to have similar facilities in other ports of the realm.[84] From the
profitable heights of massive *fournitures* and monopoly controls, Chaussade plummeted to the depths: by 1760 he had been informed that the
navy had no need for his anchors and irons at all.

Still worse was the fact, evident even before the Seven Years War, that
payments to *fournisseurs* were irregular at best. Within two years after
the declaration of war, payments on government obligations practically
ceased. The king's secretary of state for the treasury was reduced to borrowing from private bankers, meeting with them daily to obtain private
drafts to pay the absolutely indispensable obligations of the royal government. At one point in mid-war, officials at Brest had to await the arrival
by courier of a parcel of gold and silver table utensils and household or-
naments to be used to pay off the most aggressive creditors and thereby
enable the navy to continue to participate in the conduct of the war. In
such circumstances, the fate of mere merchants, such as *fournisseurs,* can
be imagined.

In fact, cash payments to naval *fournisseurs* were officially suspended
as early as 1740; thereafter payments—at least those made to Chaussade—took a variety of forms that often involved significant reductions
in actual remuneration. *Rescriptions,* "a method of anticipating future
receipts,"[85] were much abused by Louis XV's finance minister, Etienne de
Silhouette, in the Seven Years War. Chaussade said that he "lost 6 percent"
when he negotiated some navy credit instruments. Subsequently, instead of
paying in negotiable instruments, the Treasury granted Chaussade close
to a million livres in nonnegotiable government notes bearing interest of
3 percent ("a trois pour cent sur les Postes du Pays").[86] Credits due him
for deliveries of materiel thus became a permanent, nonrecoverable loan

to the crown bearing trifling interest. Only part of these notes were ever negotiated (or "cashed") for Chaussade, and then only as a special favor at heavy discounts. At Chaussade's death about half the 3 percent notes he had "purchased" in 1753 and 1754 were in the portfolio of his estate; the inventory estimated their cash value at less than 2 percent of face value.[87]

Finally, toward the end of the Seven Years War, Chaussade acquired additional "credits," unconsolidated obligations aggregating between 400,000 and 500,000 livres. These credits derived from losses he sustained as a result of enemy action, for which the crown had assumed the risk. All these circumstances, Chaussade said, made him "the most unhappy of men." He had workers in his employ (as we have seen) without having money to pay them, and he was obliged to make interest payments on debts secured by comprehensive mortgages that tied up all his real property in France and thus made it impossible to sell any parcel to meet his obligations. Most of his forges were rendered inoperative.[88]

Chaussade had the good fortune, or exerted enough pressure, to obtain a few additional payments from the navy during the crisis period of the war. An order from the minister of marine dated 6 June 1759 instructed the banker Beaujon to pay "tomorrow or thereafter 30,000 livres to the Sieur Babaud de la Chaussade on the 50,000 he is scheduled to receive this month."[89] The following January a request from Chaussade for another 30,000 livres "payable this month at Moulins, and a like sum next month," was approved by the ministers of both marine and finance: the banker "Montmartel" [*sic*] was to be asked "to conform" to this arrangement.[90] The following summer Chaussade received another payment of 40,000 livres, but nothing at all for eight months after that.[91]

Hounded by creditors, he asked the navy repeatedly for additional payments. In November 1760 the *directeur de la marque des fers* at Nevers was threatening "to seize and sell his irons, *fonte,* and charcoal" if he did not pay "within the week" the 6,210 livres in taxes he owed. Chaussade argued that the tax collector would be guilty of "wrongdoing" if his property "were seized and taken in the name of the king for a sum of 6,210 livres when His Majesty owes me 400,000. . . . I beg you, Monseigneur, to write to MM. the *Fermiers Généraux* to suspend their suits against me."[92] And to Berryer, the minister of marine, he wrote: "In the name of God take pity, Monsieur." Circumstances evidently improved for him shortly after that; yet he claimed that as a *fournisseur* to the navy, his profit consisted "only in simple interest [*revenues naturels*] on my funds."[93]

In 1760 Chaussade was perfectly aware that he was losing heavily on his large "loans" to the crown at 3 percent interest; he admitted that he would have enjoyed profits if only he had been promptly paid. "In the business world," observed the intendant Ruis Embito, "the person [who is] paid badly and rarely and late is a poorly served person in every respect. It is the same in the service of the state. . . . it is indispensable that the Sieur Babaud de la Chaussade be promised exact payment, and that the promise be kept."[94] Every responsible government official in France would have sanctioned the ideal of prompt payment, but unfortunately for Chaussade, that ideal became increasingly difficult for the government of France to achieve after the middle of the eighteenth century.

CHAPTER 6

An Industrial-Seigneurial Labor Force

Chaussade himself would have been hard pressed to determine exactly how many men he had in his employ on any particular day. Like his properties and his interests, they were widely dispersed. Even those operating forges and furnaces close at hand were not easily counted. The count would necessarily have included supervisors, resident managers and caretakers, lawyers, accountants and clerks, and a large number of external workers, some employed full-time and others part-time or seasonally: woodcutters, carters, carriers and teamsters, stevedores, and boatmen and *flotteurs* to supply and service the manufactories and transport shipments to the Ile d'Indret. Chaussade also had regular resident agents (*commissaires*) at Paris, at Nantes, at each of the Atlantic seaboard arsenals, and abroad, at Dort, Rotterdam, Amsterdam, sometimes at Riga, and even New Orleans. The number of his employees increased as the number and size of his properties and contracts grew, changing naturally with the seasons and with rises and falls in demand for anchors and irons and timber and fuel from year to year, in peace and in war. Chaussade's labor force also fluctuated radically with irregularities in payments.

The largest groups of workers were at Cosne and Guérigny. The minister of marine, Maurepas himself, who apparently visited Cosne early in 1737, found 125 men employed there in processing and producing irons for the navy.[1] Twenty years later, in 1759, it was estimated that Chaussade's five forges at Guérigny alone employed "about a hundred families, who live in houses that M. de la Chaussade constructed for them."[2] In 1778 an inspector of manufactures undertaking an inventory of manufactories in the *généralité* of Orléans classified Chaussade's workers at Cosne as follows:[3]

50 "constantly employed" at the two great forges
65 employed as "casual and accessory" employees:

40 at the nailworks ("four furnaces making large and small nails for the construction of ships")

12 at the edge-tool works ("four furnaces, producing 15,000 to 16,000 tools for the navy and for land-clearing in the colonies")

5 at the general hardware and tool works, the *serrurerie* ("two furnaces producing vices, jacks, . . . chains, and other varied hardware")

8 at the tilt-hammer works ("trimming and finishing irons")

10–50 *externes,* who worked as needed, bringing in and taking out materials and performing other unskilled labor

Thus his two major manufactories, Cosne and Guérigny, together must have employed about 250 workers, and at times in the 1770s over 300. If we include external and seasonal labor (woodland and forest workers, teamsters, carters, and porters, etc.), the figure could be raised to 500 or even 1,000.

Payment Crises

Chaussade himself recorded several estimates of the size of his work force in the 1760s, the latter part of the Seven Years War, when he and his workers were plagued by the failure of the state to pay. In May 1760 Chaussade asserted that he had "begun (three months earlier) to discharge his workers," of whom 800 had already been laid off and 1,500 were still in his employ.[4] Pleading for payment, he emphasized his need for funds "to maintain men and horses to operate numerous furnaces and fourteen forges and manufactories," and pointed to the "atrocious condition" (*affreuse necessité*) to which his workers had been reduced the previous year.

In December Chaussade wrote again, to seek payment of the 441,000 livres due to him for irons already delivered to Nantes: "permit me to call attention to the [large] number of inhabitants and families in the parishes where I am located . . . ; in a famine (*disette*), grains would be distributed to them without cost, and they are in exactly that case now, since I cannot pay them their salaries." He said he needed only 30,000 livres immediately and 15,000 livres monthly for the next year. As proof of the workers' needs, he said "I [would] consent to have this sum paid, not into my hands, but to Monsieur l'Intendant de Moulins, who would distribute it through his *subdélégué* or via the *receveurs des tailles*. This help will not break (*gêneront*) the state." If that could not be done, he begged his correspondent (probably the minister of marine), for a personal favor: "Do me the great favor, Monsieur, I beg you, send me a [bank] draft for 30,000 livres as a [personal] loan. I'll give you my note payable on demand."[5] He wrote again later on the condition of his workers: "I found on my arrival [at Guérigny] families crushed by the weight of their misery: my people [have] sustained themselves with grain that they purchased on credit. The price was very high, the quality not good. The obligation of my workers to pay their taxes [*taille et la capitation*] . . . reduced them to despair. . . . the lack of money . . . cost me 50,000 livres in last years' accounts. The modest help that I gave them and my presence revived their hopes and re-established order." But regular payments henceforth, he repeated, were an absolute need.[6]

On the occasion of another crisis (in 1768), he wrote: "The Sieur de la Chaussade has also sustained a third disaster this year. One of his forges set fire to its building and to the [adjacent] housing of workers, which was entirely reduced to ashes. In establishments of this size, with 3,000 workers, accidents and losses are inevitable." Surely, he begged, "your excellency (*Monseigneur*) would not expect a private person, who is occupied day and night with the service, to work under his orders without profit, and even with loss."[7] In August 1768 (when the navy owed him at least 60,000 for the year), he alluded again to the number (and condition) of his workers: "The Sieur de la Chaussade's workers have been paid on a weekly basis since the advent of high grain prices. It is now fifteen days since they have received anything." There was reason for "real concern (*frayeur*). . . . That is the reason the Sieur de la Chaussade came to Compiègne. . . . He begs Your Excellency most earnestly to pay him the 60,000 livres the colonies owe, as soon as possible, to help his workers, whose salaries support more than 12,000 people."[8] Another of Chaussade's *mémoires* (dated Fontainebleau, 11 October 1770) reported that the condition of his workers continued to be critical: "Bread in the province is at an excessive 3s., 6d. and to 4s. the livre. These unfortunates must be paid every day. The Sieur de la Chaussade has increased their salaries twice. Salaries are now at the maximum possible level. Yet they are earning nothing more than bread for themselves and their families. They lack all other necessities: horses, wood, coal—everything is extremely dear. You cannot buy anything or do anything [there] without hard cash."[9] Clearly many thousands of people depended directly or indirectly on employment in Chaussade's manufactories. If his concern for them was self-interested and paternal, it was nonetheless sincere and humane.

Labor Relations

Chaussade faced the common problems of employers of skilled labor: recruiting and training, managing and retaining skilled employees. Such problems were commonly eased for eighteenth-century employers by the state's willingness to use power and authority to strengthen the employer's hand. That was particularly the case with government contractors. Chaussade and other employers in the metallurgical industry were beneficiaries, for example, of the *Arrest du Conseil d'Estat du Roi* of 1729 (reissued in 1767), designed to help employers to deal "fairly" with each other by discouraging them from recruiting laborers or technicians at each others' expense. The legislation also helped the employer to control workers in the metallurgical industry in a variety of ways. Skilled and unskilled workers, forge and finery workers, carters and rivermen, were forbidden to leave an employer from whom they had received advances, to leave while furnaces were "in blast," or to leave without giving at least three months' prior notice, on pain of a 300-livre penalty. Master foundrymen and forgemasters, for their part, were forbidden to hire any workers who could not prove that they had given the required notice, on pain of a 500-livre fine and responsibility for all debts owed by the worker to the former employer.[10]

This and other *arrêts*, differing from each other in details, enabled finery and forge owners and managers to control the mobility of both skilled and unskilled labor in their employ. Provincial intendants and their *subdélégués* functioned as enforcers, giving regional application to the substance of royal decrees with rules and executive decrees of their own, applicable in their own jurisdictions.

Essentially the same policy was enunciated and implemented by the king's intendants at the royal navy arsenals. Thus the intendant Mithon at Toulon issued "explicit prohibitions" in 1730 that forbade "all workers and sailors at the arsenal to accept any service abroad, or to absent themselves from the port, without express permission [of the intendant] on pain of condemnation to [life imprisonment on] the galleys as a deserter, or to conscription [for active naval service] in accordance with an *Ordonnance* of His Majesty dated 8 February 1724."[11] Such restrictions were designed not only to prevent workers from leaving, but also to prevent employers (such as Chaussade) from recruiting or "borrowing" without official permission skilled labor from the pool available at the navy's arsenals.

More than once Chaussade himself transgressed the laws against *embauchage*, the recruitment of men in the employ of others. Extraordinary circumstances seem to have been behind each incident. In 1752, for example, the production capacities of the plants at Guérigny and Cosne were being (or had been) greatly increased, and he needed many more men. He, or a *régisseur* acting for him, then gave employment to a certain

Dubuisson, who was still in debt to his former employer, Sieur Godeau, *fermier* of the forge of Mareuil in the Berry. After litigation, Chaussade and Dubuisson were condemned to pay a penalty of 10,000 livres for damages and interest. Chaussade claimed that the law of 1729 was not promulgated in Moulins and thus did not apply; that documents inculpating Dubuisson (who could neither read nor write) were technically invalid; and that there was no documentary proof that the four horses and fourteen mules Dubuisson brought with him (only partly paid for) were handed over to Chaussade, since the animals in question could not be identified among the 250-odd animals in Chaussade's stable.[12] Chaussade continued to litigate for five years, but finally lost the case *en principe* at least; he may have paid Dubuisson's debt, but one would be surprised to learn that he had paid out the total amount assessed in the first instance.[13]

That particular case of "aggression" by Chaussade as *embaucheur* occurred when he was expanding operations; more commonly, in the late fifties and well into the sixties, he faced the opposite circumstances—insufficient demand, with consequent overcapacity and underemployment for much of his labor force. In 1765 low demand led him to put some of his skilled workers on part-time, piece-work employment, and even to discharge others.[14] But when production activity revived in the later sixties (1767–1768), we find Chaussade involved in a complicated charade of *embauchage*. Five *régisseurs* at five different forges, owned (or leased and managed) by three different firms, made illicit efforts to recruit skilled metal finishers (*affineurs*) from each other's forges.

The affair appears to have surfaced because the forge of Dazy, operated by a certain André Chastignier, was forced to close down when Chaussade and another forge operator, "La Durrie et Cie." separately hired away Chastigniers' key workers. Apparently Chastignier then located and hired a discontented employee in Chaussade's works at Demeurs; and La Durrie et Cie. took another worker from Chaussade's forges at Guérigny. The game-score in these recruiting operations then stood as follows: La Durrie et Cie. (the "winner") gained two workers; Chastignier and Chaussade each lost two, but gained one apiece.

The recriminations accompanying this affair occupied scores of folios and incidentally disclosed some significant details about the management methods of these three forge owners. Chaussade intimated that La Durrie et Cie. was a front for foreign capital: apparently Bigeot de Carcy, *fermier général* of Austria, and his brother-in-law the Sieur Boulle, held shares in it. La Durrie et Cie., without explicitly denying this allegation, retorted by calling attention to Chaussade's use of false names, notably the *prête-nom* "Sieur Ducatellier," to cover some of his operations in the

Berry and elsewhere, including the lease of the works at Grossouvres. It was also brought out that Chaussade used (as did many other entrepreneurs) the partial payment of salaries in advance and long (six-year) contracts to obligate workers to remain in his employ.[15] Finally, it was charged that forge owners sometimes held employees' goods as security. Chaussade, for example, seized (or at least detained) the furniture of the Sieur Marny, who left Chaussade's very active works at Demeurs for health reasons to take a less demanding (and also lower-paid) job at another forge.[16]

At times Chaussade apparently found it less litigious and risky to recruit skilled labor from outside the region where his manufactories were situated. He undertook an interesting but obscure venture to recruit "foreign" workers during the ministry of Machault d'Arnouville, Jean-Baptiste (1754–1757), early in the Seven Years War. At that time Chaussade had orders from the navy for more anchors and irons than he could hope to produce. Looking for workers to develop and man new forges and fineries, he turned his attention eastward. He and his late brother had for many years done business and resided in German-speaking regions of France, especially around Metz and Bitche. Earlier, Masson and the Babauds had been partners in leasing the forge of Moyeuvre from the prince of Craon in Lorraine,[17] and Chaussade himself had owned and leased forge or finery properties in German Lorraine and Alsace, near Metz. These experiences could have suggested the possibility of bringing in German-speaking skilled workers.

A plan to do so was approved by minister of marine Machault, formerly *contrôleur général des finances*. Amiably disposed to the Babauds, Mauchault was certainly aware of the growing intimacy of Austria and France as well. Early in the fifties, Chaussade was not only doubling the production capacity of his forges at Cosne and Guérigny but was building rolling mills, slitting mills, and row-housing for workers at both. He later recalled that when he built new mills at Cosne "to make strip [or strap] iron of various sizes, I brought in German workers for the purpose."[18] Some new German workers arrived around 1752, and Chaussade himself probably saw to their installation in his new factory housing blocks at Cosne.

Likewise at Guérigny, perhaps at about the same time, he settled another group of "*étrangers*," perhaps German-speaking workers also. An anonymous *mémoirist* remarked in the late fifties (probably 1759) that the two great Forges Royales and three small forges that worked for the navy in the environs of Guérigny "employ about a hundred families, who are housed in the buildings M. de la Chaussade built for them." The phrase "nearly all foreigners" (*presque tous étrangers*) was penned into the margin of this document by an unknown writer.[19] The number and precise provenance of these "foreign" forge workers, whether brought in from other parts of France or from abroad, is not known. It seems likely, however, that the presence of such workers presented retention and control problems. And the problems may not have been long in coming.

It might be surmised that at least some of the foreign workers, after a residence of only three or four years in Chaussade's employ, left his manufactories during the increasingly difficult later years of the Seven Years War—1758, 1759, 1760. He himself may have been referring to this circumstance when he said that "many [workers] are tempted to go abroad" (*de passer à l'etranger*).[20]

In fact, even as Chaussade was writing to the ministers about the unpaid, hungry, and miserable workers at his Loire valley forge and foundry works, some of whom (perhaps including the "foreigners") had already left, he himself was spending the fall months of 1760 visiting Atlantic seaboard ports. During those visits, occasioned by the need to transact other business (see Chapter 8), he took advantage of a very unusual opportunity. He hired workers from the ports and arsenals, perhaps to replace those he had lost or was losing. These highly skilled replacements belonged to a class of worker not normally available, but at that time there was no work, and no prospect of work on the coast. Naval arsenals and commercial ports alike were suffering the effects of the maritime disasters of the Seven Years War. Remnants of the navy that survived the defeats were scattered along the coast or confined to port, as were French commercial vessels in the face of Britain's close blockade. No armaments were taking place; hence, there was no activity, much unemployment at French ports, and there were many hungry workers needing work. Chaussade encountered them at La Rochelle, the navy base at Rochefort, and at Bordeaux. Visiting those ports, he could take his pick of a considerable group of highly skilled men.

In a letter written during his travels, en route from La Rochelle to Rochefort on 1 October 1760, Chaussade explained the situation:

> A great number of workers [at French ports] have been released because there is no work. The best of them are leaving daily for Spain and Germany. I have been informed that the intendant [of Rochefort] wants me to employ as many as possible. . . . The intendant considers as ideal and most important my plan to establish at my forges a nailery (*clouterie*) for the manufacture of

hardware (*des fers ouvrés*) for the building trade and the colonies. He has sent five *forgerons* [from Rochefort] to Guérigny
and wrote to me himself to say that these are excellent workers
who in no other circumstances [up to now] were ever outside
the port. Furthermore, my correspondent at Bordeaux has written
me [to say] that . . . [friends] have procured seven *cloutiers* and
taillandiers. This was regarded by the Chamber of Commerce
as most fortunate for my project. These twelve master-workers
must [soon] arrive. . . . [But,] Monsieur, they will find all my
manufactories in desolation. They are going to be disheartened
to be there. Only my presence can remedy that. But I cannot go
there without money. If I [can] bring only 15,000 livres, I will
restore everyone to duty, and that will enable me to wait for new
orders from Mr. Berryer.[21]

One can imagine that Chaussade's workers at Guérigny found it difficult to share his evident satisfaction at finding and hiring skilled outsiders
whose dire circumstances made them accept almost any offer or conditions of work. Chaussade himself remarked that the condition of his
work force in the environs of that town "would surprise you if you knew
it intimately (*tout entière*)."[22]

The Campaign for the "Privilege": Exemption from Militia Service

Chaussade's more usual method of recruiting and retaining skilled
workers was to treat them whenever possible as he and his business associates were wont to be treated at the hands of the government. He sought
and often obtained for them special advantages—in effect, privileges—
one of which was exemption from militia service. This exemption was
attractive to the employees, whatever the levels of their skills. Militia service was poorly paid; it could involve leaving home for an indefinite period; and it was as dangerous as service in the army.

The militia in eighteenth-century France was a secondary defense force
backing up the army. Most militiamen were conscripts selected by lottery
or drawing systems (*tirage au sort*) for a term of six years. Men were
drafted from parishes and towns in proportion to population. Bachelors
and widowers between the ages of sixteen and forty were the men usually
taken for militia service. A commonly used substitution system permitted
a man whose name was drawn to contribute a sum of money to buy the
services of a replacement, the cost varying at different times and places.[23]

This system was a source of much difficulty for the authorities, and additional trouble resulted when some men were declared to be exempt.

From the standpoint of provincial intendants, any substitutions and exemptions entrained trouble. The intendant Dodart (Denis Dodart II (1698–1775)) at Bourges explained:

> Replacements for the militia are always and everywhere the most distressing (*pénible*) affairs with which we [intendants] are charged. But for me the difficulty of this operation becomes [unusually] severe in the canton of La Charité-sur-Loire. The various [industrial] enterprises established there to serve the navy give rise to an infinity of exemption claims, [with] which I find [it] almost impossible [to deal]. The establishment at Cosne for the manufacture of anchors and irons and the [exploitation of] timber for naval constructions is an almost sure refuge for all the young men who want to avoid conscription.[24]

Intendants were also persuaded that many men in the community were exempted from conscription even though they rendered no essential service to the navy or the iron industry. Forgemasters (*forgerons*) were ordinarily exempt, as were certain others whose specialized services were deemed indispensable for the continued operation of the manufacturing enterprises. But the terms "necessary" and "indispensable" seem to have been used loosely and interchangeably, without clear definition. Abuses resulted from the difficulty of defining the category of workers whose services were in fact necessary.

In 1740 the administrators of the Cosne forge, then belonging to the partners Masson, Marie Boesnier, and Chaussade, insisted on the need to exempt twenty-five men who were employed in manufacturing operations. The intendant responded that "if all the workers listed are such that others cannot substitute for them, it is clearly my duty to exempt them. But . . . I have difficulty believing that in each forge so great a number are irreplaceable. . . . It rarely happens that a master worker is not married; as such he is always exempt. Even in the case of his helper (*garçon*), I would give exemption. It is not with these that we have concern. The real trouble comes with the *valets* and *garçons* employed under them."[25]

From the standpoint of the general population, the most important consequence of each exemption was the fact that someone else would be obliged to serve instead in order to fill the local quota. Difficulties and hardship were involved, and they increased with the number of exemptions. Up to 1774, the provincial intendants were allowed such latitude and sometimes used their arbitrary authority in this matter, is was said, as a threat to aid in the collection of difficult tax assessments.[26]

Their powers and problems were Chaussade's opportunity. Intendants, for all their regional prestige and power, did not awe him. Chaussade was a regional magnate himself. He had high connections, including some with the royal officials from whom intendants themselves received their orders. It was apparently a long-term objective of Chaussade and his associates, from their acquisition of Cosne (1736) onward, to multiply exemptions among their workers. Their first navy contract included an article (number 24) allowing "blanket" exemption for the workers at Cosne from "the *taille personnelle* and other obligations" (i.e., militia and *corvée* service).[27]

Prolonged and almost insuperable difficulties developed when implementation of this clause was sought. The sweeping phraseology (and the advantages implied for the partners) may be taken as a mirror of the favor they sought from Maurepas, who is known to have visited the Cosne forges about that time. It is difficult to believe that Maurepas bothered himself about the implications of article 24. Even if conscious of its existence, he could not foresee the disagreements that would develop over exemption issues involving, on the one hand, Chaussade and his ministry of marine (supporting article 24), and, on the other, the ministry of finance, prodded by tax farmers and intendants, opposing the proliferation of costly and troublesome exemptions from the *taille* and *corvée* and militia service.

Initially the entrepreneurs did not seek implementation of all the exemptions article 24 might allow; they surely understood that the concessions made to them by their contract with the navy did not bind the *contrôleur général des finances* or his subordinates: the provincial intendant and his *subdélégués*. They made no effort to have their workers exempted from the *taille personnelle,* since such exemptions involved tax-farmer interests. Instead they sought exemption only from general public obligations. Thus they sought first to get their workers exempted from militia service, a privilege that was damaging mainly to the interests of people in the region. Then they sought exemption from the *corvée,* meeting greater resistance, and last from the *taille.* Here they would encounter the most formidable opposition.

Exemption of the Cosne workers from militia service was an immediate and pressing objective for another reason as well: the War of the Austrian Succession broke out quite soon after their contract was signed in 1736. That war produced changes in the militia system as well as demands for more men and threats to the exemptions their workers had received. Other forge owners in the Berry who were involved in producing irons for the navy petitioned to obtain comparable exemptions for their workers but most were emphatically rebuffed in 1739 by the minister of marine: "I cannot obtain this concession for them, not only because of the consequences, but also because their contracts did not include the [exemption] clause, and there is no precedent, as far as the navy is concerned, for ordinary contractors' (*simples fournisseurs*) having this exemption."[28] Workers at Cosne were "extraordinary" because of their involvement in anchor production. But the partners were informed in 1743 that their privileged status would not enable them to obtain exemption for their workers at forges other than Cosne,[29] even though the exemptions they enjoyed at Cosne itself appear to have been quite comprehensive and were recognized by a succession of ministers and intendants as established practice.[30]

Over the years from 1740 to 1762, the entrepreneurs used a variety of tactics to add exemptions and to extend the Cosne exemptions to their other forges. In this campaign they were steadily held in check throughout Maurepas's tenure by reasonable, moderate policy on the ministerial level. Under Rouillé (1749–1754) and Machault (1754–1757), resistance to new exemptions was weakened on that level. In the provinces, however, intendants and some of their *subdélégués* resisted further exemptions with rigor, or so it seemed to Chaussade. Finally, in the 1760s, when the "revival" of the navy was undertaken under Choiseul, this "exemption campaign" made some significant gains.

The tactics of this campaign can be traced in detail through bundles and volumes of navy correspondence. Analysis of this evidence makes it clear that Chaussade and his *régisseurs* shrewdly manipulated a number of variables. As early as 1745 Chaussade (or his agents) sought exemption from militia service not only for a short list of highly skilled *forgerons* (approved without difficulty), but in addition for the following employees:

> *At the Forges of La Vache:*
> Michel Chevalier, *marteleur* at two forges, married, aged 30 years
> Pierre Pasquelin, worker at the forges, married, aged 28 years
> Pierre Frebault, worker, married, aged 38 years
> The person called "Le Chat," muleteer, carter of coals, bachelor, aged
>   26 years

At the Magazine of La Charité:

Sieur François Jorteaux, bookkeeper for the reception and storage of irons, bachelor, aged 17

Jean Gabriel Le Maure, arrangement of irons in the magazines, bachelor, aged 25 years [31]

The intendant Dodart of Bourges reluctantly exempted all these men, but dispatched the following comments to Maurepas: "I live in forge country, and I know forges. I also know how important it is to aid such establishments." He did not begrudge exemptions for the principal workers at forges, but he pointed to "others who do not merit any exemption," such as "the muleteer's aide [Le Chat] and that other aide who is supposed to arrange the irons in the warehouse;" either of them could be replaced on a moment's notice; "[they] are of no consequence in the manufacture of irons. I also ask you to note another anomaly in this 'authenticated' list: the two who are simply labeled 'workers' [are] the most remarkable, inasmuch as the title *worker* [underscored] is unknown in the forges, where everyone has his particular title—founder, guard, breaker, refiner, assistant refiner, etc." Dodart hoped that requests to exempt clearly nonessential workers would not be submitted again.[32] But they did recur, especially after Rouillé became minister of marine in 1749. Remarkably favorable to Chaussade in other matters, as we have seen, the Rouillé ministry decreed full implementation of article 24 of the Masson-Babaud contract of 1736, whose application had never been allowed under Maurepas. A letter from Rouillé in late 1749 interpreted that article as allowing the exemption of workers at Cosne from *all* impositions, including the *taille!*[33]

The value of such exemptions to Chaussade was multiplied when they were extended to workers at forges and foundries other than Cosne. The rationale for doing so was that many of the small works produced raw materials—the *fonte* or forged bars—that were sent to Cosne as components in the fabrication of anchors. Thus it was claimed that the workers at these small forges and fineries were also essential links in the anchor-manufacturing process. In 1752, when he bought two small forges in the parish of Raveau from M. de Mouchy, Chaussade immediately sought to have their workers exempted from "the *taille* and other impositions." Exemptions would raise the tax rates of those who were not exempt, since the tax quota would have to be paid by fewer taxpayers. Residents of Raveau had been confronted and engaged in litigation with Chaussade before. Far from deterring him, the knowledge that trouble would surely ensue seemed to encourage him. He was willful, determined, and punitive when opposed. Intendant Dodart's cocky *subdélégué* at La Charité (a certain M. de Charan) was likewise determined to see that the rules were enforced. Chaussade announced to Charan his acquisition at Raveau, adding:

> I hope that when they learn of my acquisitions, the inhabitants of Raveau will spend no more [funds for litigation]. But I foresee that I will have another lawsuit with them over the [amount of the] *taille* that they will pay after my management staff is exempted. . . . I believe the case can probably be decided at the *cour des aydes*. . . . It is sad, Monsieur—trying to do all the good I can, and doing a great deal, in a populous parish where I provide paid employment the year around, as payment they will force me into a second lawsuit. I have five other properties where my management staff and guards pay neither the *taille* nor [any] other charges.[34]

Chaussade did not mention that he was just then having serious trouble at the forges and foundry at La Vache in which that same *subdélégué* M. de Charan was involved. Charan had sent the local constables (*archers*) to oblige certain of Chaussade's workers at La Vache "to pay fifteen sous each for the three days of absence" from the *corvée* "or suffer arrest." Chaussade responded to this threat as follows:

> I did not know, Monsieur, that it was again a question of the [seasonal] *corvées* in your district, and in consequence I did not give my people orders to excuse themselves from *corvée* labor, nor did I forbid them to pay the tax due when labor was not performed. . . . If you had only had the goodness to say a word during the three weeks that I have been on my estates, I would, with your approval, have written to the intendant, or I myself could have paid [for them] provisionally. Will you let me know, Monsieur, in view of the re-emergence of this unsavory affair, if you can remain there until we can get together on my passage to La Charité, or if I must address myself to M. Dodart [Charan's chief] to ask him to treat me in his *généralité* as [I am treated] at ten [other] forges and one furnace in [the *généralité* of] Moulins. I go even farther. I will be [personally] responsible for the tax of my workers pending the settlement of this matter with the intendant, who ignored, through my error, the exemption that was accorded to me by my contract.[35]

The indefatigable Chaussade also wanted a few other exemptions and expressed the hope that a certain Bourdeau, "guard of my woodland," could be exempted from the *corvée:* "He is lodged with me, [is] my domestic and without anything but the wages I give him. I have seven [others] at other properties who have never been subject to either the *corvée* or the *taille.* If you cannot take it upon yourself to exempt them, I hope the intendant will treat me as he does my neighbors."[36]

Chaussade pressed this campaign for exemptions with energy and constancy. He gained his most signal victory with the coming of the Seven Years War, when charged with "the general provisionment of anchors and irons for the navy." Trumpeting this victory, he wrote to the intendant Dodart, who had been trying for years to hold the line on exemptions: "*M. le Garde des Sceaux* has informed you, I believe, that he has entrusted to me the *fourniture général . . .* and that the matter is so pressing and important that he has found it necessary to exempt from the *corvées* and from the militia the workers, teamsters, and boatmen and [their] *valets* who work in my service and who are attached to my establishments." That announcement to Dodart was accompanied (or soon followed) by lists of at least eighty-eight men from four parishes, nearly all of them external workers, charcoal-burners, boatmen, and helpers of varied sorts, generally easily replaceable, for whom exemption was to be granted from both *corvée* and militia service.[37] "It appears," intoned Minister of Marine Machault, writing in support of these exemptions, "that these sorts of people are no less necessary to him than those to whom exemptions are ordinarily granted."[38]

All these concessions had as their explicit or implied justification the wartime needs of the navy. As the *subdélégué* Charan put it, doubtless with chagrin, Chaussade was allowed "to give the widest possible extension to the privileges accorded; to mingle an infinity of workers of all sorts, [including] those of little use with those that are absolutely necessary."[39] In contrast to Chaussade's sweeping exemption privileges, a cannon manufactory that included several forges was allowed exemptions for only eight principal workers.[40]

Charan and Chaussade continued to feud. In late May 1757 Chaussade informed the minister of marine that the director and workers at his forges in Berry were (again) being harassed by the *subdélégué* of La Charité. Charan had again sent the constables to force Chaussade's workers to pay the monetary obligations they incurred when they failed to appear in person to do the roadwork they were assigned by the provincial authority (Charan). They could not leave work, as we have seen, with a forge or foundry in blast: that was forbidden by both their contracts with Chaussade and the edicts of the crown. Nor could they pay the penalty. The constables seized and carried away their household furniture, and could have sold it or obliged the workers to sell it themselves in order to pay their fees and penalties.[41]

Writing to the intendant Dodart, Charan's chief, the minister observed that serious consequences could flow from his subordinate's extraordinary action against Chaussade's workers: "such treatment is bound to disorganize completely this service [of iron production] which is so sensitive to the least interruption that exemption from the *corvées* for all employees who work there is one of the principal conditions of the contract of the Sieur de la Chaussade. The conduct of this *subdélégué* appears to me especially reprehensible, since I have no doubt that you . . . gave the necessary orders."[42] Later the blame for this unfortunate affair was laid to some of Chaussade's own clerical staff. For it was disclosed that none of Chaussade's workers whose names were on the "exempted" list had been ordered to do *corvée* service or been threatened by the constables, and that the names of those who were ordered to serve, and whose furniture was seized, were *not* included on that list. "In the future," the minister informed Chaussade, "you must send him [Charan] a list of *all* the workers employed at your forges, taking care to keep him exactly informed of any subsequent changes."[43]

Notwithstanding this fiasco, overall Chaussade enjoyed impressive successes in winning exemptions from militia and *corvée* service for his workers. But he obtained few exemptions from the *taille personnelle*, the most burdensome and arbitrary of all the impositions, described as "the ruin of fortunes, bodies, and souls."[44] Article 24 of the 1736 contract, when applied at all to the *taille*, touched only Chaussade's principal workers at Cosne.

Even at Cosne there were formidable obstacles to getting such an exemption. The intendant Dodart from the start firmly and emphatically disparaged article 24: "it does not and cannot confer exemption from the *tailles* as you appear to believe and point out to me positively, perhaps by inadvertence." But Dodart did point out a few technical grounds that might qualify a particular employee for exemption. The only persons with much chance for exemption, as Dodart described the situation, were outsiders who had never before been on the tax rolls for the *taille*, such as men who had been brought in as employees and given management positions in the parish where they resided. Such employees's names might be included on the list of those being considered for certification, but Dodart was wary. And he incidentally warned Chaussade that a person living on Chaussade's own premises, even if serving only part-time as a domestic, would owe the tax known as the *capitation*, to which domestics were subject.[45]

Generally, Chaussade obtained exemption from the *tailles* only for management staff, his *régisseurs* (and perhaps his clerks) at Cosne and Guérigny, his principal workers, forgemasters, and a single clerk at each forge or foundry situated elsewhere. The careful controls on exemptions from the *taille* were reinforced by the *receveurs des tailles*, who were professional collectors, highly litigious officials for whom economic interest was paramount, as it was with their tax-farmer chiefs. Their aim was to maximize the amount they collected. They were reputed to ignore appeals to sentiment and rational argument alike from petitioners and taxpayers, rarely making concessions or exceptions to their collection rules or procedures. Thus in 1761 we find Chaussade requesting that the *receveurs des tailles* "suspend their litigation to collect from his impecunious workers"; but even so influential a man as Chaussade found little flexibility in the operations of that branch of the fiscal bureaucracy. The intendant Le Nain of Moulins was unyielding: "I have no power to order such a suspension. It must come from higher authority."[46]

The powers of intendants were limited where the interests of tax-farmers and their agents were concerned. Even the powers of the *contrôleur général* of finance were restricted after the tax had been "farmed": that is, when the power to collect the tax had been sold to a consortium of bankers or other entrepreneurs. The tax-farming system depended on the tax-farmers' ability to recover the advances made, with some profit besides. The obligation of the king's intendants, in the circumstances, was simply to facilitate the collection arrangements and forestall hindrances—for example, by disallowing exemptions such as those sought by Chaussade.

The intendants' authority was even more effectively tied by "higher authority" after issuance of the royal *ordonnance* of 1 December 1774. That *ordonnance* obliged provincial intendants to conform to new restrictions and effectively removed their power to exempt men from militia and *corvée* service.[47] The heyday of exemptions of all kinds seemed to be over. The old opportunities for provincial magnates such as Chaussade to multiply exemptions by influencing intendants and their *subdélégués* were ended. New guidelines explicitly fixed the list of the exempt; the central government reserved to itself a greater measure of control, arbitrary as before, but in practice allowing fewer exceptions.

Even more significant were royal decrees of 1775 and 1778. The former ended the practice of assembling the militia, virtually "abolishing militia [service] in time of peace"; the latter expressed His Majesty's wish that men subject to militia duty would nonetheless have "liberty to go to work wherever they wish, without . . . any sort of restraint." To leave their parish they now had only to declare to local authorities where they were going.[48] Yet these new liberties were apparently not enough to dissipate hatred of militia service, a sentiment reportedly expressed repeatedly and emphatically in many of the *cahiers* of 1789.[49]

From the Seven Years War onward, the burden of *corvée* service was progressively reduced on the initiative of certain intendants concerned for "the public good" (notably Turgot, Anne Robert Jacques as intendant de Limoges), who allowed substitution of a pecuniary payment for personal service. When such substitution became possible, it effectively invalidated the claim that exemption was needed to forestall interruption of work at the manufactories. These changes were almost certainly not welcome to Chaussade, for they eliminated his exemption privileges. Once the burden of *corvée* service became less avoidable (by being made payable in cash), did Chaussade raise wages to make up the difference and thus assume the burden himself? I am confident that if he did so he then sought higher prices from the navy for his anchors and irons.

Clearly these changes reduced the utility of (and justification for) exemptions as an instrument in the hands of favored employers such as Chaussade. But these changes did not mean that working men were suddenly freed from the burdens of conscription or liberated to go where and when they pleased. Their "new liberties" conformed better to contemporary theories of natural law than to the realities of their lives.

A wide variety of methods were available to control the mobility of labor and assure forge owners that skilled workers would not leave work without notice and permission. Chaussade knew that men could not be expected to work well against their will: that was certainly one reason why he sought exemptions. Exemptions made employment at his manufactories more attractive than work elsewhere; and so much the better if exemptions were obtained for his workers at the expense of others. That was positive profit to himself.

There is other evidence suggesting that Chaussade's workers were more favorably treated than many of their contemporaries. They worked for a man interested in obtaining advantages for them so long as he obtained concurrent advantages for himself. Indeed, Chaussade appears to have had a hand in a curious "social security" (or perhaps salary supplement) scheme proposed for certain skilled workers at his forges. A mémoirist who effectively spoke for Chaussade and his interests described it as follows:

I would like to see the king pay a small pension to the principal
workers in these forges whether the forges were operating or not
to engage them to apply themselves to the work. The king might
give 100 livres a year to [each of] the four principal *forgerons,*
to the four second *forgerons* 60 livres, and to the eight others
40 livres each. This will occasion competition among these workers, who will be flattered to be pensioned by the king and with
this outlook will apply themselves to their work. I have seen this
method used advantageously in the cannon forges of St. Gervais
in Dauphiné, where a similar pension extremely excited the
workers of that forge to work and gave them status in the region
once they had obtained the pension.[50]

We find no indication that this idea for inducements was ever in fact financed by the crown at Cosne or Guérigny.

Some common long-term concerns underlie the exemption program,
the "pension plan" of 1762, and the rigorous contract terms Chaussade
imposed on some individual workers. Jacques Masson's initial contracts
for skilled labor at Guérigny in the 1720s relied on the contract provisions and phraseology that were usual in the charcoal-iron industry of the
time. In 1739, for example, the *marteleur* Joseph Bernard signed with the
partners Masson and Chaussade a contract promising (a generous) 1,575
livres of *fontes,* from which he was to produce 1,000 livres of forged iron
using 30 *bannes* of charcoal. If more charcoal was used, or less iron of
good quality was produced, the difference was to be paid to Masson at
"market prices." Conversely, if less charcoal was used or more good forged
iron was produced, Bernard's compensation would be increased in proportion.[51] Chaussade was still using similar contracts in dealings with his
principal iron workers long afterward.

Under the auspices of Masson and Chaussade, and later Chaussade
alone, *régisseurs* at Guérigny also used "pure gift" (*pur don*) contracts,
from 1741 at least until 1768, common devices in the iron industry that
effectively bound to their jobs the lower-level workers brought in to
Guérigny from outside the area. In both Masson's and Chaussade's times,
they were used to bind the long-time employee and *régisseur* of Guérigny,
"the Sieur Jacques L'Estang," who was perhaps the author of the detailed
contracts he used during his tenure there. (L'Estang's loyalty ultimately
led to his appointment as *régisseur* and *receveur* for the whole Guérigny
complex of forges and properties.)[52]

"Pure gift" contracts provided for bimonthly, *paye ordinaire* plus an
additional sum (60 or 100 livres), a *chapeau de valeur d'un écu* [3 livres],
and wines to the value of 6 livres each year given as pure gift. The mone-

tary "gifts" were to be received partly in advance. A worker who quit his job under such a contract before the term of three years was up was legally obligated to return all the pay and perquisites (*épingles*) received, these being classed as gifts if he stayed and repayable as loans if he left. The departing worker was also held liable for the legal cost of writing the initial contract and any charges involved in transporting his belongings to Guérigny; moreover, the worker freely granted the employer a lien on his belongings to guarantee execution of terms of the contract.[53]

Other workers, apparently equally skilled but perhaps better known to the *régisseur*, were given less stringent contracts. Thus the contract signed in 1741 (by L'Estang) with a certain Jean Le Gendre, *forgeron*, provided that the latter would receive the usual 1,500 livres of *fonte* and 3.5 *bannes* of charcoal, to produce a *millier* (1,000 livres) of forged iron, and the sum of twelve livres and ten sols for each *millier*, to be paid to him "every fifteen days." L'Estang promised to furnish at the forge for the term of six years certain tools, the hammer, and the leather to be used "to maintain the bellows of the said forge, and Le Gendre himself was to provide subsistence for the bellows man."[54] Later that year (28 October 1741), still another agreement was signed by this "Jacques L'Estang". He then described himself (under Chaussade-Boesnier-Goossens auspices) as "*réceveur*." That agreement was with a *forgeron* named Louis Kiesard (spelling unclear), residing at Imphy, who consented to live and work "full-time" for L'Estang at Guérigny as *valet-marteleur* for a wage of forty livres each year.[55]

Chaussade was a relatively enlightened employer. Many of his workers could count themselves fortunate to live in housing he provided and to work at his Forges Royales. Not all were content (see Chapter 7). Yet the more serious labor disturbances of the period seem to have passed Chaussade's forges by. Indeed, an *ordre du roi* issued 9 March 1776 declared that "some workers" employed for the naval service "commit infidelities [transgressions] . . . contrary to the welfare of the service" and "ruinous to the entrepreneurs who employ them." His Majesty authorized extraordinary measures to control them: workers guilty of "breach of trust or who refuse to obey the orders of their superiors" could be punished with prison "for as long as appropriate and according to the gravity of their fault."[56] It is not clear that any workers involved in such activities were in Chaussade's employ.

His employees showed little disposition to make demands or to desert their employer, as did those of a certain M. de Gribeauval, who was plagued with runaways and was at last obliged to call in troops to reestablish order at Tulle.[57] Certainly Chaussade never did what one of the highest-ranking officials of the navy implicitly recommended: keeping the payment of wages in arrears as a matter of policy.[58] That was the antithesis of Chaussade's policy as we understand it; he recognized the need for, and strove to achieve, regularity of payment to his employees.

The author of a retrospective *mémoire* of 1787 discussing the Forges Royales de la Chaussade and their management in Chaussade's own time (before 1782) observed that Chaussade's workers "were well-paid. Men of talent sought employment in his works because wages were advantageous."[59] Such assertions must be taken as simple statements of opinion, unless evidence can be adduced to show that certain of Chaussade's workmen were in fact paid more than others performing comparable work. We do not have such evidence, and for many reasons compensation scales for comparable work in different manufactories under different management would be difficult to establish at this distance in time. To say that Chaussade could afford to pay his workers more because the navy paid him high prices for his irons is hardly proof that he did so. Yet the available evidence suggests that he did pay very well, especially for skilled labor and "internal" workers, because he needed first-quality products.

To conclude, perhaps the best we can do is to cite an official opinion about the Forges Royales de la Chaussade expressed in the printed *cahier* of the *bailliage* of Nivernais at Nevers in 1789. There the deputies of the Third Estate urged the king to get rid of the Forges Royales—"that establishment, highly advantageous in the hands of a private operator [Chaussade], is very harmful to the province in the hands of the king."[60] That statement leaves untouched the particular question whether wages in 1789 were lower or higher than they had been under Chaussade; it merely expresses the dislike, commonplace among *philosophes*, for government ownership of industry and a preference for private management. Those sentiments must explain the statement's seeming nostalgia for the days when the Forges Royales were owned by Chaussade; after all, Chaussade's director remained on the job after the sale, and managed for the king.

CHAPTER 7

Chaussade: Agrarian and Industrial Lord

The Lord Pays and Collects Rents and Taxes

About mid-afternoon on 10 November 1752, Pierre Babaud de la Chaussade traveled across the town of Nevers and knocked at the principal portal of the bishop's palace. A Swiss lackey opened the door and allowed him to mount to the great hall. There Chaussade the industrial magnate assumed the humble posture of a vassal before his bishop and seigneurial lord; without sword or spurs, with head bare, one knee touching the floor, he completed the suppliant act of faith and homage, offering his *dénombrement* for Guérigny, Demeurs, and the neighboring tenures of his fief. Chaussade's *dénombrement*, notarized earlier that day, included a description of the fief and a list of the obligations he owed as a vassal. They included the payment of six livres a year for Guérigny, and for neighboring Demeurs three bushels of rye (measure of Nevers) and a fat hen. In addition he owed two sous and six deniers and a fat hen for each parcel, pasture, chateau, furnace, or forge on the fief. For the use of the road from Guérigny to Nevers, he owed six deniers, and six more for the road to Prémery over which his irons were transported to the forges at Guérigny.[1] Chaussade also had other, equally serious commitments to other regional lords, among them His High and Very Powerful Seigneur, Monseigneur Louis Jules Barbon Mancini Mazarin, duc de Nivernois, grandee of Spain, peer of France, before whom Chaussade rendered "*homage* and fealty" in 1775, as he was obliged by law to do at least once in his life.[2]

Some unpleasant surprises marked the life of a vassal, even one of Chaussade's stature; thus he found himself dunned for "unpaid" obligations to his lord when the tax collector of the bishop of Nevers, a certain Goussot, presented him in 1766 with a bill for 121 livres, 10 sous, and 9 deniers. Chaussade set his own feudal lawyer (*feudiste*) to work, using different grain prices, and estimated the amount due as 106 livres, 0 sous, and 7 deniers.[3] For Chaussade the claim was an annoying outgrowth of a feud he was having with the bishop, but he had to pay the arrears. He was again involved in long and complex litigation with the bishop in 1767, this time over a question of rights and dues in the Châtellenie d'Urzy-Demeurs.[4]

As holder of fiefs and seigneuries and a myriad of tracts and parcels of various sorts, Chaussade was deeply involved in the confused seigneurial regime of the time. The complexities of that regime provided a rich field of enterprise for landowners and their lawyers. Chaussade employed several feudal lawyers over the years, part of whose job was to help manage his holdings by discovering forgotten or neglected tangles of seigneurial relationships that might be turned to account. Furthermore, even so formidable a litigant as Chaussade might, as we have seen, be caught in tax delinquencies by lawyers in the service of others. He needed legal defenders as well as "enterprisers" on his staff. In 1753, for example, a certain Blondeau, agent of His Majesty's tax-farmers, approached Chaussade with claims for payment of an overdue tax (the *centième denier*) that he should have paid on a transaction concluded over a decade earlier, in May 1742. Blondeau cited a *déclaration du roy* of 24 October 1724 that had been transgressed and urged Chaussade to pay immediately to avoid the cost of litigation. Chaussade probably paid that one too.[5]

Of even greater magnitude and seriousness was a bill Chaussade received from agents of the prince of Condé. They demanded 3,337 livres—the costs and damages awarded for certain illicit actions by Chaussade's manorial judicial officers in the administration of *haute justice* at Guérigny. Chaussade managed with much pleading and delay to scale that penalty down. The sum due, he claimed, was only 2,919 livres, 17 sous, 9 deniers; he is known to have paid at least 2,169 livres to Condé's representatives on 20 July 1771.[6]

The seigneurial regime could require some formal public expressions of humility, even from men who were not at all humble; it could also impose costs and penalties on men of any rank, and to defend one's interests, even in the eighteenth century, could entrain long and complex litigation. Chaussade's elder brother, Jean, abhorred and sought to avoid legal entanglements of all kinds. His dislike of litigation led him to insist on a clause (article 15) in his contract with Masson and Chaussade providing that in case of any sort of difference between the associated partners or their heirs, arbiters should be chosen—two or three well-known, honest persons—to reach a settlement. Going to justice or the courts was to be avoided, and any partner taking an issue to court or appealing a decision of the arbiters was required first to pay 10,000 livres to the other partners. One quarter of that sum was to be given as charity to the poor; the rest was to be used to pay the legal expenses that ensued.[7]

Chaussade, in contrast, showed himself to be unusually litigious—inclined to manipulate legal technicalities for profit, and even to conduct litigation with neighbors as a kind of game. He did so with his neighbor de Fougis (the comte de Berthier-Bizy), who apparently had a similar disposition. These two, both forge owners and large landed proprietors, carried on a veritable jousting match in the courts, using manorial custom and law as weapons, over a period of decades. Some of the issues were trifling—matters of pretension, prerogative, and *honneur*—but they both affected to consider them important. There were perennial problems of jurisdiction, boundaries between their properties, tenures, and the like; both men employed lawyers specializing in title searches, liens, rights, and obligations that might be revived or established and on which payments and arrearages might be collected from the other to help pay for the intricate legal research they supported. Each managed to have the other condemned to pay various small sums or penalties at different times. At one point, however, they patched up their differences long enough to allow their offspring to marry.[8] In the end, they became strong allies. After the Bourbon restoration of 1814–1815, Louis XVIII was responding to the request of none other than Madame la Comtesse de Bizy, granddaughter of Chaussade, when he decreed that the manufactories at Guérigny would henceforth be designated officially as the Forges de la Chaussade.[9]

Seigneurial Justice

Contemporary critics of the French legal system condemned abuses of seigneurial justice. They deplored the excessive number and levels of jurisdictions, the multiplicity of extraordinary tribunals, the vagueness of their jurisdictions, the complexity of their procedures, the excessive number and almost unlimited duration of lawsuits, the exactions of the judicial officials, and the enormous cost of the system referred to as the "brigandage of justice."[10] In the eighteenth century many abuses flourished, particularly on the lowest level of judicial administration, in the system of seigneurial law and practice. Whether called feudal or manorial, the seigneurial justice system often entrained a "rigorous economic subjection of a host of humble folk to a few powerful men."[11]

Pierre Babaud de la Chaussade, it seems, must be numbered among those powerful few. Yet some of his actions brought credit to seigneurial justice. Some seventeenth-century appointees to judicial posts on the seigneurial level were described by Loyseau as "neither lettered nor experienced."[12] These criticisms may still have been applicable to some eighteenth-century judicial officers, but not to Chaussade's. His judicial appointees appear to have been reasonably "lettered" and in some instances seemed excellently qualified as far as judicial knowledge and experience were concerned. Chaussade appointed as his chief judicial officer a certain Jean François Roüelle, whose legal qualifications seem to have been very respectable. He had been *procureur du roy de la province de Lorraine* and *justice ordinaire gruriale et de police de la province de Lorraine.* Ultimately, he became judge and *chef de police des terres, seigneuries, et justices situées en la province de Nivernois appartenant à M. de la Chaussade.*[13] Roüelle functioned for some years and in various capacities as Chaussade's judicial officer.

If Chaussade's judicial officers were at fault in any important respect, it was for their excessive activity. At least one of Chaussade's judicial officers, as we have seen, made some costly procedural errors at Guérigny, which were detected by the agents of the prince of Condé round 1764. Good lawyers manipulate laws and can make mistakes in doing so. Chaussade habitually used the law to pressure others to do his will. The litigation and judicial phases of seigneurial management were clearly consonant with his disposition.

On his seigneuries, Chaussade's judicial officers exercised the power of high, middle, and low justice (*haute, moyenne, et basse justice*), depending on the quality of the particular estate. Around 1773, in the environs of Guérigny, Chaussade held all these powers for the barony of Villemenant, for Guérigny, Marcy, Gondelens, the fief of Biez, la Douée, Ouvrault, and Yville, but only middle- and low-justice powers for the properties of Richerand and Demeurs.[14] On some of his lands, Chaussade shared seigneurial powers with others and made conventions to clarify confusion in jurisdictions. Possession of some seigneuries conferred the power to name functionaries for the estate—sergeants, guards, notaries, and the like.

The jurisdiction and authority of seigneurs in judicial matters, even high-justice authority, were restricted and reduced in the eighteenth century by the ascendant royal system of justice. In criminal matters, *haut justice* might still deal with cases involving the death penalty, but such cases were bound to be appealed to higher courts. The most notorious criminal case handled by Chaussade's justices appears to have been a murder—a body was found in the barn of a man named Camus. Apparently the case was not solved, but more than a dozen years afterward a series of incidents took place in which Camus was involved: a sum of eighteen livres was stolen from a forest guard, a horse was stolen, and there was a theft from the Church of Saint-Aubin. Camus was condemned by local and regional "justice" (at Moulins) "to be broken alive" on the wheel, but a still higher court (Parlement) "did not find the proofs of guilt to be sufficient" and set aside the death penalty, ordering instead that Camus merely be branded (*flétri*, usually with the letters GAL) and sent to the galleys.[15] A local prison could be used in such cases for temporary detention of prisoners during trial; a note dated Guérigny, August 1762, remarked that "our prisons in Frasnay cannot be in condition to be used before the end of next week."[16]

In civil law seigneurs with high-justice authority had wide but limited competence and punitive powers; middle- and low-justice authority was further limited, even as to the size of the fines that could be assessed. But whatever the level of authority, seigneurial justice conferred important powers that reinforced seigneurial authority. Seigneurs could oblige their tenants to perform duties. And that, as Doucet remarked regarding an earlier period, was the basis of the whole feudal edifice.[17] Judicial powers that enabled the seigneur to enforce rights, prerogatives, and privileges conduced to his honor and prestige; by the exercise of judicial powers, the lord's taxes and rents became collectible, and the privileges associated with particular tenures and properties became enforceable.

His People: Renters, Tenants, and Workers

With good reason Chaussade referred to the families living on his seigneuries and other properties as "his people." They were housed on his property; they fed themselves and their livestock with feed produced on his lands; they were subject to his justice. His tenants and *censiers* were among the hundreds he employed at seasonal or part-time jobs—in lumbering and woodcutting, as teamsters, in maintenance work on farms and in manufactories. Some of his tenants worked his fields; others were employed in his furnaces, foundries, forges, or mills. Chaussade's influence and prestige, his wealth, his judicial powers, his economic controls, and his governance as manorial lord—all contributed to his ability to coordinate the lives of "his" people, his renters, tenants, and workers, so that their labor contributed to the smooth operation of his industrial and agricultural enterprises. Chaussade's labor costs, his production and balance sheets for manors and farms, forges and manufactories, were intricately interrelated; his farms and forges were mutually sustaining, semi-integrated enterprises.

Régisseurs were the men who coordinated these people, properties, and powers. They oversaw the management of scores of farms, thousands of acres of woodland and forest, and a myriad of seigneurial properties. But whether established at rural Guérigny or urban Cosne, the *régisseur's* first task was to manage the forges and manufactories. *Régisseurs* made enterprise-type contracts with forgemasters and others, as we have seen, who agreed to use Chaussade's forge and mill equipment to produce specified quantities of iron or steel products utilizing agreed-upon amounts of fuel and other materials that the *régisseurs* arranged to have delivered to the works. The irons produced, if accepted, were paid for at predetermined prices. *Régisseurs* made seasonal or longer-term contracts in Chaussade's name with woodcutters, charcoal-burners, and carters to cut and stack firewood and to burn and deliver charcoal fuel to the forgemasters at the manufactories. They oversaw these operations each year on scores of Chaussade's scattered forest and woodland parcels, planned the cycle of cuts for each, and saw to the deliveries of charcoal so that they arrived in good time to keep all the furnaces, forges, ovens, fineries, mills, and other manufacturing facilities in operation. Scores of teamsters and stablemen were employed, using their own or Chaussade's wagons and teams. Some labor was owed to Chaussade under the terms of leases; much was hired with or without equipment and teams under specially tailored contract terms.

Chaussade's notaries prepared, checked, or authenticated contract terms; reference copies were filed with the regional office, as at Nevers. For many years Claude Gilbert Bort was his notary at Guérigny. Chaussade was apparently content with his services. In 1768 he added to Bort's responsibilities those of *procureur général fiscal,* and since Bort had the confidential records in his care, he was also the logical choice as Chaussade's archivist. For Guérigny he also served as Chaussade's prosecutor in seigneurial affairs.[18]

Another notary, Hugues Anthéaume of Ecouen, was appointed *procureur général et special* with power of attorney to act for Chaussade and the comte and comtesse de Gondrecourt and other owners of portions of the fief of Gentien (in the parish of Belloy, Villaines); Anthéaume was to function as a *feudiste:* "to receive and recover arrears of the *cens sur cens,* seigneurial rents, *lods et ventes,* indemnities and other seigneurial and feudal rights" from vassals, *censitaires,* proprietors, and "*tempteurs de maisons, jardins,* lands, pastures, etc.," to receive and receipt all payments, and, in default of payment, to bring suit, cancel contracts, and generally take all necessary action to develop and obtain acceptance of the *terrier* of the said fief.[19] Evidently Chaussade had been empowered to act for all the owners in giving Anthéaume the authority to revise the rent structure and improve the general productivity of the fief. Essential to the process was the establishment of an accepted legal basis for management—hence the need to establish the terms of a legally enforceable, updated *terrier,* the *terrier* being in effect a detailed description of a property, with an inventory of all its parts, indicating the amount of rent and other obligations due for each part.

The search for "arrearages" was simply one stage of the process of renewing a *terrier,* but it was often painful for some of the parties involved. Arrears were, of course, legal obligations that had been neglected or gone unrecognized and unpaid, or were considered to be due or overdue because receipts proving that payment had been made could not be produced. Even modest accumulations of such obligations could easily exceed the capacity of humble people to pay. Small owners or tenants might then be obliged to cede, sell, or lease some plot, field, woodland, or right or make other compensatory concessions to pay off the debt. Thus, for example, Jean Fity and Marie Chamoir, his wife, transferred (i.e., sold) a parcel of land to Chaussade to pay 115 livres in seigneurial dues that had been discovered to be in arrears, and in the same act the Fitys acknowledged that they still owed the Sieur de la Chaussade 100 livres of additional arrears.[20]

All sorts of documentary tools could be used by legal officers in reviewing long-neglected rights or claims to land or usages: wills, inventories, *quittances, reconnoissances, déclarations,* and *dénombrements* in the *terriers.* Even fragments of *terriers* in the archival records could disclose bases for claims for recovery of lands, shares of land, rights and obligations forgotten, overdue rents, or shares of crops payable in money or kind; there was a myriad of possibilities.

Thus there was profitable purpose to the thoroughgoing legal research conducted by Chaussade's *feudistes* and the *notaire* Anthéaume in order to establish a documentary basis for a revised *terrier.* Researches on the fief and justice of Villemenant-Marcy were apparently pushed back several hundred years to 1341.[21] Such an investigation, hardly a game for the uneducated or the poor, could be profitable for the well-to-do; a wealthy seigneur, well served by his *feudistes,* could substantially increase future revenues from a fief. Some of Chaussade's neighbors were researching as he was and managed to oblige him to pay arrears, though his own legal officers did manage some successes in his defense.[22]

Such work in notarial archives with the *terriers* for Guérigny and Villemenant gave Chaussade grounds for claims against Jean Lanvergon, and fourteen years later against his widow, for arrears of unpaid cash (*argent*) totaling 20 livres, 15 sous, of dues payable in fowl (one hen per year) totaling 53 livres, 7 sous, and *corvées* (subject to arrears?) in the amount of 14 livres.[23]

Chaussade appears to have generally taken the offensive—energetically and aggressively—in purchasing and litigation. His continual purchases of lands and rights, even of arrearages per se, and his exchanges of property and conventions with other landed proprietors had the effect of expanding the field of legal enterprise open for his exploitation, thereby perhaps giving pause to persons contemplating action against him.

Sometimes, of course, the rights, properties, or privileges he sought to acquire were directly related to the maintenance or expansion of his industrial plant or facilities. Through an agreement with one seigneur Chaussade was constituted *subrogé,* and in effect beneficiary, of "all his rights and privileges," including the right "*de faire former toutes saisies féodales.*"[24] At least in the case of this seigneury of Beaumont la Ferrière Grenau, Chaussade found it profitable or necessary to pay 13,000 livres for the right to collect feudal dues, with concommitant control of water rights and usages. He was particularly interested in the "pool" (*étang*) of Vingeux and dependencies (a fief that was distinct from the *terre de Frasnay*), probably as a potential source of water power over which he desired control.

Surviving papers record more than a hint of opposition to Chaussade's regime in the environs of Guérigny. A certain Jean Garné complained to Chaussade that the rent he was paying on a piece of pasture (twelve livres a year) was too high; he offered eleven livres instead. Perhaps Garné's complaint was put forth to test his landlord, to see what Chaussade would say or do; perhaps Garné merely wanted to call attention to himself, to show that he could write, and think. He may also have thought it a joke. If Chaussade was amused as he sat in his chateau penning a two-page response to this proposal to reduce the rent by a single livre a year, his amusement did not show. The answer was no; referring the letter, finally, to a subordinate, Chaussade sternly reminded him that this Garné also owed payment of six deniers in *cens* and a bushel of oats.[25]

Some of Chaussade's other renters were less subtle and more blatantly hostile than Garné. Popular irreverence focused on Chaussade's judicial officers and powers and the functioning of his manorial courts. The following condemnation by Lieutenant Juge Bailly of Frasnay is eloquent: "[Having] seen the indecency of the said Pierre Foiny, *martelleur* at the new forge of La Doué, who refused to uncover [i.e., take off his hat] at the opening seance of our present assize, disturbingly insisting that others imitate him in keeping their hats on in contempt and derision for the assembly and the representative of the person of the seigneur and of Justice, and having even made several impertinent remarks; for this irreverence, [we] have condemned and [do] condemn him to a fine of three livres, applicable to the decoration of our court, with injunction made to him, and to all others whom he has insisted on stirring to similar derision at the same time and place, to be more circumspect in the future, on pain of double [the penalty]. This will be imposed notwithstanding opposition or appeal."[26]

Many similar "antisocial" manifestations were reported in the environs of Guérigny. Most, it should be emphasized, seem to have taken place in the early sixties, when the navy's postwar demand for Chaussade's anchors and irons was at a low level. Hundreds of his workers had been laid off. The salaries of workers at some manufactories were in arrears because Chaussade himself had not yet been paid for merchandise he had long since delivered to the arsenals. Jean François Roüelle, Chaussade's senior judicial officer, was expected to deal with this situation.

Roüelle called attention to the prevailing "defiance of the law (*mépris de nos Réglemens*) issued for the exercise of police and good order in many matters." Police powers, an attribute of high justice, authorized the seigneur to promulgate regulations for all the inhabitants of the seigneury. Policing rights included the regulation and management of commerce and the use of thoroughfares. Roüelle mentioned as particularly scandalous the failure to accord the respect and protection owed to the church. "Many parishioners," he said, disobey the rules "with impunity" and display a "spirit of insubordination or rebelliousness":

> [They] indecently stay outside the walls [i.e., in front of the church] during divine service . . . on Sunday and feast days, to the great hurt of our holy religion and public scandal. . . . To remedy this, and also [to control] the pernicious frequenting of cabarets, which is a common and inexhaustible source of the worst disorders . . . we command in His Majesty's name and [that of] justice that all parishioners and strangers who henceforth come to assist at the divine service of the parish range themselves immediately between the second and third bells for mass or for vespers, as close as they can to the altar of the church, the men on one side and the women on the other, without too much commotion and keeping their places; and stay there decently as all Christians should, especially during the sacrifice of the mass, . . . taking care to leave [only] after . . . the priest retires from the host, without tumult, as they should. [It is] forbidden for them to seat themselves, as is their reprehensible custom, [with] their backs turned to the host, either before or

during the sacrifice, on pain of three livres fine against either parishioners or visitors, payable either in cash or by labor service.

Furthermore, we enjoin the guards to visit and inspect carefully each and every cabaret both before and during divine service, and to arrest those found there drinking, and also the tavern-keeper who delivered the drink. And also to arrest on weekdays, Sundays, and feast days alike each and every one of the forge workers whose debaucheries and absence from work are prejudicial to their masters. . . .

The aforesaid tavern-keepers are forbidden furthermore to lodge in their houses any stranger without reporting in writing, on the day of registry, their names and the names of the places from which they have come and those where they will go and why, on pain of twenty livres fine, one-third to the informers and two-thirds to the *domaine seigneuriale*.

It is forbidden also to persons other than the officers and agents of the seigneur to invite outsiders (other than members of the household of the seigneur) to occupy the seats and the chairs . . . [presumably as distinguished from benches, the chairs being reserved for the seigneur's household], on pain of twenty livres fine.

So that the present regulation cannot be called unknown, it will be published and posted on the portal of the church next Sunday.

At the bottom of one copy of the text is an "endorsement": "I, the undersigned curé of the parish of Guérigny, attest to have published the above *ordonnance* last Sunday, the third of October 1762, with the announcements accompanying the mass for my parish." *Signé* "clerk to the Curé of Guérigny."[27]

Nearly identical ordinances were issued by Roüelle and published in the parishes of Richerand, Demeurs, and Saint-Aubin. The text for Saint-Aubin placed even greater stress on controlling forge workers patronizing taverns:

Workers from the forges and furnaces disorganize their work by their debaucheries, to the great detriment of the forgemasters and their *martelleurs;* [they can be] found drinking, eating, and feasting night and day and sometimes [are found] in these cabarets from Sunday to Tuesday . . . a proceeding that is not allowable except for travelers, and never for wage earners [*mercenaires*], who often ruin themselves at those forbidden games whose prohibition we reiterate with the penalty of an arbitrary fine against the gamblers and innkeepers collectively, with loss of

tavern privileges for the first offenders; for habitual drunkards
and children the penalty is corporal punishment.[28]

Just the sort of Sunday quarrel that Roüelle condemned in his ordi-
nance occurred at Michel Minot's cabaret in Guérigny in September
1764. (Interestingly, Chaussade himself was the owner of the tavern;
Minot had merely leased the premises from him.)[29] "The tavern was full
of drinkers, gamblers, quarrelers, and was scandalous in all respects,"
when Eustache Bouvier and Hubert Renoir, carpenter-contractors in
Chaussade's employ, began a fight. Renoir, with the aid of two companions, "so thoroughly beat Bouvier that without medical aid his life would
surely have been in jeopardy." Afterward, Renoir was condemned to pay
Bouvier's medical bills, thirty sous for each day of work Bouvier lost, and
a fine of twelve livres to the *domaine* of the seigneury; each of his companions was to pay three livres and to give three pounds of white candle
wax to the parish church. The tavern-keeper and the victim were also
ordered to pay fines of three livres and a pound of wax apiece to the parish. Renoir and Bouvier were enjoined to live in the future "in good intelligence with each other with no transgression by themselves, or by their
wives, children, companions, or domestics; for their collective good conduct in this respect, the two principals were to be held personally responsible. The tavern-keeper was forbidden henceforth, on pain of fifty livres
fine, to sell either food or drink on Sundays or feast days, or ever to receive any drunks, gamblers, or blasphemers of the holy name of God and
the saints."[30]

Hubert Renoir was apparently not moved to abandon his habit of in-
dulging in drink. One decade later (December 1774), we find him being
"rehired" by Chaussade under a three-year labor contract that carried
the following clause: "If, in spite of all the warnings given to Renoir, he
frequents cabarets on work days, even though he remains there only a
single hour, the present agreement will be void without need of any for-
mality, this clause being absolute (de rigeur)."[31]

Seigneurial Authority and Paternal Discipline

The ordinances promulgated by Roüelle, if the circumstances described
in his commission of appointment still prevailed, were issued "in the
absence of the justices of Monsieur Babaud de la Chaussade."[32] Why
Chaussade's regular justices were absent is not clear. One or more may
have been temporarily relieved of judicial duties because of the successful
action brought against Chaussade by the prince of Condé for the illicit

exercise of powers by his justices at Guérigny, as described above in this chapter. It appears that Roüelle was brought in to act as Chaussade's judicial primate in the difficult circumstances that must still have prevailed at Guérigny and neighboring communities in 1763–1764.[33] Although the particular errors committed by justices in Chaussade's name remain unclear, it appears that "police powers," usually an attribute only of *haute justice*, were used by Chaussade's officers in communities where Chaussade appears to have held only *moyenne* or *basse justice* authority—for example, Richerand and Demeurs, and perhaps Saint-Aubin and Frasnay.

Roüelle and his immediate predecessors, though caught up in extraordinary labor troubles and guilty of judicial errors, were probably conforming closely to Chaussade's expressed wishes. Chaussade, who carefully monitored conditions at Guérigny in the sixties, must have watched Roüelle's performance closely. Roüelle's policing regulations, with their intrusive, paternalistic attention to detail, probably came closer to mirroring Chaussade's thinking, attitudes, and wishes than the work of his regular judicial officials.

Judicial decisions at best served only to ameliorate the symptoms of social problems. From our perspective, however, they offer evidence of the regulatory disposition, paternalism, and benevolent will of a concerned seigneur and entrepreneur. Chaussade sought to impose social controls that he conceived to be in his interest and the interest of the community, his employees, and their wives and children, and conducive to Christian peace and order. If, for example, an employee and his wife died and left minor children, Chaussade's judge might step in to assign the children to the care and tutelage of some person judged to be responsible and competent to manage (essentially as a trustee) any property the children were to inherit when they reached their majority.[34]

Chaussade himself seems to have been involved as a humanitarian arbiter in a number of such actions: lawsuits, succession questions, matrimonial affairs, inheritance problems, post-mortem inventories, and so on.[35] These events were very important in the lives of the humble, often illiterate, members of the community. Chaussade, his *régisseurs,* his clerks and his law men (*notaires, feudistes,* and judges), and his priest were among the few people able to read and write or even sign their names. At a community assemblage held to consider the cession of an old church presbytery and land to Chaussade (described below in this chapter), only three people present were said to be able to write: Chaussade himself, the *notaire,* and the curé.

Much evidence suggests that Chaussade the seigneur was sincerely, paternally interested in helping his people, whom he considered his dependents, part of his seigneury. Though resident in Paris or elsewhere most of the time, Chaussade definitely was not an indifferent absentee lord. He personally appointed his own justices, *notaires, feudistes,* and parish priests. He took great care with estate affairs, sometimes personally selecting minor officials and even their subordinates. We have records of his interviewing and appointing suitable persons. He wrote to the officers of the *Maîtrise royalle des eaux et forêts de Nivernais,* which was not his preserve, requesting (tantamount to ordering) that one Vincent Beaufils be received and "given the oath" as "guard of our woodlands, fisheries, and hunting preserve in our *châtellenie* of Narcy." [36] He saw to the appointment of one Jacques Joseph Haly as *procureur* and *greffier* in his courts with wages of twenty-four livres a year. [37] He wrote to his *notaire* and *procureur fiscal* at Guérigny, Bort, reporting the visit to his offices in Paris of "one of the boys who work under the orders of the *capitaines des chasses* at Chantilly, where they take wolves, foxes, and other '*mauvais bêtes.*' Their wages are very small. He is very poor. But if he can really catch wolves, he would be a treasure for our parishes." [38] Very few persons were authorized to possess or use firearms to hunt—hence Chaussade's keen interest in this young man.

Chaussade went beyond interviewing, selecting, and appointing both senior and subordinate officers; he sometimes went so far as to advise them how best to get along together. On one occasion he told one of a group of subordinates who worked together that he deplored their habit of eating together. And writing to Bort, apparently on the eve of a trip, he said: "I want, on my first trip, to have nothing but reason for satisfaction and [to hear] that each [of you], in his discharge of responsibilities, earned and merited my confidence." [39]

Chaussade at times required seigneurial judges to submit to him regular reports on the docket of court cases with which they had dealt, including details of penalties and fines. Thus we have a copy of Bort's report listing the cases of illegal grazing that came before him in the seigneurial court at Guérigny:

> 23 *September 1768.* Pelletier caught eight cows in the woods of Biez, six [belonged] to Moizy, hammersmith of Marcy; the other two to Josep Henry, also employed at Marcy. M. de la Chaussade ruled [in this case], ordering fines of three livres for each animal . . . to be deducted [from the account of each animal-owner] by the office at Guérigny.
> 23 *December 1768.* Thirteen cows taken at the chateau, seven belonging to Baudry [the *régisseur*], who paid three livres, of which I gave twelve sous to the takers; six other cows claimed by Chausson, hammersmith at

Poelonnerie, three livres [fine], of which notice was given to the office for Chausson's account.

29 December 1768. Six cows taken, fines of three livres, six livres, and three livres, to be paid by owners.

4 January 1769. Note to the office: withhold two livres, eight sous from the account of Pierrot; from that of Chausson [withhold] one livre, four sous for six of the cows taken by domestics of the chateau, to whom one livre, four sous was given; remainder to the office.

10 March 1769. Assisted at inspection of some pieces of oak cut illegally by the *métayer de Chatre* in the pasture of the *domaine.* Judgment: twenty-seven livres fine, three to the forest guard, twenty-four to the office of the seigneur.

[*Date unknown*]. Four horses taken, six livres fine withheld from Guillemot, three livres paid to guard Pelletier.[40]

Rules about pasturing and foraging were intended, as one of Chaussade's magistrates put it, "to render the inhabitants more attentive to guarding their animals."[41] In Chaussade's own view, wandering animals and marauding humans alike had to be controlled to prevent damage to the property interests of the lord and to maintain customary (community) rights, but he made exceptions for pecuniary reasons. Some controlled grazing was allowed. Pasturing privileges were leased or sold, sometimes on a seasonal basis. Chaussade even permitted owners of pigs to take their marked or tagged animals into his woodlands to forage, after a pasturage fee of twenty sous was paid for each pig.[42] But no animals were to be "tethered among the vines," on pain of a thirty-sous fine for each animal. Dogs and pigs found in the vineyards without tethers were to be killed.

Evidently Chaussade's police and judicial authorities favored the use of a variable system of pecuniary penalties. Documents produced by that system, cited above, disclose significant details about the fiscal organization and management of the estates themselves and the manufactories established on them. Bort's report implies that an account was maintained at an "office" at Guérigny for every person employed in the manufactories in the region of his jurisdiction. At a separate "bureau of the seigneur," accounts relating to the administration of the lord's domains were apparently kept, along with records for persons leasing, renting, or working as laborers, cash-renters, or sharecroppers (*métayers*) on Chaussade's estates, whether they were connected with the manufactory or not.

The landed and manufacturing sectors of Chaussade's holdings were kept separate for fiscal purposes; yet they were integrated where forest, forage, food production, and housing for livestock and humans were concerned. Agricultural, pastoral, woodland, manufacturing, commercial, and governmental operations were carried on concurrently and directed by the seigneur, assisted by his functionaries. Law enforcement in the seigneurial communities was at least partly auto-financed by Chaussade and his magistrates, some of the funds deriving from fines being used to elicit help from private citizens, and to energize regularly appointed but low-salaried guards, by offering bounties. A transgressor could be certain, whether his account was with the "bureau at Guérigny" or with the "office of the seigneur," that conviction would result in substantial debiting. He was apt to pay especially dearly if he transgressed when Chaussade was on his estates and taking part in the proceedings.

Theoretically his decisions and convictions could be appealed. But appeals were expensive. Anyone contemplating an appeal might be advised to note the case of three *laboureurs* ("well-to-do" peasants)—the brothers Pierre and François Bernard and Vrain Fouchère and his wife—who jointly appealed a case involving forest law. We can assume that they collectively had considerable financial resources. Their appeal was successful in the intermediate-level courts, where it was decided that Chaussade's attorneys had provided insufficient proofs. But Chaussade's attorneys continued the case to a higher jurisdiction, "to the Siège Général de la Table de Marbre du Palais à Paris," where the decision apparently went to Chaussade by default. His opponents were then condemned to pay aggregate litigation costs.[43]

Added evidence of Chaussade's local role—some might say paternal disposition—is implicit in his decision, after many years of delay, to build a new church and presbytery for the community of Guérigny, in part at least at his own expense. The new buildings, completed and put into use around 1767 or 1768, cost, Chaussade said, 40,000 livres.[44]

The need for the new structures can be traced to problems of the Guérigny church that were evident early in the century. The problems antedated Chaussade's arrival; indeed, when Masson bought the Guérigny property in the 1720s, the church structure was (to use Chaussade's phrase) "in a state of complete destruction. The presbytery had collapsed long before."[45] Standing on low ground, near the banks of the river Nièvre, the old church was subject to flooding. A committee of inspectors reported in August 1743 that it "could not be rebuilt." The walls were weak, the timbering was in "very bad state," the foundations could "not be made good, at least without sinking piles, which would be very costly." The committee recommended "another church, built in another place."[46] But it was not until March 1746 that parishioners were informed of this report. By that date the number of persons inhabiting the parish had increased, partly in consequence of expanded activity in the manufactory. The parishioners, led by the curé (Chaussade's appointee), "humbly begged the said Sieur Babaud de la Chaussade to undertake, in an act of charity toward them, to construct at his cost . . . a new church and presbytery"; they offered to "cede and abandon to Chaussade full proprietorship of the old church, cemetery, and presbytery and the land on which they were established."[47]

Chaussade's response to this request, though affirmative, was surprisingly insensitive to the interests of the community. His counteroffer, apparently a rigorous, self-serving business arrangement, was expressed in writing, "in his name," but explained by others in his absence. Several provisions seem to suggest an intention to delay or postpone full implementation. His affairs in the transition years following Masson's death were extraordinarily complex and diverse; moreover, he was then new to many Guérigny problems. He did have a local counsellor on the church matter (perhaps M. Bort, *feudiste* and *notaire*), in whose opinions he seems to have had confidence, judging from his letter to this unidentified counsellor in March 1743: "I depend on you, Monsieur, as regards the church and presbytery of Guérigny. I have no alternative but to do what you have explained to me."[48]

In his response, Chaussade accepted the land the community proposed to cede and agreed to give the parishioners and curé suitable dry land elsewhere for the new buildings. Emphasizing that he was granting this double gratuity "purely voluntarily," he agreed also to furnish necessary construction materials, provided certain conditions were met. *First,* the cost of maintenance and repairs on the new structures would, by notarized act, henceforth be the responsibility of the parishioners, not Chaussade and his heirs. *Second,* "salvage materials from the old church and other usable salvage materials belonging to the community . . . will be used in the new constructions. [The community] can even, if it is not too inconvenient for the inhabitants, and if they are in a position to do so, be obliged to furnish the wagons, the number to be determined, required to move materials." Before construction there was also "the expense of installing bells, if there are some; or if there are none, the expense of locating and furnishing them." Moreover, "the bishop or someone commissioned by him must plant a cross on the spot where the altar will be, which must be placed so that the priest presiding at the altar looks eastward. It is also usual practice that the bishop should bless, or have blessed, the first stone." After all this has been done, an act of agreement with the inhabitants "will be made, which will contain recognition of the rights of the founder-patron and nominator of the curé."[49]

The curé and parishioners unanimously accepted Chaussade's offer. But construction of the new church was long delayed. The community was poor, without either funds or leadership to advance the work. The very terms of the contract with Chaussade alienated other potential (seigneurial) support. Ten years went by, and as late as 1755, the new church and presbytery were not yet begun. The priests appointed to the parish, being Chaussade appointees, were naturally responsive to his wishes. His first titulary was Jean-Baptiste Juniat, from Basse-Marche in the diocese of Limoges, a blood relative of Chaussade's from the environs of Bellac, Chaussade's own birthplace. Father Juniat was curé of the parish (Saint Amand) of Guérigny for about fifteen years (July 1744 to August 1759).[50] His successor was Claude Greffier, already a priest of the bishop's diocese and again, of course, the choice of Chaussade; he served until 1768.[51] Next in succession came Antoine Pifault.[52]

Until 1766, by Chaussade's own admission, the divine service at Guérigny was held in the chapel of Chaussade's chateau, which was much too small: as Chaussade later said, "three-quarters of the inhabitants and workers remained outside during the service." The poverty of the humble people of the parish made it "impossible for them to contribute to the reconstruction," and it was that fact, said Chaussade, that finally moved him late in the 1760s to undertake to construct a new presbytery and a new church twice the size of the old one. Later still, in 1779, he offered a new, more comfortable parish house to the Curé de Saint-Agnan.[53]

The site of the old presbytery, church, and cemetery, down by the river, had by the 1760s long since been ceded to Chaussade. On precisely this site, where the village itself had once stood, Chaussade built his new manufactory. It was close to the junction of the two branches of the river Nièvre, a good place to generate water power for the bellows, hammers, and other machinery installed in his new anchor forges and auxiliary facilities. Here, after the old church and cemetery had been removed, Chaussade built his new millrace and mill. Near the manufactories, as if for lack of space elsewhere, he chose to build his new chateau and along with it, very close by, auxiliary buildings to house the offices and provide lodgings for the *régisseur* and staff who directed and managed the works and for his workers.

Chaussade's chateau at Guérigny was destined never to be finished, at least in his time. The project was an ambitious one for a man whose capital was so heavily committed to business. Over the years, by his estimate, he put over 100,000 livres into the chateau. In 1769, when he was trying to sell his holdings to a group of businessmen, he estimated the cost of completing the chateau at "under 50,000 livres."[54] The fact that he was

disposed to sell his properties *in toto* (forges, foundries, forests, and chateau as well) should not be taken to mean that he was not fond of the
place. Being just a few score yards from the forges of Guérigny, however,
the chateau was inseparably and perhaps uncomfortably close. The location of the chateau, the simplicity and practicality of its design, and its
proximity to the manufactory made it better suited to housing a plant
manager and his clerks and staff with perhaps some senior workmen than
a nobleman and his family. Chaussade had conflicting inclinations. His
nature and experience alike led him to act as a plant superintendant
might. But later he came to think of himself as an aristocrat, and he liked
and wanted to live nobly; hence he may later have regretted the early decision to place his chateau so close to his Guérigny manufactories.

When Chaussade and his family were "in residence" at Guérigny, as
they sometimes were for a few weeks of the year, Chaussade seems to
have spent much time at his desk. If the season happened to be one when
water levels allowed the forges to work, he could hardly have escaped
constant reminders of business—the calls of workmen and the nearby
whirr and thump and clatter of machines, including the crash of his
thousand-pound forge hammers. Only a few minutes were required to
stroll over from his chateau to watch his machines and workers in action.
He had a long-standing interest in machines, and he may have inspected
the specialty ovens and furnaces, or the machines he had had brought in
or built, or innovative processes or products that were being tried. He
also took time away for the hunt. He owned hundreds of horses, most of
them draft animals, of course, but also some riding stock, and many
thousands of acres of accessible woodland and forest. Perhaps it is significant that he chose in his portrait to be pictured with hunting dog and
gun—as an aristocrat.

Some of Chaussade's intervals of relaxation at Guérigny were no doubt
spent on the grounds of the chateau itself, among servants and family. Of
the servants there were always many, though they were certainly most numerous when the two sets of children, by his two successive wives, were
at hand. In those days there must have been more than a score of full-time
personal servants and many maintenance people living and working about
the chateau. Later, in retirement, after the children were grown and his
wives had died and he had sold off Guérigny and much else, Chaussade
still kept nine active servants (two of them semiretired). One other personal servant had by then been pensioned off and was living elsewhere.
The list of his servants, with an indication of the sum he intended in 1787
to leave to each of them by his will, included the following:

Champagne, "my first lackey"	1,200 livres
François, "my second lackey"	600 livres
Noisette, first coachman	1,000 livres
Benoit, second coachman	500 livres
Cuisinier (no name given)	400 livres
Marie Ann, *fille de cuisine* and the wife of Champagne	300 livres
Fleuri, "my porter"	200 livres

He had with him also the Demoiselle Le Glaire, "who served my last wife for many long years as maid-servant and who has remained with me," and the Demoiselle Le Gendre, "who raised my children and who still lives with me." To each he left 1,500 livres. Living elsewhere was Nicolas Gabriel François de La Ferté, "first lackey to my late wife, whom I have kept since her decease, but who cannot serve because of his infirmities, . . . now resident at his birthplace with his wife" (pension—512 livres). Some of these people must have been with the family during its sojourns at Guérigny.[55]

We know nothing for certain of Chaussade's personal preferences in food, but a few of the expense accounts of Mademoiselle Dautrec, housekeeper at the chateau in the 1750s, have survived. They suggest an ample larder and table. The account for the chateau for 11 January 1755 included 56 livres of beef, 16 livres of veal, 4 livres of butter, and 10 dozen eggs.[56]

The contents of Chaussade's wine cellar naturally changed over time. We do not have an inventory of the cellar at the chateau, but after his death in Paris the inventory of his cellar listed the following items:

A quarter-cask of *vin blanc de Pouilly*	60 livres
102 bottles of Beaune	80 livres
40 bottles of Bordeaux	30 livres
18 bottles of misc. reds and whites	36 livres
3 *eau de vie*	5 livres
450 empty bottles	

Stored with the wines was a *balle* of 200 livres of *café moka* with an estimated value of 300 livres.[57]

On the grounds and wooded environs of his chateau at Guérigny, Chaussade was most surely in his element as seigneur. He was entitled to display, on the portals of the manufactory and beside the esplanade of his chateau, his authorized coat of arms, a copy of which he obtained around 1764, and a new copy of which he requested in 1784 from M. D'Hozier de Serigny, royal genealogist.[58] Close to the chateau and manufactory he built stables and barns for livestock and kept stockpiles of necessary fodder and hay. He also built a long line of two-story rowhouses where some of his employees lived, within sight of the manufactories and of his chateau. Preoccupied with efficiency, he observed that when workers are scattered, "they are much less prompt in appearing for work, and to prevent the abuses and prejudice that can result, it is extremely desirable that they be on hand to receive quickly the orders of the directors of the forges." At some of his works, Chaussade provided an added inducement to promptness and assiduity by installing a large iron clock on the top of one of the buildings. He was also in a position—through the priests he chose for his parishes—to influence his workers and even to determine the moral lessons they were taught. Guérigny offered many opportunities for Chaussade's paternalism. He liked to point out that workers "come from two or three leagues to work for me" at Guérigny. "I cannot get along without them, and I am necessary for them."[59] He had a special liking for a local *chirurgien,* a certain Sieur Henry, who "for twenty years was established at Guérigny, where he exercised his profession," as Chaussade phrased it, "with zeal and disinterestedness." As a bequest to the good surgeon's widow, Chaussade saw fit to leave a pension of 150 livres a year "free of royal taxes."[60]

We have seen that when he was unpaid by the state, Chaussade wrote *mémoires* and dozens of letters to the ministries of finance and marine and various intendants. It is fair to say that compassion for workers whose wages were due and past-due was one of his motives. Similarly, when local grain prices rose at Guérigny in the late sixties, the workers turned for help to Chaussade's local representative, at that time Pierre Robreget, *régisseur* for the region of Guérigny, Frasnay, Villemenant, and Demeurs. Robreget purchased a quantity of low-priced grain at a town many miles away, no doubt with Chaussade's knowledge and consent, and authorized dispatch of a "pack-train" to transport it. Eighteen horses were drawn from stables at Demeurs, and six mules and two horses from Frasnay, to go with four men to fetch the grain and bring it to Guérigny, where the cargo was destined "to be distributed to workers of different forges and manufactories." On 29 and 30 June (1770) the twenty-six animals, each carrying two large sacks of grain, were en route in four separate contingents when groups of armed men stopped and seized the grain. The four accompanying drivers were released, given a small quantity of grain for themselves, and naïvely told to go home and say nothing. Their arrival at Guérigny, almost empty-handed, generated a wave of indignation. An angry posse of sixty workers swarmed out of town, determined to use force if need be to recover the grain. Their "vigorous search" led to the sacks, in various hiding places in wooded parcels, whence virtually all of the shipment was safely brought to Guérigny. Reassuring the authorities about this affair, Chaussade declared that the people of the parish of Poisseaux, who ambushed the pack trains, "are very bad; mine are [by contrast] tranquil." If necessary, he said, "force must repel force. . . . my *forgerons* [and workers] gave examples of their formidable superiority. But they are restrained by good order, by people in authority who watch out for them; furthermore, unhappy people approach my managers with confidence about their special needs, and they regard me as their father." [61]

Further indications of Chaussade's paternal, albeit self-interested, disposition toward the Guérigny community are implicit in his long-sustained, and ultimately successful efforts to obtain authorization to hold a regular local market and an annual fair for the town. Local people urging that he seek these privileges were probably influenced by the example of their neighbors. Nearby communities in the barony of Frasnay, for example, enjoyed the double privilege of a weekly (Thursday) market and a market fair twice each year. [62] The historically smaller Guérigny had participated in the events held by more populous neighboring communities—not only Frasnay, but also the big river towns of Nevers and La Charité. Thus the merchants and elders of those communities would be apt to oppose the idea of allowing the inhabitants of Guérigny to hold their own market and fair.

Chaussade, as seigneur of Guérigny, was willing and even eager to obtain permission from regional and royal authorities to hold such markets. We have evidence that he attempted to do so in 1766. Opposition to the proposal came from nearby Nevers, where it was claimed that a weekly market at Guérigny would divert grain sales from Nevers and reduce certain tax revenues. [63] The opposition appears to have prevailed in this case, but Chaussade did succeed in obtaining a semiannual fair for Guérigny. The inhabitants of the parish learned officially of his success on 17 July 1774. That Sunday morning:

> before the principal portal of the parish church of Guérigny, the
> usual place to hold gatherings of the inhabitants of the parish,
> at ten in the morning following high mass, the assembly was
> convoked by the toll of the bell in the usual manner by Pierre
> Tericot, farmer of the domaine of Chatre. The people were in-
> formed by officers of the *bailliage* that the *Conseil Supérieur de
> Clermont Ferrand* had [finally] issued letters patent of the king
> for October 1772 establishing two fairs for Guérigny, to be held
> on 4 May and 12 November each year.

The assembled inhabitants, at the request of the officials, declared "with unanimity that they had no knowledge of any other fair for four leagues around the parish that was held on those two days," and they "consented to their establishment, which they regard as the result of the zeal of the seigneur [Pierre Babaud de la Chaussade] for their *bien et avantage.*" [64]

As lord of Guérigny, Chaussade wanted his final resting place to be there. As early as March 1746, when the community was writing the contract ceding the sites of the old church and presbytery, Chaussade expressed his interest in the "rights of the founder-patron," which commonly included that of inhumation. He did so again in the 1760s, when the new church was completed. Apparently he never changed his preference on that score. Guérigny was the place where he was known best, where he sincerely believed people had esteem for him. It was there that he had established his manufactories and by enlarging them provided many people of the community with work. Through his many kindnesses to acquaintances and friends in the town, he hoped to be long remembered as the patron-seigneur, the most famous figure in the history of the town—or even of the region. Hence he had his attorneys include in his testament, this expression of his sentiments:

> I commend my soul to God and beg the Divine Mercy of Salva-
> tion. I wish my body to be sent to Guérigny and interred in
> the vault of Guérigny, which is part of the land that I sold to
> His Majesty, and which I reserved as my sepulcher. I declare
> that vanity has no part in my intentions, but only the desire to
> perpetuate the memory in that country that I constructed the
> church and presbytery and that I gave the site, without the par-
> ish's having contributed anything. In consequence I leave to my
> children . . . the liberty to do what they judge most proper in
> execution of this wish. [65]

The desire to recover seigneurial authority and exercise it to the fullest possible extent was hardly unique to Chaussade. On the contrary— several parlements were currently giving support and encouragement to the revival and exercise of seigneurial powers. In 1736 we find an *arrêt* of the Parlement of Bordeaux "rendered in favor of seigneurs, against the peasants, for the payment of seigneurial obligations." [66] Exactly four decades later, in 1776, the Parlement of Paris urged the importance, for public tranquility, of maintaining "old and immutable principles that some unquiet souls seem to want to alter . . ." (perhaps an allusion to Turgot's attempted reforms or to agricultural "modernization" movements both in France and abroad). The court (parlement) "commands all subjects of the king, [including] vassals and ordinary subjects of particular seigneurs," to continue to acquit rights and duties as in the past, both to their king and to particular seigneurs in accord with the ordinances and declarations of the realm . . . [and] general and local customs." The *arrêt* of 1776 expressly forbade "any innovation contrary to the aforesaid legitimate and approved rights and usages on pain, for violators, of extraordinary prosecution and exemplary punishment as subverters of the laws and disturbers of public peace." Copies of this decree were ordered printed, registered, and sent "immediately" to all *bailliages, sénéchaussées,* "and even to seigneurial justices under the immediate jurisdiction of the court."[67] Chaussade should have received a copy of that document. Reading it, he would have nodded his assent. Renovators of *terriers* and investors in seigneurial lands and tenures, such as he, were bound to be pleased to see that the powerful parlements were still using the weight of their authority to ensure the continuance and even invigoration of the *régime seigneurial.* Chaussade believed, as did many *parlementaires,* that seigneuries were still one of the best investments open to enterprising men of means.

III. Market Problems, Return to Timber, and Retirement

CHAPTER 8

Markets for Anchors, Irons, and Steel

Government Markets

As long as the navy was his principal customer, Chaussade was vulnerable to drastic fluctuations in demand in war and peace. Had he been simply a merchant of irons, he could easily have adjusted to differences by increasing or ceasing his purchases of irons for resale. But as a manufacturer he had heavy investments in labor force, equipment, and plant; skilled workers at his forges and mills, hundreds of semiskilled workers, and laborers and their families depended on him for their livelihood. Moreover, at the time of his most severe crisis (1758–1760), when he was instructed by the navy to stop deliveries to the arsenals, the navy owed him almost a million livres for deliveries made over the half-dozen years preceding. Hence he had to contend not only with the collapse of demand, but also with problems of nonpayment: his workers were unpaid; hundreds were laid off and unemployed; and his own creditors were demanding payment. The very ownership of his manufacturing plants and estates was legally at risk, since all his holdings had been mortgaged—the expansion of his manufactories after 1752 had been partly financed with borrowed funds, on which he was still obligated to make regular payments of interest. Though the risk of foreclosure was probably infinitesimal, since the navy would almost certainly move to protect its suppliers, Chaussade was under great pressure to find means to continue to operate his manufacturing plants, some of them an integral part of his estates.

To that end, as we have seen, he sought to diversify. He brought in workers with new skills to re-equip and establish new plants and to introduce different processes to enable him to turn out new products. His aim was to develop a line of iron and steel goods more varied than his traditional offerings. He needed alternative markets, a broad clientele in the trades, and continuous sales in order to continue to operate his plants, keep his workers employed, and meet interest payments and ongoing costs. In the long term he meant to reduce his excessive dependence on a single customer, the navy. To do so he hoped to penetrate commercial markets with his anchors and irons, and to produce and sell a diversified line of general hardware and steel goods.

Initially the family partners took pride in the fact that the navy was their principal customer and that their manufactories were the Forges Royales, specializing in the production of anchors of the largest sizes and highest quality for the king's navy. Chaussade doubled production capacity at his anchor and iron forges in the years 1749 to 1754. For him those were the halcyon years of the Rouillé ministry, when he became "*fournisseur général.*" He coveted monopoly status because it meant less risk, assurance of a market, and the elimination of competition from the other *fournisseurs*. In fact, however, he never had a monopoly. The navy was never his private market for anchors and irons. The most he could claim was that at certain times before the Seven Years War, he was the near-exclusive supplier (but only of anchors) for the largest arsenal, the port of Brest. Other *fournisseurs* were major suppliers of irons to Rochefort. Many of the anchors and irons used at Toulon, on the Mediterranean littoral, were imported from abroad, especially from Spain.

There were really three official or semiofficial government markets where Chaussade's iron and steel manufacturers might be sold: the navy, the Compagnie des Indes, and the French colonies overseas. The principal *fournisseur* of irons to the Compagnie over a period of at least thirty years was a certain Claude Le Blanc, who leased the forges of Clavières and used them as his base of operations until after the mid-1760s. However, in May 1738, on the eve of the War of the Austrian Succession, Maurepas wrote to the navy's *commissaire* on the Loire informing him that the Compagnie had made a contract with "the Sieur [Jean] Babaud" for deliveries of anchors and had a pressing need for them in view of the likelihood that war would soon break out. As soon as possible, he said, shipments should be sent to the French colonies overseas. Maurepas, as minister of both the navy and the colonies, urged that work for the navy be suspended until the following November to expedite the Compagnie's shipments to the colonies.[1] Later that year, on 26 December 1738, the Compagnie's own forges at Lorient were destroyed by fire; as a direct result, Chaussade was granted a contract on 27 February 1739 to deliver general irons to the Compagnie.[2] That was Chaussade's first contract to supply the Compagnie's own needs; it was probably under an extension of its terms that the "widow Babaud (et Cie.)" delivered anchors to the Compagnie in August 1739 and in 1740.[3]

A decade later, in the ministry of Rouillé, Chaussade inaugurated a series of major provisionments to the Compagnie. He signed a six-year contract on 19 June 1749 promising delivery of anchors, parts of anchors, and pieces for the strengthening (*radoub*) of both anchors and iron *courbes,* used to reenforce or replace compass or curved timber and knees, which were then scarce.[4] In that contract Chaussade agreed to some unusually rigorous terms for the testing and reception of the merchandise he delivered. Article 8 provided for the testing of anchors by forge hammer blows and capstan trials in harbor conditions—the kind of testing practiced at the king's arsenals. In addition, Chaussade agreed to allow the Compagnie to return anchors judged to be defective, even after they had been used at sea: "if they do not resist the efforts of the sea during the first campaign or voyage they make, I will be obliged to take them back when they are represented to me as defective, and [I will] furnish others at my cost and risk." This provision obliged him to allow three years for the testing, since a campaign to India or China could require eighteen months (or more) each way.[5] These testing conditions were far more demanding than those the navy usually exacted from its *fournisseurs.*

Chaussade's acceptance of such severe, potentially troublesome, and costly provisions can be taken as an indication that he was very anxious to get the contract with the Compagnie. In 1749 he must have seen it as an important potential peacetime customer. Particularly in the immediate postwar period, the armaments and shipments destined for colonies overseas were apt to be active, and the Compagnie's ships and its base at Lorient were considerable consumers of anchors and irons.

Not only the eastern, but all the colonial trades, must have interested Chaussade as potential markets for anchors and irons, agricultural implements, hardware, tools, ship fittings, industrial supplies, and a variety of building materials. Irons destined for colonies could often be conveniently shipped as ballast aboard outbound ships. The colonies had, moreover, been isolated from the mother country during hostilities, allowing colonial demand to build up and offering an attractive market at precisely the time when demand from the navy was at low ebb. Thus the Compagnie and the colonies on the one hand, and the navy on the other, complemented each other nicely as markets for Chaussade's production. Clearly, he had reason to be keenly interested in the contract he sighed with the Compagnie des Indes in June 1749.

Chaussade's connection with Michel, one of the Compagnie's directors, gave him no evident advantage in the terms of the contract, but the connection may have helped in getting it. His connection with Rouillé doubtless helped him more. When the Compagnie ordered 92 anchors and, in the summer of 1751, increased that order to 254, Chaussade had to warn Rouillé that he might have difficulty filling such large orders without compromising his *fourniture* for the navy. Rouillé reassured him: "I will see what needs to be done to conciliate the interests of the two services." [6] Six months later Rouillé expressed approbation of Chaussade's arrangements with the Compagnie: "one can only approve the motives that led you to assume these obligations, and I hope that they are advantageous for you." [7]

Several years later, in 1757, after war had broken out, we find Chaussade reporting that he could not satisfy the pressing needs of both the Compagnie and the navy, because their combined needs for irons exceeded the capacity of his manufactories. He proposed therefore that the navy finance further expansion of his production facilities. That proposal was emphatically vetoed by the marquis de Moras (de Peirenc) then minister of marine, who countered with the surprising suggestion that Chaussade satisfy the needs of the Compagnie first. Moras promised, much to Chaussade's chagrin, no doubt, to ask all the ports to scale down their earlier estimates of navy requirements—which Moras thought had been exorbitant anyway. He promised to send Chaussade the revised estimates as orders (*états*) for the coming year. "By this means, I calculate it will be less difficult for you to satisfy the needs of the ports without multiplying the objects of expenditure, which the scarcity of funds does not permit." By remarking pointedly to Chaussade that he assumed Chaussade's forges would "be working only for the king," Moras revealed that he suspected (or knew) that they would *not* be. [8]

The Search for Commercial Markets

Chaussade's effort in 1757 to get the navy to finance the further expansion of his plant came at a time when he was already involved in diversification. He had doubled his anchor production on the eve of the war and was certainly aware that the naval demand for anchors and heavy irons would probably collapse with the restoration of peace, if not before; surely his thoughts had already turned to development along commercial lines. As later became clear, he was becoming interested in turning out small forgings of many kinds, in building facilities for nail production, and in creating new facilities to produce edge-tools; and he wanted the slitting mills to produce hoop or strip iron "in the German manner." These were the mills and facilities that he later declared (in 1763) he had built during the war.[9] In fact, at least as early as the spring of 1761, Chaussade remarked that he had some of those facilities in operation, and had already produced and stockpiled "pig iron, nails, and worked irons of all kinds" to the value of 300,000 livres. Those irons he intended to sell commercially as soon as practicable.[10] Thus during the period 1757–1760, Chaussade planned and developed important new production facilities, and even in the midst of the war, diversified plant and product, preparing to step briskly into new markets at the restoration of peace. By 1760 the initial phases of his transformation of production facilities had been accomplished; the market phase of his diversification program lay ahead.

Chaussade's market problems were complex, in part because very different requirements had to be met in different markets. Not only were naval and commercial requirements different; there were unique problems to be met in dealing at each arsenal, with the Compagnie des Indes, and with each commercial port, and overseas colonial market. Chaussade's manufactories were designed to produce high-quality forgings, large and small anchors, shipbuilding irons, and tools. Yet his plants were hundreds of kilometers from navy yards and the sea. Guérigny and Cosne and their environs offered adequate stocks of the resources essential to the industry—wood fuel and water for power—and although iron ore supplies were getting short, pig and bar iron could be brought in more easily than fuel or power. His two centers can probably be considered efficient, economically viable facilities capable of producing at costs competitive with those of plants much closer to the seaboard markets.

But Guérigny and Cosne, and all the other forges in the Nivernais and the Berry as well, were obviously dependent on the networks of rivers, canals, and roads for access to markets. Shipments destined for the royal navy were, as we have seen, furnished with *passeports* exempting them from tolls and tariffs. Chaussade's anchors and irons destined for commercial users, however, enjoyed no exemption. His iron manufactures not only paid the *marques des fers et sur les aciers,*[11] but also the tariffs and tolls collected at many points along the rivers, canals, and roads over which they passed in transit to their destination. Chaussade's prices had to rise to cover carriage costs plus the total amount paid in tariffs and tolls en route.

The problem was how to compete with foreign manufacturers who marketed their irons on the seaboard of France. In particular, Chaussade's goods had to be competitive with irons from Spain and those from

Sweden, the latter of which were usually brought in by the Dutch. The methods he used to try to meet this foreign competition reveal a good deal about Chaussade himself and the political, fiscal, and general commercial milieu in which he and other Frenchmen did business.

The schemes that Chaussade devised to promote commercial sales of his anchors and irons at French ports displayed both his energy and the fertility of his mind. From the very outset he sought the help of government officials. He was in an unusually good position to secure the intervention of officials in the top echelons of government in his behalf. He had the ministers of marine and finance write to the chambers of commerce at the ports to "introduce" him and recommend his products.[12] Then, by means of personal letters and *mémoires* that were in fact circular letters, he arranged a series of visits to French ports, including appearances before the chambers of commerce at Nantes, La Rochelle, and Bordeaux.[13]

The chambers of commerce at all these ports were informed, in essence, that the Royal Council and the ministries of marine and finance would see with satisfaction preference given to Chaussade's anchors over imported ones. With recommendations from such high authorities, Chaussade's visits and proposals were bound to receive serious, though not necessarily favorable, attention. Surviving correspondence reveals that by early August 1760, Chaussade had specific invitations from authorities at Nantes, La Rochelle, and Bordeaux to visit them and discuss his products. He was also urged, especially by the chamber at Bordeaux, to ship samples of his anchors and other irons to the port. He readily consented to do so and with minimum delay undertook his planned itinerary of visits.[14]

Chaussade spent three weeks at Nantes in late August and September 1760, intending, as he said, "to familiarize myself fully with the anchors and irons that enter this city, the prices at which they are sold, and the reasons for the extensive use made of them here and at other ports in peacetime while our [i.e., French] forges languish and cannot sustain themselves." The merchants and shippers consulted by the Chamber of Commerce at Nantes assured him that they wanted him to continue to manufacture anchors on the river Loire; they found all sorts of advantages for Nantes and for other ports in having him do so. But as Chaussade himself phrased it: "they are aware that I do not know how to reduce the price [of my anchors] to the [level of] the imports, and it is this fact that is the subject of their deliberation. They consulted the intendant of Brittany, who is here for the meetings of the *Etats*. They asked me for a *mémoire,* which I have given to them."[15]

Chaussade's six-page *mémoire* to the chamber at Nantes "made known," as he phrased it, "the importance of the establishments of the Sieur de la Chaussade, the reasons why he is hindered in furnishing anchors for commercial use, and the means that can procure acceptance [of his anchors]." Chaussade professed to be shocked that foreign anchors were commonly sold more cheaply at Nantes than French ones. "Spain is . . . the source of the anchors in use. Their price at Nantes is from 28 to 30 livres the quintal. The Sieur de la Chaussade cannot sell his anchors at less than 35 livres." Thus there was a difference of up to 7 livres, or 20 to 25 percent.

Spanish irons, as distinguished from anchors, were a special problem. Chaussade expressed astonishment at the "great consumption of foreign irons at Nantes, above all those from Spain. . . . What is not easy to understand is that irons from Spain are sold at Nantes at 180 to 190 livres the millier (1,000 livres) and those from Anjou, Berry, Maine, and Brittany from 20 to 40 livres less." Thus French irons were offered for sale at Nantes at substantially *lower* prices than the imports from Spain; yet the higher-priced Spanish products were heavily—indeed, almost exclusively—used.[16]

Chaussade attributed the preference for Spanish irons largely to the "misguided choices" of the buyers. "The iron of Spain," said Chaussade, is "soft (*mou*) and pliable (*sans consistance*); workers can work it with ease and that makes them prefer it. People of town and country alike suffer notable damage in consequence. They do not notice that the same piece of work in Berry iron will last three times as long. They employ it [Spanish iron] at Paris in the most important [decorative?] work, where the beauty of the iron is the essential need, and similar use is made of it in the provinces." Yet "that malleability in which the worker finds his ease . . . betrays those who are not alert to the difference in durability."[17] Chaussade's own plants, working with Berry and Nivernais pig iron, produced a good many "mild steel" products, but apparently little or none of the "soft," malleable iron preferred by smithies and artisans in France.

The Warehouse Scheme and the Search for Privilege

Chaussade knew that he could not continue to operate his Forges Royales for anchors without an assured commercial market. He was realist enough to see as well that his project of marketing anchors at commercial ports could not possibly succeed unless the prices of foreign anchors and his own were equalized. As far as he could determine during his visit to

Nantes, anchors from the north presented no great problem. None were manufactured in Russia ("siberie," as he called it). The anchors from Sweden "have always sold, without much change, at about 15–16 and 17 florins before export," bringing their price with commission and freight to 35 or 36 livres or more in France. "They send many to our ports, but rarely larger than 600 livres in weight; larger ones must be specially ordered, which is inconvenient." In the Nantes market the main obstacles were the low cost of anchors imported from Spain.[18]

At La Rochelle in late October, Chaussade had "many conferences with the Chamber of Commerce. Talks were concluded by a general assembly of shipowners and merchants; all of them said it would be very interesting for them if I establish here [at La Rochelle] a warehouse [*magazin*] for anchors of assorted sizes as soon as peace is restored. But the same thinking prevails here as at Nantes": prices must be equalized.

Chaussade waxed enthusiastic about this warehouse scheme. He envisioned an extended warehouse chain for anchors and hardware—"all sorts of irons made for the [ship]building trades, iron pins and bolts, hooks and eyes, fittings for block and tackle, ordnance tongs, anchor and capstan chains, and other ironware." Writing to government authorites, he said that he could compete in these lines with foreign irons "if the council would have the goodness, Monsieur, to relieve the irons from my furnaces [at La Vache, Chantemerle, and Grossouvres] of the *droit de marque des fers* . . . and the steels from my four small forges [La Doue, de Chamilly, La Vache, and Marteauneuf] from the *droit de marque sur les aciers,* [and] exempt me from the *droits du roi* on worked irons and on anchors transported overland and by water. I am making a proposal to the council to establish, in each maritime city, a warehouse (*magazin*) for anchors of all weights and [for] irons used in the construction and refitting of ships."[19]

All sorts of problems and obstacles and a myriad of special interests and privileges stood in the way of this scheme. Regulations, customs requirements, and rigid fiscal procedures protected many interests. The rules threatened to thwart his whole enterprise simply by limiting freedom of action and increasing costs. Even the indispensable right to warehouse merchandise was restricted. Entrepôt problems surfaced whenever shipments by water were involved. For example, if Chaussade destined a particular downriver cargo of anchors for the French West Indies, he could declare that intention to officials of the customs bureau at the inland, Loire valley city of Saumur, and the anchors making up the intended shipment could then be exempted from certain customs tolls; however, pending shipment to the colonies, they would have to be placed in entrepôt (i.e., bonded), and that was possible only at prescribed places in certain cities. Nantes was one of the cities. On the other hand, there was no right of entrepôt at Paimboeuf. Chaussade required an entrepôt or warehouse there so that ships sailing from Nantes could be prepared for sea at Paimbeuf's lower costs. Similarly, he had no right of entrepôt at Blaye for ships being prepared for Bordeaux; nor at Le Havre, for ships for Rouen; nor at Rochefort, for armaments for La Rochelle. There were other problems. If anchors destined for the colonies were not sold or shipped within one year, he could be obliged to pay tariffs, even penalties. In short, Chaussade's merchandise could not easily be stored at practicable localities, for suitable lengths of time, or shipped cheaply from practicable points. His planned warehouses could not be stocked with suitable inventory or maintained in the face of complex regional and local regulations that were stoutly defended by vested interests and officialdom. As Chaussade himself put it, "How can one deal with these distinctions and follow this detail in each city—the *impedimenta* of this commerce destroys it."[20]

The day before leaving La Rochelle, thinking of his itinerary and his prospects, Chaussade wrote: "I will be two days at Rochefort," then on to Bordeaux. "The greatest consumption of anchors and irons in this country takes place at Bordeaux. Seventy-four ships are under construction there now [Fall of 1760]. I'll be there on the eighth of the month."[21] About one month later (4 November), representatives of the merchant community of Bordeaux sent a long letter recounting the details of Chaussade's visit. Initially cooperative and polite, they had posted a placard "inviting shipowners to give preference to these anchors [Chaussade's] over those coming in from abroad." There was general sentiment *en principe* favoring the use of merchandise produced in the realm, given equal prices.

Yet the merchants of Bordeaux recalled an earlier shipment of his anchors from Nantes, "all [of which] had been recognized as being of very bad quality." This unfortunate precedent obliged the visitor to seek to reassure them: "in some measure [he] dissipated the prejudice by promising us that the anchors he proposed to send were of an entirely different quality than those we knew." Chaussade naturally emphasized that his manufactories had supplied anchors to the navy and Compagnie des Indes for many years, to their satisfaction. Later, in July 1762, he shipped (additional?) samples to Bordeaux—sixteen anchors weighing a total of 72,000 livres—hoping to refurbish the reputation of his products among the Bordelais.[22] He also promised to make available for sale irons of other sorts, both for the overseas colonies and for the shipbuilding industries of the port. The Bordelais themselves remarked that "the patriotic zeal of the Sieur de la Chaussade surely deserves to be seconded and even praised. . . . [Nevertheless,] the present state of commerce does not permit merchants to prefer the anchors of the Sieur de la Chaussade over those from abroad, unless he can sell them at the same price, and that is precisely what he told us he cannot do, as long as his irons and his anchors remain subject to certain very heavy duties that make them very much more dear."[23]

The merchants of Bordeaux urged the council of commerce to abolish the duties in question—particularly the *droit de marque des fers*—"so that the Sieur de la Chaussade and all the other forgemasters of the realm can establish prices equal to those of foreign irons, or at least in proportion to their quality." Frequent allusions to the problem of quality suggest that the Bordelais were chiding Chaussade about his earlier dumping practices and mocking his chances of future sales at Bordeaux. Even if his irons were exempted from taxes, his chances of sales at Bordeaux would be slim, since the anchors of Spain "are recognized here as the best and the strongest," and "anchors are of such consequence for the safety of ships that one always uses those recognized as being of the best quality."[24]

The fact was that the channels of trade between Spain and the French ports of the Biscay coast (Bordeaux, Bayonne, St. Jean de Luz) had flowed full for generations; the traffic in irons was just one strand of the multiple ties between France and Spain "guaranteed" after the Seven Years War by Choiseul's Family Compact. To imagine that Chaussade's products might replace imports from Spain on the commercial irons market at Bordeaux would have been naïve optimism in the extreme, and Chaussade was not naïve. He would have had to overcome not only problems resulting from his earlier dumping practices and the preference of French consumers for soft Spanish iron, but also the trading habits of communities where language, religious, and family ties (of refugees, Jews, and Basques, for example) spanned the border between France and Spain. To penetrate the market for anchors and irons at Bordeaux or elsewhere on the coast would have been difficult for any innovating French merchant-manufacturer; it was impossible for Chaussade, and he was much too perceptive and shrewd not to have known it.

When visiting the ports and afterward, Chaussade openly showed his impatience with local rules, local habits of trade, local bureaucrats, and the local businessmen who were represented in the chambers of commerce. He went to the ports as a dignitary, an outsider from the centers of power, with letters of introduction from high authorities. The gulf between himself and the locals was vast and deep—and certainly increased as friction developed during his sojourns. Chaussade undertook his visits, not as a diplomat, but as a manufacturer-trader, a businessman, knowledgeable, wealthy, privileged, and powerfully connected, lobbying for support or privileges. He cut a splendid figure. He liked to flaunt his wealth, allude to and describe his vast holdings in the prosperous valley of the Loire, and if his conversation and his comments matched the substance of his *mémoires* and correspondence, he must have referred endlessly to *his* workers, *his* paternal cares and role on *his* estates, and *his* high connections in business and financial circles in Paris and Versailles. He had "connections"; his associates could hardly have doubted that. Chaussade was aggressive, self-assured, and purposeful; his commanding presence and reputation could have made him few friends at the ports. But he did make his power absolutely clear. The plans he broached, the ideas he set forth in *mémoires* and conversation, his intelligence and far-reaching imagination, earned him respect and persuaded the members of the chambers of commerce that he was a man to be taken seriously, watched, possibly feared—in short, a person with whom the chambers must cooperate if at all practicable.

It seems to have been one of Chaussade's purposes in visiting the ports to persuade the chambers to give their support to his petitions to Versailles seeking special treatment at the hands of central government officials: exemption from production taxes at his manufactories, from transit tolls on commercial shipments within the realm, and from certain entrepôt controls. Support for these privileges, Chaussade seemed to promise, might move him to abandon other efforts to get changes that could prove costly to provincial traffic generally, such as a high tariff on imports of iron from Spain.

The merchants of the chamber at Bordeaux condemned Chaussade's declared intention of seeking the imposition of a new French tariff on imports from abroad. "Of all the methods the Sieur de la Chaussade has imagined to reduce the price of his anchors to that of those from abroad, that of imposing a new duty on anchors and irons from abroad appears to us to be the *least* suitable, the most onerous to commerce; we go so far as to say the most dangerous." At the outset of his campaign, Chaussade called for a 5 percent duty on foreign anchors brought into French commercial ports. The deputies of the chamber of commerce at Bordeaux also strongly opposed that:

> This duty will increase the price of anchors and, in consequence, the costs involved in fitting out [ships], which are too dear already; foreigners arm their vessels at very much lower cost than

the French. This new tax will infallibly occasion an increase [in impositions levied] abroad on the merchandise imported from this realm; they will import less, and thus it will be double loss for trade. The dearness of [his] anchors will never produce the preference sought by the Sieur de la Chaussade.[25]

The chamber concluded with an eloquent plea to the council to exempt all iron and steel produced in the manufactories of the realm from all export duties, all transit dues and tolls, and local levies of every kind.[26] This was more support than Chaussade really wanted; he argued, of course, only for the exemption of *his own* goods. He claimed to have paid "more than 20,000 livres a year for the *droit de marque*" on his pig iron production alone. But, he noted, a most serious threat would be posed to his warehouse chain if other forgemasters were moved (as by a blanket reduction or elimination of the *marque*) to establish magazines of their own in the port cities.[27] Other controversial proposals included a direct subsidy (Chaussade called it an "indemnity") to himself by the government, apparently to compensate him for damage caused by imports from abroad; a small tariff on imports of anchors, with the revenue to be paid over to him; and a complex "bank operation" intended to establish commercial credit for himself with certain Amsterdam bankers.[28] This last scheme would have obliged the merchant communities of the ports to take Chaussade's anchors and irons: he would have had a guaranteed market.

None of these proposals won acceptance, and the prospect for Chaussade's irons at the ports seemed accordingly bleak. Chaussade had a large inventory on hand: in December 1760, having completed his journeys in quest of markets to the ports, he declared that he had already manufactured "150,000 livres [of irons] for the commercial market, of which I am unable to sell a single one."[29] Clearly his warehouse empire was unwelcome at the commercial ports.

Nonetheless, his visits had produced testimonials and pressure from the commercial communities on the Biscay coast supporting his own barrage of arguments that he deserved special privileges because his irons could not compete with anchors and irons imported from abroad. With the support of the minister of marine and after many conferences with M. de Trudaine,[30] the *Fermiers Généraux* finally consented in June 1761 to certain exemptions for Chaussade. They agreed to moderate many *droits de traites* (taxes) on the anchors, nails, and iron work produced at Chaussade's manufactories. Furthermore, "liberty of transport" for anchors was granted, a prime concession and, Chaussade said, one without which he "could not hope to be competitive with imported anchors at the ports."[31] Chaussade now had to pay twenty-two sols on steels and eight sols per quintal on other types of iron; these charges were (usually) payable only once, at the products' exit from the *Cinq Grosses Fermes*. He was also accorded rights of entrepôt at Paimboeuf.[32] Thus the council and the *Fermiers* accorded some of the "relief" Chaussade sought, intending, as Chaussade himself said later, "to facilitate the distribution and sale of irons and steels from my forges in commercial markets"—preferential treatment justified by "the recognized utility of sustaining" Chaussade's establishments.[33]

The Seven Years War was not yet over when these concessions were made in mid-1761. Chaussade had enlarged production facilities and employed workers from afar, ready to gear up for full-scale production. He had a large inventory of hardware and irons. Yet he still carried a heavy burden of debt, much of it occasioned by the navy's failure to pay for merchandise already delivered. There was then little if any need for anchors or irons at the arsenals, even though reconstruction of the fighting fleet was being decided upon. Nonetheless, Chaussade managed to persuade France's principal minister of state, the duc de Choiseul-Stainville to take special action in his behalf. In September 1762 Choiseul himself described his concession to Chaussade: "All the ports, especially Brest and Toulon, are already sufficiently supplied with anchors and irons for many years. Nonetheless, I have decided to give work to your forges and the principal workers attached to them. Henceforth, therefore, anchors and irons to the value of 100,000 livres will be ordered [from your manufactories] by the navy each year, and you will receive your orders (*états*) in the month of October each year."[34] This remarkable promise assured Chaussade that the navy intended to place regular orders with him for a minimum number of anchors and irons every year, whether they were actually needed or not.

Colonial Shipments

With the restoration of peace in late 1762 and early 1763, Chaussade had the opportunity to begin shipments to the few colonies that remained to France. This opportunity was another consequence of his connections with the secretary of state for the navy (Choiseul), in whose portfolio colonial administration lay. Chaussade's hope of building up inventories of anchors and irons at entrepôts near major seaports to supply colonial needs was about to materialize. In April 1763 he was commissioned by the minister to supply "60,000 implements, tools, and pieces of worked iron for the pressing needs of the colonies." Chaussade shipped such materials along with rolled sheet of various sizes, to the value of 100,000 *écus* (300,000 livres), to the port of Rochefort.[35] A *passeport* issued earlier to authorize the transit of some of these materials listed the items in detail, suggesting the breadth of Chaussade's commitment to the traffic in iron and steel goods for "peaceful" purposes:[36]

1,200	Billhooks (*serpes*)
1,200	Hoes
6,000	Mattocks/pickaxes
6,500	Scoop-shovels and spades
3,000	Ordinary axes
100	Bakers' ovens and hearths
100	Harpoons
600	Gouging adzes
600	Gouging adzes (curved)
3,000	Wagon wheel pins (6-inch length)
20,000	Nails of 6-inch length
37	Anvil blocks for forges (250–300 livres) with steel-topped tables having either one or two anvils, one round and one square
230,000	Livres of iron supplies, varied sizes and shapes

This *passeport* of April 1763 may have been an "*état*" sent by Chaussade to Rochefort from Berry. The steels could have come from his four small forges (La Doué, de Chamilly, and Marteauneuf, or from La Vache where both steel and iron products were turned out), or from Chantemerle or Grossouvres. We know with certainty that less than three years afterward, Chaussade used the *prête-nom* "Sieur Jean Claude Ducatellier" to lease the extensive forges and other establishments of Cardinal de Bernis in the environs of La Charité-sur-Loire, thus expanding and further diversifying his production facilities.[37] There is, of course, a possibility that not all this novel merchandise was produced either at his home forges in Guérigny and Cosne or at those he leased. Another *passeport,* dated 4 November 1763, suggests that Chaussade was undertaking to ship additional quantities of many of the same items, and including an even greater variety of products, again without indicating where the particular items were produced:[38]

2,500	Billhooks (*serpes à douilles*)
1,200	*Serpes à mauches*
1,000	Cleavers or meat knives
1,200	Grubbing hoes (large)
1,200	Grubbing hoes (small)
80	Wagon axles (*essieux pour charrettes*)
100	Sacks of wheels (*sacs de charrues*)
700	Iron hinges (medium size)

   300 Iron hinges (large)
1,000 Iron shovels
1,000 Rakes
1,000 Spades

Another document entitled "Etat des Fers, clous et autres Ferrements" lists irons en route from Nevers to Rochefort for the colonies. Dated 3 September 1763, it clearly constitutes an addition to the others. These less specialized materials (except the steel from Berry) could readily have been produced at the anchor forges, rolling mill, slitting mill, or naileries in the environs of Guérigny: [39]

   150 *Quintaux* of nails, 5-, 6-, and 7-inch length
   250 *Quintaux* of nails, *double carreille*
   300 *Quintaux* of nails, various sizes
1,800 *Quintaux* of flat irons, round and square, rods and sheets
    10 *Quintaux* of steel from Berry
1,200 *Quintaux* "chunks" of iron
2,000 Mason's hammers, flat and toothed
1,200 Hatchets, for wheelwrights
   600 *Haissettes* (?) for wheelwrights
   150 Iron tongs
   200 Iron hooks (*crocs de fer*), pulley blocks, and eyes (*palans et cosses*)
    30 Cargo hooks (*pattes de Cargaison*)

These lists suggest that a considerably higher degree of sophistication had been achieved at the manufactories producing for Chaussade than was involved in the fabrication or assembly of "great anchors," which Chaussade himself on one occasion described as "*gross.*" His diversification had gone far and gone well. Referring to these lists in the letter that accompanied them, Chaussade called attention to his own contributions—he was not a modest man: "By means of a great deal of work and expense, I have established manufactures of all these types. As evidence of their importance, Monseigneur, you have already seen the three *passeports* that have been sent to me. This is one further evidence of the good that I have brought to the *généralités* of Moulins, Bourges, and Orléans." [40] This reference to three cities only indirectly connected with his centers of anchor manufacturing suggests the wide dispersion and diversity of his production network. Chaussade himself called special attention to Moulins as a new, or at least hitherto seldom mentioned, locale for his production: "Practically no crop is produced at Moulins, where my lands are situated. The parishes subsist entirely by the work of the forges. . . . The entire province sees with as much astonishment as satisfaction the success of these new manufactures, but it will not be sustained, Monseigneur, except with the protection of the minister."[41]

Ongoing support from the state took many forms. Minister of Marine Choiseul, as we have seen, had promised that the navy would buy anchors from Chaussade even when there was no need for new anchors at the ports. That promise was well kept. As a supplier of irons for the new naval vessels whose construction was undertaken late in the Seven Years War and afterward, Chaussade was strongly recommended by Choiseul. The Sieur de la Ferté Bernard, for example, charged with the construction of *Le Diligent* and *Six Corps* at Lorient, was told that he "could hardly find irons elsewhere of quality and price that matched Chaussade's."[42] Furthermore, Choiseul (as Chaussade himself specifically said afterward) "gave orders in 1764 to the Sieur de la Chaussade to establish nail manufactories on his properties for the *service des colonies*." Whether these orders were accompanied by a subsidy, loan, or any other form of financial aid is unknown. New naileries, in any case, were a further step in the diversification of Chaussade's product line. Beginning with Choiseul and continuing under his successors, the navy showed itself disposed to help him by agreeing to buy the new products. We know, for example, that some samples were provided to Chaussade so that he could manufacture to the exact specifications required at the port of Toulon, which differed from those required for other ports. We also know that the nailworks he established were employed continually for at least ten years after 1764, filling orders for the colonies and supplying the needs of Toulon (perhaps only until 1766) and Brest, Rochefort, Lorient, and Havre.[43]

The ministry's preferential treatment extended to taking a contract from another *fournisseur* (Petel et Cie.) and transferring it to Chaussade. Petel held earlier contracts for deliveries of certain irons to Brest and Havre. Financial difficulties made his continued production difficult.[44] In May 1764, just before a new naval contract was to be issued, Petel signed an *acte de cession* for the forges of Sauvage in Berry belonging to the comte de Torcy, for the manufacture of irons to be delivered to the Atlantic seaboard arsenals. This, he obviously hoped, would bring him the contract award. Instead, the minister wrote:

> Whatever assurances you give me of the good quality of these irons [from the forges of Sauvage], they have never been used at the ports; since we have always been content with those delivered by the Sieurs Babaud de la Chaussade and Le Blanc de Marnaval, I am the more firmly determined to renew the con-

tracts of those entrepreneurs because they themselves are
proprietors and forgemasters, whereas you have no knowledge
of forge management. Furthermore, the *fourniture général des
bois* with which you are charged . . . requires your serious
attention.[45]

When Petel wrote to importune the minister again, he was told: "I have
decided [to renew the Chaussade-Marnaval contracts] . . . because I am
informed that the solicitude shown by these entrepreneurs for the needs
of the ports has never left anything to be desired. . . . I cannot therefore
consider your offers."[46]

The ministry's esteem for Chaussade became further evident in 1769
when it was a question of using port facilities to reduce the thickness
of the iron plates being used to install new galleys aboard ships-of-the-
line. Rather than have the forges of the port do the work, the duc de
Choiseul-Praslin (César-Gabriel), cousin to Choiseul Stainville charged
Chaussade with furnishing stoves ready-made for installation. Praslin
willingly consented to pay a high price for the work, confident that
Chaussade would do a good job: "Irons of these sorts have been executed
very well [by Chaussade]; but since [they] are not included in his contract, I consent to the estimate [of] 400 livres the *millier*."[47] In 1764
Chaussade had received a general price increase on the unneeded anchors
he was being allowed to deliver to the ports.[48] And late in 1769 he was
given various other contract advantages, including the provisionment of
certain types of irons to Rochefort that had hitherto been supplied by
other contractors.[49] Earlier he had been offered the opportunity to supply
irons for use in fabricating *courbes* (52,500 livres of them) to be used in
construction at Lorient.[50] It is clear that in many respects Chaussade
received favorable and privileged treatment at the hands of the Choiseul
administrations.

Probably none of the privileges was more significant than the opportunity to ship merchandise to the colonies. The merchandise, as we have
noted, was of many kinds immediately after the war and became even
more varied during the two decades that followed. He was able to furnish
the usual variety of commonplace irons: round, square, and flat irons were
ordered in bulk, with nails, tacks, "bands" (*cercles*) for masts and spars
(especially for made-masts or *mâture d'assemblage*), and iron *courbes*.[51]
Anchors and *grapins* (oversized grappling hooks) were also ordered for
shipment to the "East" (Ile-de-France, Pondicherry, Chandernagor) from
Lorient. These staples made up the greater part of the volume of many

shipments. At least as early as 1773, the lists of merchandise shipped became much more varied. Orders for 1773 included the following items: [52]

```
       Steel from Berry, 1,000 livres
   4   Augurs (for wheelwrights)
  25   Vices (for coopers)
       Spades (nonhafted)
  27   Anvils (various sizes and kinds)
  12   Long-nosed nippers (for ironmongers)
 100   Woodworker's vices (in components)
  25   Axes, double-edged mortising (besaignes), for carpenters
  10   Jacks, assorted
 200   Chisels, for carpenters (6- to 15-ligne edge)
  50   Chisels, for wheelwrights
  30   Chisels, with handles
  —    Wedges (coignées?), for wheelwrights
  50   Dividers/compasses, for coopers
  50   Clamps (chiens), for coopers
 250   Tentes de forge
   6   Broadaxes
   1   Durands pour chyarons
  12   Bench vices
   6   Hand vices
   6   Anvil blocks for forges
  10   T-squares (18-inch arms), for carpenters
   4   T-squares (18- to 24-inch branches), for carpenters
 100   Sickles
 600   Quintaux of square irons
 200   Quintaux of round irons
 820   Quintaux of flat irons
 460   Quintaux of strap irons
  90   Quintaux of irons galopine (?)
 300   Quintaux of irons en taule (shackle irons: manacles, ankle irons, col-
         lars for prisoners and slaves)
       Metal dies, assorted, for forges
       Screws, for vices
       Metal dies, for cutlers
       Assorted irons and metal products
 400   Capstan spindles (?)
  12   Hammer heads, malls
  12   Hammer heads, for metal working
  12   Hammer heads, à soyer et moulures
       Misc. tools for foundry and forge workers
       Misc. tools for barrel-makers
       Assorted ripsaws (scies de longs)
       Assorted cross-cut saws (de tarpoints), 13–42 inches
       Syphons ou trompes (horns or funnels?), in copper
       Locks, 3.5 to 6 inches
```

```
   12 Tongs, blacksmith's, large
   12 Tongs, blacksmith's, small
  200 Tongs, for carpenters (?)
   30 Pins or lag screws, for coopers
1,000 Villes assorties
   75 Small anchors/hooks (100–200 lbs.)
      Anchors, assorted weights
        2  4,000-livres                    2  1,800-livres
        4  3,000-livres                    4  1,200-livres
        1  2,500-livres                    6    600-livres
        3  2,000-livres                    6    400-livres
```

Chaussade's provisionments for eastern colonial markets increased in volume and value in the middle 1770s. In 1773 he supplied materials valued at 27,890 livres to Lorient for the Isles of France and Bourbon. In each of the next two years he shipped similar merchandise valued at twice that sum to the colonies and to French ports in India.[53] In 1776 hardware for the artillery service was added to the shipments destined for the colonies and thereafter remained an important item.[54] In 1777 exceptional quantities of iron strip, square, round, and flat irons, and 3,500 livres of "German steel" were included in orders he executed for the colonies, along with large quantities of barrel-makers', forgers', and shipwrights' equipment and tools, and, again, there was much material for the artillery and fortification services in India and the eastern islands.[55]

The available sources do not enable us to establish the exact provenance or the manufacturers of many products furnished by Chaussade. He owned, leased, or otherwise operated many foundries, forges, and mills with varied capabilities. His *régisseurs* operated the manufactories that he himself owned in the Nivernais, while his surrogates or their *régisseurs* managed those he leased; some independent forge owners and forgemasters contracted with him to supply particular products, and merchant-producers sold him some hardware and general merchandise for inclusion in his provisionments. Chaussade himself was an important manufacturer of specialties, and one is intrigued by Sartine's (Antoine-Raymond-Jean-Gabriel de Sartine) remark in June 1777: "I have charged M. de la Chaussade to have manufactured and placed at your disposal twenty-four German-style saw blades (*lames de scies d'Allemagne*)."[56] The blades may have been manufactured at one of Chaussade's own steel works; we know that he produced steel and had (or had had) German workmen in his employ.[57] Whether he was the manufacturer and supplier of such materials as sheets of *fer blanc* (tin-plated or enameled iron) is a matter for conjecture.[58]

These orders involved Chaussade in much technical detail, and also some problems. Packers sent roofing nails of the wrong size and type (lead instead of iron) to India; moreover, the nails commonly used at Bordeaux differed from those used at Toulon—"in the Levant the woods are extremely hard, so the nails used at Toulon are very thick"—and these, rather than the longer, more slender *cloux de Bordeaux,* were the ones wanted for India.[59]

To the French ports of India, heaters were sent to melt lead for bullets, with 4,000-round shot for cannon of six different calibers (six to thirty-six pounders), elevating screws for cannon, 2,000 livres of sheet copper, and tools and equipment for carpenters, barrel-makers, and blacksmiths. Also included in the shipments were twenty-five livres of emery dust; the delicate tools and supplies needed to assemble and repair compasses and clocks; violins, bows, and strings, destined for use in chapels; and much else to satisfy the wants of Europeans in the East. Purchased and gathered from various suppliers, at least one shipment was prepared under direct orders of Minister Sartine,[60] who placed a certain M. de Granville in charge. Sartine remarked to Granville that he was sending lists of the different tools that the Sieur de la Chaussade was to supply. "I urge him to consult you about overall sizes and shapes he will need to know. . . . when these various tools reach you, you [Granville] will pack them with the material I have asked you to buy." For his part, Chaussade was ordered (on each shipment) to see that the cases containing the tools and other equipment he was supplying were specially marked with identifying markings. Chaussade, although only one of the many suppliers of the colonies, provided immense quantities of irons from his own manufactories and from other forgemasters of the Berry and Nivernais regions—not only via Lorient to the East, but perhaps also via La Rochelle, Rochefort, and Nantes to the Caribbean colonies, and possibly (via St. Malo and Brest?) to tiny St. Pierre et Miquelon. He may also have sent some supplies to the modest stations at Gorée and Albreda after 1763. Perhaps he traded even more extensively via Rochefort to Louisiana, where a correspondent bilked him of substantial sums (see Chapter 9).[61]

Colonial markets were open to Chaussade because he enjoyed privileged status. He was a manufacturer with close connections in the ministry of marine, where responsibility for both the navy and colonial administration lay. This is not to disparage his talents or business acumen, still less his entrepreneurial capacity. On the contrary, he must be credited with devising and developing an imaginative program of diversification in his manufacturing business. But in spite of all his efforts, Chaussade had little success in the commercial markets for irons at the ports of France. The ports especially, but also the inland towns and cities, were difficult markets for him, notwithstanding the extraordinary competitive advantages he had acquired in the form of privileges.

Even the commercial component of his colonial shipments seems to have been transitory. His initial postwar shipments to the colonies included agricultural implements and building hardware, as well as considerable quantities of industrial supplies, made, as we have seen, on the explicit orders and with the approbation and approval of the ministry of marine and colonies. But those initial shipments seem to have satisfied most of the accumulated wartime demand. Thereafter, colonial demand for his commercial hardware was evidently thin.

Chaussade continued to dispatch shipments to the colonies. He obtained new and renewed contracts with the ministry for goods to satisfy the needs of colonial government and its officials: provisionments for the maintenance and refitting of naval craft; parts for gun carriages and field artillery; materials for the construction of fortifications, the furnishing of government buildings and other government enterprises. If some part of his colonial traffic was thereafter conducted independently (i.e., apart from government), and could be considered an authentic commercial operation, neither its size nor its importance is evident in the documents that have come to light. If Chaussade engaged in commercial traffic at all, it is difficult to believe that it was of much consequence compared with his provisionments for official purposes.

Notarial records in Paris relating to Chaussade's business affairs offer very little evidence that he was involved on any significant scale in commercial iron sales. It is, of course, likely that some local and regional consumers of agricultural implements, foundry and forge equipment, and building hardware in the environs of his manufactories made some purchases from him. Moreover, a single Parisian notarial act reveals that he was involved in the Paris market—and with a novel project to construct a building largely or entirely of iron: "a covered and incombustible hall in this City of Paris."[62] The year of that contract was 1768—very early in the industrial revolution to find mention of a structure in France (or elsewhere) designed to be built of iron. It is unclear whether cast iron or forged iron members were to be used—Chaussade could probably have made and supplied either type, though forgings were his specialty.

In either case, this instance of innovative design, industrial or commercial, is one more indication that the reputed backwardness of French technology in the third quarter of the century stands in need of some reexamination. Chaussade and his entreprises clearly demonstrate that the metallurgical industry in France was not uniformly primitive or backward. The iron and steel industry included a wide range of businessmen and manufacturers, foundry- and forgemasters and other technicians, with a comparably wide range of competence and skills. French entrepreneurs and technicians innovated imaginatively when circumstances moved them to do so.

Bureaucrats and Taxes

Adverse business conditions must have been the fare of most businessmen. Even a man as well-connected as Chaussade, favored as he was with special privileges and guarantees from his major customer, the government itself, had to contend with serious problems. He carried an enormous burden of debt, largely government-imposed, including heavy obligations to both his family and commercial lenders, and that must have darkened his private estimate of business conditions. He had grounds to complain about the bureaucracy, and he did complain. But he survived the multiple problems of the 1760s. Well past sixty years of age by 1770, he still enjoyed good health.

In 1770 Chaussade resumed his campaign to move the government to modify the taxes that burdened his business and (though he seldom wrote of them) the iron trades generally in France. He was still thwarted by the intransigence of a certain tax collector at Nantes who was a representative of the interests of the *Cinq Grosses Fermes*. In 1761, as we have seen, Chaussade obtained from them the ruling that his irons descending the Loire would receive special treatment: his irons coming downriver, after paying the usual tax at Saumur if destined for commercial sale, were to be allowed, without any obligation to pay further duty, to be warehoused at Paimboeuf, below Nantes. But this privilege did not leave Chaussade free to import his own tax-paid irons from the entrepôt *back into* the sprawling jurisdiction of the *Cinq Grosses Fermes,* as he would do if he sought to market (or even store) them, for example in the province of Poitou. Chaussade found this interpretation of the tax rules by the director-agent of the *Fermes* at Nantes particularly annoying, and in 1770 he again appealed over this functionary's head, via Trudaine, for a more favorable interpretation of the rules.[63] It is uncertain whether he obtained the reinterpretation of the rules he sought; it is equally uncertain whether it was the principle or the modest economic benefit that concerned him most. Few merchants without Chaussade's high connections would dare to oppose such an official or carry complaints over his head.

In 1771 Chaussade revived his appeals to the deputies of trade for action to help him meet the competition of imported anchors. He claimed to have insufficient orders for his anchor forges. The Compagnie des

Indes was by then defunct and in state receivership. The arsenals at Brest, Rochefort, and Toulon were still heavily oversupplied. The needs of the commercial ports were apparently being supplied with anchors from Spain and the Netherlands at better prices than Chaussade could offer. Bourgeois de Boynes, the new minister of marine, gave strong support to Chaussade's appeal, saying that it was "indispensable" for the Deputies of Commerce "to decide either to augment the levies collected on anchors coming from abroad, or to diminish those taxes to which the irons used by the Sieur de la Chaussade are subject." [64] This same appeal had been made by Chaussade in 1760. But this time, surprisingly, it received favor and endorsement. It was sent along to the *contrôleur général* in the treasury department, and thence to the Royal Council. There the decision was finally taken in early 1773 to impose an additional tariff of forty sous per hundred-weight (twenty livres per thousand) on imported anchors. [65] This welcome action still left a large differential between Chaussade's costs and foreign anchor prices: in Chaussade's words, the new tariff "was too low and cannot be the basis for competition between the anchors of the Sieur de la Chaussade and those that merchants import from abroad." His position remained much the same. [66] In July 1773 another manufacturer of irons, a Sieur Rivaltz, resident of Carcassonne in Languedoc, petitioned for an increase in the tariff in the name of "all the proprietors of forges in Languedoc," all of whose forges, he said, were "inactive because foreign irons sell at a price so low that it is not possible to compete." [67]

In February 1775 we find Chaussade renewing his representations to obtain exemption (he had earlier been granted a reduction) from the industry-wide tax on iron production, the *droit de la marque des fers.* Again the minister of marine (now Sartine) strongly supported Chaussade's plea. "It is very generally recognized," Sartine observed, "that the anchors produced at his forges are very superior in quality to those imported from abroad. But the various taxes, and above all that of the *marque des fers* to which he is subject, oblige him to sell at a higher price." This letter accompanied Chaussade's *mémoire* and was addressed by Sartine to the *contrôleur général.* But on the margin of a summary of the letter is this note: "Keep [i.e., file this]. It is not possible to grant this request. 28 mars 1775." [68]

In the years that followed, this problem of Chaussade's, though surely not forgotten, gave way to other concerns. Again there was war. He no longer had need to compete with foreign irons, because orders from the navy accelerated furiously. The war years after 1776 saw Chaussade's manufactories inundated with orders for quantities that went far beyond any he could possibly produce or buy in France. After 1778 Chaussade himself became a major buyer and *fournisseur* of Spanish and Baltic anchors and irons for the navy. In the rush to produce for the colonies and the navy, amid the renewal of wartime demand, his effort to sell irons in the commercial markets fell from view. Apart from small local and regional sales in the environs of the works, Chaussade was again producing almost exclusively for his major customer, the state.

CHAPTER 9

The Business in the Decade of the American War

Delegating Authority

In 1769 a group of French entrepreneurs offered to buy Chaussade's Forges Royales and all their dependencies: the forges, fineries, seigneuries, forests, and lands. Chaussade was then in his sixties, an advanced age in eighteenth-century France and one at which most businessmen were concerned with arranging their affairs to accommodate their heirs. Chaussade's debts to individuals probably amounted to close to 500,000 livres, and the complexity of his affairs gave him good reason for wanting to liquidate his major holdings.[1] The price offered was reasonable, and Chaussade accepted the proposal. He undoubtedly welcomed the opportunity. When the buyers proved at last to be unable to raise all the necessary funds, he must have been deeply chagrined.

We cannot know what Chaussade would have done had he actually consummated the sale in 1769. We can guess that he would *not* have retired. In the event, after the failure to sell he undertook to transform the management of his Forges Royales. Thenceforth, much more responsibility for executive control was delegated to others. He unburdened himself of most of the problems of managing his complex aggregation of manufactories. But in the years that followed—the decade of the seventies—he involved himself increasingly in a variety of other enterprises.

Chaussade remained the owner and ultimate authority in the management of the Forges Royales, designating Martin Michel Sionville, Sieur de Damfreville, as his director-general in February 1771. Sionville was empowered to operate and administer the manufactories and all dependent facilities and lands in the provinces of Berry, Orléanais, and the Nivernais; all daybooks and accounts were subject to his inspection and correction, even retroactively as far back as July 1762.[2]

Paris was Sionville's headquarters. By 1780 he had five assistant directors under him, replacing the earlier, less numerous *régisseurs* and *sous-régisseurs;* the five, each with particular responsibilities, had their divisional headquarters at Guérigny, Demeurs, Frasnay, La Vache, and Cosne.[3]

- *Guérigny (including the estates of Guérigny and Villemenant)*

   Personnel: Director-*caissier,* 3 clerks for the forges and forests, a *chef aux travaux* for anchors and irons
   Facilities:
      3 Anchor forges
      1 Large forge
      3 Small forges
      12 Edge-tool *feux*
      The vineyard of Garchizy

- *Demeurs (the estate of Demeurs)*

   Personnel: Director-*caissier,* 1 clerk
   Facilities:
      1 Furnace
      1 Large forge
      1 Small forge
      4 Domains, pastures, mill, and woodland reserve
      Naileries, with tilt hammers and hand forgers

- *Frasnay (the estates of Frasnay and Douée)*

   Personnel: Director-*caissier*
   Facilities:
      3 Iron forges
      1 Forge for *acier commun*
      2 Domains, a mill, an enclosed pasture, and forest and pasture reserve

- *La Vache (the domains of La Vache; domains of Bleterie, du Toreau, and de Beauregard; the domains of Narcy and the forge of Marteauneuf depending on it; the furnace and forge à aciers communs de la Vache, pasture and forest reserve)*

   Personnel: Director-*caissier*

- *Cosne*

   Personnel: Director, serving as *contrôleur du caissier;* 1 assistant-director-*caissier*
      1 *contrôleur* for the naileries
      1 clerk
   Facilities:
      2 Large anchor forges
      1 Large slitting mill, "pour passer les fers en verge, et gros feuillards pour cercles de mats"
      1 "Slitting mill *à l'Allemande,*" to cut strip for barrel/cask hoops
      8 Tilt hammers for finishing work

   1 Small forge to convert trimmings and old irons
 12 Furnaces for edge-tools and specialty hardware
  4 Furnaces for nailery

The fiscal management of the first four director-*caissiers* was "to be verified by a *contrôleur;* all registers will be communicated to him when requested."[4]

The two domains of Richerand and Ouvrault, including a tile works, vineyards, pasture, and woodland, provided building materials, wood, and feed for livestock used by the forges and manufactories. Both were managed by a single *régisseur.* In all, the woodland and forest dependencies of the Forges Royales aggregated 6,000 *arpents.* In addition, Chaussade and his son Jean Pierre Babaud (de Guérigny) owned other woodland and seigneurial lands that were not considered dependencies of the Forges but were under Sionville's management. They must also have supplied fuel.[5]

The magazines at Nevers, on the *fief de Medine,* were also part of Sionville's responsibility, an establishment tended by a warehouseman-guard with a clerk and one laborer. The smaller magazines at La Charité were confided to a warehouseman-guard with one laborer. Guérigny and Demeurs shipped their product to Nevers when it was destined for Cosne or the ports; the warehouseman-guard at Nevers was required "to receipt the bottom of all shipping papers, thereby discharging the directors" of responsibility. Bills of lading for all shipments were to be sent to Sionville, who also received monthly accounts, each to include a summary-inventory of all property and supplies on hand, to be worked into a year-end (fiscal year) accounting (the calendar year ran from 1 October). We know these details about Chaussade's management because when he finally did sell out to the king in 1781, his procedures were meticulously described to facilitate the takeover. The king's administrators were ordered to follow them "in form and principle."[6]

The industrial organization and management methods were apparently developed ad hoc and progressively as the family acquired properties. In the 1770s Sionville took over most of the executive functions Chaussade himself had previously performed: all details related to procurement, production, and furnace, forge, and estate management. In short, Sionville was director of manufacturing operations. Chaussade himself remained active in the iron business only in marketing and negotiating contracts and prices. Responsibility for the fiscal aspects of the business, including payments from the *trésoriers de la marine* and the collection of sums due from commercial sales, was not specifically included in Sion-

ville's portfolio. Had they been his province, he would infallibly have incurred Chaussade's wrath when embezzlement led to serious losses. Since
neither Sionville nor any other inspecting authority received even a whis-
per of criticism, we can conclude that the fault, if any, was Chaussade's
own. He gave his correspondents too much leeway, too little surveillance
and control. The fiscal phase of Chaussade's organization proved defective on several occasions.

Chaussade's agent at Nevers handled large sums deriving from navy
payments and the transfer of funds, and in 1773 it was discovered that
this *dépositaire* had embezzled the sum of 40,000 livres.[7] Five years later
it was revealed that Chaussade's Nantes correspondent, the merchant
Louis Huguet, was engaged in peculations at Chaussade's expense. Chaussade ordered the trusted and overworked director-general Sionville to inspect the accounts of sums due from Huguet, the records of shipments
made by him to the colonies, his purchases and disbursements, and any
accounts connected with the descent of timber to Nantes for Chaussade's
account, all of which had passed through Huguet's hands. Sionville was
empowered to demand correction of the accounts "in case of errors,
omission, double-entries, etc."[8] Chaussade's fears were justified. Over a
considerable period, apparently using lateness of payments as a pretext,
the disbursements by his correspondent at Nantes had been slowed,
creating confusion in the accounts and leaving large sums illicitly in the
correspondent's hands.[9]

After this experience, his third major loss in about a decade at the
hands of embezzlers, Chaussade sought new means to achieve tighter
control of his fiscal affairs while relieving himself of direct supervisory or
executive responsibility. He took one step in that direction late in 1778
by naming Jean Mathias Deveaux *procureur général et special* to deal
with creditors: "to receive from the paymasters of the navy and private
persons all sums due."[10] Shortly afterward he appointed a second *procureur général et special*, Master Nicholas Chanu, *avocat au Parlement*,
whom he empowered "to assist at all assemblies of debtors, to draw up,
and sign all their deliberations," and to receive the sums involved.[11]

Throughout the 1770s Chaussade passed as much responsibility as
possible to subordinates and surrogates. He also assigned to others, as he
had in the past, power to exercise judicial authority on his estates, sometimes on a temporary or trial basis, with the appointment being subsequently confirmed if performance was satisfactory.[12]

Chaussade continued the practice of using surrogates in various capacities. In 1768 he leased the forges of Grossoeuvre, formerly the establishment of a competitor, under the *prête-nom* "Sieur Ducatellier"

(sometimes "du Cathelier").[13] He held major contracts to supply the navy with both timber and irons in the names of surrogates. Those surrogates, in turn, subdivided the operations among several persons who saw to field operations in different geographic areas. These practices transferred managerial responsibility and effectively masked Chaussade's entrepreneurial role, while complicating the job of the historian. For example, a certain Sieur François Hebre, a merchant of Rochefort, signed a series of contracts for Chaussade, some in his own name, some in Chaussade's, agreeing to deliveries of irons and equipment of various kinds to Rochefort and to the French colonies.[14] In another instance, we have a revealing letter from the minister, who was then concluding negotiations for one of Chaussade's contracts to supply timber to the navy: "Send me six copies signed with your assumed name ["Sieur Barrois"], and [also signed] by you and your son as [his] *cautions*."[15] The names "Barrois" and "Nion" we know were assumed by Chaussade and used in his contracts of the 1770s, and there are indications that other, more prominent contractors of the time may also have been front men or partners of his.

Hence, although an examination of the registers of naval correspondence might suggest that Chaussade had become less active, he had in fact a very active director-general and various "taken names" or surrogates. Our direct knowledge of certain aspects of his business (and general) activity is correspondingly diminished: the navy's letters to his director-general and directors, *prête-noms*, and surrogates became more succinct and brief, without the details or the personal touches to be found in exchanges between Chaussade and earlier ministers. Yet Chaussade's *rapport* with Minister Sartine was excellent, and he had easy access to court circles after the accession of Louis XVI, through the count of Maurepas, *de facto* prime minister. Maurepas, former minister of marine, was one of Chaussade's oldest friends, and Sartine was a Maurepas protégé.

Of the many reasons for using *prête-noms* and surrogates, discretion was among the most important. Connections and influence in high places and the relatively privileged character of Chaussade's contractual relationships made discretion advisable. Moreover, as in earlier periods of international war, some contracts in which Chaussade had an interest involved shipments of materiel by river and road through neutral areas or states such as the Rhineland region. Such contracts could best be carried by surrogates using assumed or false names to avoid easy identification of the *fournisseur*. Chaussade's own name must also have been prominently associated with the embezzlement cases discussed above. He was doubtless remembered in the merchant communities of Nantes, Lorient, La

Rochelle, and Bordeaux for his high-pressure salesmanship and his agitation for tariff rises on imported irons. A further reason for placing much of the business in the hands of surrogates may have derived from Chaussade's problems with some officials of the naval bases at Brest and Rochefort.

The Port of Brest

Brest was a difficult market for Chaussade in the 1770s because of friction between himself and successive chief administrative officers of the arsenal. Ruis Embito was intendant at Brest from 1 December 1770 until 29 May 1776, when illness necessitated his replacement.[16] His path had first crossed Chaussade's four decades earlier during the Masson-Babaud timber exploitations in Lorraine (see Chapter 2). Embarrassed, not to say humiliated at that time, relieved of his post and sent back to Rochefort, Ruis had over the years proved to be competent. His talents carried him through successive promotions to the highest grade attainable and eventually to the post of intendant at Rochefort, whence he was ultimately transferred to Brest to assume the intendancy there in 1770.[17]

Ruis Embito was seriously ill at increasingly frequent intervals during 1775 and 1776. In his place on those occasions, *Commissaire Général* Marchais assumed the command. It was a time of crisis, the eve of war. As usual, the navy had placed large orders for new provisionments of anchors and irons. The quantities sought far exceeded the capacity of Chaussade's production facilities, especially the orders for iron plate and sheet iron, and above all for rods and for hoops or strips for use as bands on masts, spars, hogsheads, barrels, and kegs. These were among the most labor-intensive and costly of the bulk irons supplied from Chaussade's plants, nearly all of them being products of his slitting mills at Cosne.[18] He had several slitting mills—the large one producing rods and heavy strip, and the slitting mill producing strap iron and strip of smaller dimension "*à l'Allemande*" for barrel hoops and casks—with no less than eight tilt hammers, all being used at Cosne for the metal finishing. The volume of such products he could supply was therefore limited, as Chaussade informed the minister and the administrators at Brest.

Intendant Ruis Embito and his *commissaire général* apparently estimated the capacity of Chaussade's works to be much higher. In December 1775 or January 1776, *Commissaire* Marchais, evidently to satisfy orders received, did not hesitate to ship from Rochefort to colonies overseas, French and others (the "Thirteen"?), materiel including about twenty-four tons of irons from Chaussade's specialized mills at Cosne. The arsenal at Brest also contributed to those shipments and was apparently cleaned out. The subsequent shortage of these irons, which was to last for two and a half years, was apparently set off by these peremptory overseas shipments.[19] The ministry ordered a special inventory of equipment and supplies at the port of Brest, carried out "with the greatest exactitude" in early February 1777. Some significant and disquieting shortages were revealed: among the missing items that could not be accounted for were 300 *milliers* of irons.[20]

Subsequent correspondence made it clear that supplies to replace the irons that were missing or that were known to have been shipped out could easily have been purchased (at higher prices than Chaussade was paid) on the commercial market at Nantes or elsewhere. But the correspondence also suggests that the new intendant at Brest, M. de Laporte (November 1777 to November 1781) was bent on obliging Chaussade himself to deliver the irons needed at the relatively low prices that were stipulated in his contract with the navy.[21] Laporte blamed Chaussade for the poor assortment of irons that he found in the magazines. "This *fournisseur*," he said, "during many years in succession, has delivered irons of dimensions and types not used every day, which make up the bulk of the current contents of the magazines, without being of much use to the service. For some time and with reason we have thought of obliging him to deliver what is needed, which undeniably would somewhat disrupt the work at his forges, but is essential to the interests of the king." [22]

Obviously an imbalance in the assortment on hand should not have been simply blamed on Chaussade. As the inspection reports revealed, the administrators themselves could not account for all the materiel, including irons, that they were known to have received. It was evident, however, that some of the port administrators, in an apparent effort to ensure that territories overseas would be adequately supplied in the hostilities that were soon to break out, had precipitously shipped out all the irons of certain crucial strategic categories (especially those used in the manufacture of hogsheads, barrels, and kegs) that were on hand at the arsenals. They seem to have made no effort to replace the supplies of irons thus shipped, from other sources. Instead, they tried to represent that the "imbalance" in the assortment of irons on hand was Chaussade's responsibility. And they sought to persuade Sartine to oblige Chaussade to replenish the depleted stores with newly manufactured irons, even though they knew that would be difficult and costly for him. Laporte, especially, seemed disposed to criticize Chaussade. Laporte must be credited, of course, with the desire to obtain irons needed from the most economical source.

If Chaussade did not supply the required irons, Laporte proposed importing Russian ("Siberian") irons to France. (He appears to have expected Chaussade to find the idea threatening.) Irons from St. Petersburg, Laporte said, "will cost 25 percent less than those of P. B. de la Chaussade." The freight would cost "very little," since the irons could be laden as ballast in shipments of masts currently coming from the same Baltic markets.[23] Chaussade no doubt concurred with Sartine's decision to approve the contract that had been made in May 1777 at Brest with the Sieur Du Buat, a merchant of St. Malo, for the provisionment of about twenty tons of sheet iron from Siberia. Sheet iron, the administrator at Brest claimed, was in short supply in part because "the irons of that type delivered by the Sieur de la Chaussade are breaking and of bad quality."[24]

Earlier, in August 1776, a Stockholm exporter had proposed delivery of various irons, nails, and copper at prices substantially lower than those the navy was paying to French manufacturers, but on one condition: the company was to be paid cash on delivery. The navy's initial response was that "it appears essential to support our domestic manufacturers, from whom we get many of the items offered by this foreigner."[25] The navy also, however, proposed to refer the Helensius offer to the Royal Council. Delay ensued. On 18 October it had still not been referred, and over a year went by before the council reported in favor of M. de Laporte's proposal that a test shipment be requested of Helensius, for which cash was promised.[26] By December 1777 the samples had apparently been received and tested at Brest. Laporte reported as follows:

> "In the test that was made for me by the forgemaster, in the
> presence of the director of constructions, they [the samples] were
> recognized as fully adequate, even as *cercles des mâts*. Moreover,
> they are less dear by fifty livres the hundred-weight than those
> from France furnished by P. de la Chaussade for the same ser-
> vice. These considerations led me" said Laporte, "to decide to
> keep them for the service, and I propose in consequence to di-
> minish proportionately the orders for this materiel to be made in
> the year to come from the Sieur de la Chaussade."[27]

Meanwhile, in December 1777, the Sieurs Gautier frères, merchants of St. Malo, were reported to be proposing to deliver from Sweden a provisionment of small squared rods (in short supply at the arsenal), thus diminishing the use of Chaussade's irons of that type.[28] Earlier that fall a batch of round and square irons from Sweden, brought into Le Havre as part of a cargo of other merchandise, was purchased by the navy from Vve. Homberg et Cie., merchants of Le Havre.[29] In December 1777 permits were issued for the entry at Le Havre of 350,000 livres of Swedish irons, most of types Chaussade found it difficult and costly to supply in adequate quantities.[30]

Chaussade had repeatedly indicated, as we have seen, that he could not possibly produce additional irons of these types beyond those he was already committed to deliver. But his critics (or, more accurately, his enemies) in control of the administration of the base at Brest were bringing to a climax their campaign against him: not only the intendant Laporte, but also the "interim administrator" who served during Laporte's illnesses, the *commissaire général* Faisolle de Villeblanche.[31] From Brest to the minister went reports that essential supplies of irons, especially iron strip (*feuillard*), were so seriously short that ships could not be prepared for sea. On 13 April the intendant at Brest sent the ministry a report that might have made real trouble for Chaussade. It asserted that ten vessels were ready, or almost ready, for sea, including crews, but that six (other?) vessels could not be armed and would remain in port because "the lack of strap iron [for barrel and cask hoops] does not permit us to think of actually arming these six vessels. We have counted on the Sieur de la Chaussade. We have not ceased for four months to remind him of the need of the port for this type of iron, [and to ask him] to send some if he had any available. If we do not receive irons of these types, the vessels in question cannot be armed immediately."[32]

The farcical, not to say fraudulent, nature of this "crisis" was revealed four days later when Laporte was able to inform the ministry that all the vessels ordered were in fact armed and ready to sail after all! As for the irons they lacked, the intendant then admitted that he had 100 *milliers* on hand. Henceforth, he reported, "we will supply ourselves by means of the [local?] forges of *la ville neuve* and those of the *fort* where we extrude iron." That was slow work, he said, but some irons were being sent from Lorient. "However, all the vessels whose armament is ordered are today supplied with barrels and casks. There are even enough to arm another vessel, and with the help of our forges we could even manage a second vessel. . . . Our forges are always at work, daily furnishing strap iron; and it is hoped that some will finally come from the forges of the Sieur de la Chaussade."[33]

Sartine was, or pretended to be, incredulous. Seeing the "crisis" evaporate, he demanded an explanation: "In [your] response, tell me what has happened; give me an exact account of the measures that you have taken." He bombarded Laporte with queries and demands, sending him four letters on 30 April, nine letters on 1 May, six on 2 May, and one or two others undated.[34] This onslaught of nineteen or twenty letters in three days put extreme pressure on Laporte. In one of the letters Sartine said that he was disposed to accord Chaussade an increase of 40 sous per quintal on iron sheets 2.50 to 2.75 *lignes* thick, from which straps and hoops could be cut. Laporte responded meekly: "this increase appears to me to be just; these irons will then cost 240 livres per *millier,* and it is certain that it would not be possible to buy irons of these dimensions from forges other than those of the Sieur de la Chaussade at less than 250 livres per *millier.*"

Chaussade had warned that he could not guarantee absolute uniformity in the exterior dimensions of these pieces: allowance should be made for a range of 24.0 to 25.0 *lignes* in width; thicknesses might vary from 2.5 to 2.75 *lignes,* but would not exceed 3.0 *lignes.* Again Laporte was compliant: "this appears equally just." These variations, he intoned, are commonplace, "well-established usage," and he seemed to echo Chaussade's words when he observed that it was not possible to subject a forge-master to a precision of a quarter of a *ligne.* In another letter the minister indicated that he had relieved Chaussade of any further obligation to deliver irons of these sorts to Brest at any time in 1778.

Chaussade must have been pleased and gratified by the minister's decision. He had had by 1778 several years of severe stress and strain as a result of rising domestic and foreign competition and harassment by the administrators at Brest.[35] An indication of his position and disposition in that period appears in two letters he wrote in September 1777 to Sartine. He proposed to quit, to sell out, and suggested various expedients to transfer to the king his anchor and iron manufactories and their dependencies. Realizing the difficulties bound to ensue if he sought payment in cash, Chaussade envisioned various possibilities. He especially favored an *exchange* of his own properties for state properties. Presumably in response to a *mémoire* he prepared on the subject, it was remarked: "M. le Cte. de Maurepas assuredly will agree to any suitable expedient that is proposed . . . but M. de la Chaussade has [perhaps] not considered that this method of selling by means of property exchanges is always subject to long delays that could only increase the complications that he is trying to forestall." A comment penned at the bottom of this letter suggested that Chaussade's best course might be to offer to sell or transfer his forges at Cosne alone, "since they are the most interesting for the naval service," but the discussion was concluded with the (minister's?) bottom-line note: "the King will not buy them."[36]

Foreign Irons

Not only Russian and Swedish, but also Spanish and German imports were then being offered for sale in France. Spanish anchors and irons had been formidable competition for Chaussade in the 1760s. Since then, sales of Spanish irons in France had increased. The French naval base at Toulon, especially under the Hocquart intendancy, had frequently imported Spanish anchors and irons for the arsenal. It was difficult for Chaussade or other French iron merchants to supply Toulon; Spain was a practicable source of supply. Chaussade himself appears to have been authorized in 1776 to acquire and supply 18,000 livres of *fers quarrés d'Espagne* that year. And in June 1777, with the consent of the Conseil de Marine, he signed a major contract to import Spanish irons and anchors for use at Brest.[37] Alluding in 1781 to Chaussade's importation of anchors to Rochefort, the intendant observed that Chaussade "had been obliged to have recourse to Spain, his forges not having been able to satisfy the considerable demands placed on them for this specialty." Six large Spanish anchors (6,000–6,500 livres each) had just been found to be defective; "the others," of the thirty-two Chaussade had just delivered, "did not have the [same] defects, but they were for the most part for frigates [i.e., smaller]."[38] It is an interesting commentary on Chaussade as a businessman that by 1780 he himself had become a major importer of Spanish anchors and irons: many *passeports* issued in the first half of 1780 attest to his extensive imports.[39]

Such importation was good business for him. Chaussade had succeeded over the years in obtaining repeated increases in the prices he was paid by the navy for various categories of anchors and irons.[40] The prices called for in his contracts were supposed to cover his manufacturing and transit expenses and give him a reasonable profit, the latter being presumably scaled to reflect interest on capital investment and risks—including (when he dealt with the state) that of partial payment, delays in payment, and even nonpayment when irons were not accepted by inspectors at the ports. Other contractors at times sought rises to match the prices paid (on a *pro tem* or wartime basis) to Chaussade, and in some instances obtained them.[41]

Clearly, when Chaussade could purchase foreign irons for the navy at costs that were lower than his own aggregate manufacturing costs, plus taxes, transit, and transportation expenses, he stood to profit substantially by importing. Moreover, imports could often be brought to France as ballast or supercargo—in cargoes of wool from Bilbao, with masts and spars from Stockholm, Riga, or St. Petersburg. Low freight costs were among the circumstances that underlay low prices and sustained demand for foreign irons in France. One wonders whether similar practices prevailed in England: when John Paul Jones's *Ranger* took the *Lord Chatham* as prize, the English vessel's cargo included "Siberian" irons—which the French navy did not buy because their auction price went to 165 livres, more than Chaussade received for comparable irons of his own manufacture. Sartine afterward wrote to Intendant Laporte, "You did well to let them go." [42]

But there were other times when the intendant did less well with foreign purchases. In November 1778 Intendant Laporte was ill and *Commissaire Général* Faisolle de Villeblanche was substituting in the interim. Chaussade had just begun buying irons abroad on a large scale, at low prices. When about a ton of these imports were delivered at Brest on his account, Faisolle de Villeblanche, being conscientious and wanting to do well for the navy, discounted them because they were imported, even though they were judged to be of good quality and suitable to be received. Chaussade complained to the minister, who reacted with vigor: "I find it hard to believe," he wrote to Faisolle, "that he [Chaussade] could have had this difficulty. But if he did, you must stop it. It suffices that the irons this entrepreneur delivers are recognized as proper for the service." M. de la Chaussade was to be credited with the full prices prescribed in his contract regardless of the prices at his sources of supply. [43]

Being well paid for them, Chaussade naturally sought to expand the volume of his imports, and his earlier experience and apparent contacts in eastern France and the Rhineland region turned his attention to that area. He knew that the great rafts of tree trunks and timber descending to the Netherlands offered easy downriver transit for irons. In 1778 we find him buying irons from a certain Sieur Gonvy of Saarlouis, who owned numerous forges in Lorraine and the principality of Nassau. In connection with their joint interests, Gonvy wrote to the French authorities seeking help in his efforts to avoid double payment of the *droit de marque des fers* on his irons produced in Nassau: charged when his irons entered Lorraine, he was taxed again when they entered France. Stopping at the toll stations also resulted "in delays and risks for the *fournisseur*." By special dispensation and at Sartine's request, Jacques Necker, then *contrôleur général des finances* in France, consented to omit the tax collected at the French frontier. [44] *Passeports* ordered for the Gonvy irons suggest that they could descend from Saarbrücken in *flottes* carrying plank destined for the navy, thus keeping downriver transit costs at a minimum. [45] Chaussade assured Sartine that orders for certain irons would be filled if the transports from Holland do not create "unforeseen obstacles to the arrival of those I have purchased in Germany."[46]

Manufacturer and Merchant

Other specialized products were purchased by Chaussade using other French middlemen or surrogates. He entered into a series of agreements with a merchant of Rochefort to supply for that port (and perhaps ultimately the French colonies) such diverse materials as twenty-four grills on which "red-hot shot" could be heated, 2,000 livres of specially fabricated nails to be used in constructing gun carriages, six large and six medium-sized jacks, 1,900 steeled hoes, and 300 iron sheets of various sorts (including *fer blanc*).[47]

The variety of Chaussade's activity is further indicated by his connection with a M. Cornic, to whom he was supplying, from his own manufactories, "irons of large dimension" for use in fabricating beacons or markers (*balises*) at the entrance to the roadstead of the port of Morlaix; by the end of May 1776, Chaussade reported that "the fifty-six bars of iron" manufactured in his forges were in transit and had been charged on a boat at Paris going via Rouen.[48] Chaussade also provided irons, nails, and "pieces of worked irons" (whether from his own forges or not we do not know) for His Majesty's service of the "Machine at Marly" (pumps for the water supplied to the Chateau at Versailles).[49]

Chaussade was one of many *fournisseurs* in France and abroad who provided the materials needed to build and operate the Wilkinson foundry and boring mill for cannon manufacture on the Ile d'Indret at the mouth of the Loire. This enterprise appears to have been initiated in 1776, with William Wilkinson, operating (at first) as "M. l'Abbé MacDermott,"[50] sending eight cannon of his own manufacture to Brest to be tested.[51] The foundry operated, not with ore, but with old irons, including old cannon, for which Sartine had the naval arsenals scoured systematically, seizing all those being used as ballast in ships or lying in port. In 1777 D'Orvilliers and Laporte at Brest reluctantly shipped to William Wilkinson at Indret all the old guns and ingots ordinarily used on naval craft laid up at the arsenal: "we believe we can assure you that the short durability of vessels derives in great part from the use of stones (*mauvaises pierres*) with which vessels [now] are ballasted when they are disarmed."[52] Nevertheless, the orders were that all were to be sent to Indret, and Chaussade was informed that in addition to the 40,000 livres of iron building materials already supplied by July 1778,[53] he should hold himself in readiness to increase his shipments of ingots. "You can make your arrangements to cast 200,000 livres in ingots of the same proportions as those you have already delivered."[54] Three weeks later the order for Wilkinson's works at Indret was increased to 500,000 livres of ingots, "but I urge you to see that the *fonte* is *très grise et pas trop minée,* since the Sieur Wilkinson complains that some of those in your last shipment, while of good service, were inferior to the first."[55] In November Sartine wrote to Chaussade regarding the dimensions of the lumber required to construct a large, open-faced utility building (perhaps a loafing barn) on the Isle d'Indret to shelter the animals employed in the work.[56]

Demand for his irons finally led Chaussade to the emergency expedient of establishing a third finery at Demeurs so that he would be in a position "to furnish to the *département* [*de la marine*] the materials that are daily being ordered for the fabrication of cannons and the anchors and irons needed in the construction of vessels."[57] Before doing so he was obliged to ask permission, not only of the navy, but also of the *contrôleur général.* He apparently received it in 1778 or early 1779.[58]

The actual extent or volume of Chaussade's aggregate sales of irons cannot be known, but the provisionment he was asked to make to the navy in 1778 was estimated by the minister himself at 5,266,000 livres. This figure did not include his very substantial shipments of ingots to Indret.[59] In March 1779 it was said, on the basis of orders given to him, that his aggregate deliveries of irons to the navy that year, from his own forges and (apparently) from foreign sources, "will exceed by 2,859,000 livres."[60]

In August 1779 Chaussade was told that "one could presume" he would receive equally large orders for 1780, and in due course he was informed that the provisionment in irons for 1781 would be "as great as it had been in the current year."[61] It is clear that the demand for Chaussade's irons was sustained at a very high level on the eve of his sale of his forges to the king.

Equally apparent is the fact that Chaussade's forges and mills worked at or near full capacity throughout the seventies. Being disposed to avoid further expansion, he seems to have added only one new furnace. But erratic demand, a severe problem in the 1760s, was not evident in the seventies. Even payment problems were less severe, as far as Chaussade was concerned.

Chaussade, being both manufacturer and merchant, combined sales of his own products with the purchase and sale of ingots, industrial and agricultural tools, equipment, and instruments manufactured by others. In the seventies he appears to have continued to seek diversification of his product line, but not by introducing changes in his own manufactories. He concentrated increasingly on the production of basic goods to satisfy the navy's perennial and predictable needs. He could not predict, as he had tried to do earlier, its future demand. Instead, he seems to have been intent in the seventies on functioning as a flexible provider, furnishing materiel from his own plants when he profitably could, otherwise buying from other producers. He became more the merchant industrialist, with progressively greater stress on his role as middleman.

By 1770 Chaussade was a veteran contractor with over forty years of experience behind him. He owned dozens of seigneurial estates and parcels of land, was certainly one of the great noble landowners of the upper Loire, and commanded a small army of vassal tenants and industrial workers. He had had dealings with half a dozen ministers of marine, and his ties with them generated confidence in his capacities as an entrepreneur. Most ministers of marine came to office with little knowledge of the navy, and less of marine technology. The best of them in Chaussade's time—Maurepas, the Choiseuls, and Sartine—after a period of testing, came to have confidence in *fournisseurs* who could take on a difficult task and be depended upon to finish the job.

Timber *fournisseur*

Chaussade's reputation among the ministers of marine in the seventies enabled him to win not only contracts to supply his own products, but special contracts that gave him a role as organizer and the profits of a middleman. In effect he became a supervisor and manager of other entrepreneurs dealing with the navy in that period. Chaussade was pleased to perform such a supervisory role among *fournisseurs* of irons under Sartine; and Sartine was to hand him a similar role as a *fournisseur* of timber in 1775. The minister, from the beginning of his tenure, faced pressure to enlarge the navy and fleet, to build ships, repair and reconstruct the old, and arm them all. For these purposes timber was needed. Ship timber from Alsace, Lorraine, and Flanders was generally regarded as "less suitable for construction than that from the interior of the realm."[62] But Sartine was advised by many persons, including one Charlot de la Grandville, that good timber—perhaps 100,000 cubic feet a year—could be purchased at the auction sales held regularly by the officials of the royal forestry service in the Gatinois, Blaisois, Berry, Bourbonnais, and Nivernais provinces close to the rivers Loire and Allier.[63] Chaussade, consulted by the minister, confirmed this counsel.[64] Sartine sent a timber specialist from Rochefort to Nevers to see what suitable timber could be found, giving him explicit orders to see the Sieur Babaud de la Chaussade for information and guidance in locating suitable trees.[65]

Chaussade appparently advised that they start where they were—with the examination of some local timber stands. A considerable amount of timber was easily found belonging to Chaussade himself and to M. le Duc de Cosse, M. le Marquis de Brunoi, and the Chapter of Nevers. The minister urged Chaussade to find an entrepreneur to take it out: "I know your zeal well enough to be persuaded that if you have a wood merchant in your area who possesses the skills and intelligence to accomplish this task, you will do your best to engage him to treat with the navy. You can assure him that he will be paid for his provisionments with the greatest exactitude."[66] This guarantee of prompt payment was very effective; within a month Chaussade himself had purchased 1,800 suitable trees in the Berry, close to the Allier, and the navy's inspector, a man named Fouché, was sending complaints to the minister about the numerous surreptitious (illegal) cuts hitherto made. Sartine thanked Chaussade for his help and "the manner you have chosen to second my views," and asked him to continue to guide the several naval officials who by then (November 1775) had been sent to intensify the search. By December Chaussade had purchased several thousand additional trees near the Allier.[67] The minister and field officials alike were by then receiving "daily propositions" from other merchants and landowners, offering to contract to deliver suitable timber to the navy.

Fearing that the "great number of *fournisseurs*" and "the multiplicity of their contracts" would cause "embarrassment," Sartine accepted Chaussade's offer, in effect allowed him exclusive (monopoly) rights to furnish all the timber that could be exploited from the three provinces of the Berry, Bourbonnais, and Nivernais.[68] Although there were rules against "exclusive" or monopolistic contracts, "the more I reflect on this," Sartine wrote, "the more I think that this affair—which I regard as very important for the service—could not be put into better hands." Chaussade requested an increase of nine sous per cubic foot on the prices being paid for three types of timber and eleven sous on a fourth. Sartine accepted his proposed price schedule less two sous for each category:

Type 1: 60 sous/cubic foot (up 7 sous)
Type 2: 55 sous/cubic foot (up 7 sous)
Type 3: 50 sous/cubic foot (up 7 sous)
Type 4: 45 sous/cubic foot (up 9 sous)

"My intention being to treat you as favorably as possible," he wrote, "I consent without further discussion." [69]

But there were further talks, both then and later. Chaussade asked that his "*prête-nom* be used in all sales and auctions for the purchase of trees." [70] He agreed to deliver about 350,000 cubic feet from the three provinces over a period of six years, using the name Barrois. The final agreement carried no limit on the total amount of timber to be supplied, allowing delivery of "all wood proper for the construction of the king's ships." [71] The timber was to be sent downriver in boats, not by *flottage*. Chaussade was given a choice: all or part of his deliveries could be received definitively either at Rochefort or at the Ile d'Indret. If he chose the latter, the price would be reduced by 10 sous (Sartine's tentative proposal) or 7 (Chaussade's proposal). Sartine finally allowed 8 sous. But, as he pointed out, "the [ocean] freight, the landing fees, cost of unloading, the commission, risks of the sea [i.e., insurance], and the easy disposal of rebutted pieces" at Indret/Nantes are considerations whose estimated value will certainly exceed the 10 sous per cubic foot reduction allowed if timber was inspected or definitively received by the navy at Indret. [72]

Chaussade asked that his transport workers be exempted from militia service, but the navy replied that such a clause "would not have any effect on the intendants of provinces"—that is, would not be honored by them. An article of the *Ordonnance* of 1 December 1774 disallowed such exemptions. Chaussade also sought inclusion of a clause limiting to 20 percent of the shipment the amount of timber that could be rejected, but that too was disallowed. [73] In a postscript the minister observed that "I have only the naval service in view in seeking to conciliate the interests of the king with those of the entrepreneurs, whose labor and concern must be compensated by an honest recompense." [74]

During each of several years of the six-year contract, as much as 250,000 cubic feet of timber were descended by Chaussade's own surrogates (operating under *prête-noms*) to the entrepôt at Indret. Deliveries of that magnitude required enormous capital, large and relatively long-term advances, and sufficient credit to survive the long period between the purchase of standing trees and the actual transfer of funds for timber accepted by the inspectors at the arsenals. It was a dangerous business for merchants expecting or needing to receive their money on delivery of the goods.

There were a few very small operators among Chaussade's "competitors." Some of them were probably proprietors of forested land: some of the *passeports* issued for downriver transit were for as little as 2,000 or even 500 cubic feet. (Since the average timber tree of the region produced between 15 and 25 cubic feet of timber, 500 cubic feet could be derived from twenty or thirty trees.) Other merchants or landowners commanding small capital formed an association to sign a contract with the navy.[75] Two wood merchants of Nantes, MM. Donard and Benache, went up-river into the provinces and apparently made trouble by offering excessively high prices for standing trees and by trying to get liens on available timber to force Chaussade (or his *prête-noms*) to buy through them. Later Donard asked the minister for a contract with the same terms as Chaussade's, but requiring him to deliver only 100,000 cubic feet in eight years. His proposal (which was rejected) was thought to be a cover for his purchases of liens on trees that had been marked as naval reserve. Still later, these two showed interest in the by-products of cuts—in pieces *not* intended for naval use. Without a contract themselves, they wanted to pass the navy-destined timber to Chaussade or his agent and take the remainder of the trees for private trade. Chaussade charged these "interlopers" with obstructing his operations, which they certainly tried to do.[76] Chaussade also made some charges against one of the navy's timber inspectors, but the minister's inquiries were "not sufficient," in Sartine's words, "to move me to use rigorous means." But he added that if the inspector in question were caught in illegalities, "this affair will probably have consequences disagreeable for him."[77]

In the first months of the contract, the work proceeded slowly. Chaussade informed the minister in April 1776 that in spite of difficulties, his agents estimated that 40,000 cubic feet would surely be delivered that year. But it was probably to make sure that all was going well, and to speed up his own agents, that Chaussade visited the Nivernais in mid-May, "to look over the work of the sawyers and axmen and see to the transport of the timber." His personal experience in the management of such operations extended back almost half a century, and he may have enjoyed getting back into the field, if only briefly.[78] It was probably Chaussade himself while in the area who gave the order to use horses from the stables of his forges to transport the timber in order to hurry the work. The navy's forest inspector on the site reported that Chaussade's presence "gave to the operation all the action of which it is susceptible."[79] It was perhaps during his visit in May that he decided to sell all the timber trees, whatever their age, from many of his own lands in the Nivernais.[80] And during that same visit to the region, or shortly afterward, Chaussade entered into an agreement with "three merchants of timber" by which they agreed to deliver to the "ports of the Loire" 200,000 cubic feet over a period of three years, beginning 1 November 1776. The contract made it clear that the marked (naval reserve) timber that they were to bring out of the forests to the river was to be delivered by Chaussade himself rather than his surrogate. Chaussade took the occasion to remind Sartine that he had earlier asked for a rise in prices of five sous per cubic foot, and that the rise had become more necessary than ever.[81] The ministry noted that the requested increase would occasion an added expense of over 80,000 livres "just for the contractors that M. de la Chaussade has hitherto procured." Evidently he had found suitable subcontractors. But he did not receive the substantial increase he wanted until December 1776.[82]

In December he announced that he had a special problem. He was assured of 125,000 cubic feet of trees situated "a great distance from the Loire and the Allier"; but "their extraction will cause extraordinary and ruinous expense . . . unless Monseigneur grants . . . the five-sou increase . . . requested." The navy's field inspector confirmed his description of the situation. It was decided to allow the increase "for all cuts more than four leagues [about ten miles] from the rivers." War was coming, and the navy was prodigal.[83]

Chaussade and his agents (*prête-noms* and subcontractors), conducting extensive and widely scattered exploitations, ran some of the navy's inspectors almost ragged, examining and marking "bouquets" and even single trees, as well as selections from extensive woodland and forest stands. Timber inspectors were "on circuit" for weeks, months, all year long, "obliged to eat and to sleep continually in different cabarets." They were exhausted; they complained about the four livres, ten sous *per diem* they received, which they called inadequate.[84] The pursuit of suitable timber by Chaussade's agents led one *contremaître charpentier* (inspector) to sell two horses that he had "carelessly ruined on his continual trips." Sartine granted him a *gratification* of 150 livres, which he took care *not* to call compensation for loss, since that might establish a costly precedent, saying, "I am furthermore persuaded that this mark of my satisfaction will lead this man Fouché to redouble his zeal and activity."[85]

Sartine was generous and helpful to Chaussade and rigorous in dealing with people who created problems for him. For example, when the horses and oxen needed to transport his timber were not made available, Sartine wrote to tell the intendant de Bron (April 1777) that it was "of the greatest consequence that the wood . . . furnished this year by the Sieur de la Chaussade . . . be transported as promptly as possible to the river-ports. . . . I have reason to believe that this entrepreneur, who has made purchases in your department, has the greatest desire to fulfill his engagements, and that in such pursuit he spares neither care nor expense. But you can see by the enclosed *mémoire* that the measures he takes so as not to allow the escape of a single piece of wood suitable to the construction or refitting of the king's ships will not produce any satisfactory result if the transport of which he has need is not furnished in time. It being the most favorable time of year, I ask you with fervor to give to your *sub-délégués* the most precise orders in this regard [so that] the service will experience no delay. You will, I assure you, do something very agreeable to the king in according to this entrepreneur all the facilities to which the importance of the service confided to him entitles him."[86] De Bron had been reluctant to assist Jean Babaud during the Lorraine exploitations, but he was apparently cooperative in the 1770s; Chaussade's accounts of the partners' earlier experience may have moved the minister to write this letter.

The following year Sartine again used the weight of ministerial authority to activate another intendant and get the timber moving. The problem arose when workers in two parishes of one intendancy rejected the price fixed by the *subdélégué* for the transport of timber destined for the naval service. "*Laboureurs,*" Sartine wrote,

> have no reason to complain when their vehicles are rated [for payment purposes] according to prices current in the district. The entrepreneurs will exact indemnities [through the courts] if they are obliged to accept arbitrary conditions from people of the countryside. This service cannot be considered a corvée, since the vehicles are paid for. [If] the intendant of the king believes that the parishes receiving orders are either refusing to furnish [vehicles] or are exacting prices that are too high, then that intendant should use his authority and fix transport prices in an equitable manner. Present circumstances require that the timber be delivered promptly to the ports. I would be very much obliged to you if you would give the necessary orders to your *subdélégués* so that nothing hinders the transport.[87]

Another sort of exploitation problem emerged when Chaussade and his associates moved to acquire timber in the forests of Grosbois and Ménage. Very large resources were found, but the Grand Master of Waters and Forests of Cirilly objected to extra (or irregular) cuts apart from their annual auctions.[88] In order to oblige the reluctant forestry officials to allow them, Sartine asked Jacques Necker, *contrôleur général des finances,* to give the necessary orders. Apparently Necker did so.[89] Later Necker again asked the *maître particulier* in charge of the two cantons in question, a Monsieur Moniot, to allow the exploitation of naval timber, and Moniot appears to have complied.[90]

The next year Chaussade again acquired the trees suited for naval use in the regular cut at Grosbois. He was evidently moved by their quality (and price) to commit himself to bid for all suitable materials as they became available in cuts of subsequent years. Because such roads as existed in the region were poor, Chaussade managed to persuade the forest administration (under Moniot) and the navy to divide the cost of bringing them to usable condition.[91]

As early as the spring of 1778, Chaussade reported that he and his employees "in the four provinces" had contracted with proprietors to acquire about 700,000 cubic feet of timber. But he expressed concern about reports from Rochefort that future deliveries would be given "the most severe inspection." He pointed out that he could probably double his deliveries in the next four years, but was hesitant to proceed without assurances regarding the attitude of the port: "I could not stand to lose the fruit of a *fourniture* as painful and arduous" as this one.[92] His shipments grew smaller.

Sartine was informed early in October 1778 that 240,000 cubic feet of timber was assembled at the ports of the Loire and Allier, with more en route.[93] Intensive exploitations continued in the period following. For example, *passeports* were issued in January 1780 for 200,000 cubic feet, and in May 1780 for 300,000.[94] Chaussade and his *prête-noms* renewed contracts in the fall of 1780 for *fournitures* to extend over a period of six years to supply Rochefort, Brest, and Lorient with all the shipbuilding timber that could be found and descended on the rivers Allier, Arron, Arroux, and Loire.[95]

In the middle years of the seventies, some suggested resuming the importation of timber from abroad. Proposals to bring in timber from the Rhineland region—Alsace, Lorraine, and specifically Cassel—were initially received with skepticism, if not hostility. A *conseil de marine* had, as we have seen, laid down a general condemnation of timber from Lorraine.[96] Nonetheless, in 1776 proposals from Hamburg merchants were favorably received, and it was reported in the summer of 1777 that sixteen ships had arrived at Rouen and Nantes carrying timber from Hamburg, and more was en route.[97] The timber coming from Hamburg merchants was declared to be of excellent "proportions," but much of it was also found to be "*gras*," and inspectors declared that it would be dangerous to use it for members in construction. Other counsellors pointed out, however, that "the time has come when one counts oneself fortunate to receive timber of any usable quality whatsoever." It was recalled that twelve years earlier, in the Choiseul administration, timber had been extracted from the forest of Normale in "Haynault," and two-thirds of the first shipments were rejected as "*gras*." That contract had been canceled, but afterward all the timber rejected was purchased by the English. So a timber inspector was sent off to Hamburg, apparently to assist the merchants there by selecting the pieces to be shipped to French arsenals.[98]

These imports evidently encouraged Chaussade to propose to transport to Holland and deliver in France 100,000 to 300,000 cubic feet of young trees from a "new forest near Sarrelouis belonging to a German prince." He would do so for the same price he received under his contract for the Loire cuts. One difficulty was that the young trees produced finished timbers only about ten inches square (hence, fourth-class timber).[99] The ministry urged Chaussade to have a sample of about thirty pieces sent covertly to France, "to the address of Monsieur Mistral," presumably a naval official at Le Havre. If the pieces proved usable, an *ingenieur constructeur* would be sent to make an exact inventory at the forest site.[100] The following December (1778), a *passeport* was issued to Chaussade for the passage of "timber from the principality of 'Saarbruck.'"[101] Chaussade probably undertook the proposed exploitation under an assumed name.[102]

Shipbuilder and Owner

In those years (1777–1781), Chaussade also showed an interest in the construction of the cargo vessels known as *gabarres*, which were sometimes as large as 350–400 tons. Such vessels were commonly used as carriers of timber, irons, and such bulk commodities as hemp, masts, and spars from Baltic ports to France or from Nantes to the naval dockyards. Though no document indicating why Chaussade ventured into the shipbuilding and shipowning business in this period has turned up, a report to the minister dated August 1779 states that about 170,000 cubic feet of "beautiful timber" was piled up at Indret.[103] Much of that timber must have been delivered to Indret by Chaussade's *prête-noms* and surrogates, and all of it must have been awaiting transportation by sea, either to the naval dockyards or to some commercial port or market where it could be sold. Chaussade's own deliveries of both timber and irons from French domestic sources were inspected and received by the navy at Indret during the war; there may also have been stockpiles of timber that were not in fact beautiful—that had not met the naval inspectors' exacting standards and were therefore on Chaussade's hands.

He could not easily move this timber out, much less sell it, for months or even years to come, given the international maritime struggles then going on. Moreover, crews for the navy were taken on around Indret and Rochefort and the coastal environs of the region. Hence, the arming of private craft for the transport of such surplus timber and irons as he had on hand was likely to be delayed. Chaussade himself commented in 1780 about the difficulty of the navy's own shipments.[104] "I don't have much hope that the barks out of Nantes will be able to move this wood and conduct it to Rochefort. They only carry 2,000 or 2,500 cubic feet, and if they are not helped by the [cargo-carrying] ships of the crown [usually *gabarres*], which carry 8,000 cubic feet, the removal [of this timber] will be very slow, and regardless of the care taken for its preservation, the timber deposited at Indret will suffer damage."[105] This comment could be interpreted as a discreet suggestion that extraordinary steps be taken to move the navy's timber out, perhaps in Chaussade's own newly built *gabarres*. More timber, hundreds of thousands of cubic feet of it, as we have seen, was to arrive at Indret in the two years that followed. The pressure to remove it efficiently to the arsenals was certain to increase. A desire to participate in and profit from that process, perhaps stowing some of his own irons as ballast, was, we can guess, part of Chaussade's immediate purpose, and part of the reason why he undertook to build four *gabarres* at Nantes.[106]

Chaussade may also have seen the development of the Wilkinson works at Indret as creating a longer-term need—a postwar need—for ships to bring coal and iron ingots to supply the needs of the newly created industrial plants. All of the coal and iron used there during the war was necessarily brought in by water. Opportunities as obvious as those in the shipping business would surely not have been missed by such a man. *Gabarres* based at Nantes in peacetime could carry exports (e.g., wines) from France to the Netherlands, Scandinavia, or even England, and return with northern masts or timber and irons or even Newcastle coal for Indret. Or his *gabarres* could go south, taking French exports to Spain and perhaps returning with Spanish woolens and irons.

As a *fournisseur* of timber and manufacturer of anchors and irons, Chaussade could certainly keep to a minimum his real shipbuilding costs, especially if the construction took place at Indret, where he could draw on his own stocks of *rebut* anchors, irons, and timber and whence the cost of transportation to Nantes would be minimal. Rejected materiel generally consisted of pieces or units that did not meet navy standards, which were exacting and objective in some matters, subjective in others. As regards both wood and iron, there was concern for uniformity, often extending to an insistence on specific texture, color, density, or hardness. Navy regulations, some of them printed, dictated size and proportions.

Much materiel judged unacceptable or drastically reduced in appraised value by inspectors went to commercial markets, but in wartime a *fournisseur* might become saddled with an embarrassing (and costly) superabundance of unwanted material, in which he had money tied up.

On 16 July 1781 Chaussade remarked in a letter to the new minister of marine, the marquis de Castries, that he had built four *gabarres* at Nantes to be employed exclusively for transporting his timber to Rochefort.[107] The likelihood is that they were built with material that Chaussade himself had on hand at Indret, much of it *rebut* material that he was unable to move out or sell commercially because of the war. Such material, having been exempted from river tolls in descending the Loire because it was destined for the navy, became subject to them when used for any commercial purpose. We can be confident that the tax collectors at Nantes, with whom Chaussade had an ongoing feud, were watchful and anxious to collect the taxes due if the material was put to commercial use. We can surmise that it was probably to avoid the payment of commercial tolls on the material he used in his ships that Chaussade accepted the condition, stated above, that his ships would be used only to transport his timber to Rochefort—that is, they would not engage in any operations as commercial carriers. Chaussade may have thought that acceptance of that condition would not disqualify him as a carrier of cargo, other than his own, for the navy. If so, he must have been jolted when the navy, probably at the behest of the tax-farmers, interpreted it as meaning that his ships could *not* be freighted by the navy for any purpose, since that would effectively make them commercial carriers, competing with other commercial carriers for navy cargoes.

Hence we find on 19 and 20 July, just days after the date of Chaussade's letter, Minister De Castries taking the trouble to write several letters, including one to Chaussade, saying that he was instructing officials at Brest and Rochefort *not* to use Chaussade's *gabarres*, even in lieu of the royal *service de gabarres*.[108] De Castries, it seems, was requiring the ports to freight exclusively the *gabarres* or *flûtes* of the navy, or other carriers, and explicitly forbidding them to use Chaussade's ships.

Since Chaussade's *prête-noms* and surrogates continued to hold contracts for the delivery of timber well into the eighties, they were probably able to make some use of Chaussade's *gabarres*. Chaussade's later contracts to deliver timber always carried clauses giving him the option of delivering it either to Indret (the preferred destination in wartime, to avoid risk of capture at sea) or to the arsenals themselves at higher prices. Whether he could make use of his own vessels in that traffic is uncertain.

What happened to Chaussade's four ships? Once his and his surrogates' contracts ran out, perhaps before, he would probably have gladly sold them to the crown at a good price. He may well have done so, and afterward they would have been used by the navy itself or by the Company of the North, organized by the navy after the war (in 1783) to bring timber from Hamburg and other foreign sources, and even masts and spars from Riga and St. Petersburg. Some might have been sold to Anthoine for his Black Sea enterprise, which aimed to import timber from the eastern Mediterranean.[109] It is hard to imagine Chaussade unable to dispose of those ships at a reasonable price.

CHAPTER 10

Chaussade in Retirement: Real Estate and Revolution

Selling Out

Chaussade finally sold the Forges Royales and their dependencies in 1780–1781. Since he still held important contracts to furnish anchors and irons for the navy, the negotiations with prospective purchasers included interviews between them and various "high personages" of the state, among them were the comte de Maurepas, then de facto first minister to Louis XVI; Sartine, secretary of state for the navy and colonies; and Daniel-Marc-Antoine Chardon, minister of marine (and later *directeur, forges aux ancres du Nivernais*). An acceptable proposition was finally tendered by the prospective buyers, a company of merchant-manufacturers represented by the Sieurs Sabatier and Desprez. The ministry of marine consented to renew the contract that Chaussade held for *fournitures* of irons to the navy, due to expire at the end of 1780.[1] Then, all the terms having been agreed upon by the buyers and Chaussade, the buyers deposited on 12 September 1780 the downpayment of 1.5 million livres that Chaussade intended to use immediately to pay off some of his creditors.[2]

One of the persons most affected by the sale of the Forges Royales was Champion de Cicé, bishop of Auxerre. He was not only the spiritual, but also the temporal, seigneur of the City of Cosne and its dependencies. Chaussade was his vassal and therefore obliged to obtain Cicé's assent to the transfer of the fief to a buyer, whether person or company. After considerable discussion and bargaining, on 4 June 1780 Cicé gave (in effect sold) Chaussade his formal written consent to the transfer of the forges to a purchaser not as yet selected. For this consent Cicé required 12,000 livres in cash, to be paid in three equal installments in December 1780 and the following January and February.[3] This transaction took place three months before the actual sale of the forges to Sabatier and Desprez.

Under the terms of the purchase contract, Bishop Cicé was to continue to collect from the new buyers the same feudal dues, *lods et ventes* and *cens*, and to receive *soumission* as he had from Chaussade. In short, the fief was transferred with all rights and obligations intact.

In the meantime, however, powerful persons in French government circles had decided that the Forges Royales should be acquired by the crown, rather than by a commercial company. The *contrôleur général des finances*, Jacques Necker, was the main promoter of the idea of purchase by the king. Maurepas, Sartine, and others in the royal councils opposed it. Necker, however, ultimately prevailed. With the king's sanction, he informed M. Chardon on 26 December 1780 that the king was purchasing the Forges Royales. The sale to Sabatier and Desprez was canceled, and the payment they had made to Chaussade was to be returned. The royal acquisition was backdated, but the definitive contract was not passed until March 1781.[4]

By substituting the king as purchaser of the forges, Necker effectively extinguished the seigneurial rights and perquisites, judicial powers, and *mouvances* that Champion de Cicé had hitherto enjoyed as lord. The king would not be Cicé's vassal: officially, the fief was extinguished by the act of acquisition by the crown. Cicé felt that he had been duped by Chaussade, against whom he undertook a campaign, demeaning himself by his three-year pursuit of an "indemnity." Finally he accepted 4,000 livres from the Royal Treasury to supplement the 12,000 he had already received from Chaussade, but insisted that he did so "without prejudice to the right to other compensation or to our rights." Thus he went back on his commitment to Chaussade and persisted to the bitter end in seeking more money.[5]

The duke of Nivernais, lord of Nevers, was similarly injured by the sale to the king, but an earlier royal *déclaration* (22 September 1722) gave him a serious claim to compensation. The indemnity paid to the duke amounted to 150,000 livres, which he consented to receive as a *rente viagère* (annuity) paying 5 percent, or 7,500 livres *per annum*.[6]

The Treasury evidently found it less easy to pay the 2.5 million-livre purchase price of Chaussade's forges. Chaussade had several major obligations secured by the properties being transferred, and these had to be paid off when the transfer was made. Over 215,000 livres in treasury funds was used to pay off such obligations and claims in June 1781, 188,000 of it going to the comte de Pierrecourt to repay a family loan of long standing. Later, 100,000 went to other relatives by marriage, the family Berthier de Bizy.[7] In all, at least 460,000 was paid to Chaussade's creditors in the first two years, and another 431,000 was paid to them later.[8] In 1785, several years after the sale of the forges, the full purchase price had still not been paid, but a payment plan was inaugurated calling for regular annual installments to Chaussade, then almost eighty years of age.[9]

Few payments, if any, were in fact made before 1789. In May 1791 half the purchase price was still unpaid. This fact was brought to the attention of the National Assembly, which apparently passed a private bill recognizing the obligation on 17 May 1791. Even in the best of circumstances, payments by the state could be slow, and circumstances were not then good. Several published sources suggest that Chaussade was never fully paid, and that contention seems to be part of family tradition. Curiously, Chaussade appears to have executed a receipt acknowledging payment in full of all sums due him from the crown. This receipt, dated 23 March 1792, is in the archives of Chaussade's notary (Aleaume); even if that receipt is authentic, it remains uncertain whether Chaussade received full payment for the forges in that eighty-sixth (and last) year of his life.[10] The receipt could, for example, have been readied by Chaussade (then in poor health) in hopeful anticipation of the payment promised in 1792 and placed in the hands of his faithful notary for possible use. The fact that it remains in the notary's files might in fact argue that payment was *not* made.

In the years between 1780 and 1790, Aleaume's records show, Chaussade (then between seventy-four and eighty-three years of age) was busy with various money-raising and investment enterprises. Thus in March 1780 he raised 52,000 livres by selling an office he had acquired for his son, Pomponne Marie Pierre Babaud de la Chaussade de Villemenant.[11] In October 1781, under the name of his familiar *prête-nom* Jean Barrois, he subleased to the king for 25,000 livres a year the barony and seigneury of the comte Desbordes with the forge of Gué and 153 *arpents* of woodland that he himself had leased from the widow Antoinette Crozat de Thiers on 10 June 1780, the summer he sold the forges.[12] He also persuaded some of the creditors whose claims on him were secured by his lands to renounce immediate claims and accept *rentes en perpetuité* at 5 percent interest,[13] the usual rate paid in contracts with the state. However, in that period of government financial crisis, Chaussade was able to purchase four treasury certificates of 9,000 livres denomination each, paying 27,000 livres for the first three and (apparently) 8,000 for the fourth. Those certificates paid him 9 percent interest. Thus he was borrowing at 5 percent and buying government securities paying 9 percent.[14]

Apparently some of his creditors disapproved of Chaussade's methods and priorities in paying off obligations and took legal action, but the minister of marine, De Castries, asked the *procureur général*, Joly Fleury, to cease to push further suits against Chaussade.[15] At one point Chaussade disbursed 46,000 of 100,000 he received from the king to pay off all that remained of a debt to the estate of the duc d'Orléans.[16] And he was the leader of an association of creditors cooperating to try to obtain settlement from a certain St. Joseph de Guerennet, paymaster (*tresorier*) to the late prince of Conty. It is doubtful that the association enjoyed much success.[17]

Chaussade also attempted to raise money by going after sums due him for materials delivered to the navy. Emphasizing the "heavy expenses he incurred every month for the service" and his need for regular payments (he suggested the tenth, twentieth, and thirtieth of each month), he said that he was persuaded that he "merited this preference."[18] We also find him insisting to Minister De Castries in April 1781 that the navy should buy his irons at the higher prices to which Sartine, the minister's predecessor, had agreed in 1780.[19] A month later Chaussade begged De Castries to include 60,000 livres for him on the next scheduled disbursement of funds (*état de distribution*) to *fournisseurs*, which was due to be published soon; that amount, he said, would be due on the timber he was currently delivering to Toulon.[20]

Chaussade sought to turn to his advantage the change in the minister for marine. The knowledgeable Sartine was out, and soon afterward Chaussade's long-time friend and patron Maurepas died. Chaussade's relations with Sartine had been amiable. One senses them becoming increasingly intimate in the 1770s as the vagaries of officials at Brest and Chaussade's losses through fraud were revealed. Sartine, though principled and honest, made many concessions to Chaussade. He spent heavily for the American War, and Chaussade was, of course, one beneficiary of that spending. Sartine's successor, De Castries, was under great pressure to economize expenditure. Chaussade must have wondered what to expect from this new administration, but he was not reticent in seeking to protect his interests.

Indeed, in March 1781 he sought some form of compensation from De Castries (perhaps a *gratification;* Chaussade called it "*un dédommagement*") in lieu of "the benefice he would have hoped for" from his operations (had he not sold his forges?), and "for having provisioned in 1779 and 1780, with anchors and irons of all kinds, the ports of the navy, the colonies, and India."[21]

Chaussade had already received some significant recognition. With Sartine's support he had been commended by the king for his work as director of the establishments at Cosne and Guérigny and for "the zeal he had always shown for the well-being of His Majesty's service . . . over more than fifty years." His Majesty also recognized that the Sieur Babaud de la Chaussade had "arrived at an age which will no longer permit him to carry on the difficult work such great enterprises require," but had given "new proof of his disinterestedness in consenting to transfer property and manufactories to buyers who were judged the most capable of maintaining them in the flourishing state to which he had brought them." In consequence His Majesty, as a mark of his satisfaction, accorded Chaussade a pension in the amount of 5,000 livres a year, beginning 21 September 1780.[22]

That De Castries was favorably disposed to the "retiring" *fournisseur* of irons and timber is suggested by a summary of the navy's accounts for 1781, where Chaussade was carried for a provisionment of irons (his last year) valued at 1.1 million livres, nearly all of which he had already received.[23] Hence Chaussade was paid relatively promptly and fully for his *fourniture* of irons under De Castries. As a *fournisseur* of timber and plank—with which he was still involved—he was paid in 1781 at least as well as the other *fournisseurs* in the realm.[24] Toward the end of 1781, timber was needed for construction at the manufactory of M. Wendel, a plant familiarly known as the *établissement de Montcenis*. De Castries called on Chaussade, who no doubt gladly agreed to supply the necessary timber. Accordingly, in November 1781, Chaussade was asked "to give the necessary orders" for timber deliveries to Wendel's manufactory.[25] Chaussade not only built manufactories himself, but was called to supply construction materials to help other industrialists build theirs.

When pulling out of the iron business, Chaussade concurrently transferred to others most of his responsibilities and ties in the timber business. Surrogates and *prête-noms* thereafter handled the details and soon carried the contracts in their own names, but with Chaussade often serving as *caution* (i.e., their financial guarantor and very likely also silent partner). One such semi-independent successor-*fournisseur* was Brillantais Marion, who was referred to in 1783 as "*cessionnaire* of the contract of M. de la Chaussade for provisioning the ports of the [Atlantic] Ocean with timber."[26]

By the end of 1783 Chaussade was suffering from that common malady of government contractors of the old regime—financial stringencies resulting from slow payment or nonpayment by the state. To deal with forest proprietors, even to bid for marked trees at auctions, where cash payment was usually required, was becoming impossible by the end of 1783: his resources and credit were exhausted. The minister could do little to help him except to order subordinates to restrict the marking of trees to those that could provide curved timber or pieces of the first type, thus slowing the work. The wartime need to hasten provisionments no longer existed: De Castries wanted to be helpful but could offer no prospect of early payments.[27]

Though officially retired from the iron business and in the process of unburdening himself of timber *fournitures,* Chaussade still found himself saddled, in February 1783, with quantities of timber at Indret. The stockpile probably comprised pieces that had been rejected for some cause by the inspectors at Indret and had not been used up in the construction of his four *gabarres.* It was reported the next month that five *gabarres* had brought cargoes of defective timber and other stores belonging to Chaussade to the port of Lorient, where, it was said, there was a good deal of resentment at his saddling the port with these mountains of rejects. Orders were given to suspend such shipments.[28] It was finally decided that the port could accept for use only fifty-eight planks, twenty-eight *bordages,* 300 barrels of tar, and selected other stores; there were eleven masts, and even though Lorient was "sufficiently stocked with pieces of those sizes," the minister ordered the port to accept them anyway, "but effort should be made to reduce the price."[29] Chaussade probably managed to unload much of this material eventually, because much commercial shipbuilding was going on at Lorient and other ports in those postwar years. But after the first half of 1782, the Babaud name—for the first time in over half a century—became rare in the correspondence files of the navy.[30]

Real Estate Investments

Chaussade, though retired from timber and irons, was still busy. The suggestion in the king's pension decree that he was no longer capable of difficult work was mistaken. Chaussade was in Paris. His age and physical condition probably prevented him from undertaking much travel, even within the city, but he had notaries, lawyers, accountants, clerks, bailiffs, *régisseurs,* and leg-men at his command, and he still had an active intelligence and "spirit of enterprise."

Principally he busied himself with buying and managing property both in Paris and in the provinces. He turned up some attractive investment opportunities. For example, in December 1780 he bought a property in the village of St. Gervais, "on the main street of the parish of Pantin" (in Paris), comprising a building, courtyard, *orangerie,* barns, a large garden, trees, promenades, and ponds, "the whole enclosed by walls and containing about five acres with a small house and garden and various scattered pieces of ground nearby." The price was 55,000 livres, plus assumption of various rents and feudal or seigneurial rights and obligations.[31] He bought for 60,000 livres a second property in St. Gervais in 1788 (one large house and one small, with their dependencies) on the same street as the 1780 purchase.[32]

South of Paris, in his old stamping ground in the valley of the Loire— the Nivernais—Chaussade still held several properties: the seigneuries of La Boue, acquired in 1770 for 115,000 livres, including 80,000 in cash; and the seigneuries of Bolz (acquired for 36,000 livres). To these, in 1783, he added Beaumont la Ferrière and dependencies (46,800 livres)[33] and the fief and seigneuries of Guichy, situated in the parish of Nanoy in the Nivernais, for which he paid 102,000 livres, with payments spread over four years.[34]

Chaussade's largest and most costly purchase was made in 1785, not in the Nivernais, but northwest of Paris near Calais. From Charles de Rohan, prince of Soubise, Chaussade acquired Mons-Boubers, a group of associated seigneuries (Mons, Boubers, Arret, Franleux, Lesquesnoy) and their dependencies situated close to Abbeville (Ponthieu). Possessed for many centuries by the House of Melun, they came after the last duke died in 1724 to the prince of Soubise. Chaussade paid 330,000 livres for them. They paid substantial feudal dues to the crown, amounting to 35,000 livres a year, and Chaussade assumed that obligation in making his purchase.[35]

Significantly, nearly all his properties, even his parcels in Paris, were seigneuries. Statements made in the contracts, or the terms of payment themselves, indicate that many of the purchases were made with hastily borrowed funds and a minimum of cash. After his purchases, Chaussade appointed *régisseurs* to manage the estates according to carefully detailed instructions. The management of seigneurial estates in eighteenth-century France involved no military or significant political functions aside from the maintenance of law and order through the exercise of police and judicial authority when "high-justice" powers were conferred. But the exercise of such authority and powers was sure to be helpful—indeed, critical—to the goals of a "feudal" tenant like Chaussade. He was comfortably well-to-do but without the independent means required to make large annual outlays without receiving substantial rents himself. His objective in purchasing was bound to be to make the property pay. He was a middleman, a tenant with tenants of his own; he and his surrogates saw profit as their essential purpose.

The importance of this economic motive was made clear after his acquisition of the Mons-Boubers properties near Abbeville. He immediately set his feudal lawyers to work on "the up-dating (*la renovation*) of the *terrier* of Mons-Boubers and dependencies."[36] To that end he handed over available titles and records and made an agreement with a certain Sieur Dumesnil, *commissaire à terrier,* "to make a *terrier général* of the domains of Mons-Boubers and its dependencies." Chaussade "paid in full the agreed price for the said *terrier.*"[37] Paying more than 10 percent of the value of the seigneury in rent (35,000 livres *per annum* on a 330,000-livre purchase), Chaussade was understandably anxious to have Dumesnil work fast and well in order to get the "exploitation" of the seigneury under way as soon as possible. Unfortunately, Dumesnil did not accomplish all the tasks required by Chaussade. Chaussade himself was unusually experienced in such matters and may have set standards that Dumesnil did not foresee. In any case he did not meet them. The Mons-Boubers dossier found among Chaussade's effects at his death does not reflect his insistence on systematic procedures and meticulous, thoroughgoing attention to detail. This jumble of residual papers consists essentially of models of *procurations* and *procurations données* by the late Sieur de la Chaussade to different persons for the *régie* of the domains of Mons-Boubers: accounts, *mémoires,* receipts from workmen, receipts for taxes, estimates for work to be performed, contracts, and so on.[37]

Late in the same year he bought Mons-Boubers (1785), Chaussade acquired, and immediately renewed for the period from 1786 onward, a nine-year lease already held by a certain Cesar Delorgue Delisle, merchant of Abbeville, which entitled him to take young trees (*taillis*), except oak, from the woodlands of Mons-Boubers. The contract also allowed Delisle to lease the arable (*terres à labourer, champarts, ou terrages*) and mills from 1787 on, and to collect the *cens et rentes* due on the crops. Delisle agreed to pay Chaussade 8,500 livres *de loyer en fermages* per year, in two equal installments at six-month intervals; to furnish him with a certified accounting of the taxpayers (*censives payées*) and the amounts paid to the previous seigneur of Boubers (Soubise); and to continue to provide such accounts henceforth.[39]

Subsequently, Chaussade bought other properties in the environs of his Abbeville holdings. In 1786 he acquired "one-half of the fief of Abrancourt, situated at Franleux, for 4,000 livres plus 144 livres *épingles* and 24 sous contribution to the poor"; the next year he bought the other half. Another property was acquired from a certain Aclot of Abbeville for 9,012 livres in 1788.[40] Amid the momentous events of 1789, we find Chaussade picking up parcels of property, small and large, including a piece of about two *journaux de terre.* Since a *journal* commonly comprised the amount of land a plow could work in a day (the exact dimensions varied with the locale), this was a distinctly small parcel situated in the Franleux area, near Boubers, and Chaussade paid 184 francs for it on 8 June 1789.[41]

Nor did the advent of the revolution bring these proceedings to a halt. On the contrary, in 1791 he submitted tenders, using the name Isaac Greson, to purchase twenty-two *journaux* of land in twelve parcels close to Mons-Boubers. These had been owned by the Chapel of Boubers but passed to the state after the legal take over of church property. For the twelve parcels, Chaussade paid 13,200 livres.[42] The same year he bought a much larger unit of tillable land for 110,000 livres (or francs), referred to as being in the département de la Somme; other land he acquired was close to Calais. And in 1792, amid full-scale revolution and at eighty-six years of age, we find Chaussade busy collecting the parchment titles, deeds, and leases of property formerly owned by religious of the priory in order to establish the amount of acreage held by tenants, farmers, and sublessees in the environs of property he already owned.[43]

Though he showed special interest in his Abbeville holdings, Chaussade did not neglect the Nivernais; he was concerned that the properties be well administered and the accounts correct. To that end he appointed two carefully selected men, Grenot and Sebastien Guay, as his special representatives in 1781.[44] Guay was Chaussade's choice as *régisseur* of the *terre* of Boue, whose previous *régisseur*, a certain Sieur Millot, had held the post for less than two years (1780 and the first seven months of 1781). Millot may have embezzled funds during that period and certainly spent money without Chaussade's approval. Millot insisted that he had used 3,861 livres to buy rye on Chaussade's account from a person in the village of Lameny and 264 livres to purchase wood for the navy. He was relieved of his authority, and Chaussade instructed Grenot and Guay to sell the rye and the timber, "if it can be found," *à la folle enchère* (an auction of the possessions of an incompetent) "for the account of the Sieur Millot." The accounts must be balanced, "if need be by the sale of any or all of the household goods, real estate, or other possessions of Sieur Millot or his wife *solidairement*, all proceedings to be at the expense of the Millots."[45]

It was Guay who was inadvertently responsible for uncovering Millot's mismanagement, for in comparing Guay's accounts with his own (based on Millot's) Chaussade found that the receipts and expenditures did not balance, making it appear that Guay himself was about 4,000 livres short. Chaussade ordered the Sieur Guay, his newly appointed *régisseur* to come to Paris, bringing all papers relevant to his accounts. Guay duly arrived with registers and papers, and "after having employed a great deal of time examining the said accounts, the Sieur de la Chaussade decided to return the Sieur Guay to his post." He gave him a new set of books (*modèle de comptabilité*) to use from then on; thereafter, Guay was to send his receipts and records of expenses month by month.[46]

Chaussade was more careful, it seems, in dealing with estate managers than he had been with certain earlier correspondents in distant places. He watched the *régisseurs* with exacting, meticulous attention, and was stern with subordinates who stepped over the bounds. Even minor transgressors were treated with rigor. Among his papers is a dossier containing no fewer than twenty-six documents connected with his legal action against a certain Sieur Guerville, a *fermier* who had illicitly felled a single tree "in the woodland of the late Sieur de la Chaussade at Mons-Boubers."[47] However, when a good and faithful job was done, Chaussade was willing to reward a subordinate with a certain watchful confidence. Guay won a promotion, becoming *régisseur* of both La Boue and Bolz, with an annual salary of 900 livres, just a trifle less than the designated salary of De Vaux, *régisseur* of Chaussade's largest, most complex estate, Mons-Boubers. A certain C. Signière, *régisseur* of Beaumont, Guichy, and La Ronce, earned a salary of 600 livres. (The salaries were probably only part of the remuneration received by the provincial *régisseurs;* each was also supplied with housing and enjoyed such perquisites as domestics and transportation.) Among Chaussade's papers are hundreds of pieces relative to the work of the Sieur Baudard, inspector-general of his estates in the province of the Nivernais. Chaussade also had in his employ in 1792 Citizen Jean Mathias de Vaux, *caissier* at Paris. He affirmed after Chaussade's death that the master account books (*Grand Livre*), and also the "greater part" of the other accounts that he had kept for Chaussade, "were balanced."[48] Even in the last year of his life, Chaussade maintained an office in Paris, with a headquarters staff of at least four people: his *chef de bureau* (with a salary of 3,600 livres); a comptroller (*caissier,* 1,500 livres); a secretary (*commis aux écritures,* 900 livres); and an *agent de bureau* (500 livres). Their relatively high salaries probably reflect the minimal perquisites attached to their posts and the relatively high cost of living in Paris.[49]

Chaussade's preference for seigneuries and his concern for the intricacies of *terriers* and feudal relationships can be traced, as we have seen, to his preoccupation with exploiting the potentiality of all his properties. He was no doubt following a well-established pattern of the period. Some of his own predecessors—the Soubise family, for example—had employed *régisseurs* and *terriers* to manage the Mons-Boubers complex. Chaussade worked through some of the agents (or lessees) of Perier, the Soubise *régisseur,* to obtain established lists of taxpayers. Taxes had been collected

under the auspices of absentee-owner Soubise, but probably no more efficiently than under the next absentee, Pierre Babaud de la Chaussade,
whose thorough-going system required: (1) an inventory of available
records and titles; (2) the development of a general *terrier* by his own attorneys or a *commissaire;* (3) examination of existing tenures and leases
and their revocation or renewal as required; (4) rehabilitation of facilities
(buildings, mills, mill ponds, roads); (5) appointment of a loyal *régisseur*
with bailiffs and judicial officers; (6) the use of every opportunity to
strenghten the owner's hand and maximize the revenues from the property, whether paid in money or in kind.

Revolution

Chaussade's management had been in effect at Mons-Boubers for less
than three years when he received a report, dated 17 May 1789, confirm-
ing earlier warnings and no doubt causing him serious concern: the
Abbeville vassals were said to be "murmuring" against him. When that
news reached him, angry crowds in his own quarter of Paris must have
been both audible and visible to him from the window of the house where
he lived. He habitually sat overlooking the street. He already knew that
his vassals at Mons-Boubers were "pretending that the agent of the late
prince of Soubise [d. 1787] had already required them to render *aveux et
reconnaissance* in the name of the prince;" they claimed that they were
not obliged to do so again, except at Chaussade's cost and without any
cost whatsoever to themselves.[50]

Chaussade cannot have been pleased by this resistance to the payment
of assessments. But what could he do? Perhaps he counseled his *régisseurs* to be cautious, reasonable, and calm. The violence in and near the
quarters where he himself resided continued in the weeks and months following May 1789. He was retired, quiet, but also alert and watchful. He
has described his own situation on the rue Bondi (now the rue R. Boulan-
ger, near the Place Republique). The house where he lived was owned by
a man in the entourage of the prince of Soubise. Chaussade's window, as
he himself described it, "offered a view on the street and boulevard" (now
Boulevard St. Martin). There he sat in 1787, aged eighty-one, "in an arm-
chair by the fireplace, feeble in bodily health, suffering the infirmities of
age, but still healthy in soul and memory and mind."[51] Chaussade quietly
managed his affairs from his comfortable chair. He may have been seated
there on 13 January 1789 when Nicolas Chaillon, *conseiller* and *secrétaire du roy,* "assumed the posture and state of a vassal [bowed head and

bended knee?] and made and offered the faith, homage, and *fidélité* he [as vassal] owed to Chaussade [his lord] by reason of the fief he held." [52]

Chaussade could also act from that chair, as we have seen, through surrogates and attorneys, seeking payment of sums due (long overdue) from the state, and purchasing still more property. He used both *prête-noms* and (on several occasions) his own name to buy substantial parcels of land that before nationalization had belonged to the church. Many of his contemporaries condemned such purchases; some members of his own family, if they knew about them, probably disapproved.

His family, in any case, was divided. Many were well-established *noblesse;* he had selected such families when seeking prospective husbands for his daughters. His daughter Louise Rose Babaud de la Chaussade, for example, had become the wife of Etienne François, comte de Berthier-Bizy; his grandsons, the brothers Pierre Charles Auguste Goujon (chevalier marquis de Gasville) and Jean Prosper Camille Charles (chevalier de Gasville), likewise bore distinctly aristocratic names; and his granddaughter, Dame Cécile Rose Françoise de Guiry, was the wife of Charles Amedée Gabriel (chevalier marquis de Brossard). Even Chaussade's son Pomponne Marie Pierre Babaud de Villemenant classed as *noblesse*. Chaussade had acquired offices for him that implied, if they did not confer, *noblesse*. Chaussade himself, as we have seen, for almost half a century owned the office as *secrétaire du roy au Grand Collège,* that had conferred *noblesse* on him, a status he still relished, for in the eighties he wrote again to d'Hosier, the genealogist, to obtain a new copy of his official coat of arms.

The course of revolution in France after 1789 put members of Chaussade's family at a crossroads. Some became *émigrés;* others remained in France. [53] Chaussade himself showed no disposition to leave, even had he been physically able to get away. But after he died, in August 1792, the revolutionary government, having decided to seize the property of *émigrés* and others classed as enemies of revolutionary France, did seize much property belonging to his heirs. [54] Not until 1839 were the resulting difficulties and divisions finally settled by his descendants, and then only in circumstances described as disastrous.

Epilogue: Comparisons and Reflections

Significant comparisons can be made between Chaussade's firm and two other major iron manufacturers of the period—the Crowley firm of London (and Birmingham, Sourbridge, Winlaton, and Durham) and the Söderfors anchor works of Sweden.[1] Like Chaussade, the Crowleys and Söderfors were manufacturers of anchors and therefore important naval contractors. Söderfors furnished anchors and iron to the Swedish navy, and also to the British; the Crowleys furnished to the British navy and to merchant shipbuilders and shippers in the Americas. All three suffered from fluctuations in naval demand and from late or depreciated payment by the navy they principally served. Chaussade suffered the most prolonged and greatest damage because the promissory notes and scrip he received were nonnegotiable. The Crowley and Söderfors works were established some decades earlier than Chaussade's, but all three were prosperous and prominent in the four decades after 1748, especially in the years of the American War. Afterward, all three passed into the hands of successor managements and declined.

While they lasted, each of these industrial firms was a giant for the time, employing thousands of men, including outworkers, who clustered around several concentrations of producing units, working either in them or as carriers between them, bringing in raw materials and conveying production toward entrepôts and the navy's seacoast arsenals. The navy yards were their principal customers, but each firm also shipped to distant markets overseas. Both Chaussade and the Crowleys looked to colonies overseas to absorb surplus production in peacetime. The Crowleys dispatched to English colonies dozens of products of types almost identical to those named on the bills of lading (or *passeports*) for Chaussade's shipments destined for French possessions overseas. Söderfors also supplied an Indies company and some merchant shipping requirements, and exported anchor overstock and much bar iron to England.[2]

Products and Quality

The remarkable similarities between the Chaussade and Crowley firms deserve detailed examination. In comparing their shipments we need to note that the documentation on the Crowleys was not abundant for their historian M. W. Flinn, and that more than three decades separate the documentation available on the exports of the two firms.[3] However, the character of demand in the North American, West Indian, and Indian Ocean colonies of the two powers probably did not undergo major change in the period. The advancing industrial revolution, at least in the ferrous metal trades, did not much affect the form or type of products used. Hence considerable significance may be attached to the fact that the items named on the export lists of the two firms were very similar; this evidence puts the firms very much on a par.

Ideally, we would like to be able to compare the quality of the export items produced and shipped by Chaussade and the Crowleys, since such comparison might throw light on the level of technical expertise at their respective manufactories. Unfortunately, this is not possible, because both firms employed numerous subcontractors whose products, for the most part, cannot be distinguished on the lists from the products of the units managed by Crowley and Chaussade themselves.

Perhaps the best general comment we can manage on the relative quality of their iron and steel is that the Crowleys made very extensive use of foreign irons: American, Russian, Spanish, and especially Swedish. The use of Swedish bar iron was considered desirable when a high-quality end-product was sought, as in steel manufacture. For the Crowley firm the costs of English and Swedish bar iron, all considered, may have been similar; their persistent preference for Swedish iron must have been based on its superiority over much of the bar iron available in England.[4] "For some purposes," reported M. W. Flinn, "particularly steel-making, only Swedish iron could be used, so that it was never possible for the Crowleys to do without their Swedish supplies."[5]

In Chaussade's manufactories, on the other hand, all the iron used was smelted in France. Situated far up the Loire, his works were remote from seaports; though importing Swedish or foreign iron was doubtless possible, via the rivers and canal of Briare, for example, it was not economically practical for Chaussade to import stocks of semifinished materials, as it was for the Crowleys and many other English producers of iron and steel. Chaussade as a steel producer lacked the Crowleys' easy option, the advantage of using high-grade imports as primary materials. He had to depend on pig iron or bars fabricated from French ores, the best of them reputedly being from nearby sources in the Berry. That fact might raise estimates of the quality of Berry iron-smelting operations generally; or, conversely, it might justify lower expectations about the quality of his finished product. We do not, in fact, know much about the processes he and his suppliers of semifinished materials used, and (as will be seen) we can only guess about the quality of his steel.

We do know, however, that *passeports* for his shipments (c. 1760) referred to "German steel" and later to "common steel." The term "German steel" had by the mid-eighteenth century become a blurred, generic phrase implying (in England) either cementation or shear steel quality. In France the term probably had different meanings, and in Chaussade's terminology might even have been simply descriptive of the fact that German (or German-speaking) workers had been employed in its production. In the early 1760s Chaussade was operating several steel-processing facilities. The steel produced at a facility operated by his German-speaking workers could have been of cementation quality, the cementation process having been commonly used in German ironworking even in the seventeenth century. Chaussade, we know, had good local clay, much-used for tiles on his estates, that could have been employed, as clay needed to be, in the preparation of the chests then employed in the cementation and "German" processes of steel making.[6]

The first references we find to steel making at his manufactories followed (but did not precisely coincide with) the introduction of German workers, suggesting at least the possibility that the German newcomers did introduce the manufacture of steel and perhaps participated in its production at his manufactories. The evidence suggests that they were probably most involved in introducing other industrial processes there. Chaussade himself referred in one document to a slitting mill he had just built at Cosne (1760) with two accompanying reverberatory *feux*, where he said he was producing thin strip iron (*feuillard mince*), "thereby procuring for France a type of iron that before my time was imported from Germany and Sweden." A later (1780) reference to the same facility (by then enlarged) alluded to the unit as a "German-type slitting mill" (*fenderie à l'allemande*) producing hoops for casks, with eight tilt hammers for finishing work. Some of his German workers may therefore have been employed in the production of thin strip iron as well as hoops for casks and barrels.

Most of the few references to German steel on *passeports* issued for Chaussade's shipments involve several types of uncertainty. First, we know that not all items listed were of Chaussade's own manufacture (e.g., the musical instruments and parts for them on some later *passeport* lists).

The German steel listed on *passeports* may actually have been imported from German sources, though I think that this is very unlikely and that German steel very probably was manufactured at Chaussade's plants either by workers he brought from Germany or from German-speaking parts of France, or by French workers using one or another of the so-called German processes. Yet when we read that the minister of marine Sartine charged Chaussade "to have twenty-four German-style sawblades manufactured," we cannot know whether Chaussade produced such blades at his own manufactories or had to turn to some other maker. Two of his steel-producing plants (Frasnay and La Vache) were early and definitely identified with the production of German steel, but by 1780 they were simply reported as producing common steels (*aciers communs*). Taken together, these scattered references suggest, I think, that at different times his manufactories probably turned out steels of different grades.

Various grades of steel may have been precisely what Chaussade intended to produce. Intentionally or not, a variety of steels, each made differently and having different characteristics, would have been a natural outcome of the interplay of the many variables in steel making, then little understood. Steel production was complex; uniform quality was extremely difficult to achieve. Steel is an alloy of iron, carbon, and other elements; small variations in carbon content and in the procedures used in heating, cooling, casting, or forging could change the properties of the end-product considerably. Chaussade had little or no use for steels of fine quality—crucible steel, for example. Even the contemporary Crowley firm (admittedly not particularly innovative) did not introduce the production of crucible steel until 1810, seventy years after the process was discovered by Benjamin Huntsman.[7] But Chaussade and the Crowleys did have many uses for lower grades of steel in the wide variety of products they turned out. Both firms must have made or used most of the steels that modern metallurgists identify as "mild," "tempered," "medium," "high-carbon," "thin-layered," and "case-hardened."[8] Important questions remain concerning the steel-making processes and product of Chaussade's works; some combination of industrial archaeology and local records can perhaps produce more detailed knowledge of the processes used in his time and the specific quality of the steels his works produced.

I have here placed special stress on the quality of the iron used and the steel produced at Chaussade's works. It must have been generally good, if only because the goods produced from those materials seem usually to have satisfied those very critical inspectors at the royal arsenals at Brest and Rochefort. To manufacture products acceptable to those fastidious navy inspectors was Chaussade's prime objective, as it was Ambrose Crowley's in his dealings with the officials at the dockyards of the British navy. Even our limited knowledge of the production processes used at his forges and fineries suggests that a large proportion of the metal in his products, his hardwares and tools as well as his anchors, was of quality that would be classed, in modern technical terminology, as being one or another of the various grades of steel (mentioned above). But it is also worth remembering that in France steel was much more heavily taxed at the producer level than was iron; Chaussade would surely have taken care to see that as much of his product as possible was classed and taxed as iron, rather than as steel.

Chaussade was, above all else, a businessman. He was no Darby or Huntsman, nor could he have had much use for the processes in which they specialized, whatever their value for others. Unlike those two remarkable innovators, Chaussade did not and could not develop his own processes for production and then base his business and career on them. When Chaussade took the helm of the family business, the industrial firm he was to control was already well established. The first great anchor forge at Cosne was already in use. Most of the processes he was required to utilize to fabricate anchors (the pyramid process in particular) had been developed and perfected as far as the navy was concerned long before. His principal customer was waiting; Chaussade had only to deliver the goods to it. It was, we might add, a tough customer, having very definite, fixed standards of quality. The iron and steel he delivered had to pass scrutiny and testing, in the dockyard and at sea, by an organization prepared to discount or reject any product believed to fall short of its standards.

Both Chaussade and the Crowleys, we may be sure, strove to have their forgemasters exercise every care to meet those standards; both knew well that the king's ships and the lives of the crewmen aboard them must sometimes depend on the quality of the anchors that they had forged. It was no mean task to forge an anchor, and the larger the anchor the more difficult the task. Not even the best processes and heaviest water-powered hammers of the time could achieve a uniform strength in the entire thickness of the shank and branches of the largest pieces. But a weak or uneven anchor was a perilous one. The French navy's solution to this problem, the pyramid system, employed carefully preforged bars about one inch thick and varying in width. The largest anchors were fabricated with shanks composed of as many as thirty-five bars, which were individually forged, then stacked and forged together, layer after layer in many successive heats. Preforging the bars and welding each layer to those adjacent ensured that the metal in the members was well forged and welded throughout. The system appears to have been capable of producing steel anchors of excellent quality. Some of the best metallurgical technicians in France, and even members of the Académie des Sciences, applied themselves to its development over many decades; it was the outgrowth of an authentic "research and development" program, sanctioned and financed by the navy. Officials of the French navy were no doubt confident that Chaussade, using that process, was forging anchors that no one could then have bettered.

The documents available to M. W. Flinn did not permit him to explain in detail the methods used by the Crowleys or to state whether the British navy prescribed any method for forging anchors. Hence we do not know whether their methods could produce anchors as strong and dependable as the pyramid system so carefully developed and so much depended upon and praised by the French. We know, however, that both the Crowleys and Chaussade produced anchors of comparable size that passed the tests of inspectors at the arsenals and of use at sea.

Commercial and Colonial Markets

Perhaps the most significant differences between the Chaussade and Crowley firms emerge when their commercial marketing opportunities are compared. Both firms sought to sell not only to the navy, but to semi-governmental Indies companies, private commercial shipbuilders and shippers, and consumers in overseas colonies as well. The Crowleys, conducting their business far and wide over Britain, were "unique in catering for a national market in an era of regional economies."[9] Chaussade could not supply a national market where none existed—France was a vast composite of virtually autonomous regional markets. Even with the close collaboration of the ministry of marine, Chaussade never made important sales to commercial consumers at the Biscay ports of the Atlantic seaboard, still less at those of the Mediterranean. Though the French colonies seemed a promising market to Chaussade when he undertook to expand and diversify around 1750, subject as they were to control by the ministry of marine, all the commercial markets in France and the French colonies proved disappointing to him.

Opportunities for overseas sales were drastically reduced for him by the Seven Years War. Not only was France cut off from the colonies during the war, but the failures of the armed forces of France and its allies resulted in the amputation of many overseas possessions and markets. Those colonial losses were confirmed at the peace table. Afterward the Louisiana colony was transferred to Spain, France's ally and partner in the Bourbon Family Compact. Thus after 1763 Chaussade had only the residual of the French empire as a market. The postwar atrophy and collapse of the ailing Compagnie des Indes closed off one more of the remaining prospects.

To these disappointments, the decade of the sixties added others. His plan to establish warehouses at the major ports where his products could be stocked and sold as demand arose—similar to the method of warehousing and sales employed by the Crowleys—failed utterly because the chambers of commerce at French ports resisted it. The shipbuilding, shipping, and other iron-consuming industries of the ports and their environs habitually used anchors and irons imported from Spain, Sweden, and Russia. Chaussade turned to Versailles and over a period of years won a few valuable concessions: limited duty reductions for his irons; relief from some duplicate taxes; entrepôt privileges below Nantes at Paimboeuf on the lower Loire; and a very modest tariff on foreign irons. Yet these concessions did not enable Chaussade to sell to the shipbuilding and shipping industries of the coasts. His inability to find any large commercial market in France, even at the easily accessible commercial ports of Nantes, La Rochelle, and Bordeaux, was a grave commercial handicap.

Chaussade may have had limited regional markets in the environs of his manufactories. Surrogates and his own *régisseurs* sold some agricultural implements, tools, building hardware, and even household irons in the Berry-Nivernais, and even in the more distant localities where he leased or sublet facilities. Local notarial archives might reveal the extent of such sales. A handful of other commercial transactions, of which we know, may have been especially significant: he is reported in notarial acts to have agreed to supply parts to repair the "machine at Marly," and is reported to have agreed to supply components to fabricate harbor markers at the port of Morlaix, and structural and other components for an innovative "incombustible hall" in Paris. Moreover, a recent study of the locksmiths of Paris has disclosed the existence of Chaussade's own name (apart from the names of possible *prête-noms*, who may have acted for him) among the wholesale suppliers for that trade in Paris.[10] The bulk of the evidence suggests, however, that his privileged transactions with the Atlantic seaboard naval arsenals and other state-connected buyers overseas were as close as Chaussade came to having a "national market." His limited success in commercial markets was a striking contrast to the commercial successes of the Crowley firm in England.

Labor

Finally, we should compare Chaussade, the Crowleys, and the Söderfors firm as regards the number of workers each employed and their labor policies and practices.

In the heyday of their operations—the second quarter of the eighteenth century—the Crowleys employed about 1,110 men.[11] The Söderfors works in the same period are reported to have had "at times about 4,000" workers and employees. This figure, cited by L. E. Hedin, seems very large even as a total for the owner's Osterby and Söderfors manufactories together; it may include employees associated with his other manufacturing and commercial interests as well.[12] Chaussade's labor force can be estimated at between one and three thousand, depending on the method of counting.[13]

The conditions of work were difficult and dangerous for some "internal" workers in smelters, forges, foundries, fineries, and other iron works of that era, whether in England, Sweden, or France. Yet none of the firms lacked adequate numbers of men for that mostly skilled work, though all three sometimes depended on skilled workmen from outside. The fact that none of the three experienced problems in recruiting and retaining an adequate labor force can be variously explained. For all three, semi-skilled and unskilled labor was abundantly available; insofar as there was a recruitment problem, it would have concerned skilled workers alone. We know a good deal about the methods used by Ambrose Crowley in recruiting and retaining such labor; Chaussade used many of the same methods. Both found that providing company housing could be helpful, as were leases of tools and wage advances (*don gratuit* contracts in France) that could bind an employee to stay or to reimburse all value received if his contract was broken. Chaussade had much more help from government regulations and privileges than the Crowleys apparently did where retention of employees was involved.

Although we know little of employment policies and practices at Söderfors, we can compare those of Chaussade and the Crowleys. The owner-entrepreneurs of the three firms seem to have had similar motives: profit and paternal control. "Executives" of the firm saw themselves as both businessmen and aristocrats of a sort, with rights as employers to manage their business and as masters or lords to preside over the management of the seigneurial estates. These dual roles, they believed, conferred the paternal obligation to provide leadership and dispense justice and benevolent help to employees and tenants, whom they considered to be their people.

Historians of business might class all these firms as examples of aristocratic entrepreneurship. From London, Stockholm, and Paris (or Versailles), all three entrepreneurs superintended managers who administered their iron works, landed estates, manors, or fiefs. The *Law Book of the Crowley Ironworks* offers detailed evidence that Crowley was an aristocratically inclined and extremely exacting employer. Chaussade, as far as we know, prepared no comparable manual for his managers, but other evidence suggests that his rules, rigor, attention to detail, and aristocratic inclinations approximated those of Ambrose Crowley III. Yet our knowledge of Chaussade's methods relates to the management of his manorial estates and other holdings in the environs of rural industrial Guérigny, and the lives of people living in or near communities where his manufactories were situated, rather than the sort of factory management that preoccupied Crowley.[14]

As a seigneurial lord and vassal, Chaussade was presumably bound within the jurisdiction of his "feudal" masters, as well as by the ducal rules of his neighbors and the regulations of his king; there were definite legal limitations on the authority such seigneurial vassals as he could exercise. But Chaussade and his appointed judicial officers did not always adhere strictly to the rules, especially in the exercise of police powers. In the 1760s, at least in rural Guérigny and its environs, his justices promulgated regulations not only for inhabitants of his own seigneuries and other persons in the community, but even for people in other neighboring communities who happened to be employed by him in some capacity, whether Chaussade possessed high-justice (and police) powers over them or not. Chaussade intended his decrees to be as inescapable as were Crowley's rules for his people, but the network of Chaussade's attempted controls was wider. He sought to oversee civil life in the communities where his workers lived, using methods that would seem extreme even in some company towns of a later age.

Both Chaussade and Crowley offered medical services to employees; the former, however, did so only to the extent of encouraging a physician to be available for employees at rural Guérigny, whereas Crowley's provisions for the education of his workers' children seem unique. When Chaussade was present on his estates, he did participate with his legal officers in settling family problems for his people. Moreover, he did take a serious view of a lord's (his own) obligations to assist workers in emergencies. When local grain prices rose extraordinarily high, for example, he organized and financed grain importations and distributions. And like Crowley, he showed a serious interest in the religious life of his people. Both erected houses of worship for the use of the community, and, of course, both saw afterward to the selection and appointment of a chaplain or priest to lead the community in worship and help individuals to follow the right road.

Conclusion: Tradition and Innovation

As an entrepreneur, Chaussade built and sustained a diversified large-scale business in the face of severe handicaps using privilege as his principal tool. Thus advantaged, Chaussade combined the considerable strengths of the traditional charcoal iron industry of the Loire valley region with a selection of adaptations and technical innovations, locally devised or brought in from outside. He adapted elements of the old and the new to create a diversified conglomeration of manufactories and merchant enterprises that were profitable as long as he dealt with the state. But the locational advantages of his industrial establishments, proximity to good Berry irons and abundant fuel and water supplies in a thinly settled region, became handicaps when he sought to compete in commercial iron and steel markets on the coasts. His large-scale facilities, located deep in the interior of France, were hemmed in by road and river tolls. The tolls added greatly to transit costs and were an important element in the negative business climate in which he found himself. They enfeebled his ability to perform in many of the commercial iron and steel markets.

Yet Chaussade's manufacturing establishments did link the economics of producing iron and steel with the economics of managing seigneurial lands and estates. He and his family partners turned the dispersion and remoteness of their industrial sites into advantages; privilege was the principal tool they used to make those sites more economic. The "tyranny of wood and water," that Ashton and Sykes and others saw as a drag on England's development, was not tyranny at all for Chaussade and his partners in France. The use of wood fuel and water power was advantageous for them. Coal was available, but they chose wood (charcoal) fuel; steam engines doubtless could have been purchased and installed, as they were at some other localities in France, but for Chaussade water power was available and cheap, the rational choice for him.

Chaussade committed himself to carefully selected technical innovations, preferring to draw skilled workers and innovative manufacturing processes from areas with which he was personally familiar in eastern

France or the Rhineland region and the naval arsenals. He chose to rely on "German" or French rather than "English" sources for workers and technical knowledge, and his failure to draw additional technical innovations from contemporary English (or other foreign) industry must be interpreted as deliberate abstention from innovation on grounds of economic self-interest. His particular decisions as an entrepreneur, to adopt an experimental process or to abstain from an innovation, in each instance needed to be motivated by his perception of the unique circumstances of his business, and his understanding of the conditions he faced in France in his time. The fact that Chaussade judged some innovations unsuited for adoption in his particular manufactories should mark him, not as a "backward businessman," but rather as a discriminating innovator; such decisions added to his stature and historical importance as one of the giants of the iron and steel industry of his time.

When other entrepreneurs in iron and steel, or other industries in France, made comparably discriminating choices in the management of their businesses with a view to profit, they must also rank as businessmen who were trying to participate in the complicated process now called the "industrial revolution"—a process that was everywhere the product of particular decisions made in unique circumstances by individual entrepreneurs, whose profit possibilities were sometimes aided, but were also very widely restricted, thwarted, or entirely crushed in the old regime by the existence of privilege in the hands of a favored few.

Notes

INTRODUCTION

1. These general remarks are taken in large part from my "Entrepreneurship in Seventeenth- and Eighteenth-Century France: Some General Conditions and a Case Study," *Explorations in Entrepreneurial History* 9, no. 4 (1957): 207–19.
2. Quotations in this paragraph from P. H. Beik, *A Judgment of the Old Regime* (New York: Columbia University Press, 1944), pp. 150, 154.
3. I am indebted to my former colleague Robert H. Bremner for discussions on the nature of privilege and for permission to quote from his stimulating unpublished paper "Privilege and Labor."
4. Herbert Lüthy, *La Banque protestante en France de la révocation de l'Edit de Nantes à la Revolution,* 2 vols. (Paris: SEVPEN, 1959–1961), 1:22; 2:151n, 412–13. Untold numbers of individuals whose ancestors had been Protestants or who had themselves been Protestants, and who were moved to accept the prescribed Catholicism, were classed by contemporaries, and are classed by some historians, as "new converts" or "new Catholics." Many individuals and families, and even remote descendants in the eighteenth century, evidently continued to think of themselves as a distinct group; though Catholics, their "new convert" status remained a fact of business life. Their common ex-Protestant background could have importance and utility as a link to the world of the *banque protestante,* and perhaps to other relationships as well.
5. Lüthy, *La Banque,* 1:23.
6. Ibid., 1:vii–viii.
7. Ibid., 1:ix.

CHAPTER 1

1. Lüthy, *La Banque,* 2:412; but see Bertrand Gille, *Les Origines de la Grande Industrie métallurgique en France* (Paris: Domat Montchrestien, n.d.), p. 181.
2. His marriage contract provided for a dowry of 6,000 livres, with the value

of furnishings calculated to be 10,485 livres (property *non-commun*), in a contract passed before Gaillardie, 11 Nov. 1719, cited in CII (Linacier): *Inventaire après le decès de Marie Ann Duru,* 23 May 1732.

3. John Law (1671–1729), a Scottish financier, persuaded the French regent, Philippe II, duc d'Orléans, to found a national bank issuing notes that temporarily raised government credit; he also originated the Mississippi scheme, a plan for the exploitation of France's American colonies. Both bank and Mississippi schemes failed, and thousands of speculators were ruined.

4. Jacques Masson, *Mémoire justificatif pour le Sieur Masson, cy-devant chargé par Feu S.A.R. de plusiers affairs concernant l'administration de ses finances* (*imprimé,* Tours Notre-Dame de Nancy, 30 Nov. 1729), passim (hereafter *Mémoire justificatif*). In preparing the material that follows relating to Masson, I received help in the form of correspondence, *deplacements* of documents, and the opportunity to use the master's thesis prepared for the Ecole des Chartes in 1948 by Jean Colnat, "Les Finances des duchés de Lorraine et de Bar sous le règne des Ducs Leopold 1er et François III (1698–1737). See also Michel Antoine's recapitulation and guide-commentary on *Les Fonds du Conseil d'Etat et de la chancellier de Lorraine aux Archives Nationales* (Nancy: Editions Berger–Levrault, 1954).

5. *Nouvelle Biographie Général* (1836 ed., reprinted 1968), vol. 39, s.v. "Paris (frères)," p. 206; Colnat, "Les Finances," pp. 111, 143, 156–57; Meurthe-et-Moselle, 3F^1 290: *Mémoire de Mrs. Paris sur le payement de neuf millions de dettes,* 17 Feb. 1725, with letter of the same date.

6. André-Hercule, cardinal de Fleury (1654–1743) was *de facto* first minister to the young Louis XV.

7. Lüthy, *La Banque,* 2:38.

8. *Mémoire justificatif,* pp. 7–8; Meurthe-et-Moselle, 3F^1 290: *Mémoire de Mrs. Paris.*

9. *Mémoire justificatif,* pp. 7–8, passim; Meurthe-et-Moselle, 3F^1 290: *Mémoire de Mrs. Paris.*

10. Colnat, "Les Finances," p. 140.

11. Archives Nationales (hereafter AN) E 3180 Lorraine: *Edits et arrêts,* fols. 51–55; Antoine, *Le Fonds,* p. 23.

12. Meurthe-et-Moselle, B 168, fols. 145–46; *Régistre: naturalité pour de Sieur Masson,* Lunéville, 20 Nov. 1727; and the act of appointment to the *conseil des finances,* Lunéville, 20 Oct. 1727, fols. 149–50.

13. Other revenues controlled by Masson were half of the *octrois* (i.e., income from municipal and other concessions, privileges, tolls, etc.), income from the increase in the price of salt, profit from the coinage and the mint, and other funds raised by special levies and destined for the payment of debts. "His Highness decrees that [the said funds] . . . will be managed and administered in conformity with the declaration, separately from other revenues and finances, by a director charged with that *Régie*." AN E 3180 Lorraine, Lunéville, 8 May 1726, *signé* Maheu (?).

14. E 3180 Lorraine, decree art. 5, 6, 8, 9.

15. E 3182^B Lorraine: *Arrêts du Conseil d'Etat,* 13 May 1726, fols. 366–67.

The *arrêt* appointed as *commissaires* Nicolas Joseph Lefebvre (president); Affricaine Henart (*conseiller*); Louis Barbarat (*conseiller*).

16. Colnat, "Les Finances," pp. 141–51, passim.

17. Colnat, "Les Finances," pp. 141–51, 156; Meurthe-et-Moselle, 3F¹ 290: *Copie d'un ordre de Son Altesse Royale*, Sept. 1728.

18. As Masson himself argued, in reporting to Leopold by *mémoire* during his mission to Sampigny: "Your Royal Highness ordered me to explain to MM. Paris the situation of his finances in detail and without reserve. We have worked together since Thursday morning, and since these men bring much exactitude to everything they do [we are not yet finished with the work]. . . . MM. Paris stress particularly the importance of putting Your Highness in a position to avoid the necessity of imposing the capitation. . . . In fact, to avoid the capitation, only 1,500 thousand livres [de France] are needed." Meurthe-et-Moselle, 3F¹ 290: *Sur les mesures a concerter avec Mrs. Paris pour le payement des debtes de l'état*, 7 Oct. 1728; Colnat, "Les Finances," p. 156.

19. Meurthe-et-Moselle, 3F¹ 290: *Sur les mesures;* Colnat, "Les Finances," p. 156.

20. E 3181 Lorraine: *Edits et déclarations, Ordonnance touchant l'ordre que S.A.R. veut être observée dans l'administration de ses finances*, Lunéville, 9 Feb. 1729.

21. Ibid., art. 20, fol. 69.

22. *Mémoire justificatif*, p. 1.

23. E 3181 Lorraine: *Edits et déclarations, Ordres pour faire conduire le Sieur Masson à Nancy*, 20 Sept. 1729.

24. *Mémoire justificatif*, pp. 1–5.

25. Meurthe-et-Moselle, 3F 296: *Etat sommaire des dettes de Son Altesse Royale*, May 1729, *signé* Masson; Colnat, "Les finances," p. 141 and passim.

26. *Mémoire justificatif*, pp. 11–13.

27. *Mémoire pour le Sieur Masson, 13 Novembre 1729* (Paris, 1729).

28. *Mémoire justificatif*, p. 29.

29. Ibid., pp. 16, 25–27.

30. Ibid., p. 21.

31. Ibid., p. 28.

32. Ibid., p. 4.

33. Antoine, *Les Fonds*, pp. 20–21.

34. Meurthe-et-Moselle, 3F 296: *Observations sur le recueil des billets paiables aux porteurs*, n.d. Samuel Levi was a banker who had lent money to Leopold; hence the presence of his name on the list is more easily explained than some of the others.

35. The *séjour* of François III in Lorraine began 29 November 1729 and extended to April 1731, when he left, never to return. (Colnat, "Les Finances," pp. 169, 172.) The dating of his stay suggests that the Council and the Regents, before his arrival, had a hand in planning and executing the early stages, at least, of the "reaction."

36. Colnat, "Les Finances," pp. 169, 172.

37. *Mémoire justificatif,* p. 4.
38. Masson's claim was that the *lettres* were approved by M. de Coussey shortly before Leopold's death. But the letters apparently were not recorded as required, for the claim does not seem to be substantiated in the records of *lettres d'anoblissement accordées*. That claim gave his enemies a sweet victory.
39. These arrangements are alluded to in CII (Linacier): *Constitution et quittance, Masson à C. de la Motte,* 23 Sept. 1721.
40. CII (Linacier): *Vente, Guillaume de Lange à Jacques Masson,* 18 Jan. 1724.
41. CII (Linacier): *Vente de bois, Marie de Berthier à Jacques Masson,* 16 May 1724.
42. Marine, B^3 326, fol. 376, including a *mémoire* reporting appraisals of the assets they had listed as security for the 100,000-livres advance that the navy finally allowed them so that they could meet the start-up costs of the Lorraine timber enterprise.
43. During the crisis in Lorraine in 1728–1729, Masson claimed that his acquisition of a share in the partnership was the result of a gift that the late Duke Leopold had personally directed him to accept. Masson's published statement about this is unclear, ungrammatical, and illogical. But apparently almost anything could be believed of Leopold, and so Masson could assert: "His Highness the late duke, having desired to reserve a quarter-share in the latest contract [with the Sieur Babaud for forest exploitations], in order to understand and follow the progress of the undertaking of the Sieur Babaud, which was entirely new, placed this quarter-share at the disposal of M. le Prince de Craon. The prince did me the honor of telling me that he had begged His Royal Highness for leave not to accept this opportunity, because he would or could not raise the cash for such an affair, as he would have been obliged to do. After which His Royal Highness ordered me to [re-]arrange the matter so that the Sieur Babaud would be obliged to pay a fixed sum each year to repurchase the share in question. . . . We agreed on a sum of 10,000 livres a year. . . . I reported this to His Royal Highness, who ordered me to accept this as a gift." *Mémoire justificatif,* p. 27.

    Masson claimed in 1729 that he had not yet received any of the annual payments due him under this scheme.
44. Such officials were normally preoccupied with forest conservation and caretaker functions: to ensure the regular regeneration and replenishment of stands, to prevent illicit cuts and entry into the forests, and to control users of wood and water resources. The extraordinarily heavy forest cuts that Masson planned to authorize for the sake of increased revenue (and to meet Jean Babaud's requirements) were bound to violate in gross fashion the established practices of forest administrators.
45. Masson's authority derived from the following decrees, among others; AN E 3180 Lorraine: *Edits et déclarations,* 8 May 1726, art. 2; E 3182^B Lorraine: *Arrêts du Conseil d'Etat,* 13 May 1726, fols. 366–67.
46. XCVI (D'Aoust): *Procuration deposée, Jean Babaud à Jacques Masson,* 4 Dec. 1733.
47. CII (Linacier): *Inventaire de Marie Anne Duru,* 23 May 1732.

48. CII (Linacier): *Mariage, Mlle. Masson et [Pierre] B. de la Chaussade,* 4 Mar. 1734. Also present was one Pierre Gaudron, officer of the late Monseigneur Duc d' Orléans, *regent du royaume,* godfather of the bride-to-be. Named among the relatives present were Jacques Masson's mother-in-law, Marie Ann Martin, widow (apparently since 1732) of the late Sieur Jean Duru; and several persons named Blumenstein: "a maternal aunt and germain cousins." The bride's grandmother Martin apparently had at least one sister who married a Blumenstein.

49. Regarding Masson's "portion," the dowry clauses of the marriage agreement cited a notarial act passed before Junot et son Confrère de Paris, by Masson and Me. Antoine Paris, dated 18 Sept. 1733 (this date being corrected in the text to *treize* and in a marginal correction to *vingt trois,* in lieu of *trente trois*): "The Sieur Masson declaring that, although by the aforesaid act it appears that the said Sieur Antoine Paris ceded to him the entire third of the said concession for a consideration amounting to 50,000 livres that the said Sieur Paris declared he had received, the truth is (*la verité est*), however, that the said Sieur Masson actually paid nothing whatsoever for the said conveyance, although that same day *dix-septième* [?] *septembre mil sept cens trente trois* [here too the *trente* is crossed out, and a cross in the text refers to a left-margin change to *vingt*] he filed an amending letter to declare that the one-third interest belonged to the Sieur Antoine Paris, with the exception of one-sixth part of the third of the aforesaid concession, which the said Sieur Masson retained with the consent of the aforesaid Sieur Paris, which sixth of the said third the Sieur Masson herewith relinquishes in favor of the said bride-to-be, subject to the conditions of the arrangements made with the Sieurs Boutin et Boisson, proprietors of the other two-thirds of the said concession." CII (Linacier): *Mariage,* 4 Mar. 1734.

50. CII (Linacier): *Obligation,* 6 Aug. 1734.

51. One accounting included such trifles as an item of 3 livres paid for notarial services by Chaussade for Masson, who seemed short of "pocket money." Another item recorded Chaussade's outlay of 49 livres for a trip made with Masson from La Charité to Nevers; one of 72 livres paid by Chaussade to a certain Sieur Mangin for preparing certain documents for Masson; and one of 24 livres for sending an express to Moulins and St. Pierre (Le Moûtier) in connection with the *donnation* of the Sieur Marquot de Machy to Jacqueline. CII (Linacier): *Compte, Masson à Pierre Babaud,* 4 Feb. 1736, recording 27,000 livres in transfers by Masson to Chaussade, all items of under 2,000 livres each.

52. CII (Linacier): *Convention,* 14 Feb. 1735.

53. CII (Linacier): *Transport,* 31 Jan. 1735.

54. CII (Linacier): *Compte,* 4 Feb. 1736, lists scores of items compiled over a period of eleven months "according to the journal of M. de la Chaussade," including 2,000 livres in interest on the unpaid dowry Masson owed to Chaussade.

55. CII (Linacier): *Vente, procureur de Philibert du Bouchat à Masson,* 14 June 1736; and *Vente de terre, C. Berger à J. Masson,* 4 June 1741.

56. VI (Silvestre): *Vente,* 19 Feb. 1738.

57. CII (Linacier): *Déclaration par Jacques Masson,* 9 Aug. 1738.
58. CII (Linacier): *Déclaration par Masson,* 9 Aug. 1738.
59. C. 351 and C. 351 (6) (Bas-Rhin) *Lettres de Jean Babaud,* 1732–1733 passim.
60. XCVI (D'Aoust), *Procuration deposée, J. Babaud à Masson,* 4 Dec. 1733.
61. The cash settlement to Jacques Duportal included 60,000 Dutch florins (124,137 livres de France on 31 Jan. 1735), to be paid to Jacques's brother, Daniel Duportal of Rotterdam; 3,200 staves were to be delivered gratis to Daniel "for his house," and 80,000 French livres were to be paid in France. CII (Linacier): *Société deposée* (appendix, *Dissolution de société*), 1 Oct. 1733.
62. VI (Silvestre): *Inventaire après decès de Dame Jacqueline Marie Anne Masson, épouse de Chaussade,* 18 June 1744, quoting their act of society, Bitche, 24 Aug. 1733.
63. CII (Linacier): *Transaction, Masson et B. de la Chaussade,* 25 Sept. 1736.
64. AN, F⁴ 1962: *Compatabilité générale* [administrative note—pension petition], 2 July 1741.
65. Marine (Paris), D³ 31: *Mémoire sur la fixation des prix des ancres,* 1 Dec. 1735.
66. CII (Linacier): *Dissolution de la société,* 8 Dec. 1738; "S. Gossins" was described as "*commis* of J. Babaud" in CII (Linacier): *Inventaire après le decès de Jean Babaud,* 10 Jan. 1739.
67. CII (Linacier): *Inventaire de Jean Babaud,* 10 Jan. 1739.
68. Claude Prieur, for example, served as a partner with a one-third interest in the Montbéliard timber operation (only), following the terms of agreements of 1735–1737, but sold out to the full partners in 1739 for 36,000 livres and was replaced by Nicholas Doyen and Pierre Goossens. (CII [Linacier]: *Transport,* 11 Aug. 1739; *Association, Masson, Vve. Boesnier et N. Doyen,* 6 Jan. 1740, with *Annexe.*) One outside partner (Doyen) was paid off within two years, but Pierre Goossens was kept on. On 19 August 1741 Goossens was made principal *commis* of the *société* known as "Pierre Babaud et Cie." (CII [Linacier]: *Procuration, Chaussade à Pierre Goossens,* 19 Aug. 1741.) Thereafter, Chaussade seems never again to have used the Linacier *étude.*
69. On the preliminaries, terms, and general character of the "northern" contracts: Marine (Paris), B³ 367, fol. 169; B² 308, fols. 523–24, 542, 549–550, 570; (Rochefort) 5E² 18, passim.
70. Marriage contract: CII (Linacier), 3 Dec. 1739, with community of property; VI (Silvestre): *Liquidation des droits et abandonnement,* 1 Oct. 1742.
71. CII (Linacier): *Société, P. Babaud et Marie Boesnier,* 9 Feb. 1739.
72. VI (Silvestre): *Inventaire de Jacqueline Masson,* 18 June 1744.
73. VI (Linacier): *Inventaire après decès de Jacques Masson,* 23 June 1741.
74. CII (Linacier): *Vente de terre, Claude Berger, seigneur de Frasnay, à Jacques Masson,* 4 June 1741.
75. LXXXVI (Magnier): *Transaction, procureur de Marie Boesnier et P. Babaud de la Chaussade,* 7 Sept. 1755.
76. The petition goes on to say: "represent . . . that the Sieur Masson, having been chosen in 1736 to work under the orders of M. le *Contrôleur Général*

with the affairs of Lorraine, was obliged to maintain establishments both at Versailles and at Paris at great cost, and to increase considerably his expense thereby. The appointments attaching to his office were mediocre. He was charged with many different operations in grains, and the travel he was obliged to undertake in that connection entirely ruined his health." AN F⁴ 1962: *Comptabilité générale* [administrative note], 2 July 1741.

77. Marine (Paris), B² 314, fols. 586–87.
78. VI (Silvestre): *Renonciations* [Boesnier], 16 Nov. 1741; [Chaussade], 22 Nov. 1741.
79. VI (Silvestre): *Liquidation*, 1 Oct. 1742; LXXXVI (Magnier): *Transaction, Boesnier et Chaussade*, 7 Sept. 1755 (summary description).
80. This global figure may have included the respective shares of Jean and Pierre in the modest inheritance they had received from their parents, originally of Bellac.
81. Bibliothèque Nationale (hereafter "BN"), Fonds Fr. 30,279, p. 11: *Titre de Babaud du 22 mars 1743 (parchemin)*.
82. VI (Silvestre): *Inventaire Jacqueline Masson*, 18 June 1744, including two *constitutions* by Chaussade, dated 1 and 8 Feb. 1743, each for 2,500 livres annual *rente* on 50,000. See also AN, V² 42: *Secrétaire du roy*, 12 Mar. 1743.
83. AN, V² 49, p. 132; V² 70, p. 631; V² 71, p. 700.
84. LXXXVI (Magnier): *Cie. des Secrétaires du Roi à Chaussade*, 11 Mar. 1772.
85. LXXXVI (Aleaume): *Retrocession et transport*, 13 June 1787. Cf. Marcel Marion, *Dictionnaire des institutions de la France aux XVIIe et XVIIIe siècles* (Paris: 1968), pp. 505–6, who indicates that the total initial cost of the office was 150,000, apparently including the special assessment of 40,000 (1755) as part of his global figure.
86. He sold this office—*conseiller au siège de Bellac*—in 1759. LXXXVI (Magnier): *Traité d'office de conseiller*, 28 Jan. 1759.
87. Nièvre, A²: *Lettre, signé* Chaussade, 19 Mar. 1743, called to my attention by Bernard Gaulejac.
88. VI (Silvestre): *Inventaire de Jacqueline Masson*, 18 June 1744.
89. LXXXVI (Magnier): *Transaction, Boesnier et Chaussade*, 7 Sept. 1755.

CHAPTER 2

1. Marine (Paris), B³ 326: *Lettre du président de la Chambre des Comptes de Bonn*, 18 Nov. 1728, alluding to their Rhine River timber floats.
2. Marine (Paris), B³ 326, fols. 376, 484, 486, and passim.
3. *Mémoire justificatif*, pp. 4, 26–27.
4. Marine (Paris), B³ 326, fol. 476.
5. Marine (Paris), B² 293, fol. 1085.
6. Bas Rhin, C. 351(6): *Marché*, 22 Aug. 1728.
7. Marine (Paris), B³ 326, fols. 474, 476 (reports of M. de la Tour, intendant at Poitiers, and M. d'Orsay, intendant at Limoges); and B³ 335, fols. 277, 279, 281, 288–89 (reports of M. de Pomereau, intendant de Tours), all on Duportal's father-in-law, a "rich" merchant residing at Montreuil. Some of

the reports included hearsay and innuendo: from Tours came a copy of a letter from one Fonsson (?) of Saumur, who declared that "the Sieur Boynier du Portal . . . is constantly associated with the Sieur Babaud in many wood contracts; these, it is always said, have not been very profitable, to which I can add that the Sieur du Portal, who was formerly a merchant of wine and spirits on a commission basis, has not found the change [from wine to wood] to be profitable. He is a young man of about forty years, married for many years, without children. . . . it appears to me doubtful that Duportal and his wife could put together 20,000 livres. He is an honest man, of integrity, conducts his life with *aisance* and in such a way as to suggest, at least, that the profits of his business are considerable. He has not been able to increase his fortune." B³ 326, fol. 486.

8. Marine (Paris), B³ 326, fol. 372: cf. fols. 368–78, 474–89, passim. On the ancestry of the Babaud families of Bellac and Confolens in the seventeenth century, see BN, Fonds Fr. 30,279, item 8: *Babauds, de Bellac et Confolens,* fols. 10, 12. Two years afterward (1731) the bankruptcy of the Paris banking house Donnadieu et André Chambon compromised the credit of both partners (and Masson as well) and produced a new, even more searching investigation of their assets, producing additional details about this affair. Again, however, the reports were affirmative. (Marine, (Paris), B³ 348, fol. 346.) On the effects of the Donnadieu et Chambon failure on the partners, see CII (Linacier): *Société deposée,* 14 Feb. 1735.

9. Marine (Paris), D³ 8, fols. 173–74.

10. Marine (Paris), B² 279, fol. 383.

11. Marine (Paris), B³ 321, fols. 214, 228–29; B³ 322, passim. The navy also sent timber experts to Lorraine and Alsace to select and mark the trees to be cut by the entrepreneurs' crews. Hence by order of the king in late December 1727, two seats (*places de fond*) were reserved on the coach to Nancy for the Sieur de Francy, *commis principal de la marine,* and Poirier, *maître constructeur des vaisseaux,* his aide; they probably carried with them a copy of the *mémoire* of instruction that had been prepared for Lorraine. B² 269, fols. 23–24, with *Mémoire pour servir d'instruction,* 23 Dec. 1727. See C⁷ 168: *Dossier La Rue de Francy,* which shows that family's three generations of service to the navy.

12. Jean Babaud apparently traversed the river routes in person and consulted officials at Trier on the Moselle and Bonn on the lower Rhine, among others, before going on to Dordrecht to consult with Daniel Duportal, the timber merchant (their correspondent), and then on to Amsterdam to deal with other details. Marine (Paris), B² 281, fol. 28; B² 287, fol. 712 (D. Duportal), with correspondence resulting from this trip, much of it concerned with the tolls.

13. Marine (Paris), B³ 326, fol. 183.

14. Marine (Paris), B² 281, fol. 28.

15. Marine (Paris), B³ 341, fol. 7; B² 283, fol. 416.

16. Marine (Paris), B² 289, fol. 524.

17. Marine (Paris), B² 281, fol. 28.

18. Marine (Paris), B² 286, fol. 340.

19. Marine (Paris), B² 279, fols. 534–35.

20. Marine (Paris), B² 281, fols. 29–30, 33–35, 292.
21. Ibid., fols. 309, 312.
22. Ibid., fols. 35–36.
23. Ibid., fols. 39–40.
24. Ibid., fol. 314: *Minister to Francy,* 20 Nov. 1729.
25. Marine (Paris), B² 286, fol. 336.
26. Marine (Paris), B² 283, fol. 228.
27. Ibid., fol. 275.
28. Marine (Paris), B² 286, fol. 150.
29. Local labor and machinery no doubt had to be employed, if only for the sake of good will. There were six sawmills in the environs of the Comté of Bitche. Bitche was a town of about 4,000 people situated in a forested region where the partners cut thousands of trees and where Babaud kept his headquarters for all their exploitation enterprises in the region. Throughout Babaud's lifetime, part of the sawing was done near the cutting sites in Lorraine, and part of it in Holland. The *flottes* assembled at Bitche for descent on the river might routinely include (as did the Sieur "Schaaff's" *flotte* of 1733):

> 150,000 cubic feet of naval timber;
> 100,000 staves for La Rochelle;
> 100,000 staves for Bordeaux;
> 14,000 pieces for *tonneaux;*
> 325 trees (to be sawn downriver);
> and "some planks."

CII (Linacier): *Etats deposée, Jean et Pierre Babaud et Masson,* 14 Feb. 1735, enclosures; Marine (Paris), B² 302, fol. 99.
30. Bas-Rhin, C. 351(6): Babaud contract, 22 Aug. 1728.
31. Compare (Bas-Rhin, C 351(6): *Mémoire,* 25 Mar. 1733, and Marine (Paris), B² 290, fols. 590–91. The latter describes a shipment arriving at Brest, 3,044 pieces equaling 96,745 cubic feet. The tariff, or schedule of prices, in Babaud's contract with the navy specified the three usual grades of timber. Pieces classed as first grade were priced at 48 sols per cubic foot; second grade, 47; third grade, 44.
32. Bas-Rhin, C. 351(6): *Observations sur la demande du Sieur Babaud* (1733).
33. Ibid. A specially prepared *mémoire* described several types of "Wagenholz" or *rebuts:* the first, and apparently most common and best known, took the form of a *bahus* and was made by sawing a tree trunk lengthwise, producing pieces 12 feet long and 12 inches thick; other sorts of "half-logs" were 6 to 8 feet long and 9 to 10 inches thick. Then there was *Pfeifolholz,* "whisle" or hollow wood that was defective at the core; *Knapholz,* pieces that were in one way or another defective; and finally *kloks,* the smallest type, 5 feet long. Bas-Rhin, C. 351(6): *"Mémoire pour rendre compte,"* 25 Mar. 1733.
34. The wood, he said, came from several sources: "First, from the large and old trees, of which the owners want to be rid, being identified as defective by rotted knots, cup-shake, or coloration. These [trees] are abandoned by

officers of the king entirely; [*second*] . . . timber initially selected for the navy as useful, but found in the processing to be defective.

"From these . . . the Sieur Babaud cuts blocks two [feet] wide and [about] six feet long, or two by twelve. These blocks, called *Wagenuenscholtz* [*sic*], are converted in Holland into boards for joinery and millwork, or into staves that the Sieur Babaud ships to the seaboard vineyards of France; these are the types of wood that serve as *flottage* for the naval timber. . . .

"As regards the construction timbers that are rejected after being worked . . . [they] are . . . sold at a great discount for merchant shipbuilding. The Sieur Babaud earlier proposed to furnish them to the *Compagnie des Indes de France,* which would not accept any more after the first trial shipment. . . .

". . . it is easy to see that the Sieur Babaud's private traffic in this wood is a necessary by-product of his contract with the navy, and that if he were not free to make this use of trees that are not suitable for the [naval] service, his provisionment would become entirely impracticable. The Sieur Babaud would then be burdened with quantities of trees and *rebut* timber for which no local use could be found, which would become for him a pure loss.

"The removal of these trees cannot entrain any disadvantage whatsoever. On the contrary, all cutting of trees, including those employed for the [naval] service, facilitates the regrowth [*recrue*] by young trees coming up from below. Far from causing degradation, it ensures the re-establishment of the forest." Marine (Paris), B³ 355: *Mémoire du Sieur Babaud au sujet du bois d'Alsace,* with letter of Intendant Bron of Alsace, 12 Nov. 1732.

35. Bas-Rhin, C. 351(6): *Mémoire de Jean Babaud,* Strasbourg, 15 Mar. 1733. One can compare Babaud's description with another report from the pen of an inspector. He examined a particular forested region where Babaud's crews were at work (the comté de Dabo). According to his report, less than 10 percent of the wood being cut in that forest was fit for use by the navy; the remaining 80,000 cubic feet cut was *bois d'Hollande* destined for Babaud's private trade. Ibid.: "*Mémoire,*" signé François, 25 Mar. 1733.

36. Marine (Paris), B² 289, fol. 199.

37. CII (Linacier): *Convention, J. Masson de Guérigny et MM. Babaud,* 6 May 1738. Neither Babaud nor the navy correspondents made much mention of fir (*sapin*) as a component of the *flottes* descended to Dort, except in the *flottage* of lumber that was hand-sawn upriver, but there is mention of fir being cut for that specific purpose. (Bas-Rhin, C. 351[6]: *Lettre, Maurepas à M. de Bron,* 31 Aug. 1732.) The fir had its uses—in the building industry, for example—but did not usually figure significantly in the markets for either merchant or naval shipbuilding materials. We can assume, in any case, that Babaud minimized the use of fir in his *flottes;* overaged oak was much preferable. In fact, it was one of his complaints that when he used fir rafts to float sawn lumber to Coblenz, he was obliged to sell it at a loss after the *flotte* reached that junction. (Marine [Paris], B² 286, fol. 386.) Judging from Babaud's claims and competence, oak *Wagenholz* rather than fir provided the buoyancy we are told was so essential in the pieces that accompanied the timber destined for the navy. Since the moisture content of oak decreases gradually but substantially with advancing age, the specific

gravity of the wood in the trunks destined to produce *Waguenscholtz* must have been less than that of the naval timber (though more than that of fir). White oak, which is now known to possess *tyloses* (blocked pores), must have had the greatest resistance to water absorption and good buoyancy when rafted to Dort, even though it was heaviest in terms of specific gravity (as much as 0.71, compared with 0.66 for the red oak group). (H. P. Brown, A. J. Panshin, and C. C. Forsaith, *Wood Technology* 2 vols. [New York: McGraw-Hill, 1952], 2:588–89. I am indebted to Dennis Dark for this reference.) Overaged oak, in any case, and especially dead trunks of this highly rot-resistant wood, must have been ideal for *flottage* from Babaud's point of view. Obviously some sites could provide a higher percentage of overaged trees than others; these must have been especially attractive, and the proportion of navy wood and *bois d'hollande* would vary accordingly.

38. Marine (Paris), B² 290, fols. 590–91; cf. B² 289, fol. 583. About two months later Potin reported that the Sieur Schaaf's shipment had indeed made a successful descent and had just arrived at Rotterdam, and that sea transport to France was being arranged. With his letter he sent an *"état"* of the timber descended by "Jacob Staat" [*sic*] to Coblenz, consisting of many small *flottes*, apparently the components of the next major *flotte* that was to be formed at Coblenz, which was destined for descent to the other major Rhine timber port, Dort. Marine (Paris), B⁷ 316: *Lettre de Potin*, 28 Aug. 1732.

39. Marine (Paris), B² 295, fol. 396.

40. Marine (Paris), B² 298, fol. 345. But Babaud was allowed to continue his own personal traffic, and orders were issued allowing him "to take even the trees reserved for the service that are not of [much] consequence." In November (1734?) the navy's own inspectors and constructors were "retired" to Phalsbourg. *Ibid.*, fols. 303, 384, *bis.*

41. Marine (Paris), B³ 488, with copies of receipts and *passeports* for scores of ships, Dutch, English and French, engaged in this traffic.

42. Marine (Paris), B² 289, fol. 537.

43. Marine (Paris), B² 290, fols. 662–63. Maurepas saw this loan as an experiment: "From this first voyage, we will be able to decide whether or not it is practicable to continue to use these little vessels instead of the Dutch." (Ibid.) By the end of August, the two *gabarres* in question, *La Tourterelle* and *La Becassé*, had arrived at Dort and were to be laden "immediately." Ibid., fol. 703; B⁷ 316, *Lettre de Potin*, 28 Aug. 1732.

44. Marine (Paris), B² 286, fol. 39. This was perhaps unusual, occurring early in the Lorraine exploitation. Normally, Salomon would have cash in his account or could draw bills of exchange in payment for freight. When defective timber arrived, or reception was refused for any reason, Babaud's correspondent was involved. Thus in 1733 Babaud's agents at both Rochefort and Brest had on hand, apparently in private storage yards, an accumulation of rejected timber valued at 66,690 livres, principally at Rochefort, to which most early shipments of Lorraine timber were sent. (CII [Linacier]: *Etat des mairains et rebuts de bois de construction*, 14 Feb. 1735.) Part of this *rebut* timber was sold privately to commercial shipbuilders at St. Malo,

for example, to which a cargo of *rebuts* was shipped in August 1731. (Marine [Paris], B² 287, fol. 839.) But much of it had to be cut up into staves and cask wood for the cooperage trade. B² 286, fol. 99.

45. Marine (Paris), B² 302, fol. 105–7.

46. Marine (Paris), B² 290, fols. 742, 749, 838.

47. Marine (Paris), B² 290, fols. 742, 749, 838; B² 302, fols. 105–7; D³ 8, fols. 207–15; XCVI (D'Aoust): *Marché de marine, 5 Jan.* 1737, with *copie de procès verbal de Brest sur le qualité de bois de Lorraine,* 1730.

48. Marine (Paris), B² 286, fol. 150.

49. Ibid., fols. 204, 336.

50. Ibid., fol. 335.

51. Ruis Embito was transferred from Lorraine to Rochefort on 9 June 1732. Marine (Paris), B² 290, fol. 535.

52. Marine (Paris), B² 287, fols. 664, 676–79. As he said, "I have not found the necessary security to give him additional help. I seek expedients to obtain release of the wood by M. le Duc de Lorraine and its passage to its destination without running the risk of seizure by other creditors."

53. Ibid., fol. 676.

54. Ibid., fols. 664, 711–12.

55. Ibid., fols. 1208–9. At one point Maurepas clearly believed that there would be no risk of the timber's being seized if the king owned it, and from some source he learned of the existence of an imperial edict that was supposed to forbid seizures of great *flottes* during their navigation. Ibid., fols. 866–67.

56. Ibid., fols. 866–68, 874.

57. Ibid., fols. 977–78.

58. Ibid., fol. 999.

59. Ibid., fols. 999–1000.

60. Ibid., fols. 1122, 1159; there was no danger of Babaud's private *bois d'Hollande* being seized en route, since it was tied up as part of the surety required for the "advances" being made by the crown. Maurepas also wrote to Ruis Embito, Babaud's old enemy, ordering that he or Ollivier must accompany Babaud's *flotte* down the rivers to the Netherlands "to see that all goes as planned." At the same time he wrote to Holland to ensure that the seaborne passage was being planned (Ibid., fol. 678), and he also suggested that Babaud be told never again to get himself into "the embarrassment from which he has been saved." B² 289, fol. 199.

61. Marine (Paris), B² 287, fol. 1208.

62. Marine (Paris), B² 289, fols. 561–62. That agreement called for a minimum delivery of 600,000 cubic feet, and a maximum of 750,000. At the outset (1728), Maurepas indicated that the navy would much prefer to receive the lesser quantity. (B² 279, fols. 383–84). But it was affirmed by October 1732 that 10,400 trees had been cut or marked for cutting. The court of Lorraine claimed that that number would produce a total of over 785,000 cubic feet for the navy; Babaud, with tacit support from the navy, claimed that those trees would furnish only 420,920 cubic feet. (B² 290, fols. 893–94.) Under pressure, the duchy apparently consented to allow another 330,000 cubic feet to be marked and cut. Ibid., fol. 812.

63. Ibid., fols. 1062–64.
64. Babaud and Company may have been encouraged to broaden the area they had under exploitation by the reported activity of a company of Dutch merchants in the Rhine basin in the spring of 1732. The Dutch, indeed, offered to buy trees on the lands of the comte of "Hanau" in Alsace, on condition that he would obtain permission from the French government for them to export the product of their cuts to Holland. (Marine (Paris), B² 289, fol. 462.) The permission they sought was immediately refused on the grounds that the export of wood from French territory was forbidden by the *arrêt* of 1722. Babaud alone was being permitted to make cuts of timber for sale to the navy. But the Dutch presence and offer, whether authentic or not, led the minister to encourage Babaud to explore wider possibilities (ibid., fols. 462, 485), even though the navy had no immediate need for additional timber.
65. Marine (Paris), B³ 355, fol. 224.
66. Ibid., fols. 206, 208–11, passim.
67. Marine (Paris), B² 290, fols. 1094–95.
68. Marine (Paris), B³ 361, fols. 373–76.
69. Marine (Paris), B² 293, fol. 702.
70. Ibid., fol. 905.
71. Ibid., fols. 905, 907, 908.
72. A certain "Sieur Tervenus," *conseiller au Grand Conseil de Lorraine,* had been a member of the commission assigned to examine Masson's papers when he was imprisoned in 1729, but a few days after the commission convened to undertake its work, he "fell dangerously ill" and was unable to participate in the proceedings that resulted in Masson's indictment. Masson, *Mémoire justificatif,* p. 1; Antoine, *Le Fonds,* p. 30 and note.
73. XCVI (D'Aoust): *Convention et resiliation, Maurepas à Jean Babaud,* 14 Dec. 1733, with enclosure dated 4 Dec. 1733.
74. Marine (Paris), B² 295, fol. 711.
75. Bas-Rhin, C. 351(6): *Babaud à intendant Bron* (?), Pfalzbourg, 12 Mar. 1734. The *passeports* of this personage were vital because "the prince de Beveren has command of the armies of the emperor and the Empire." Marine (Paris), B² 295, fols. 402, 709.
76. Marine (Paris), B³ 367, fols. 496–501, passim.
77. Marine (Paris), B² 295, fols. 439–440, 633.
78. Ibid., fol. 802.
79. Marine (Paris), B² 298, p. 82, fol. 343.
80. BN, Fonds Fr. 29,594: *Marché (Babaud),* copy, signed by *notaires* d'Aoust and Bucault, 11 Feb. 1735.
81. Ibid., arts. 30 and 31, 11 Feb. 1735.
82. Marine (Paris), B² 295, fol. 590.
83. Marine (Paris), B² 296: *minister à Maréchal de Noailles,* 15 Aug. 1734.
84. Ibid., fols. 149–51, 199.
85. Marine (Paris), B² 300, fol. 84.
86. Marine (Paris), B² 296, fol. 213.
87. Ibid., fols. 509–10.
88. Marine (Paris), B³ 367, fols. 503, 506–8, 597–98.

89. Bas-Rhin, C. 351(6): *Le comte de Hanau à M. le comte de Maurepas,* Hanau, 24 Nov. 1734.
90. Ibid.: *Babaud à de Bron,* Strasbourg, 12 June 1739.
91. Ibid.
92. AN, K 2092 XI Montbéliard, *Ordres* of 26 Jan. 1726, 15 June 1736.
93. Marine (Paris), B³ 379, fol. 232.
94. AN, K. 2197 XI Montbéliard, passim; Marine (Paris), B³ 389, fol. 107.
95. Marine (Paris), B³ 389, fol. 108.
96. AN, K. 2197 XI Montbéliard.
97. Marine (Paris), B³ 367, fol. 358.
98. Marine (Paris), B³ 389, fols. 59–60; this item for 1735 was mistakenly filed in the 1738 letterfile.
99. Marine (Paris), B³ 371, fol. 361.
100. Ibid., fols. 359–65.
101. Marine (Paris), B³ 389, fol. 61.
102. Marine (Paris), B³ 371, fols. 359–65.
103. Vanolles wrote to the minister of marine in early August from Montbéliard, "where I have brought the Sieurs Masson and Le Vasseur. They came to Besançon to see me, and I am benefiting from their knowledge and their advice regarding the erection of a sluiceway [*digue*] on the Doubs at the forge of Audincourt, which will be solid and suitable for the *flottage* of naval timber.

    "In their company, Monsieur, I have also visited many other localities on this river, and I know through the different discussions I have had with the Sieur Masson that he is infinitely knowledgeable (*au fait*) on the subject of *flottage,* and on dams and other works that will be needed. This persuades me that we can do without the engineer that you were going to send here, and also that it will suffice if I name a knowledgeable *subdélégué* and experts in navigation, carpentry, and masonry to accompany the Sieur Masson on the visit you refer to as preliminary, to draw up a *procès verbal* sufficiently detailed to enable you to make a final decision. Looking over all the things I have to deal with, it appears to me essential to profit from the remainder of the summer [August] and the coming fall. I await your orders to go ahead even before the return of the Sieur Masson, who asked for eight or ten days to take care of business he has in Lorraine. If you approve my proposal, Monsieur, the Sieur Masson told me he will advance the cost of the visit." Marine (Paris) B³ 389, fols. 84–85.
104. Ibid., fols. 108–9.
105. AN, H¹ 159 (*Administration provinciale*): *Procès verbal de visite de la rivière du Doubs faite par M. Masson en Septembre 1735,* 58 pp. (67 articles), 22 pp. appendix, and forty-four maps and illustrations in color; see also Marine (Paris), B³ 379 fols. 194–203.
106. Marine (Paris), B³ 389, fols. 107–24.
107. Marine (Paris), B³ 379, fol. 196.
108. Marine (Paris), B³ 389, fol. 121.
109. Marine (Paris), B³ 379, fols. 197–98.
110. The provisions of the contract were as follows:

    1. All oaks deemed proper for naval use found in the *parc* and *do-*

maine, and in the forests of the dependent communities of Montbéliard, would be made available by Würtemberg forest officers, who were allowed to reserve only the crest or branches that could not be used by the navy or for Babaud's commercial traffic or converted to firewood or charcoal.

2. Prices proportional to circumference of the trunk, ranging from seven to twenty livres per tree; measures were to be taken (as customary) with a chain or cord at a man's height.

3/4. Babaud's workers would be furnished with the wood needed for their *chauffage* in the forest and for the construction of barracks.

5. Babaud's clerks and workers from outside the locality, with their families, would, while in his employ, be exempt from all the taxes and impositions that the subjects of Montbéliard pay; the property and products of the exploitation would likewise be exempt.

6. The poles, harness, and oars needed for *flottage* would be provided at prices determined by the office of the governor, Tornaco.

7. Babaud had no responsibility for damage done to other trees in the exploitation.

8. The governor had full powers to regulate all difficulties and contestations, notably those incident to cartage and *flottage.*

9. "Since it is just that the subjects of the said *comté* of Montbéliard are employed by preference in cartage and transports, the government of the *comté* of Montbéliard will give orders to allot [the obligation to provide] vehicles in proportion to the *facultés* of the populace of the villages and communities nearest to the forests; and if the Sieur Babaud cannot obtain agreement on the price [to be paid] for vehicles by negotiation, the price will be regulated by the governor or officers appointed by him. . . . the carter and vehicle services [will] be paid for in cash." . . .

13. Trees of the *parc* and *domaine* of Montbéliard would each be purchased at twenty sols more than trees from the communities' woodlands.

14. The government of the duchy would pay communities for wood sold and claims made; "the Sieur Babaud cannot be delayed or disturbed in his exploitations."

AN, K. 2092 XI Montbéliard: *Marché,* Tornaco, Governor of the Principality of Montbéliard (for Mgr. le Duc de Würtemberg) with the Sieur Jean Babaud, Paris, 20 Oct. 1736; *ratifié* Stuttgart, 12 Nov. 1736.

111. Marine (Paris), B² 309, *Arrest,* 30 May 1739; XCVI (D'Aoust): *Marché de marine pour les bois de Montbélliard,* 5 Jan. 1737.

112. AN, K 2092 XI Montbéliard: *Mémoire responsive aux observations sur le traité du 12 novembre 1736 par le Sieur Prieur* [Masson-Babaud surrogate]; see also BN, Fonds Fr. 29,594: Arrest du Conseil d'Estat du Roy concernant le flotage (sic) des bois de marine sur la rivière Doubs, 5 Nov. 1737 (*imprimé*), 7 arts.

113. AN, K 2092 XI Montbéliard: *Lettre, Hertzog, Hatzel,* et al. [forest officers], Montbéliard, 31 Jan. 1737.

114. The *régisseurs* of the cuts finally procured permission to bring in some grains from Burgundy, but "the quantity was not anywhere near sufficient to provide for the workers and their families." Ibid.: *Lettre signé* De Lamprecht and De Rossel, Montbéliard, 21 May 1739.

115. Ibid.: *Mémoire du directeur à M. le Conseiller Beuttel*, n.d.; cf. ibid., *Copie d'une lettre de M. Babaud*, Paris, 28 Aug. 1737.
116. Ibid.: *Etat des arbres qui doivent martelés*, 3 Dec. 1738.
117. Ibid.: *Remonstrance de Grand Forestier Sattler*, Stuttgart, 22 Jan. 1738.
118. Ibid.: *Babaud lettre*, 24 Apr. 1738.
119. Ibid.: *Etat général des arbres exploités dans le comté de Montbéliard par le Sieur Monzé* (surrogate of J. Babaud), n.d.
120. Ibid.: *Convention, Babaud et le Conseil de Montbéliard*, Paris, 15 Oct. 1738, *signé* J. Babaud.
121. The actual value of individual trees was at times estimated as high as 120 livres (Marine [Paris], B^1 84, fol. 392); in the Montbéliard exploitation, private owners sold trees for about 10 livres each (B^3 383, fol. 295). Thousands, of course, were given without any payment.
122. Marine (Paris), B^3 394, fols. 200–201.
123. Marine (Paris), B^3 399, fol. 204: Charron to minister, Lyon, 11 Feb. 1740. Two of the fourteen mills outside the city posed a perennial problem for rafts descending the Saône to Lyon. The response to Charron's complaints was always that the mills were essential to the city and that there was no other place to put them. In 1734 Charron reported that about a year earlier a boat had been lost close by these mills with seventy persons aboard, and another since then with six or seven persons.
124. Marine (Paris), B^3 367, fol. 584: Charron to minister, 20 Nov. 1734.
125. Marine (Paris), B^3 399, fols. 207–8, 213, 217, 218, 222.
126. Ibid., fols. 223 ff., passim.
127. Shipments of wood passing these stations in 1719 were subject to the following tolls:

Oak wood, pieces of 48 ft.^{3}	14 *l.*, 11 *s.*, 10 *d*
Cask wood (staves), per 100 of 3-ft. length	8 *l.*, 15 *s.*, 8 *d.*
"Prussian" plank, per doz.	63 *l.*, 0 *s.*, 10 *d.*
Masts, per 300 ft.^{3}	117 *l.*, 16 *s.*, 4 *d.*

Marine (Paris), D^3 6, fol. 53: *Tarif général des droits que le roy etant en son Conseil veut et ordonne etre payez a l'avenir, et à commencé du premier Janvier 1718 (bois pour Marseille et Toulon)*; cf. B^3 367, fols. 105–14: Proposed Rhône improvement works with cost estimates, Orry letter, 19 July 1734.
128. Marine (Paris), B^3 348, fol. 394.
129. Marine (Paris), B^3 409, fols. 306–9, 331.
130. Marine (Paris), B^3 382, fol. 104.
131. Ibid., fols. 73–75; cf. fols. 104, 204–5, 206–21.
132. Marine (Paris), B^2 309, fols. 204–5.
133. E.g., Marine (Paris), B^2 302, fol. 105.
134. Marine (Paris), B^3 321, fol. 214, 228–29; B^2 279, fols. 383–84.
135. Marine (Paris), B^2 290, fol. 1027; B^2 298, fols. 226, 418–19.
136. Marine (Paris), B^2 302, fols. 71, 112.
137. Ibid., fol. 158.

138. Ibid., fol. 195.
139. Ibid., fols. 206–7; cf. B² 304, fol. 8: purchases in the forest of "Rosestaye" in Alsace.
140. Marine (Paris), B² 304, fols. 157–58; (Rochefort) 5E² 18: Mémoire de M. l'Intendant, Juin 1738.
141. Marine (Paris), B³ 384, fol. 209; B² 305, fol. 419.
142. XCVI (D'Aoust): *Marché de marine, pour la fourniture des bois dans les ports du Ponant,* 26 June 1738.
143. Cf. Augustin Jal, *Glossaire nautique: répertoire polyglotte de termes de marine anciens et modernes* (Paris: Presses Universitaires de Frânce, 1858), p. 628.
144. In referring to that clause himself, the minister alluded to the requirement that "three-fifths must be in *bois tors.*" (Marine (Paris), B² 305, fol. 81 of the table of contents at the head of the volume; but see fol. 410, the minister's letter to Pomet, 6 Aug. 1738.) The precise term that would unequivocally have required Babaud and Company to work toward supplying the navy's pressing need for curved timber was not included in the legally binding document placed in the notary's files (XCVI [D'Aoust]: *Marché de marine* [for provisionment of the Ponant ports with timber], 26 June 1738). There also appears to have been clerical error or tampering with the register of out-letters in the navy's files; the phrase in the table of B² 305 (fol. 81) differs from the phrase appearing in the actual copy of the letter (fol. 410).

CHAPTER 3

1. Marine (Paris), B³ 405, *Mémoire au sujet des bois des seigneuries seques-treés,* joined to Vanolles' letter dated 25 (actually 15) Nov. 1741.
2. Ibid.
3. Marine (Paris), B³ 412, fol. 76: Vanolles to minister, 17 Jan. 1742.
4. Marine (Paris), B³ 392, fols. 371, 376.
5. Marine (Paris), B³ 402, fol. 379, and passim: Charron correspondence.
6. Marine (Paris), B³ 409, fol. 306 and passim.
7. Marine (Paris), B³ 411, fols. 02, 14, 93–94, and passim.
8. Marine (Paris), B³ 438, fol. 117.
9. Marine (Paris), B³ 412, fol. 79; B³ 409, fol. 280.
10. Marine (Paris), B³ 399, fols. 222, 224–25, and passim.
11. Marine (Paris), B³ 488, fols. 178–79.
12. Marine (Paris), B³ 382, fols. 73–74, 104–6, 206–21, passim, esp. letters of *Commissaire Général* Villeblanche at Toulon; B³ 393, fol. 273.
13. Marine (Paris), B³ 494, fols. 63–64. Le Tessier's contract (i.e., the partners') allowed 5 percent substandard deliveries without loss, a clause criticized at the arsenals. B³ 398, fol. 509.
14. Marine (Paris), B² 315, fol. 605.
15. Ibid., fol. 121.
16. Marine (Paris), B³ 494, fols. 63–64.
17. Ibid., fol. 56.
18. XVCI (D'Aoust): *Marché de marine,* 26 June 1738. Cf. Marine (Paris), B² 304, fols. 157–58.

19. Marine (Paris), B² 305, fol. 298.
20. Marine (Paris), B² 310, fol. 86.
21. Ibid.
22. Ibid., fols. 455–56, 509; cf. B² 298, fol. 226.
23. KK 1005ᴱ (Lorraine): *Projet d'arrest concernant les bois propres pour la marine dans les forêts de Lorraine et Barrois,* Sept. 1738; Marine (Paris), B² 305, fols. 87, 446; B³ 388, fols. 78–82; B³ 389, fols. 278, 284.
24. *Arrêt [par Sa Majesté Polonaise],* 18 Sept. 1738; quoted and discussed in relation to Babaud and *subrogé* Mangin in references in note 23 and B² 310, fols. 518–19.
25. Marine (Paris), B² 310, fols. 518–19; B³ 389, fol. 284.
26. Marine (Paris), B² 310, fols. 518–19.
27. Marine (Paris), B³ 389, fols. 278, 284–86.
28. Marine (Paris), B³ 405, fols. 222–23; Bas-Rhin, C. 351(6): *Note à garder,* undated reminder that Chaussade "must not touch trees marked . . . 'for the service of the king in Alsace.'"
29. Marine (Paris), B² 314, fols. 586–87.
30. Ibid.
31. Ibid., fols. 593, 615.
32. Ibid., fol. 615.
33. See above, and Bas-Rhin, C. 351(6): *Mémoire du Sieur Babaud,* 11 Mar. 1738.
34. Marine (Paris), B² 304, fols. 111–12; Bas-Rhin, C. 351(6): *Mémoire du Sr. Babaud,* 11 Mar. 1738, and notes, Strasbourg, 19 May 1738.
35. Bas-Rhin, C. 351(6): Notes headed "Paul Esprit Feydeau," Strasbourg, 19 May 1738.
36. Ibid.: Letter to Babaud, 24 July 1739.
37. For example, *passeports* and correspondence relating to "permission for the Sieur Babaud [de la Chaussade] to exploit the wood he has purchased from the Sr. Deist, one of the *adjudicataires* of the [routine] cuts from the forest of Haguenau" involved 160 pieces of timber cut from 134 oaks; Chaussade dealt with Deist throughout the forties. Bas-Rhin, C. 351(6): *Passeport,* Strasbourg, 1 Aug. 1740.
38. Ibid.: *Passeport,* Paris, 10 Feb. 1741, *signé* Pre. Babaud et Cie., with notation: "*Le passeport* sent by M. le Maréchal [Du Bourg?]."
39. See, for example, the note in Bas-Rhin, C. 351(6): *A Mettre . . . au bas du mémoire par [pour?] M. Paullin,* referring to an *ordonnance,* dated 9 Feb. 1747 by M. de Vanolles.
40. Ibid.: *Passeport,* 13 Mar. 1748.
41. On the *intendances des pays d'imposition,* see Albert Mirot, *Manuel de géographie historique de la France,* 2 vols. (Paris: Picard, 1948–1950), 2:373–74.
42. Papers related to the lease of this large seigneury, together with the lease itself and at least one sublease, were apparently left by Chaussade with his wife when he went abroad to the Netherlands or Baltic Europe in 1743–44; Jacqueline died during his absence, and the papers were therefore gathered up, catalogued, and preserved in a notarial file as part of her invento-

ried effects: VI (Silvestre): *Inventaire de Jacqueline Masson,* 18 June 1744 (appendix).

43. Marine (Paris), B² 308, fol. 610; cf. B² 305, fol. 298, the offer of 2,000 pieces of curved timber, perhaps from Rodemacher.

44. Signed on 10 Nov. 1740 before notaries at Metz; cf. VI (Silvestre): *Déclaration deposée,* Chaussade, 24 Sept. 1742. The lease ran from 1 January 1741 to 1 January 1751. Chaussade paid 18,000 livres in cash for the first two years of the lease, and agreed to 9,000 for each of the other seven.

45. VI (Silvestre): *Declaration deposée,* 24 Sept. 1742 (enclosures).

46. VI (Silvestre): *Procuration, Chaussade à Sieur René Duval, Sieur de Villeray,* 21 Feb. 1742. See also VI (Silvestre): *Inventaire de Jacqueline Masson,* 18 June 1744; *Etat estimatif des bois, dependens de la seigneurie de Rodenmacker et Hesperange* [*sic*].

47. Both these properties were acquired from Jean François Rouelle and his wife by contracts before notaries of Metz, the papermill for 15,350 livres and a bonus or commission (*epingle*) of 850 livres, and the old (ruined?) chateau for 4,645 livres (*argent de France*). VI (Silvestre): *Inventaire de Jacqueline Masson,* (with appendix), 18 June 1744.

48. Marine (Paris), B² 326, fol. 835; Bas-Rhin, C. 351(6): *Memoire à Monseigneur de Vanolles* (Ind d'Alsace), Bitche, 3 Dec. 1749, *signé* Du Pasquier (Chaussade surrogate).

49. Feb. 1749; see Marine (Paris), B² 337, fol. 449.

50. Marine (Paris), D³ 8, fol. 224.

51. For example, Bas-Rhin, C. 351(6): *Etat des arbres de la forest de Meukelbac,* 1746/47; Marine (Paris), B³ 486, fols. 312 ff.

52. CII (Linacier): *Association,* 6 Jan. 1740, referring to the contract of July 1739.

53. Marine (Paris), B² 308, fols. 523–24 (*états* for Rochefort), 542 (Brest), 549–50, 570 (Havre), etc.

54. On the limited French mercantile activity in the northern markets, see my "French Shipping in Northern European Trade, 1660–1789," *Journal of Modern History* 26 (1954): 207–19.

55. Lüthy, *La Banque,* 2:321–22.

56. CXV (Doyen): *Rouillé à Gabriel Michel et Pierre Babaud de la Chaussade,* 5 June 1750; Marine (Paris), B² 337, fols. 474, 480, 496.

57. A company correspondent (*procureur*) named Charles Chocquain de Lessart died at "Nouvelle Orléans Capitale de la province de la Louisiane" on 4 November 1740; on 22 June 1742 Chaussade gave power of attorney to a certain M. Salmon, *commissaire ordonnateur de la marine* at Nouvelle Orléans, to "faire reclamation des touttes marchandises" and, as successor to Lessart, to receive and act on orders from Sieur La Molie of La Rochelle. (VI [Silvestre]: *Procuration, Chaussade à M. Salmon,* 22 June 1742.) A Monsieur Salmon was resident agent of Dame Veuve Babaud et Cie. at Rochefort as late as January 1740. Marine (Rochefort), 5E² 18: *Facture d'une Cargaison,* Jan. 1740.

58. Jacques Masson's old associates, the Paris brothers, were involved in provisionments of lead; procurement may thereby have been "facilitated." Marine (Paris), B² 308, fol. 613.

59. Ordnance (esp. cannon) was another Paris brothers specialty. Marine (Paris), B² 313, fol. 675.
60. Ibid.
61. Marine (Paris), B² 314, fol. 560.
62. Ibid., fol. 592.
63. CII (Linacier): *Procuration, Chaussade à Goossens,* 19 Aug. 1741.
64. Marine (Paris), B² 314, fol. 633.
65. Ibid., fol. 691.
66. Ibid., fol. 759.
67. The minister informed Chaussade that "this copper cannot be employed. . . . [It will be] turned over to your correspondent at Brest for your account, to be disposed of as you judge appropriate. It will not be necessary to replace the 700 [*sic;* actually 698] of defective copper, . . . the [intendant] having informed me that it is not needed now." Marine (Paris), B² 316, fol. 404.
68. Ibid., fol. 434.
69. Ibid., fol. 448.
70. *Planches de Bergue* had to be 7 to 8 feet long, 8 to 9 inches wide, and 12 to 13 *lignes* thick. *Planches de Coperwick* were larger: 9 to 10 feet long, 11 to 12 inches wide, and 14 to 16 *lignes* thick. (A *ligne* was equal to one-twelfth of an inch, or 0m .0023.) (Marine (Paris), B² 308, fol. 524.) Maurepas wrote, "The proportions were specified in the *état* sent to the late M. Masson, which must be available to you. This is the type of plank you are asked to supply—24,000 pieces. I cannot accept any that you send of any other size." Marine (Paris), B² 316, fol. 465.
71. Marine (Paris), B² 317, fol. 479.
72. Ibid., fol. 505.
73. Marine (Paris), B² 319, fol. 329.
74. Marine (Paris), B² 320, fols. 393–94: *Mémoire sur les éclairissements que l'on demande par raport aux droits qui sont payés dans les ports de Hollande,* n.d. (mid-Oct. 1743).
75. VI (Silvestre): *Procurations, Chaussade à Jean Rivet,* 28 juillet 1743, 14 avril 1744.
76. VI (Silvestre): *Inventaire de Jacqueline Masson,* 18 juin 1744 (appendix).
77. Marine (Paris), B² 325, fol. 740.
78. For example, he had brought in many cargoes of masts during the later years of the war; he was reported to have shipped six cargoes of masts from Riga (one of the principal Baltic mast markets) in 1747, five cargoes of masts in 1748, and four of hemp in the same year. (Marine [Rochefort], 5E² 19: *Mémoire de Sieur Michel,* Sept. 1749, and passim.) Those were wartime provisionments, with Michel being granted "economy" (i.e., commission) contract arrangements; the navy thereby consented to bear much of the risk and cost, including costs engendered by long delays en route, as in 1747–1748, when six cargoes of Michel's masts were tied up in Holland at one time, the carrier being unable to proceed to France. (Ibid.; Marine (Paris), B² 332, fol. 498.) With peace restored, Michel reverted to enterprise provisionments. (Marine (Rochefort), 5E² 19: *Mémoire,* 1749, passim; 145, fols. 559, 649, 751.) Successful though he seems to have been,

Michel had some problems comparable to Chaussade's: he too had difficulties, even in peacetime, with his "Bergen planks," many thousands of which were rejected by the navy in 1749, obliging him to market them elsewhere "with the least possible disadvantage." (Paris), B² 337, fol. 438.

79. Marine (Rochefort), 5E² 19, printed copy of contract, 1750; (Paris), B² 337, fols. 480–81, 618; CXV (Doyen): *Marché, Rouillé à G. Michel et P. Babaud de la Chaussade,* 5 June 1750.

80. Chaussade had earlier sold the navy 100 pieces of fir timber 50 to 70 feet long and 24 to 30 inches square from those Black Mountains more cheaply than they could be had from the Baltic. VI (Silvestre): *Inventaire de Jacqueline Masson,* 18 June 1744; Marine (Paris), B² 322, fols. 19, 41, 62.

81. Marine (Rochefort), 1E 148, note dated 31 July 1750.

82. Marine (Paris), B² 343, fol. 428; cf. (Brest), 1E 505, fols. 5–6, 85–86, reporting that of thirty-two masts inspected, only fourteen were acceptable. A later report indicated that "the greater part were rejected." Marine (Paris), B¹ 66, fol. 8.

83. Douglas K. Reading, *The Anglo-Russian Commercial Treaty of 1734* (New Haven, Conn.: Yale University Press, 1938), ch. 8 and passim.

84. Marine (Paris), B³ 509: *Observations des Srs. Michel et Babaud de la Chaussade,* 1751; my *Forests and French Sea Power, 1660–1789* (Toronto: University of Toronto Press, 1956), pp. 135–57, passim.

85. G. Lacour-Gayet, *La Marine militaire de la France sous le règne de Louis XV* (Paris: 1910), pp. 224–35.

86. Ibid.

87. Marine (Paris), B¹ 66: Summary of Michel-Chaussade request, and the decision: "Bon," Mar. 1751.

88. Marine (Brest), 1E 505, fols. 88, 120, and passim.

89. First in the forests of Auvergne (1719–1720), then in the Pyrenees (1722), at Riga (1723), and at Amsterdam (1728). Barbé also worked for many years as an inspector at the arsenals. Marine (Paris), B³ 509, fols. 485–86.

90. Ibid., fols. 435–37: *Mémoire pour servir d'instruction au Sr. de Senac* (by Hocquart), Brest, 1 Apr. 1751, *signé* Rouillé, 14 fols.

91. The *bourgeois* later lost control of the trade.

92. Marine (Paris), B³ 509: *Mémoire servant de réponse aux instructions de Mgr. et aux observations des fournisseurs,* Berlin, 6 Dec. 1751, *signé* Senac (copy).

93. Ibid., fols. 471–72. Sieur Barbé, Riga, 20 June 1751.

94. Ibid., fols. 517–18.

95. Marine (Brest), 1E 505, fol. 271. The French were apparently the principal buyers in the market that year: it was reported that the British navy had not made any purchases of masts at Riga since the previous war (1749). (Marine (Paris), B³ 509, fol. 440.) Britain was then developing the "broad arrow policy," designed to ensure North American supplies for the royal navy and thereby reduce or eliminate Britain's dependence on the Baltic ports for masts and spars. Robert G. Albion, *Forests and Sea Power: The Timber Problem of the Royal Navy, 1652–1862* (Cambridge: Harvard University Press, 1926), chs. 4 and 6, passim.

96. Marine (Paris), B² 341, fol. 375.

97. Marine (Brest), 1E 505, fol. 150.

98. Ibid., fols. 239–40.

99. Ibid., fols. 344–45, 363. The supplier of domestic hemp was allowed to contract to bring in 400 *milliers* from the north in 1753.

100. Marine (Paris), B² 341, fol. 412.

101. Ibid., fols. 484, 502, 585.

102. Marine (Brest), 1E 505, fol. 227; (Paris), B² 341, fol. 514.

103. Marine (Brest), 1E 505, fol. 308.

104. Marine (Brest), 1E 506, fol. 160.

105. Ibid., fols. 54–55, 61, 82.

106. Ibid., 1E 506, fols. 271, 281.

107. Marine (Paris), B² 352: Jan.–June 1756, passim.

108. Ibid., fols. 281–82.

109. CXV (Doyen) *Quittance* (Goossens-Chaussade), 5 May 1751.

110. LXXXVI (Magnier): *Traité et transport,* 23 Apr. 1752.

CHAPTER 4

1. Marine (Paris), B³ 326: *Etat des forges situées auprès de Nevers,* Nevers, 27 Aug. 1728.

2. Nièvre, AO *Fonds de Guérigny, Catalogue des domains,* Villemenant.

3. AO *Fonds de Guérigny* (supplementaire), *Catalogue des domains,* 1775.

4. Marine (Paris), B² 381, fols. 317–19, 471. This figure did not include the *Bretagne*'s complement of 100 guns but did include some of the components of its gun carriages.

5. Marine (Paris), D³ 31, fols. 57–59: *Proportions d'ancres pour servir aux vaisseaux du Roy,* 1672; fols. 60–61: *Mémoire sur les Ancres,* 1674; fols. 62–63: lists of shipments from "the Nivernais." For later period, with some retrospective comment, see René-Antoine Ferchault, "Fabrique des ancres," read before the Académie des Sciences, July 1723 (Paris, 1761), with notes by Duhamel de Monceau.

6. Comparable views were expressed in the early eighteenth century by Ambrose Crowley, supplier of anchors to the British navy: "'Tis certain that the miscarriage of all anchors proceedeth from using an improper sort of iron, coals, and careless or insufficient workmanship. Iron is the main article, and no man can provide proper iron like him that knoweth the nature of the several mines, and from great experience can give proper direction for the making of it." Crowley went on to remark, as "I have often done to my Surveyors and workmen, that the making of anchors as they ought is a matter of conscience, and that he who maketh an anchor that through short performance breaketh, is accountable for the lives lost thereby." M. W. Flinn, *Men of Iron: The Crowleys in the Early Iron Industry* (Edinburgh: University Press, 1962), p. 189.

7. Marine (Paris), B³ 31, fols. 108, 110–14, 116, 131.

8. Pontchartrain was successor to his father in that ministry, serving from 1699 onward. Joannes Tramond, *Manuel d'histoire maritime de la France des origines à 1815* (Paris, 1947), p. 305.

9. Marine (Paris), D³ 31, fols. 116 (recto/verso) and 110–31, passim.

10. Marine (Paris), B¹ 27, fol. 217. Among the other technicians and entrepreneurs involved in anchor manufacture before and during Trésaguet's time were the master anchorsmith Gomain with Lefebvre de Chassenay, the Sieurs de la Prevostière and Du Chartre, Pierre Gautier and Guillaume Berne (both master anchorsmiths), and the Sieurs Grandguillaume, Deslongchamps, and Arnaud. D³ 31, fols. 68–69, 127–28, 155, and passim.

11. Marine (Paris), B³ 326, fols. 418–65, passim.

12. Marine (Paris), B² 304, fols. 32–33. *Commissaire* Truguet observed later that "the forge at Cosne-sur-Loire was selected for anchor fabrication over eleven other forges [including Guérigny in the Nivernais], which were not found to be equally suitable for such an establishment." D³ 5, fol. 38: *Mémoire* by Truguet, 15 Jan. 1759.

13. Marine (Paris), B² 304, fols. 32–33.

14. XCVI (D'Aoust): *Marché de Marine pour les Ancres,* 19 Nov. 1736, referring to the earlier Arnaud agreement of 10 July 1729.

15. Marine (Paris), B² 283, fols. 553, 644, 768, 814; B² 284, fols. 984–85; B² 302, fol. 111; B³ 326, fol. 418; B³ 342, fols. 128–29.

16. Marine (Paris), B² 283, fol. 553.

17. Ibid., fols. 644, 768, 814.

18. Marine (Paris), D³ 31, fol. 154–55.

19. Marine (Paris), D³ 5, fols. 39–40: *Mémoire* (retrospective) by Truguet, 1759.

20. In secondary sources, Chaussade is reported to have been sent abroad around 1734 "on important missions" by the Minister of Marine Maurepas "to study industrial processes used in England, Austria and Spain." (C. Corbier, 1870) Several subsequent writers have reiterated such reports, with variations. Bertrand Gille indicated that Chaussade was sent, at an unspecified date, "to England and to Holland" by his father-in-law Jacques Masson "to study the method of manufacturing anchors." The present writer has seen no confirmation in contemporary documents that such important missions were undertaken by young Chaussade; if he was sent the experience could have been an important component of his technical education, and a precedent for G. Jars' well-known later technical missions; the fact remains, however, that the pyramidal process of anchor fabrication (as we have shown) can be seen developing in France at least as early as the first decade of the century. C. Corbier, "Notice historique sur les forges impériales de la Chaussade," *Bulletin, Société nivernaise des sciences, lettres et arts,* 4 (1870), 368; Bertrand Gille, "Un exemple de la formation de la grande industrie: les forges de la Chaussade," *Bulletin, Société nivernaise des sciences, lettres et arts,* 30 (1938–42), 366.

21. After comparing the costs involved in producing anchors under navy management and considering "all the expenses and details to which the king was subject for the lease of the forge and for the transport, the risks, the difficulty of all the inconvenience that the Sieur Arnaud occasioned while charged with the same provisionment, it appeared to me," said the minister, "on all counts to be more advantageous for the king's interest and the

naval service to accept the offers of the said Sieur Babaud who is *en estat* to execute [the work] and maintain this establishment." Marine (Paris), B² 300, fols. 213–14.

22. Marine (Paris), D³ 32, fol. 72. One naval official remarked cynically when the prize was won by M. Bernouly, *professeur de géometrie* at Basle, "No doubt the *mémoire* having the most [geometric] problems had the preference." Ibid.: M. de la Mothe à M. de Boynes, 17 Sept. 1771.

23. XVVI (D'Aoust): *Société Jean Arnaud et J. Masson, Charles Michaut et Octavien Souchet*, 7 Aug. 1734.

24. XCVI (D'Aoust): *Dissolution de société, Masson et ses associés et Jean Arnaud*, 24 Mar. 1736. Cf. 22 Apr. 1736.

25. XCVI (D'Aoust): *Procuration déposée, Arnaud à Chaussade*, 20 Apr. 1735; Marine (Paris), D³ 31: *Mémoire sur la fixation du prix des ancres qui peuvent être fabriquées dans la forge de Cosne*, 1 Dec. 1735.

26. VI (Silvestre): *Liquidation des droits et abandonnement*, 1 Oct. 1742.

27. CII (Linacier): *Mariage, Masson et Chaussade*, 4 Mar. 1734; *Compte, constitution et partage*, Jean et Pierre Babaud et Pierre Gallicher [representing their sister, Louise], 31 Aug. 1735; LXXXVI (Magnier): *Traité d'office de conseiller*, 28 Jan. 1759.

28. Chaussade and his wife, Jacqueline, had communal property. Therefore Chaussade would seem to have temporarily derived resources from a legacy coming directly to Jacqueline from her maternal grandfather (Jean Duru), which included some substantial properties in the Nivernais. (VI [Silvestre]: *Liquidation des droits*, 1 Oct. 1742; CII [Linacier]: *Inventaire de Marie Ann Duru*, 23 May 1732.) As we have seen, Jacqueline's dowry included the seigneury of Guérigny itself and much else in which, incidentally, her children by Chaussade would have had an interest at her death. Masson effectively dispersed all the major accessible assets of his estate, apparently to protect (or hide) them from his numerous creditors. Other machinations of his, very late in his life, appear to have channeled considerable cash and property more or less surreptitiously to Jacqueline and Chaussade.

29. Her death in 1744 (VI [Silvestre]: *Inventaire de Jacqueline Masson*, 18 June 1744) had complex, and probably compromising, effects for Chaussade's holdings and general circumstances.

30. The act of society was passed before Robineau and Silvestre on 29 March 1742. (VI [Silvestre]: *Inventaire de Jacqueline Masson*, 18 June 1744.) The society consisted of Chaussade (five sols, or shares), Dame Vve. Masson (two sols), and the outsiders (fourteen sols), for a total of twenty-one sols.

31. Vi (Silvestre): *Vente des forges et moulins* [Cosne], *Chaussade et épouse à Marie Boesnier*, 5 Nov. 1743, 1 Oct. 1742.

32. XCVI (D'Aoust): *Marché de marine, Antoine Louis Mangin*, 3 Oct. 1748.

33. VI (Silvestre): *Vente de moitié de forges, fenderies et moulins, Boesnier à Chaussade*, 21 Apr. 1749; LXXXVI (Magnier): *Vente de moitié de forge, Boesnier à Chaussade*, 23 Apr. 1752.

34. The preference for Berry irons was written into the standard contracts for provisionings of anchors after 1736. XCVI (D'Aoust): *Marché de marine pour les ancres*, 19 Nov. 1736; Marine (Rochefort), 5E² 21, *Marché des fers*, 14 Aug. 1774; (Paris), D³ 31, fol. 196; Cher, C. 137 and 316; *Marché*,

Sieur Claude le Blanc, seigneur de Marnaval, fermier sous le nom de Jacques Thoreau, des forges de Clavières, 30 Nov. 1756.

35. Marine (Paris), C⁷ 316, *Dossier Tassin: Instruction au Sieur Tassin . . . envoyé en Berry,* 10 Sept. 1722.

36. Marine (Brest), 506, fols. 34–35.

37. The furnace at La Vache, according to Georges Bourgin's sources (c. 1780's) was then capable of producing 4,000 kilograms per annum. Hubert and Georges Bourgin, *L'Industrie sidérurgique en France au début de la Revolution* (Paris, 1920), p. 300.

38. VI (Silvestre): *Inventaire* (1744), appendix, contract, 1 May 1743; Marine (Paris), B² 322, fol. 103.

39. Marine (Paris), B² 328, fols. 769, 778, wherein the minister remarks, "I have no reason to be content with you in this affair."

40. Marine (Paris), B² 308, fols. 657–60: *Le Blanc, fournisseur.*

41. Cher, C. 316: *Marché (imprimé),* 14 Feb. 1751 (providing for renewal of the original arrangement), with inked annotation dated 13 June 1752 indicating that Denis was no longer involved; confirmed in C. 137: revised *marché,* 17 June 1756, after Denis' death.

42. Cher, C. 316: *Marché, Le Blanc,* 30 Nov. 1756; Marine (Paris), B¹ 69: *Choiseul à Petel et Cie.* (re Marnaval), 28 May 1764.

43. Marine (Paris), B² 337, fol. 646: *Passeport,* 28 Mar. 1749, referring to Berry irons "in part *convertie* in the forges of the Nivernais."

44. The contract that Chaussade (and Denis) signed with the navy in 1751 (art. 2) specified that the signatories, as suppliers to the navy, had priority over all other purchasers of iron in the province of Berry when they were purchasing irons for fabricating their naval provisionments. Thus, rather like timber buyers purchasing for the navy from forest proprietors, Chaussade and his associates enjoyed priority as buyers of iron from smelters or foundries. (See Cher, C. 316: *Marché, Srs. Denis et Chaussade,* 14 Feb. 1751, with annotations by Tassin, 13 June 1752; Marine [Paris], D³ 5, fol. 37.) The sale price was presumably established by negotiation. Theoretically all the contractors supplying the navy with irons might get together to agree among themselves on prices, as did Chaussade, Denis, and Le Blanc. But there must have been limits to the pressure they could safely apply on outside operator/owners; they, as *fournisseurs* to the navy, had an interest in purchasing irons of first quality. They were paid relatively high prices by the navy for the irons they supplied. Chaussade's first contract to supply anchors allowed him fourteen sous a livre, in lieu of the ten sous paid for anchors previously. Hence it should not have been difficult to pay good prices to suppliers.

45. Marine (Paris), B² 353, fol. 10.

46. Marine (Paris), B² 355, fol. 313.

47. Marine (Paris), B² 316, fol. 459; B³ 413, fols. 644–45.

48. Marine (Paris), B² 313, fol. 431.

49. Marine (Paris), B² 320, fol. 379.

50. VI (Silvestre): *Vente des forges et moulins,* 5 Nov. 1743.

51. Marine (Paris), B² 325, fol. 789.

52. Marine (Paris), B² 328, fol. 778; cf. B² 325, fol. 812; B² 332, fols. 474–78.

53. Marine (Paris), B² 325, fol. 823.
54. Ibid., fol. 853.
55. Marine (Paris), B² 326, fol. 747.
56. Marine (Paris), B² 335, fol. 295.
57. Marine (Paris), B² 335, fol. 295.
58. Ibid., fol. 295.
59. Marine (Paris), B² 341, fol. 452.
60. Ibid., fol. 452; (Brest), 1E 505, fols. 104–5.
61. Marine (Paris), B² 341, fol. 452.
62. Ibid., fol. 452; VI (Silvestre): *Société,* 29 Mar. 1742; LXXXVI (Magnier): *Traité de transport,* 23 Apr. 1752.
63. Marine (Paris), B² 341, fol. 466.
64. Ibid., fol. 452.
65. Marine (Paris), B² 399, fol. 431.
66. Marine (Paris), B² 341, fol. 415.
67. AO *Fonds de Guérigny, Terrier de Guérigny,* no. 39, 3 Mar. 1740, and many other entries in the *terrier, controllé* by Baudry. Indeed, Baudry received a *procuration* from Chaussade, showing a considerable degree of mutual trust between the two, as early as September 1737. (CII [Linacier]: *Procurations* [two], *Franc. de Blumenstein et Chaussade à Alexandre Baudry,* 28 Sept. 1737.) In May 1741 Baudry was referred to as Chaussade's *commis.* (Nièvre, D⁴, *Forges* [Guérigny], no. 134 [*liasse*]: *Marché,* 5 June 1741.)
68. The Everats of La Charité-sur-Loire were François Everat, merchant of irons and *fournisseur* of timber to the navy; his brother, Jean-Baptiste, also a merchant of that town; and Louis Everat, son of François, who did business in Paris and served as Paris agent for the Grossouvres-Sauvage society, comprising the Sieurs Boisleve, Mouchy, Janellet, the Everats, and Baudry. Baudry, as noted above, was its *régisseur général and caissier.*
69. CII (Linacier): *Quittance, François Everat à MM. Masson et Babaud,* 26 July 1737. On the Everats see also Marine (Paris), B³ 519, fols. 141–44: *Joly de Fleury à Rouillé,* 2 Feb. 1753, with a *mémoire* on the case at hand from M. de Bese de la Blouse, *conseiller de la quatrième chambre des Enquestes* [*sic*].
70. Marine (Paris), B³ 514, fol. 151; the *procureur général* of Paris estimated that Baudry owed the Everats "more than 300,000 livres" (fol. 154).
71. On this affair: Ibid., fols. 144–45, 146–54, 157–59; B³ 519, fols. 141–44; B² 343, fol. 416.
72. A copy of one *sauf-conduite* in Baudry's name, 15 Sept. 1752 (in Marine [Paris], B³ 514, fol. 159) refers to Baudry as director of the Forges Royales of Cosne.
73. Ibid., fol. 153: *Mémoire,* Joly de Fleury to the minister of marine, 12 July 1752.
74. AN, F¹² 1302; Letter, Paris, 9 Apr. 1764; F¹² 1234ᴮ: *Chargements de M. de Baudry,* 1772. For a possibly related connection of Chaussade's, see LXXXVI (Magnier): *Constitution, Chaussade à Marie Jeanne Elizabeth Rouillé,* 8 Aug. 1752.

75. Marine (Brest), 1I 506, fols. 271, 281.
76. Marine (Paris), B² 339, fol. 431: Minister to Tassin, 11 June 1750.
77. VI (Silvestre): *Vente de Moitié*, 21 Apr. 1749. The price, 55,000 livres, covered buildings, lands, and equipment.
78. LXXXVI (Magnier): *Devis et marché de forge à Cosne, Blaise Ravot et P. B. de la Chaussade*, 13 Apr. 1752.
79. LXXXVI (Magnier): *Vente de moitié*, 23 Apr. 1752. The price for the second half was 72,000 livres, in four payments with interest at 5 percent.
80. LXXXVI (Magnier): *Traité et convention, les associés* (Simon Bonfils, André Grincourt, and Pierre Prevost), 5 Sept. 1752.
81. LXXXVI (Magnier): *Quittance, Marie Boesnier à M. le Marquis de Pierrecourt*, 13 Feb. 1753. In this transaction Chaussade's father-in-law (i.e., his second wife's father) paid 105,400 to Marie Boesnier on behalf of Chaussade's and Boesnier's surrogate, Antoine Louis Mangin, *régisseur* of the Cosne forge.
82. Nièvre, AO *Fonds de Guérigny, Forges de la Chaussade, Chartrier de Villemenant, Grosse du contrat d'acquisition*, 5 Mar. 1750; *Serie de Villemenant:* description and drawings of the property, c. 1775 (Nièvre AD, accession 1973).
83. LXXXVI (Magnier): *Devis et marché de forge à Villemenant*, 13 Apr. 1752.
84. LXXXVI (Magnier): *Vente de la terre de Richeran, Louis Antoine du Creuzet à P. B. de la Chaussade*, 8 Apr. 1751; Nièvre, AO *Série de Richerand*.
85. Nièvre, AO *Série de Demeurs* (accessioned 1973).
86. LXXXVI (Magnier): *Bail à rente, Louis Sebastien Bernot de Mouchy et son épouse à Chaussade*, 30 Dec. 1750.
87. Cher, C. 316: *Chaussade à Charron (subdélégué à la Charité)*, 12 June 1752.
88. Gille, *Origines*, p. 131.
89. Thus, for example, LXXXVI (Magnier): *Constitutions (rentes sur les postes), le roy à Antoine Louis Mangin*, 16 Feb. 1753 (245,000 livres to Mangin); 22 May 1753 (118,450 livres to Chaussade); and 7 June 1753 (270,000 livres to Chaussade), all at 3 percent! Regarding the variable business connections between Boesnier, Chaussade, and Antoine Louis Mangin, see LXXXVI (Magnier): *Procuration, Chaussade et Anne Rose Le Conte de Nonant à Antoine Louis Mangin*, 7 Sept. 1752, with marginal notes; and XCVI (D'Aoust): *Marché, A. L. Mangin*, 3 Oct. 1748, with both Chaussade and Boesnier as his *cautions*.
90. Marine (Paris), B² 341, fol. 498.
91. Marine (Paris), D³ 31, fols. 177–78.
92. Ibid., fol. 188.
93. For example, Marine (Paris), B² 362, fol. 452: *Etat des payements ordonnes* (first eight months of 1759); Chaussade received 198,000 livres, almost as much as all other *fournisseurs* of irons put together. Cf. B² 358, fol. 358, and B² 359, fols. 353, 419.
94. Cher, C. 316: *Lettre, Babaud de la Chaussade*, Paris, 7 Sept. 1752.

95. Born c. 1740, Chaussade's second daughter by his first wife.
96. AN, T. 308: *Papiers sequestrés: Emigrés et condamnés (Brossard) contract*, 29 Jan. 1756.

CHAPTER 5

1. Gille, *Origines*, p. 74.
2. Ibid.; and AN, F¹² 1302: *Lettre à Chaussade*, Paris, 9 Apr. 1764.
3. AN, F¹² 1302, Chaussade letter, Paris, 16 Apr. 1764.
4. Ibid.
5. Gille, *Origines*, Introduction (by Dolléans), pp. x, 81, and passim.
6. Flinn, *Men of Iron*, pp. 116–17.
7. Marine (Paris), B³ 591, *Mémoire*, joined to Chaussade's letter, Fontainbleau, 16 Oct. 1770.
8. Louis Gueneau, *L'Organisation du travail à Nevers aux XVIIe et XVIIIe siècles, 1660–1790* (Paris, 1919), p. 11; Gerard Martin, *Le Mariage à Cosne au XVIIIe siècle Mémoire de maîtrise* (Besançon: dactylographié/Xerox, 1979–1980), p. 35.
9. Rumor had it, however, that at La Charité there was sometimes connivance between forgemasters to keep prices down during auction sales of wood fuel. (Cher, C. 316: Letter of Charaud, La Charité, 3 June 1757.) Auction sales, incidentally, were commonly conducted using the *main fermé ou la chandelle éteinte*.
10. Masson as a specialist in seigneurial management, and the Babauds as timber merchants, were skilled appraisers of wooded lands; such skills were obviously useful to owners of forges. From the time of his acquisition of Guérigny until the last year of his life, Masson's name was continually associated with purchases of woodland and the acquisition of forest exploitation rights around Guérigny.
11. Nièvre, D¹ and D², *Forges de la Chaussade, pièce* 49: *Vente par Le Loup à Masson seigneur de Guérigny* (1740), and *pièces* 50, 51–62, for example, all in the 1740s.
12. Nièvre, E⁴–E⁵, *Forges (Nièvre) Frasnay: Inventaire des acquisitions faites par M. de la Chaussade (Paroisse de Frasnay)* (n.d.); (*Villemenant*—many woodland purchases in the 1750s, when the new forges were being built); D³ and D⁴ *Forges (Nièvre), pièces* 123, 124 ff. (many purchases, some to provide grainstuffs, and fodder for livestock).
13. In the 1770s, on the eve of the American War, Chaussade owned "many bouquets of trees" in the environs of Guérigny, where, he said, one of the navy's timber inspectors, for whose services he asked, would find high-grade pieces that Chaussade wanted taken out for sale to the navy. (Marine (Paris), B² 401, fols. 416, 443.) As late as the seventies, after he had tried unsuccessfully to sell out, Chaussade was still actively purchasing wooded lands. Nièvre F³ *Forges (Nièvre) La Vache*: purchases, 31 Aug. 1777, 12 Sept. 1778, 23 July 1779, 16 Apr. 1781.
14. Nièvre, H⁴ *Forges (Nièvre): Quittance . . . livrés payes par M. de la Chaussade au greffier de la maîtrise Royale de Nevers*, 31 Oct. 1755; H⁵: *Mémoire*

des syndics des bois et usages de Narcy contre M. de la Chaussade, 1759; ibid.: *Exploits pour M. de la Chaussade d'après sentence rendue . . . contre les syndics et usagers de Narcy*, 1760; A² *Forge (Nièvre) Douesque (?): Notaire de Sancergues à Merceret, régisseur de La Vache*, 12 Dec. 1771; *Copies des provisions de l'état et office de Juge Gruyer de la Chatellenie de Narcy*, La Charité, 21 (or 26) Oct. 1756; H⁵ *Forges (Nièvre) Narcy, Liasse* (1773, 1774) amusingly labeled *Exploits de M. de la Chaussade contre divers*.

At one point (1766), Chaussade learned of "a sack of papers and contracts concerning the *terre* de Narcy" found in far-off Corbigny, and he sent his faithful notary and agent to fetch them: "I charge M. Bort, guard of my archives [also his *notaire royal* and *procureur général fiscal de Guérigny*], to go for me and fetch them, and to present my thanks to M. de Pogany." A² *Note*, Paris, 14 Aug. 1766, *signé* Babaud de la Chaussade.

15. Marine (Paris), D³ 31, fols. 181–82.
16. Cher, C. 316: *Enquête* (questions posed to intendants), 1783. Wood merchants of Nevers persisted in using their own measures; attempts to achieve uniformity implemented in 1742 had to be renewed in 1770. On the complexities of these efforts, see Gueneau, *L'Organisation du travail*, pp. 362–364. The situation was different in Berry, where three types of measure were employed for firewood, according to a *mémoire* of 1783:

> *Bois de moulle* (Paris measure): 10 *pieds* long, 4 *pieds* high, 42 *pouces* long (pieces sawn at each end)
> *Bois de cuisine:* 8 *pieds* long, 4 *pieds* high, 4 *pieds* long
> *Charbonnage* (charcoal): 2 *pieds* long (log or *rondin*); or 4 *pieds* high and 8 *pieds* long (*corde*)

Cordes of wood destined to make charcoal were worked at the site of cuts, the price for the cutting being 8 *sous* per *corde*. The total for charcoal was 30 to 40 sols, bringing a *banne* of charcoal to 12 to 14 livres. Add for transportation at least 30 sols, and perhaps as much as 3 livres (60 *sous*), depending on the distance to its destination.

17. Marine (Paris), B² 289, fol. 361; B³ 348, fols. 361, 365–66, 373; B³ 355, fol. 137.
18. Jars, whose Christian name is not now known, has not been fully identified; the name Jars is associated with Lyon and the two brothers of that name who, later, undertook and published the famous reports on industrial technology: Gabriel Jars, *Voyages métallurgiques; ou, Récherches et observations sur les mines et forges de fer . . . faites depuis 1757 et compris 1769*, 3 vols., (Lyon, 1774–1781).
19. Marine (Paris), B³ 400, fol. 287: *Arrêts*, 8 Dec. 1724, 1 Apr. 1738.
20. Ibid.: 21 Oct. 1738.
21. Marine (Paris), B² 307, fol. 428, B² 308, fol. 649: *Passeports*.
22. Marine (Paris), B² 310, fol. 662.
23. Marine (Paris), B² 311, fol. 739, and B³ 400, fol. 289: *Passeports*, 3 July, 11 Oct. 1740; *Mémoire*, from M. Pallau, intendant de Lyon, 13 Sept. 1740.
24. Marine (Paris), B² 319, fol. 299; Gille, *Origines*, p. 183.

25. Marine (Paris), B^2 319, fol. 324.

26. Marine (Paris), D^3 31, fol. 182. He again referred to *feu reverbère* in the context of reheats in fols. 184, 185.

27. AN, F^{12} 1302: Chaussade letter, Paris, 16 Apr. 1764; it is of course conceivable that Chaussade could have conducted experiments or trials using mineral fuel in his *feux reverbère*. Such fuel was used in England. In one method, according to Raistrick, pig or cast iron was placed in the furnace; then, "without the addition of anything else than common pit coal, [it] is converted into good malleable iron, and being taken red-hot from the reverberatory furnace to the forge hammer, is drawn into bars of various sizes and shapes." (Quoted in Arthur Raistrick, *Quakers in Science and Industry* [Newton Abbot: David and Charles, 1968], 136.) Rhys Jenkins has pointed out, however, "not only that there was more than one form of reverberatory furnace in use, but that there were differences in the smelting process adopted in the different works." He concluded that the "reverberatory furnace" was first used for lead and copper smelting; in 1702, or within a year or so, it was in use for smelting tin. By that date it had come into use for remelting pig iron and we begin to find iron foundries, as distinct from iron-smelting works, springing up in the British Isles. (Rhys Jenkins, "The Reverberatory Furnace with Coal Fuel, 1612–1712," *Transactions, Newcomen Society* 14 [1933–1934]: 74, 78.) As early as 1681 "a more or less satisfactory construction of coal-burning reverberatory furnace had been arrived at" (p. 71). But Chaussade would appear to have been using charcoal principally or exclusively in his reverberatory *feux.*

28. René de Lespinasse, *Dépêches et mémoires du ministère de la Marine* (Nevers: G. Vallière, 1895), pp. 3–4, 20–21, 54–55; Marine (Paris), D^3 31, fol. 83. A report of 1783 indicated that the coals of Decize had been "tested" at various times by forgemasters, who "were not satisfied." At one time the forgemasters and the proprietors of the mines at Decize discussed the possibility of conducting more thorough (year-long) tests, but could not agree on terms—evidently the forgemasters had not yet experienced a serious shortage of fuel. It might be added that after coking processes became generally understood and accepted in the 1780s, Decize coals and coke did come into extensive use in the Nivernais region. Favorable opinions of Decize coals (from the proprietors of the mines) were also on the record, in D^3 30, fols. 2–4: *Mémoire pour Mgr. Le Comte de Pontchartrain,* 1705.

29. Contracts must have been signed for such coal purchases by Chaussade or his *régisseurs.* Some of those contracts may be buried in the notarial archive at Decize, not yet transferred to the Archives Départementales at Nevers; that archive was inaccessible to me.

30. Even in 1788 (seven years after Chaussade had sold out), the forges at Cosne were still only partly fueled with coal, "which arrives at Cosne via the river Loire"; whereas the provisionment of charcoal fuel was said to be "very easy" (*très facile*) at that time. (AN, F^{12} 680: De Cheville letter, Orléans, 25 July 1788.) Manufacturers in the adjacent province of Berry were less abundantly supplied. In Berry, the reports of the intendant in 1783 show wood supplies to have been particularly scarce at the heavily industrialized town of La Charité-sur-Loire. Charcoal fuel at La Charité was "ex-

tremely dear—fifteen, eighteen, and up to twenty livres the *banne*." No mineral fuel was reported as being used at La Charité, even though Decize was only a few miles up the Loire. It was likewise reported that at Donzy, a small town with three furnaces, ten (small) forges, and a *fenderie*, only forest fuels were in use. Even at the large city of Bourges, it was reported in 1783, "no mineral fuel is used; it is too dear." At Sancerre that year, coal was "rare and dear." Well-supplied indeed was St. Arnaud, from which coal supplies were distant, but wood was still abundant: 27,615 *arpents* of woodland and forest were used almost exclusively to produce wood fuel. See, e.g., Cher, C. 316: Letters from La Charité, 8 Sept. 1783; Le Chatre, 29 Nov. 1783; St. Arnaud, 13 Sept. 1783.

31. Marine (Paris), D³ 30: *Avis aux maîtres de forges,* 17 Apr. 1780 (De Suvigny).

32. Marine (Brest), 1E 523, fols. 312–13.

33. Alfred Massé, *Monographies nivernaises: Canton de Pougues* (Nevers: Ropiteau, 1912), 210. Bertrand Gille published figures showing the tonnages of pig iron and iron produced in France using wood and mineral fuels from 1819 to 1860.

	Pig Iron (Tons)		Iron (Tons)	
	Wood	Coke	Wood	Coal
1819	110,500	2,000	73,200	1,000
1830	239,257	27,103	101,613	46,814
1840	270,710	70,063	103,304	134,074
1847	339,000	252,000	97,000	280,000
1860	316,000	582,000	96,000	436,000

Bertrand Gille, *La Sidérurgie française au XIXe siècle* [Geneva: Droz, 1968], pp. 51, 55, 69; cf. pp. 128–29, 233–34, and passim).

34. Marine (Paris), D³ 31, fol. 211, 1762.

35. Ibid., fols. 210–11 (an intendant describes the role of the *commissaire*).

36. Marine (Paris), B¹ 73, fol. 110.

37. Marine (Paris), D³ 31, fol. 177.

38. Guéneau, *Organisation du travail,* p. 346.

39. Ibid. Prior to 1750 Chaussade used rented property in Nevers as a materiel depot. Marine (Paris), B³ 474, fols. 42–43.

40. Guéneau, *Organisation du travail,* pp. 346–47.

41. Mirot, *Manuel de géographie historique,* 2: 375, 376, 386, 392, and passim.

42. Two who persisted were the Sieurs Pernet and Dreu. "The latter, brought to [ducal] court, allowed himself to be intimidated. But Pernet defended himself. He refused to sell his concession. He even sought to exact passage through the *terrain* of "Babeu" [Chaussade]. The latter had a palisade erected surrounding Pernet's parcel and allowing him no outlet but the boat landing road (*chemin de halage*). But the *bailliage*, on rather bad terms with forge owners, condemned [Chaussade] by decree of 16 November 1756 to tear down his palisade." This opposition was "very irritating" to Chaussade: "I have never seen," he said, "such sorry, self-willed people."

He appealed the decision and carried the case to the Parlement, which on 24 November 1756 voided the judgment of the ducal court, "forbade the ducal court to concern itself with this question again on pain of a fine of 1,000 livres," and ordered the reconstruction of the palisade at Pernet's expense. The obstructionist Pernet had to capitulate. Guéneau, *Organisation du travail,* pp. 346–47.

43. Jean Lyonnet, *Les Gens de métiers à Nevers à la fin de l'ancien régime* (Paris, 1941), p. 367.
44. Bernard Gaulejac, "La Loire commerciale," *Annales des Pays Nivernais,* no. 20, (1978): 26 and passim.
45. Marine (Paris), B² 307, fol. 435; B² 397, fol. 478.
46. AN, F¹² 1316: *Mémoire,* n.d., with letter dated 14 Aug. 1761.
47. VI (Silvestre): *Inventaire de Jacqueline,* 18 June 1744 (appendix).
48. Marine (Paris), B² 353, fol. 53.
49. Marine (Paris), B¹ 71, fol. 42.
50. Lyonnet, *Gens de métiers,* pp. 371–72.
51. Marine (Paris), B² 394, fol. 457.
52. Marine (Paris), B² 385, fols. 421, 499.
53. Marine (Paris), B² 387, fol. 468; cf. B² 341, fols. 494, 631.
54. Some boats could be used to ascend the river in trains, commonly as far as Orléans, occasionally as far as Roanne. Gerard Le Bouedec, "Nantes et La Compagnie des Indes," pp. 36–37. (Unpub. Thesis, dactylographié), 36–37.
55. Marine (Paris), B² 343, fol. 431.
56. Marine (Paris), B² 350, fols. 30, 54.
57. Marine (Paris), B¹ 72, fols. 65–66.
58. AN, F¹² 1302: Chaussade letter, Paris, 16 Apr. 1764.
59. Marine (Paris), B² 356, fol. 411.
60. Marine (Paris), B² 373, fols. 529, 615; B² 375, fols. 452, 489.
61. Gille, *Origines,* p. 108.
62. Marine (Paris), B² 387, fol. 495.
63. Marine (Paris), D³ 31, fol. 213.
64. Ibid., fol. 213.
65. Ibid.
66. Marine (Paris), B² 360, fol. 145; cf. B² 326, fol. 797, an overland shipment of twelve anchors (1745).
67. AN, F¹² 1316: Chaussade (to Trudaine), La Rochelle, 1 Oct. 1760.
68. Marine (Paris), B² 401, fol. 442.
69. Marine (Paris), D³ 34: *Mémoire sur le projet d'establissement des magazins de marine à indrette,* 8 Mar. 1692. In 1733 the rent on the island, paid by the navy to the tax-farmers of the domain of the province of Brittany, amounted to only 760 livres a year. (B² 305, fol. 468.) The navy's payment rose to 1,200 livres about 1768. (B¹ 75, fols. 33, 48.) It was then said that the increase was not passed on to the province but retained by the *commissaire de la marine* serving at Nantes.
70. Marine (Brest), 1E 505, fol. 118. Some *fournisseurs* claimed losses of 25,000 cubic feet. Fols. 25–26.

71. Marine (Paris), B¹ 75, fol. 33. That rule evidently did not apply in 1763, when the crane, installed and maintained at the king's expense, was broken while one of Chaussade's 6,000-livre anchors was being disembarked. Choiseul, then minister of marine, told Chaussade that he would not pay for repairs to the crane, though he did authorize the entrepreneur to use wood from the navy's timber yards to make the repairs. B² 373, fol. 463.

72. Cher, C. 316: *Marché (imprimé), Fait et passé à Versailles au chateau, en l'appartement de Mondit Seigneur Rouillé,* 4 Feb. 1751. Article 3 of that contract provided that "the [purchase] price of the irons embarked will be paid to the said *fournisseurs* on the simple bill of lading, carrying the visa of the *commissaire de la marine* at Nantes, without any other documentation."

73. Cher, C. 316: *Marché (imprimé)* 1751, art. 4.

74. Ibid.

75. Marine (Paris), B² 411: *Etat des Navires qui ont été fretés; passeports,* nos. 5, 55, 60, and passim.

76. Marine (Paris), B² 413: Marine minister to Dujardin de Ruzé, 24 July 1778.

77. Cher, C. 316: *Marché,* 4 Feb. (1751), art. 7.

78. Ibid., art. 2.

79. Cher, C. 137: *Marché,* 17 June 1756.

80. Marine (Paris), B² 345, fol. 324.

81. Marine (Paris), B² 353, fol. 27.

82. Marine (Paris), D³ 31, fols. 177–88.

83. Marine (Paris), B² 361, fols. 323–24; on the volume of Chaussade's shipments, 1756–1758, see B² 353, fol. 68; B³ 355, fols. 309, 330, 344–45; B² 356, fol. 440, the last of which reduced the number of large anchors on order.

84. Marine (Paris), D³ 31, fols. 193–94.

85. Marion, *Dictionnaire,* p. 486.

86. This "payment" took place in 1751, 1753, 1754 recorded in acts with the *notaire* Magnier; most of the acts involved sums of 10,000 livres, carrying 3 percent. Rouillé's influence must have helped in getting so large a percentage of the obligations consolidated. A few of these were paid off by the Treasury over the years in special circumstances; thus three notes with a total face value of 25,000 livres were discounted in 1768 by 25 percent and ordered paid in execution of the *Edit* of December 1764 on state debts. LXXXVI (Magnier): *Remboursement,* 5 Jan. 1768.

87. LXXXVI 885 (Aleaume), passim to 29 May 1793.

88. Marine (Paris), D³ 31, fol. 212: copy of a long *mémoire* by Chaussade, with extensive marginal commentary by his long-time critic, Ruis Embito, now *intendant de la marine* at Rochefort, Rochefort, 18 June 1762, *signé* Ruis Embito.

89. Marine (Paris), B² 361, fol. 409.

90. Marine (Paris), B² 364, fols. 25, 431.

91. AN, F¹² 1316: Chaussade to minister, Paris, 1 Apr. 1761.

92. Nièvre, D² and D³, *Forges de la Chaussade, Pièce* 90: *Extrait de la contrainte decerné par M. . . . Directeur et réceveur général de la Nièvre contre*

M. Babaud de la Chaussade, 3 Nov. 1760; AN, F¹² 1316: *Chaussade à controlleur général,* 8 Nov. 1760.

93. AN, F¹² 1316: Chaussade letter, 15 Dec. 1760.
94. Marine (Paris), D³ 31, fols. 211–12.

CHAPTER 6

1. Marine (Paris), B² 310, fol. 464; B² 302, fols. 133, 179.
2. Nièvre, A²: Untitled, undated draft of letter beginning, "*Les sindics et collecteurs de la paroisse*" (after Apr. 1759); half a century afterward (1807), in the Napoleonic wars, the number of families at the works at Guérigny was calculated as 133: Villemenant (87), La Poelonnerie (10), and Guérigny proper (36). AN, F¹² 1568: *Departement de la Nièvre: Etat des usines à fer,* Nevers, 30 June 1807.
3. AN, F¹² 561: *Manufactures: Généralité d'Orléans, signé* Montaut, Orléans, 18 Dec. 1778; a later *mémoire* compared numbers of employees and operations in 1787 with operations under the Chaussade administration: BN, Fonds Fr. 20,701: *Observations particulière sur l'exploitation des forges de la Chaussade,* 1787.
4. AN, F¹² 1316: *Mémoire à Mgr. le Controlleur Général* (by Chaussade), n.d. (c. May 1760).
5. Ibid.: Chaussade letter, 24 Dec. 1760.
6. Ibid.: Chaussade letter, Guérigny, 5 Mar. 1761.
7. Marine (Paris), B¹ 72, fol. 66.
8. Ibid., fol. 67.
9. Marine (Paris), B³ 591, fols. 450–51.
10. Cher, C. 316: *Arrest du Conseil,* 29 Septembre 1729; Nièvre, D² and D³, *Forges* (Nièvre), no. 93: *Extrait de l'arrest du conseil d'état du Roy,* 27 Dec. [*sic*] 1729; *lettres patentes* issued on 2 January 1749 expressly forbade *compagnons* and workers in all manufactories of the realm to quit a job or to work elsewhere "without having obtained an explicit *congé* [permission] in writing," on pain of a 300-livre fine (art. 1).
11. Marine (Paris), B³ 340, fol. 262.
12. An undated *mémoire* (probably first half of 1761) by Chaussade alluded in a rather jocular, loose way to the fact that he then had "less than 1,500 of the 3,500 [or 2,500?] workers he employed in the month of January 1761; [and] less than 1,000 horses." AN, F¹² 1316: *Mémoire,* passim.
13. Nièvre, C⁴, *Forges Demeurs: Lettre de M. de la Chaussade à l'intendant . . . au sujet d'un procès,* n.d. (1756), in effect admitting the charges; Ibid., other papers, 1752–1756, passim.
14. Marine (Paris), B¹ 71, fols. 32–33.
15. Cher, C. 316: *Mémoire* (by Andre Chastignier), 1768; *Reponse du Sieur La Durrie au mémoire presente contre luy par M. de la Chaussade,* 1768; Chaussade's *mémoire,* 6 Dec. 1768.
16. Ibid.: *Mémoires* of Chastignier and Chaussade.
17. *Mémoire justificatif,* p. 4.
18. Marine (Paris), B¹ 85, fols. 80–81: Chaussade letter, Paris, 15 Apr. 1778.
19. Nièvre *Forges de la Chaussade* A²: untitled, undated draft of a letter. This

information and the accompanying reference to "a hundred families" needs other confirmation; the piece is unsigned. The term *étrangers* could simply have referred to persons or families not native to the Nivernais, whose names incidentally did not appear on local tax rolls—as they likely would have had they come as the king's subjects from Alsace, Lorraine, or French ports—but any of these "outsiders" might also have been referred to by local people as *étrangers. Cher, C. 316: Dodart à Chaussade*, 17 June 1752, referring to *étrangers* not on tax rolls for the *taille*, etc.

20. AN, F¹² 1316: Chaussade letter, 5 Mar. 1761.

21. Ibid.: *Chaussade à M. Pellerin*, 8 Dec. 1760.

22. Ibid.: *Chaussade à controlleur général*, 8 Nov. 1760.

23. Lyonnet, *Gens de métiers*, p. 178 and passim; Marion, *Dictionnaire*, pp. 476–79.

24. Marine (Paris), B³ 400, fols. 185–86.

25. Ibid., fol. 186. In 1738, for example, the *collecteurs des tailles* tried to name an anchor forger as a collector of taxes, but he was exempted from that duty so that anchor production would not be interrupted. Marine (Paris), B² 305, fols. 456, 476.

26. Marion, *Dictionnaire*, p. 377.

27. Marine (Paris), B² 300, fol. 241, art. 24 of the contract dated 19 Nov. 1736; cf. B³ 499, fol. 15.

28. Marine (Paris), B² 307, fol. 432.

29. Marine (Paris), B² 320, fol. 360.

30. Marine (Paris), B³ 420, fols. 157–58 (M. Pajot, intendant d'Orléans, 1743); B² 328, fols. 739–40 (Maurepas, 1746); B³ 499, fol. 15 (M. Barentin, intendant de l'Orléanais, 1750).

31. Marine (Paris), B³ 450, fol. 274.

32. Ibid., fols. 272–73; cf. B² 328, fols. 739, 740, 762.

33. Marine (Paris), B² 337, fol. 594, 1 Dec. 1749.

34. Cher, C. 316: *M. de la Chaussade à M. de Charan, subdélégué à la Charité*, 12 June 1752.

35. Ibid.; see also Chaussade's letter, Paris, 7 Sept. 1752.

36. Cher, C. 316: *Chaussade à Charan*, 12 June 1752. Cf. *Etat des gens d'affaires de [Sieur] de la Chaussade employés et travaillants aux forges et fourneau de La Vache, de Mouchy, et des Traines, paroisse de Raveau et de Varenne (généralité de Bourges)*, 1 Sept. 1752. The "Bourdeau" list included a *régisseur*, several forgers and founders and their aides, six carters "with harness" (teams), and their helpers, and ten "furnace workers."

37. Cher, C. 137: *Etat des ouvriers*, Guérigny, 3 Oct. 1756, and *Etat des ouvriers*, 23 Jan. 1757.

38. Ibid.: *Machault to Dodart*, 23 Dec. 1756; Marine (Paris), B² 353, fol. 68 (to Chaussade).

39. Ibid.: Letter of De Charan (to Dodart?), 8 June 1757.

40. Marine (Paris), B² 355, fol. 336.

41. Ibid., fol. 325: Minister of marine to Dodart, 31 May 1757; cf. Minister to Tassin, 30 June 1757.

42. Marine (Paris), B² 355, fol. 325.

43. Ibid., fol. 345.

44. Marion, *Dictionnaire*, p. 527.

45. Cher, C. 316: *Dodart à Chaussade*, 17 June 1752.

46. AN, F¹² 1316: *Le Nain, intendant de Moulins, à Trudaine*, Salligny, 10 Oct. 1761.

47. Marine (Paris), B² 409, fols. 534–35; cf. B¹ 83, fol. 309, and B¹ 99, fol. 123 (1784), pointing to the transfer of power to the ministerial level.

48. Marion, *Dictionnaire*, p. 179.

49. Ibid.

50. Marine (Paris), D³ 31, fols. 207–8: *Reponse de M. de la Croix, commissaire du magasin général au mémoire du Sr. la Chaussade*, 7 May 1762.

51. Nièvre, D⁴ *Forges (Guérigny) (Nièvre) Laisse: Anciens marchés faits par M. de la Chaussade avec les marteleurs de ses forges* (contract with Joseph Bernard), 28 May 1739.

52. See VI (Silvestre): *Bail et marché, Chaussade et Jacques L'Estang*, 18 Jan. 1745, for L'Estang's later appointment; for 1741, see below.

53. Nièvre, D⁴ *Forges, Guérigny (Nièvre)*: contracts of 13 Jan. 1741 (3) and 7 Aug. 1768.

54. Nièvre, 3E 1-1461, *Notaire François Boury, Nevers: Marché de Forgeron, Masson et Jean Le Gendre*, 11 May 1741; *Marché de forgeron*, 11 May 1741, *Masson et Claude Parene*, a very similar contract, also with bimonthly payments to the *forgeron*.

55. Ibid.: *Marché, L'Estang réceveur, et Kiesard, forgeron*, 28 Oct. 1741.

56. Marine (Paris), B² 409, fol. 870.

57. Marine (Paris), B² 413, Nov. 1778, passim.

58. C. 1782, quoted in Geneviève Beauchesne, "La Construction navale et la Compagnie des Indes," manuscript, chap. 3, p. 11.

59. BN, Fonds Fr. 20,701: *Supplement aux observations sur les forges de Cosne, dites les forges de la Chaussade*, 3 pp., n.d. (c. 1787).

60. Nièvre, Bᴬ 58 (Nièvre): *Cahier des remonstrances et doleances du tiers-état du bailliage de Nivernois et Donzois, à Nevers*, 1789 (*imprimé*), 38 pp. (the official *cahier*).

CHAPTER 7

1. Nièvre, C⁴, *Forges (Nièvre) Demeurs, pièce* 134.

2. Nièvre, *Notaires, François Morlé: Aveu et dénombrement, Chaussade à Mazarin Mancini*, 1 Oct. 1775.

3. Nièvre, A²: *Il resulte du mémoire envoyé par M. Goussot au sujet de directes . . . comme receveur de l'évêché*, n.d. (late 1765 or 1766).

4. Nièvre, C⁴, *Forges (Nièvre) Demeurs: Procédure faite à Nevers dans le procès contre l'Evêque de Nevers, liasse*, 1767; and *Procès de la cause pour le Sieur Babaud de la Chaussade contre M. l'Evêque de Nevers*, 1768, 16 pp., *imprimé*, and another *liasse*, 1767–1768.

5. Nièvre, A²: *Blondeau à M. Boury, notaire royal de Nevers*, Prémery, 19 Feb. 1753.

6. Nièvre, A², *Forges de la Chaussade, Pièces Divers* (Nièvre): *Extrait des registres du Conseil de S.A.S. Mgr. le Prince de Condé*, 30 Aug. 1764.

7. CII (Linacier): *Société deposée, J. Babaud, J. Masson et Chaussade,* 14 Feb. 1735.

8. Among the thousands of pages pertinent to the Chaussade–Berthier-Bizy (de Fougis) litigations, one might cite Nièvre, B², *Forges (Nièvre) Villemenant: Précis, pour l'administration des Forges Royales de la Chaussade* (summary after sale of the properties), 1781; C⁴, *Forges (Nièvre) Demeurs: Procédure entre M. Desfurgis et les Chatillon demandeurs contre M. de la Chaussade (liasse),* 1743, 1744, 1745–1747; *Procédure et sentence qui conddamne M. de la Chaussade à payer à M. Desfourgis 132 livres* and *Etat de ce qui est deub par M. Babaud;* D³–D⁴, *Forges (Nièvre) Guérigny,* 1761–1772, pièces 81, 82, 94 (1761): *Pièces divers du procès jugé par arrêt du Parlement* (the result: "Sr. de Fougis henceforth to pay Chaussade a rent of twenty-one sols and a *boisseau d'avoine*"); E³–E⁴, *Forges (Nièvre) Frasnay: Contestations entre M. de la Chaussade et M. de Fougis,* 1749–1750 (*laisses* of hundreds of pages).

9. C. Corbier, "Notice historique sur les forges imperiales de la Chaussade." *Bulletin, Société Nivernaise des Sciences, Lettres, et Arts* 4 (1870): 400 n.

10. Marion, *Dictionnaire,* p. 314; and J. Q. C. Mackrell, *The Attack on "Feudalism" in Eighteenth Century France* (Toronto: University of Toronto Press, 1973), pp. 66–67.

11. Marc Bloch, *Feudal Society,* trans. L. A. Manyon (Chicago: University of Chicago Press, 1961), p. 443.

12. Quoted in Jacques-Henri Bataillon, *Les Justices seigneuriales du bailliage de Pontoise à la fin de l'ancien régime* (Paris: 1942), pp. 153–54.

13. Nièvre, A², *Pièce* 267, June 1764, and *pièce* dated 19 Jan. 1764; VI (Silvestre): Act dated 18 June 1744 (appendix), showing Chaussade's purchase of the Farelmeyer papermill and dependencies (1742), and the old chateau of Hombourg (*sic.*) (1744) from Roüelle and spouse for c. 20,000 livres.

14. Nièvre, E⁴–E⁵: *Acte confirmant les provisions de procureur postulant et de greffier civil, criminel et de police au bailliage de Frasnay accordees au Sieur Dufaud par M. de la Chaussade,* 1773, and a similar *acte* with Morlé, 1773, enumerating Chaussade's judicial powers.

15. Nièvre, A²: *Chaussade à M. Le Brelon,* Paris, 3 Feb. 1762.

16. Ibid.: *Note,* Guérigny, 6 Aug. 1762.

17. R. Doucet, *Les Institutions de la France au XVIe siècle,* 2 vols. (Paris: Picard, 1948), 2: 503, and passim.

18. Nièvre, A²: *Chaussade à Bort,* Paris, 20 Feb. 1768, and passim.

19. LXXXVI (Magnier): *Procuration,* 21 June 1756.

20. Nièvre, D⁴, *Forges (Nièvre),* no. 131.

21. Nièvre, B², *Forges de la Chaussade (Nièvre), Chartrier de Villemenant: Pièces servant à etablir des fiefs et justices de Villemenant, et fiefs et justices de Marcy,* 1746.

22. Nièvre, D⁴, *Forges (Nièvre),* No. 130: *Etat de ce qui doit être remboursssé à Monsieur de la Chaussade, qui à payé et acquitté en entier au fermier du Comte de Prémery, tous les arrearages et frais fait pour raison des Directes et droits seigneuriaux affectees sur le village des Riaux, Bois de la Robinerie,*

et les Bois et accrues des Brenais, conformement à la Reconnoissance du
15 novembre 1773, 1776; Quittance par le Sr. Petit à Mr. de la Chaussade,
d'arrérages des directes due au Comte de Prémery sur les bois des Brenet et
de la Robinière, 1776.

23. Nièvre, A²: Pierrot et La Vve. Lanvergon doivent par chacun an 3 Baux
    depuis St. Martin 1754 jusqua 1769; two untitled pages of Lanvergon ac-
    counts (c. 1766, 1768); Pièce 129: Recouvrements resultant des acquisi-
    tions faites par Mr. de la Chaussade (1774); cf. F²–F³, Forges (Nièvre) La
    Vache: Etat explicatif des RedevanceDhues à la terre De la Vache (c. 150
    livres, about 1747).

24. VI (Silvestre): Accord pour droits féodaux, 16 July 1742; Jean Joseph de
    Beze Seigneur de la Belouze, [etc.] et Chaussade; Nièvre, A², Chaussade
    lettre, Paris, 19 Mar. 1743.

25. Nièvre, A²: Note, 25 Nov. 1771, signé La Chaussade.

26. Ibid.: Jugement de Lieutenant Juge Bailly de la Baronie de Frasnay, 12 Nov.
    1760. This decision may be from a neighboring part of Frasnay whose
    forges did in fact supply irons to Chaussade's works, but were actually
    operated by Chaussade's neighbor, M. de La Belouze. Thus this judge
    (Bailly?) may not have been Chaussade's justice or his appointee. However,
    Chaussade did at the time hold part of the Frasnay property as a fief; the
    tenor of this decision is similar to others (cited below) known to have been
    handed down by judges who were certainly Chaussade's appointees. This
    document was found among papers classed in the Nièvre archive as Forges
    de la Chaussade (Nièvre), Pièces Divers. Cf. Provision de Greffier des
    Justices de Guérigny, Nevers, 27 Dec. 1764, signé Chaussade, by which
    Chaussade appointed one Jacques Joseph Haly his clerk of court; and
    Greffier en nos justices de Guérigny, Frasnay les Chanoines, Saint Aubin,
    Villemenant, et Desmeurs et dependences.

27. Nièvre, A²: Forges de la Chaussade, Pièces Divers.

28. Nièvre, A², Forges de la Chaussade: Ordonnance de police Pour la paroisse
    de Saint-Aubin, promulgé le 9 Octobre 1763 au prone de la Paroisse de
    Saint-Aubin.

29. Nièvre, D⁴, Forges de la Chaussade, Guérigny (Nièvre), liasse no. 136:
    Beaux, fermages et accenses relatifs aux divers proprietés de M. de la
    Chaussade, 1756–1776; Bail de l'auberge pour 6 ou 9 annees à com-
    mencer du 1er May 1775 moyennant 400 livres (to Minot) (some pasture
    included).

30. Nièvre, A², Forges de la Chaussade, Pièces Divers: Jugement de Police pour
    le Cabarets, 1 Oct. 1764.

31 Nièvre, D⁴, Forges de la Chaussade: Marché passé entre M. de la Chaus-
    sade et Renoir, Mr Charpentier, 11 Dec. 1774, signé (in margin) "Renoir"
    and "Bd" (Babaud?).

32. Nièvre, A², Forges de la Chaussade, pieces dated Jan. and June 1764.

33. The case was filed in Condé's judicial register on 30 August 1764; hence
    the mistakes could have been made either by a predecessor or by Roüelle
    himself.

34. Nièvre, A²: Decision of Jean François Roüelle, l'auditoire de Frasnay, 8 Feb.
    1764.

35. Nièvre, 3E 1-179, Claude Gilbert Bort, *notaire de Guérigny,* examples taken from acts of 1767; A²: *Inventaire des Effets mobiliers qui se sont trouvées chez Pierre Guemppe* (?), *voiturier demeurant au Village de Gouvelin* (on decease of wife), Sept. 1758.
36. Nièvre, A²: letter dated 15 Dec. 1768.
37. Ibid.: *Provision de Greffier de Justices, fait à Notre Hotel à Nevers,* 27 Dec. 1764, *signé* B. de la Chaussade.
38. Ibid.: *Chaussade à Bort,* Paris, 20 Feb. 1768.
39. Ibid.
40. Ibid.: *Releve Des Amendes que j'ai reçue Depuis Mon dernier Etat fourni à M. De la Chaussade.*
41. Ibid., *Forges de la Chaussade, Pièces Divers: Ordonnance du Bailly concernant la garde des porcs, chiens, vaches, etc.,* 31 Aug. 1763.
42. Ibid., n.d. (probably 1760s).
43. Ibid. The case was settled by "a decree rendered against them, to the profit of the said Seigneur de la Chaussade, 31 Dec. 1767."
44. AN, F¹² 1302: *Mémoire,* untitled and n.d., written in 1769 by Chaussade, accompanying his letter to Trudaine; also *Copie du p.er mémoire presenté à Monseigneur Le Chancelier en 1765.*
45. F¹² 1032: *Mémoire* (by Chaussade) (retrospective); D⁴ Forges (Nièvre) Guérigny: *Report of Inspectors of the Church,* Nevers, 7 Aug. 1743.
46. D⁴ Forges (Nièvre) Guérigny: *Report of Inspectors,* Nevers, 10 Aug. 1769.
47. *loc. cit.*
48. Nièvre, A²: *Lettre, signé Chaussade,* Paris, 19 Mar. 1743.
49. Nièvre, D⁴, *Forges (Guérigny): Chartrier de Guérigny* (contract dated 14 Mar. 1746); *Déliberation,* Paris, 12 Apr. 1755, *signé* Durand.
50. VI (Silvestre): *Presentation à Mgr. l'Evêque de Nevers par Pierre Babaud de la Chaussade, de la personne de Jean Juniat, Prestre,* 13 July 1744.
51. LXXXVI (Magnier): *Presentation, Pierre Babaud de la Chaussade à Mgr. la curé de Guérigny,* 29 Aug. 1759.
52. Ibid.: *Presentation, Chaussade à Curé de St. Pierre* [the new church/chapel] *de Guérigny,* 4 Mar. 1768.
53. AN, F¹² 1302: *Mémoire* (by Chaussade); the *copie du p.er mémoire presenté à Mgr. Le Chancelier en 1765* gives the cost as 50,000 livres. It has been said that the church at Guérigny was built facing the wrong way, thus disqualifying it as a church; there is some suspicion that Chaussade's quarrels with the bishop of Nevers may have been related to the problem. The size of the new church made it a welcome improvement, nonetheless. In fact, the orientation of a structure built for worship does not necessarily disqualify it as a church. Strict adherence to one orientation or another "was, necessarily, in many instances impossible; the direction of streets in cities naturally governed the position of Churches. Some of the most ancient Churches of Rome are directed toward various points on the compass." Herberman, Pace, et al. (eds.), *The Catholic Encyclopedia,* vol. 1 (New York: Appleton, 1907), p. 365. The reference to Saint-Agnan was kindly supplied by Gérard Martin, deriving from the Archives de Cosne, Régistre des déliberations de la Municipalité.
54. AN, F¹² 1302: *Mémoire* (by Chaussade), n.d. (c. 1769).

55. LXXXVI (Aleaume): *Chaussade, Testament,* 26 Nov. 1787.

56. Nièvre, A²: *Etat de la Dépense [Dautrec] pour le Chateau de Guérigny,* 11 Jan. 1755.

57. LXXXVI (Aleaume): *Inventaire après decès de Mr. Babaud de la Chaussade,* 5 Mar. 1793.

58. Fonds Fr. 30,297, 9 Feb. 1784.

59. Nièvre, D³ and D⁴, *Forges de la Chaussade, Pièce* 120.

60. LXXXVI (Aleaume): *Chaussade, Testament,* 26 Nov. 1787.

61. Nièvre, D³ and D⁴, *Forges de la Chaussade, pièce* 120. A similar incident had taken place the previous year (1769), when some of the comte de Berthier Bizy's people were mistreated by the same Poisseaux culprits. The stolen grain was recovered, but the thieves apparently were entirely unscathed.

62. Nièvre, A²: *Judgment de Lieutenant Juge Bailly* (Frasnay), 12 Nov. 1760.

63. Nièvre, E² Ville de Nevers, *Opposition à l'établissement d'un marché à Guérigny, demandé par le Sieur B. de la Chaussade* (1766/1767).

64. Nièvre, D⁴, *Forges de la Chaussade: Chartrier de Guérigny, Procès verbal,* 17 July 1774, and *Lettres Patentes portant Etablissement des deux foires à Guérigny,* Oct. 1772, *signé* Louis, issued "at the request of the Sieur Pierre Babaud de la Chaussade."

65. LXXXVI (Aleaume): *Chaussade, Testament,* 26 Nov. 1787.

66. AD IV 5, *Droits Seigneuriaux: Etrait d'un arrest du Parlement [de Bordeaux] du 27 mars 1736.*

67. Ibid., *Eaux et Forêts: Extrait des registres du Parlement,* 30 Mar. 1776.

CHAPTER 8

1. Marine (Paris), B² 304, fol. 126; cf. Bouedec, *Nantes et la Compagnie,* pp. 55–56.

2. Marine (Paris), B³ 385, fols. 105, 195–96.

3. Marine (Paris), B² 308, fol. 314; B² 310, fol. 445.

4. 1P4 Lorient fols. 110–11.

5. Ibid.: *Marché,* 19 June 1749.

6. Marine (Paris), B² 341, fol. 471.

7. Ibid., fol. 539.

8. Marine (Paris), B² 356, fol. 440.

9. AN, F¹² 1316: Chaussade letter, Guérigny, 6 Dec. 1763.

10. Ibid.: *Mémoire* (by Chaussade), n.d., but before June 1761.

11. These taxes on iron and steel dated from an edict of 1626; an *ordonnance* of 1680 fixed the levy at 20 sous per quintal on steel, 13 sous, 6 deniers per quintal on iron, but in practice these sums were not collected equally throughout the realm. Nine-tenths of the total product of the tax derived from levies collected from the producer. Marion, *Dictionnaire,* p. 366.

12. Among others, AN F¹² 1316: *Lettre à Mrs. Les Deputés du Commerce, 1 Juin 1760;* Ibid.: *Trudaine à Mrs. Les Deputés du Commerce,* 1 June 1760.

13. Ibid.: *Circulaire aux Chambres du Commerce,* 11 Aug. 1760.

14. Ibid.: *Chaussade à Trudaine,* Paris, 6 Aug. 1760.

15. Ibid.: *Chaussade à Trudaine,* Nantes, 16 Sept. 1760.
16. Lore-Atlantique, C. 768: *Mémoire, B. de la Chaussade,* 11 Sept. 1760.
17. Ibid.
18. Ibid., fol. 6; cf. AN, F^{12} 1316; *Mémoire, Chaussade à M. Trudaine,* 22 May 1760.
19. AN, F^{12} 1316, Chaussade to Trudaine, La Rochelle, 1 Oct. 1760.
20. Ibid.
21. Ibid.
22. Marine (Paris), B^2 371, fol. 679.
23. Loire-Atlantique, C. 768: *Copie de la Lettre Ecrite par les Directeurs du Commerce de la province de Guyenne à Mr. Trudaine,* 4 Nov. 1760.
24. Ibid.
25. Bamford, "French Shipping"; AN, F^{12} 1316: *Chaussade à Trudaine,* Paris, 20 July 1760.
26. Loire-Atlantique, C. 768: *Directeurs du commerce à Trudaine,* 4 Nov. 1760.
27. AN, F^{12} 1316; *Chaussade à Trudaine,* La Rochelle, 1 Oct. 1760.
28. A fund in the amount of 100,000 florins (c. 200,000 livres) would be allocated to finance purchases of his anchors and irons by the ports; Nantes would contribute 30,000, La Rochelle 30,000, and Bordeaux 40,000 livres, and each city would receive Chaussade's anchors and irons on credit up to the amount contributed. The other 100,000 would give Chaussade some working capital. He and the cities would repay the Dutch bankers in due course. "Nothing is more usual in business than to generate funds by means of credit; one can hardly put it to better use, or to any more significant object, than to support establishments of the greatest utility." He referred, of course, to the manufactories of the Sieur de la Chaussade. (AN, F^{12} 1316: *Mémoire,* n.d.; *Plan de l'Opération de Change,* with Chaussade letter dated 14 Aug. 1761. Chaussade suggested that a certain M. Le Coulteux, *député de la Ville de Paris,* could make the 100,000 florins available in Paris; alternatively, he suggested the same change operation made by means of the Amsterdam correspondents of M. de Montmartel and M. de la Borde, both very well known Paris bankers.
29. AN, F^{12} 1316: *Chaussade à M. Pellerin,* 8 Dec. 1760.
30. AN, F^{12} 1302: *Mémoire, Traites, Forges de la Chaussade,* 13 June 1761 (*imprimé*), in margin: "Decision: Bon comme il est proposé."
31. Ibid., *Mémoire,* n.d. (1770).
32. AN, F^{12} 1302, *Mémoire,* unsigned and undated, by Chaussade (1770); this *mémoire* was occasioned by Chaussade's assertion of his claim to the right of free re-entry into Poitou (within the *Cinq Grosses Fermes*) from his Nantes and Paimbeuf entrepôts. A convenient map is in George T. Matthews, *The Royal General Farms in Eighteenth Century France* (New York: Columbia University Press, 1958), pp. 82–83.
33. AN, F^{12} 1302: *Chaussade à Trudaine,* Paris, 20 Sept. 1770.
34. Marine (Paris), B^2 371, fol. 637.
35. AN, F^{12} 1316: Chaussade letter, Guérigny, 6 Dec. 1763.
36. Ibid.: *Passeport,* Versailles, 12 Apr. 1763.
37. LXXXVI (Magnier): *Bail à ferme,* 29 Apr. 1766 (to take effect 1769); Le

procureur de M. le Cardinal de Bernis [François Joachim] *à Sr. Jean Claude Ducatellier;* and *Déclaration, Jean Claude Ducatellier à Pierre Babaud de la Chaussade,* 29 Apr. 1766.

38. AN, F¹² 1316: *Passeport,* 4 Nov. 1763.
39. Ibid.: Chaussade letter, Guérigny, 6 Dec. 1763. The two *passeports* and the *état* detailed above accompany this letter.
40. Ibid.
41. Ibid.
42. Marine (Lorient), E⁴ 55, fol. 58: *Instruction pour le Sr. de la Ferté Bernard,* 1762.
43. Marine (Lorient), E⁴ 68, fol. 100; (Paris), B² 381, fol. 409.
44. Marine (Paris), B² 373, fol. 514; B² 375, fols. 502, 503.
45. Marine (Paris), B² 375, fol. 507. Chaussade himself was later to hold both the wood and iron contracts; see Chapter 9.
46. Ibid., fol. 528. The minister did, however, allow Petel to deliver irons already contracted for that the ports could immediately use. Cf. Marine (Paris), B¹ 68, fols. 213, 244, 259.
47. Marine (Lorient), E⁴ 67: *M. le Duc de Praslin à M. de Ruis,* 21 Jan. 1769 (copy sent accompanying dispatch of Boynes to De la Croix, 22 Feb. 1774.
48. Marine (Paris), B² 375, fol. 406; B¹ 68, fol. 213.
49. Marine (Paris), B² 392, fol. 218.
50. Marine (Paris), B² 387, fol. 479.
51. For example, in 1768: Marine (Paris), B¹ 73, fol. 156; B² 387, fols. 461–62.
52. Marine (Lorient), E⁴ 65, *De Boynes à Cie. des Indes,* 12 Aug. 1773, and *Etat de diverses fournitures . . . à envoyer pour le Service de l'Isle de France pendant* 1774.
53. Marine (Lorient), E⁴ 67, fols. 103, 182–83, 262.
54. Marine (Lorient), E⁴ 70, fols. 164–67; E⁴ 73–74: *Etat des Diverses Munitions, Effets et Ustensiles aux Fournier . . . pour les comptoirs de l'Inde,* 1776; E⁴ 81, fol. 25.
55. Marine (Lorient), E⁴ 78, fols. 105–9.
56. Ibid., fol. 193. I am indebted to Geneviève Beauchesne, retired *archiviste en chef* at Lorient, for this reference and others.
57. Marine (Lorient), E⁴ 91, fol. 3.
58. Ibid., fols. 102, 103 (1780).
59. Marine (Lorient), E⁴ 73, fols. 41, 43–45.
60. Marine (Lorient), E⁴ 83, fols. 19, 75, 132, 165–68.
61. The Crowleys, supplying irons to the British navy and colonies, also sustained extensive losses in the colonial export trade, with profits "thrown away in bad debts" in Pennsylvania, New York, Maryland, Jamaica, Nevis, and Madras. Flinn, *Men of Iron,* pp. 145–46.
62. LXXXVI (Magnier): *Procuration, Chaussade à Jean François Lucas, bourgeois de Paris,* 3 Sept. 1768.
63. AN, F¹² 1302: *Mémoire* (by Chaussade), n.d., and his letter to Trudaine, Paris, 20 Sept. 1770.
64. AN, F¹² 716: *Advis des Deputées du commerce sur le Mémoire du Sr. de la Chaussade,* 23 Aug. 1771.
65. AN, F¹² 1302: *Arrest du Conseil d'Etat du Roi,* 22 Feb. 1773.

66. Marine (Paris), B¹ 81, fol. 226.
67. AN, F¹² 1300: *Petition,* 7 July 1773.
68. AN, F¹² 1302: *Sartine à Contrôleur général,* Versailles, 3 Feb. 1775.

CHAPTER 9

1. LXXXVI (Aleaume): *Remboursements, Chaussade à divers,* 8, 13, 18 Aug. 1781 and passim to 28 Dec. 1781, showing over 250,000 livres borrowed in the period 1753–1763 alone, repaid by him only after the later, definitive sale of the forges to the king (1781); the greater parts of the dowries to his daughters were to be paid from his estate at his death.
2. LXXXVI (Magnier): *Procurations,* 16 Feb. 1771 and 13 Jan. 1780, in which Sionville's powers as director-general were confirmed and renewed.
3. Marine (Paris), D³ 31, fols. 237–41.
4. Ibid.
5. LXXXVI (Magnier): *Procuration,* 21 Apr. 1773.
6. Marine (Paris), D³ 31, fols. 237–41.
7. Chaussade obtained through the navy an order from the king for the seizure of the stolen funds, but too late and to no avail; the culprit died two months after being discovered. Marine (Paris), B¹ 88, fol. 74 (retrospective, dated 1778).
8. LXXXVI (Aleaume): *Procuration, Chaussade à Martin Michel Sionville,* 17 Feb. 1778.
9. Shortly after Sionville was commissioned to investigate, Huguet also died, having been, as Chaussade phrased it, "utterly ruined by conduct he had kept secret [gambling?]. The whole City knows that I have lost 60,000 livres through him. . . . How much work it will take, how many years, to recover so large a loss." Marine (Paris), B¹ 88, fol. 74.
10. LXXXVI (Aleaume): *Procuration, Chaussade à Jean Mathias Deveaux,* 7 Sept. 1778.
11. LXXXVI (Aleaume): *Procuration, Chaussade à M. Chanu,* 30 June 1779.
12. Nièvre, E⁴ and E⁵, Frasnay: *Actes confirmant les provisions de procureur postulant . . . accordées au Sieur Defaud,* 1773; cf. Chaussade's appointment of François Morlé as *notaire royal,* installed 4 Feb. 1773.
13. Cher, C. 316: *Reponse du Sieur Durrie au Mémoire presenté contre luy par M. de la Chaussade à Mgr. l'Intendant du Berry,* 1768.
14. Marine (Rochefort), 5E² 21, 22, 23, contracts dated 28 Sept. 1776, 8 July 1778, 10 Mar. 1780.
15. Marine (Paris), B² 409, fol. 549, letter of 1776 mistakenly dated 15 Jan. 1775; cf. letter of 26 Jan. 1776, fol. 570.
16. Ruis Embito apparently died in June 1776. Marine (Paris), B² 409, fol. 827.
17. There are indications that Ruis never lost his zeal for the maintenance of high standards in administration, which underlay some of his criticisms of the Babauds' conduct of timber exploitations in Lorraine c. 1731–1732. In later life, notwithstanding periodic bouts with illness, Embito seems to have imposed a rigorous control in his arsenal at Brest. His regime was sometimes onerous for associates. In 1775 Ruis Embito wrote a *mémoire* against allowing the horses and carriages of high officers to enter the prem-

ises of the arsenal—at a time when Admiral de Grasse, who could not walk (or did so only with great difficulty) was commander in chief of the squadron based at Brest. Ruis also claimed that the domestics attending high officers were not to be trusted in the arsenal; nor did he want the meetings of the local *Académie de la Marine* to be held there. (Marine (Brest), 1E 521, fols. 83–89 passim.) Intendant Ruis Embito also had troubles with another officer, M. le Vicomte du Rochechouart. Rochechouart was sharply critical of Ruis Embito's *munitionnaire*, who, he said, was supplying defective victuals to his command. The wine was "weak" (*faible*—probably watered), the lard was newly salted or "resalted," breadstuffs were wormy, and the firewood supplied on board ships was too fine-cut (kindling, not firewood, said Rochechouart, who ordered it disembarked and replaced with authentic firewood from a merchant ship in port, at the *munitionnaire*'s expense). Ruis Embito, though with some reluctance, admitted that "this new *munitionnaire*" was a "very disturbing man, even dangerous in his methods." (Ibid., fols. 183–88, passim.)

Ruis Embito also crossed horns with the distinguished naval architect Groignard, claiming in June 1775 that the dimensions called for in some of Groignard's plans were "unorthodox." Ibid., fols. 190–96, 240–44.

18. Marine (Paris), D³ 31, fols. 237–41.
19. Marine (Brest), 1E 521, fols. 309–10.
20. Marine (Brest), 1E 523, fols. 19–20.
21. Ibid., fol. 6.
22. Ibid., fol. 98.
23. Ibid.: letters of 23 and 30 Apr. 1777.
24. Marine (Brest), 1E 187, fols. 235, 345.
25. Marine (Paris), B¹ 83, fol. 195.
26. Ibid., fol. 255; B¹ 84, fol. 52.
27. Marine (Brest), 1E 523, fol. 325.
28. Ibid., fols. 325, 352.
29. Ibid., fols. 276, 279.
30. Marine (Paris), B² 411, fol. 50.
31. Guichon de Grandpont, "Les Intendants de la marine au port de Brest," *Bulletin de la société académique de Brest*, 15 (1890) passim.
32. Even small-caliber cannon ("*pièces de 4*") could not be mounted; Laporte attributed this inability not to lack of wood or workers, but to "lack of *fers feuillards* necessary for four pounders. I myself had hoped to be able to procure them from Morlaix or from Nantes. Not a single *bar* was found in the first of these two ports; only 17,000 [were obtained] from different private sources at Nantes that we will receive, but being only two *lignes* thick, [they] are good only for *pièces de 3*. ["three pounders," an almost unheard-of caliber almost certainly little used at Brest]." Marine (Brest), 1E 523, fols. 458–59, 8 Apr. 1778.) It is unclear exactly how the strip iron was to be used to mount the four and "three" pounders. Two days later (10 April 1778), this contrived assault on Chaussade was carried further: "I must report to you, Monseigneur, . . . the difficulties in which we are thrown by the lack of iron [hoops] for casks. I have sought them at St. Malo, at Morlaix, at Nantes, at Lorient. I have found no supplies. I have pressured the

Sieur de la Chaussade's correspondent at Nantes; but he told Monsieur de la Villeblanche that M. de la Chaussade will make such shipments only on specific order from you. I do not understand this resolution on the part of the Sieur de la Chaussade, and I have reason to believe that there are bad relations (*il y à du mal entendre*) either on his part or that of his correspondent [Chaussade did in fact have trouble with his embezzling correspondent at Nantes], since you have given him orders to deliver all the irons listed on the *état*, which included 1,200 *milliers de fers feuillards* because the service needs them—and by the fault of the Sieur de la Chaussade, who for five months has not delivered to Brest a single *bar* of these irons. I am going to write to him, and it is perhaps necessary that you give him positive and precise orders either to complete the provisionment ordered or to indicate the types of iron that he cannot furnish so that measures can be taken to obtain them elsewhere." (Ibid., fols. 460–61, 10 Apr. 1778. The Brest intendance report appears in fols. 462–63, 13 Apr. 1778.)

33. Ibid., fols. 471–72, 17 Apr. 1778.
34. Marine (Brest). The correspondence appears in 1E 191, passim; 192, fol. 41; 523, 6 May 1778.
35. Marine (Paris). For indications of Chaussade's low level of remuneration, see B^1 84, fol. 7 (1777); B^1 89, fol. 112. Cf. B^2 419, fol. 57 (price increases received in 1780).
36. Marine (Paris), B^1 84: *Terres et forges du Sr. de la Chaussade,* 16 Sept. 1777, with appended papers.
37. Marine (Brest), 1E 523: Intendant to minister, 9 June 1777.
38. Marine (Paris), B^3 708, fols. 129–30.
39. E.g., Marine (Paris), B^2 417: *Passeports,* 18 Feb., 5 May, 30 June 1780; cf. B^2 419, fol. 56 (table).
40. On price rises requested and/or accorded with justifications, and comparative discussions of quality and prices, 1762–1780: Marine (Paris), B^1 68, fols. 213, 244, 259; B^1 71, fols. 32–34, 54, 210; B^1 73, fol. 141; B^1 74, fols. 294, 302–4; B^1 87, fols. 208, 271; B^1 90, fols. 237–38 (with table); B^2 387, fol. 413; (Rochefort), 5E^2 21: *Prix accordes au . . . Chaussade,* 1780; 5E^2 23: *Soumission,* 1 Jan. 1779; (Brest), 1E 193, fols. 219–20.
41. Marine (Brest), 1E 193, fols. 219–20.
42. Marine (Brest), 1E 192, fol. 539. The ship's cargo of hemp, on the contrary, was purchased for the French navy.
43. Marine (Brest), 1E 193, fol. 283; implementation of this policy *vis-à-vis* other importers of irons: (Paris), B^1 85, fol. 170. Cf. B^2 413, fol. 18 (table only).
44. Marine (Paris), B^2 413, no. 80: Sartine to Necker, 8 Aug. 1778. This concession by Necker, in behalf of Gonvy, Chaussade's supplier, apparently moved the French tax-farmers of the Nassau-Saarbrücken district to offer, in early 1779, to sell the French navy irons "superior to those provided by the entrepreneur of the navy" (i.e., Gonvy-Chaussade). Marine (Paris), B^1 89, fol. 31: *Mémoire,* Feb. 1779.
45. Marine (Paris), B^2 413, fol. 18: Minister to Chaussade, 6 Nov. 1778 (table only).

46. Marine (Paris), B¹ 92, fol. 93: Chaussade to Sartine, Guérigny, 20 Aug. 1779.
47. Marine (Rochefort), 5E² 21, 22, 23, *Marchés,* 28 Sept. 1776, 8 July 1778, and 10 Mar. 1780.
48. Marine (Paris), B² 409, fols. 674, 687.
49. LXXXVI (Aleaume): *Procuration, Chaussade à Deveaux,* 7 Sept. 1778.
50. Marine (Paris), B² 409, fols. 64, 837, and passim.
51. Marine (Brest), 1E 194, fol. 1105.
52. Marine (Brest), 1E 523, fols. 286–87, 361.
53. Marine (Paris), B² 413: Sartine to Chaussade, 24 July 1778.
54. Ibid., fol. 157.
55. Ibid., no. 218.
56. Ibid., B² 413, 6 Nov. and 12 Dec. 1778 (table only).
57. Marine (Paris), C⁷ 14: *Dossier B. de la Chaussade.*
58. Marine (Paris), B² 416, Minister to Chaussade, 18 Jan. 1779 (*registre* of tables only).
59. Marine (Paris), B² 413, fol. 27.
60. Marine (Paris), B¹ 90: *Fers: Forunitures du Sr. de la Chaussade,* 12 Mar. 1779.
61. Ibid., B¹ 90: *Fourniture du Sr. de la Chaussade,* 27 Aug. 1779; B² 419 (tables only).
    Some indications of the composition of these massive provisionments is given in the commodities listed on the *passeports,* issued for Chaussade's *foruniture* for a single month (January 1780): anchors, nails, bar and/or chain shot (*boulets ramés*), *platincourts, pattes d'ancres,* jacks, *enclumes,* irons (round, square, flat, rods, and sheets), and 600,000 livres of iron ingots (*saumons*), for use at the cannon foundry at Indret. The above order weighed three million livres. B² 417: *Passeports,* 7, 21, and 22 Jan. 1780.
62. Marine (Paris), B² 409, fol. 100.
63. Marine (Paris), B¹ 81, fol. 232.
64. Marine (Paris), B² 407, fol. 425.
65. Marine (Paris), B¹ 81, fol. 271.
66. Marine (Paris), B² 407, fol. 466. Cf. fols. 425, 459.
67. Ibid., B² 407, fols. 505, 578–79.
68. Ibid., fols. 578–79.
69. Ibid.
70. Marine (Paris), B¹ 83, fol. 16.
71. Ibid., letter to Chaussade, 26 Jan. 1776.
72. Marine (Paris), B² 409, fols. 534–35, 549.
73. Marine (Paris), B¹ 83, fol. 16.
74. Marine (Paris), B² 409, fol. 535, 26 Jan. 1776.
75. Marine (Paris), B¹ 83, fol. 39.
76. Marine (Paris), B² 409, fols. 636–38.
77. Ibid., fol. 686.
78. Ibid., fol. 756.
79. Ibid., fol. 801.
80. Nièvre, D⁴ *Forges de la Chaussade, pièce* 135: *Declaration faite au Greffes*

de l'election de Nevers par M. de la Chaussade du defrichement de plusieurs terrains, 13 Aug. 1776.

81. Marine (Paris), B¹ 83: *Bois des environs de la Loire,* 23 Aug. 1776.
82. Ibid.
83. Ibid.: *Bois du Berry, du Bourbonnais et du Nivernois,* 13 Dec. 1776.
84. See Marine (Brest), 1E 521 and 1E 522, esp. 10 Oct. 1777.
85. Marine (Paris), B² 413, fol. 49.
86. Cher, C. 137: De Sartine to De Bron, 13 Apr. 1777.
87. Marine (Paris), B² 413, No. 184: Minister to M. de Reverseaux, 18 Sept. 1778.
88. Ibid.: Minister to M. Nion, 3 July, 9 Oct. 1778.
89. Ibid., 9, 17 Oct. and 6 Nov. 1778.
90. Ibid., 4, 21, and 25 Dec. 1778 (table only).
91. Marine (Paris), B¹ 92, fols. 54, 61.
92. Marine (Paris), B¹ 88, fols. 69, 71–73.
93. Marine (Paris), B² 413, fol. 13 (table only).
94. Marine (Paris), B² 417, fols. 2, 53: *Passeports.*
95. Marine (Rochefort), 1E 210, fol. 95; 1E 215, fol. 117; 1E 216, fol. 115; 5E² 28: *Marché,* 24 Mar. 1780 (plank); (Paris), B² 417: *Passeports,* 7, 11 Jan., 26 May, 5 June 1780 (for plank), and passim; B² 419: Sartine to Nion and Chaussade, 22 Feb. and 21 Mar. 1780; B² 421: Sartine to Chaussade, 15 Apr. 1781, 22 Dec. 1781; B³ 708, fols. 30, 52 (transaction involving Chaussade's *prête-nom:* Barrois).
96. Marine (Brest), IE 521, fols. 102 ff., 119–20, 356–57 (Ruis Embito); (Paris), B² 409, fols. 100, 816.
97. Marine (Brest), IE 523, fols. 191–92.
98. Ibid.; (Paris), B² 409: *Mémoire pour servir d'Instruction au Sr. Guinau, Ing. constructeur des Vaux du Roi* (detached to Hamburg, 1776, fols. 807–8).
99. Marine (Paris), B¹ 88, fol. 139.
100. Marine (Paris), B² 314, fol. 127.
101. Marine (Paris), B² 413, fol. 24.
102. Ibid., B² 413: Letter, 18 Sept. 1778, M. le Baron Taubenheim's inquiries, indicating that "many forests" on the estates of the Empress require exploitation; but see 12 Dec. 1778 (her Highness decreed that the wood should be used locally).
103. Marine (Paris), B¹ 92, fol. 91.
104. Marine (Rochefort), 1E 215, fol. 117.
105. Marine (Paris), B¹ 92, fol. 91.
106. We have a contemporary estimate of the quantity and cost of material and labor required to construct a *gabarre* at Nantes in 1777:

Materials/Labor	Value (livres)
15,000 cubic feet of oak	35,750
Plank	3,000
Other wood	2,600
Masts and spars	9,000

Coal and charcoal	600
Irons and nails, incl. casks	15,400
Staves, clapboard	1,000
Anchors	3,500
Utensils, equipment	3,500
Tools, cook stoves, heaters, hardware, tinned sheets	3,250
Labor	22,000
Total	99,600

Marine (Paris), B¹ 84: *Devis estimatif d'une Gabarre de 350 à 400 ton-neaux*, May 1777. This estimate from an unknown source (possibly Chaussade) seems high; an estimate for the construction of a similar craft at the Breton port of St. Malo (apparently including labor) was only 84,540 livres.

107. Marine (Paris), B¹ 95, fol. 214.
108. Marine (Paris), B² 421, fols. 66, 33: Minister to Chaussade, 20 July 1781, and to others, 19 July 1781.
109. See Bamford, *Forests,* pp. 111–12 and notes (Hamburg imports); 170–72 (Cie. du Nord); 196–200 (Anthoine and Black Sea imports).

CHAPTER 10

1. BN, Fonds Fr. 20,700: *Chaussade à Mgr. l'Evêque,* Paris, 19 Dec. 1782, *signé* Chaussade.
2. René de Lespinasse, "Question de droit féodal entre le roi et Champion de Cicé, Evêque d'Auxerre, à propos de la vente des forges de M. de La Chaussade, à Cosne et à Guérigny," *Bulletin de la Société Nivernaise* 18 (1898): 84–85.
3. BN, Fonds Fr. 20,700: *Copie du Deprix entre M. L'Evêque d'Auxerre et M. de la Chaussade,* 4 June 1780; accompanying the document, copies of the three notes, each for 4,000 livres, drawn by Chaussade to L'Evêque d'Auxerre, with the *quittance* signed by Chaussade and Cicé, dated 23 Sept. 1780.
4. Nièvre, D⁴, Forges (Guérigny), *pièce* 143: Contract of sale to the king (*signé*), 31 Mar. 1781 (*notaire* Doillot); other dates are given for this contract in printed accounts.
5. BN, Fonds Fr. 20,700: *De Calonne à Monsieur l'Evêque d'Auxerre,* 31 Jan. 1784, and passim; cf. Lespinasse, "Question," pp. 92–96.
6. BN, Fonds Fr. 20,700, fols. 17–18. But cf. Lespinasse, "Question," p. 89 (200,000 livres).
7. LXXXVI (Aleaume): *Quittance, Chaussade à Pierrecourt,* 8 June 1781; also ibid., *Remboursements* (by Chaussade), 8 Aug. 1781 (2), 13 Aug., 18 Aug., etc., most dating back to 1752–1753 when Chaussade borrowed to expand his physical plant. For the Berthier payment, see n. 8 below.
8. LXXXVI (Aleaume): *Consentement de mainlevée, Les Creanciers délégués sur le Roy de M. de la Chaussade,* 12 Jan. 1792.
9. AN, Y. 473: *Registre d'Insinuations,* 1785, fols. 213–20.
10. LXXXVI (Aleaume): *Remboursement, L'Etat à Pierre Babaud de la Chaussade,* 23 Mar. 1792.

11. LXXXVI (Aleaume): *Traité d'une charge . . . Chaussade à Valleton de Boissière,* 30 Mar. 1780.
12. LXXXVI (Aleaume): *Transport de Bail, Chaussade au Roi,* 6 Oct. 1781.
13. LXXXVI (Aleaume): *Constitutions,* 1 Nov. 1780; *Reconstitutions,* 20 Nov. 1780.
14. LXXXVI (Aleaume): *Constitutions Viagères,* 22 Nov. 1781 (four certificates of 9,000 each).
15. Marine (Paris), B² 421, fol. 93 (table only).
16. LXXXVI (Aleaume): *Quittance au Roy par M. de la Chaussade,* 30 Mar. 1787.
17. O¹*: *Lettres, patentes, scellées, Minutes,* Oct.–Dec. 1780, fol. 21; this suit, to recover 118,000 livres, was apparently not settled in Chaussade's lifetime. LXXXVI (Aleaume): *Inventaire après decès de M. Babaud de la Chaussade,* 5 Mar. 1793.
18. Marine (Paris), B¹ 95, fol. 88.
19. Ibid., fol. 92.
20. Ibid., fols. 123, 154.
21. Ibid., fol. 56.
22. Marine (Paris), C⁷ 14: *Dossier Babaud de la Chaussade, Brevet d'une Pension de 5000 livres,* Versailles, 21 Sept. 1780, *signé* "Louis" (XVI) and (below) "Castries." C⁷ 288 includes a document signed by Chaussade himself, certifying that he had obtained from the king a pension of 6,000 livres [?], "according to the letter that Mgr. De Sartine had very kindly written to him the 21st of September last." Cf. AN, T. 1684: *Papiers Sequestrés: Emigrés et Condamnés.* Item no. 1223 mentions "a brevet de pension" by the last "tyrant au profit dud. Babaud la Chaussade [*sic*] de la somme de neuf mille livres." Paris, 26 Brumaire, *l'an troisième de la république une et indivisible.*
23. Marine (Brest), E. 205: *Dépenses par Apperçu de l'Année 1781.* By contrast, as early as March 1781 it was reported (by M. de La Porte) that the Sieurs Sabatier and Desprez were being placed in an "embarrassing position" by nonpayment, and their situation had not improved by year-end, when they were still owed 1,175,000 of the 1,500,000 livres due them. B¹ 95, fol. 14.
24. *Fournisseurs* importing from the north, like Dujardin de Ruzé and Lambert, and Vizeau, Grand et Cie., and the *munitionnaires* (of foods) absolutely had to be paid promptly, or else they would immediately cease to be able to buy and provision.
25. Marine (Paris), B² 421, fol. 93 (table).
26. Marine (Lorient), 1E⁴ 103, fols. 112–13; this document and much other material at Lorient, and some at Rochefort, was called to the author's attention by G. Beauchesne, then *archiviste en chef* at Lorient. Judging from his name, Beauchesne commented to me, Marion was probably a Malouin.
27. Ibid.; cf. Denise Ozanam, *Claude Baudard de St.-James: tresorier général de la marine et brasseur d'affaires (1738–1787)* (Geneva: et Paris Droz, 1929), pp. 93–95, showing Marion to have been powerfully connected, yet still unable to obtain payment and very much in financial trouble.

28. Marine (Lorient), 1E⁴ 101, fol. 100; 1E⁴ 103, fol. 142; (Paris), B² 425, fol. 67 (table)
29. Marine (Lorient), 1E⁴ 108, fol. 90.
30. Marine (Paris), B² 422, *passim*.
31. LXXXVI (Aleaume): *Vente des Maisons auprés St. Gervais, Berluc et al., à M. de la Chaussade,* 12 Dec. 1780.
32. LXXXVI (Aleaume): *Vente des Maisons, Papillon d'Autroche a Chaussade,* 2 July 1788.
33. LXXXVI (Aleaume): *Inventaire Chaussade,* 5 Mar. 1793.
34. Ibid., and LXXXVI (Aleaume): *Vente de terre de Guichy à M. de la Chaussade,* 12 Mar. 1783.
35. LXXXVI (Aleaume): *Vente de Terre, M. le Marèchal Prince de Soubise à Monsieur Babaud de la Chaussade,* 1 Feb. 1785 (an eight-page description of the properties and transaction).
36. LXXXVI (Aleaume): *Inventaire de Chaussade,* 5 Mar. 1793.
37. Ibid. Apparently the Dumesnil *traité* with Chaussade was filed with Wattel, *notaire* of Abbeville, 22 Aug. 1786; cf. Aleaume, *Inventaire,* 5 Mar. 1793.
38. Ibid.
39. LXXXVI (Aleaume): *Bail à ferme, Chaussade à Louis Cesar Delorgue* [?] *Delisle,* 29 July 1785.
40. Wattel, *notaire* of Abbeville, 7 Apr. 1788, appendix in LXXXVI (Aleaume): *Inventaire de Chaussade,* 5 Mar. 1793.
41. Augier, *notaire* of Amiens, papers in LXXXVI (Aleaume): *Inventaire de Chaussade,* 5 Mar. 1793.
42. LXXXVI (Aleaume): *Inventaire de Chaussade,* 5 Mar. 1793.
43. LXXXVI (Aleaume): *Fixation du dit arpentage passe devant notaire à St. Valery,* 29 May 1792.
44. LXXXVI (Aleaume): *Procuration, Chaussade aux Sieurs Grenot et Guay,* 14 Dec. 1781. Grenot was *notaire royal* at Decize, a town twenty kilometers up the Loire, to the southeast of Nevers.
45. LXXXVI (Aleaume): *Inventaire de Chaussade,* 5 Mar. 1793.
46. LXXXVI (Aleaume): *Inventaire de Chaussade,* 5 Mar. 1793.
47. LXXXVI (Aleaume): *Inventaire de Chaussade,* 5 Mar. 1793.
48. Report, signed and certified J. M. de Vaux, in LXXXVI (Aleaume): *Inventaire de Chaussade,* 5 Mar. 1793.
49. LXXXVI (Aleaume): *Inventaire de Chaussade,* 5 Mar. 1793.
50. Bib. Municipal, Rouen: *Collection Martainville,* nos. 2897 and 2980, Y. 102: *Dossier Babaud,* Franleux, 17 May 1789.
51. LXXXVI (Aleaume): *Testament de Pierre B. de la Chaussade,* 26 Nov. 1787.
52. LXXXVI (Aleaume): *Foy et Hommage, M. Chaillon à M. De la Chaussade,* 13 Jan. 1789.
53. Regarding Chaussade's two sons, one by each wife: the first was Jean Pierre Babaud de Guérigny (died 1775); the second was Pomponne Marie Pierre Babaud de Villemenant; neither son had any evident long-term connection with any phase of their father's timber and iron businesses. However, Chaussade did have good grounds to esteem the business enterprise of his daughter Louise Rose. Had he lived, he would have seen her operating on

her own in the Revolutionary milieu (1793–94, Yr II), living in the rented premises where Chaussade himself resided in late years, 65 rue de Bondy. In that time of "suspects" and terror, her husband (Berthier-Bizy), son, and their "agent" were all arrested, and the Revolutionaries undertook to seal the Berthier business papers. Louise Rose resisted, complained to the authorities, seeking delays and access to them so that operations of the family forges would not be hindered. Later in the Yr II she herself sought and obtained commissions from the *Comité des Armes* to set up drilling machinery and gun lathes (*foreries*) at their forges to manufacture arms ("Approved, but at her own expense"). Concurrently, as Chaussade had done earlier, she was seeking payment of sums due from the state! F¹⁴ 4436 *Louise Rose la Chaussade, femme Berthier, aux citoyens composent l'administration du Comité des Armes*, 8 Germinal, An 2ᵉ; *Requisition*, 16 Germinal, an 2ᵉ; *Decision*, 16 Prairial an 2ᵉ.

54. AN, *Papiers séquestrés:* T 308 (Brossard) and T 1684 (Lumière); cf. Lezardière. Among the assets in Chaussade's estate when he died were nonnegotiable *rentes* received in "payment" for merchandise he delivered to the navy in the years 1753–1754; their value in May 1793 was estimated at 5,700 livres/francs, on face values of over 300,000 livres! LXXXIII (Aleaume): *Inventaire de Chaussade*, 5 Mar. 1793 (dossier).

Epilogue

1. M. W. Flinn has published two volumes on the Crowley firm: *Men of Iron*, and *The Law Book of the Crowley Iron Works*, Surtees Society no. 167 (Durham and London: B. Quaritch, 1957). "The History of the Söderfors Anchor-Works," based on a contemporary (1791) business history by Johan Lundström, (1768–1848), was edited and published by Lars-Eric Hedin and Fritz Redlich, both of whom wrote introductory essays for the reprint of Lundström's history (Boston: Baker Library, Harvard University, 1970).

2. Flinn, *Men of Iron*, pp. 138–43, 153, and passim; Lundström, "Söderfors," pp. 30–33, 36–37; see Chap. 8 above.

3. Chapter 8 above, and Flinn, *Men of Iron*, pp. 138–43 passim.

4. Swedish bar iron, including Söderfors', was then produced from highly reputed ores, charcoal smelted, and charcoal forged.

5. Flinn, *Men of Iron*, pp. 104, 107, 116; cf. H. R. Schubert, *History of the British Iron and Steel Industry* (London: Routledge, 1957), pp. 426, 328.

6. Flinn, *Men of Iron*, p. 131, seems to dissociate cementation from the "German" processes, apparently including shear steel in the latter category.

7. Flinn, *Men of Iron*, p. 94.

8. W. K. V. Gale, *The British Iron and Steel Industry: A Technical History* (Newton Abbot: 1967), pp. 14–15, and passim.

9. Flinn, *Men of Iron*, p. 252.

10. Claude Maire, "Commerce et marché du fer à Paris d'environ 1740 à environ 1815" (Ph.D. Dissertation, McGill University, 1986).

11. Flinn, *Men of Iron*, pp. 75–76.

12. L. E. Hedin, Introduction, "The History of the Söderfors Anchor Works," pp. 35–36, and passim.
13. Marine (Paris), B¹ 72, fol. 66, where Chaussade himself estimated 3,000; but see Chapter 6.
14. Flinn, *The Law Book*, p. xxvi.

Glossary

Allègue—lighter, also a seagoing coasting vessel

Banne—measure of charcoal

Billon—fir balk, rafter or beam

Bois d'hollande—in the terminology of our sources, wood judged unsuited for sale to the navy, but marketable to commercial buyers in the Netherlands (cf. *Kloks, Wagenholz, Pfeifolholz*)

Cens—tax paid to the king or a lord; two types of *cens* were: (1) *cens principal* paid once in a tenant's lifetime, and (2) *cens periodiques* (or seigneurial rent) that the champart sometimes replaced (cf. *champart*)

Censive—person or lands subject to the obligation of paying *cens*

Champart—in seigneurial law, a tax on "part of the field" and on "part of the crop," described as an obligation of a *censive* requiring payment (often in grains) of a share of the crop when the soil is cultivated (the *champart* was not usually subject to arrearage, but was especially burdensome when payment in kind was exacted)

Charbonnage—wood charcoal; royal *ordonnance* decreed that wood cut for *charbonnage* be two feet long, and a *corde* be eight feet long and four feet high

Clou, -oux—nail, nails

Commissaire—supervisory official

Compass timber—see *courbes*

Contrôleur général—secretary of state or minister of finance

Corde—measure of wood (*bois de moulle*) to be ten feet in length, four feet high, pieces forty-two inches in length (and sawn at each end)

Corde—bois de cuisine—firewood for the kitchen, stacked "in the forest" eight feet long, four high with the pieces four feet long

Coupon—raft or small *flotte*

Courbes—curved or "compass" timber; typically, angled knees for supporting decks of a ship

Ecrivain—purser or clerk performing record-keeping or accounting functions at an arsenal, at forest exploitation sites, on special missions or on shipboard

Embauchage—the illegal recruitment of a person in the employ of another

Entreprise—method of conducting government work using contractors, entreprise contractors sometimes being selected by competitive bidding (cf. *régie*)

Etats—assessments, inventories; also annual estimates of prospective needs submitted by each port arsenal

Fenderie—slitting mill for cutting ribbon, strip iron or plate from sheet iron or steel

Fer-blanc—tinplate, tin-coated or -lined iron

Feudiste—lawyer or solicitor specializing in seigneurial (manorial) law and practice, commonly employed by owners of seigneuries to prepare or renew *terriers*

Feuillard mince—ribbon or strap iron

Fief—tenure, obliging holder to render *homage* and fealty and other obligations to a seigneur/lord

Flotte—large raft, of logs or semi-quarried trunks

Flûte—shallow-draft cargo vessel, originally of Dutch design (cf. *gabarre*)

Fourneau—furnace, large-sized heating unit at a smelter or forge

Four—small heating or "reheat" unit

Gabarre (gabare)—*flûte*-type cargo vessel built in France, often shallow draft to facilitate coastal and river operations

Gueuse—pig, produced when iron was poured into a mold

Kloks—small pieces of oak timber, unsuited for navy use (cf. *bois d'hollande*)

Ligne—linear measure (see *pied cube*)

Ligne de la Loire—the Loire valley or basin

Livre (poids de marc)—measure of weight, equivalent to 489 grams (measure of Paris)

Lagement des gens de guerre—much feared public obligation to house and feed transient military personnel

Marinier—in *flottage*, a waterman, raftsman charged with maneuvering and binding logs; a riverman

Marque de fer, marque d'acier—a tax on iron and steel often collected at the producer level, steel paying twenty-five percent more than iron (see these terms in index)

Mâteur, maître mâteur—technician, master craftsman specializing in fabrication of masts (cf. *mât d'assemblage*)

Mât d'assemblage—a made-mast, fabricated by carefully cutting, trimming and fitting component sticks to compose a large-diameter mast when bound with iron rings

Mâtereau, -eaux—small mast, spar

Millier—one thousand

Pfeifolholz—"Whistle" or hollow wood, defective over-mature tree trunks hollow at the core (cf. *bois d'hollande*)

Pied—linear measure, a foot, about three quarters of an inch larger than the contemporary English foot (cf. *pied cube*)

Pied cube—the contemporary English cubic foot was said to be "only eleven *pouces* and three *lignes* by our measure, with twelve *pouces* to the *pied cube*"; a *pouce* was composed of twelve *lignes*

Planche de Bergue—Bergen plank, not less than seven *pieds* long, eleven to twelve in width, twelve to thirteen *lignes* thick

Planche de Coperwick—plank nine to ten *pieds* in length, eleven to twelve *pouces* in width, fourteen to sixteen *lignes* thick

Quintal/-aux—measure of weight, one hundred *livres de Paris* ("instead of being, as in our own metric system, 100 kilos." M. Marion, *Dictionnaire,* 375)

Radeaux—rafts, small *flottes*

Régie—method of carrying on government work using salaried officials to manage or direct operations instead of private contractors (cf. *Entreprise*)

Taillandier—maker of edge-tools; *taillanderie*—edge-tools

Terrier—a document or collection of documents such as avowals, recognitions and lists, declarations and admissions of economic and judicial relationships between tenants and the lord of a *seigneurie* with exact indications of boundaries, tenures and all obligations

Tirage au sort—lottery or drawing, used in conscription

Voye—measure of bulk coal

Wagenholz—literally "venture-wood," commercial timber unsuited to navy needs but judged to be marketable

Sources

This is a study of a series of business enterprises that engaged the attention of one family in eighteenth-century France. The firm's principal customer was the government. For over half a century it was a major supplier of timber and masts to the French navy. Even more important, it was the principal manufacturer and supplier of anchors, irons, hardware, and steel to the French navy in precisely the period of European history now called the industrial revolution. Hence the history of this firm deals with important phases of both naval history and the industrial history of French society.

The business must have been one of the largest of the time and was certainly on a par with the Crowley family business in England. The Crowleys were provisioners of anchors and irons for the British navy and played a key role in the economic and naval history of Britain, as the published works of M. W. Flinn have shown. But in writing the history of this business family, I have been more fortunate than was Professor Flinn, France offering far more extensive and detailed sources than he found in England.

Manuscript Sources

The ledgers, account books, most purchasing, payroll, sales, and shipment records, and other internal papers of the firm's partners have not surfaced. Fortunately, the main lines of the business and many significant operational details can be reconstructed and traced over time using the large number of public and private (notarial) records that do survive.

The archives of the French navy have been indispensable for this study. They include a long series of letterbooks containing copies of communications sent and received, including many *mémoires* and notes to partners in the firm and a parallel series of hundreds of original letters and *mémoires* from the firm. These documents cover the six decades from 1720 to 1781. Thus much of the firm's correspondence with its principal customer is available. Those papers have been supplemented by the archives of French notaries, which record transactions by family members. The surviving acts include copies of contracts, loan agreements, partnerships, and a multitude of other business papers, along with such family documents as dowry and marriage agreements, testaments, and postmortem inventories of estates—all valuable because family affairs, in a family firm, often explain business arrangements, relationships, and history. Finally, the holdings of the general collections of the Archives Nationales and the manuscript collection of the Bibliothèque Nationale have proved rich, with some valuable nests of papers in the *départements* serving as supplements.

Archives Nationales

E 3180 Lorraine: *Edits et arrêts*, Lunéville, 8 may 1726

E 3181 Lorraine: *Edits et déclarations, Ordonnance touchant l'Ordre que S.A.R. veut être observée dans l'administration de ses finances*, Lunéville, 9 fevrier 1729

E 3181 Lorraine: *Edits et déclarations, Ordres pour faire conduire le Sieur Masson à Nancy*, 20 septembre 1729

E 3182^B Lorraine: *Arrêts du Conseil d'Etat*, 13 may 1726

F^4 1962 *Comptabilité générale*, 2 juillet 1741

F^{12} 561 *Manufactures: Généralité d'Orléans* (1778)

F^{12} 680 *De Cheville lettre*, 25 juillet 1780

F^{12} 716 *Advis des deputées du commerce sur le mémoire de la Chaussade*, 23 aout 1771

F^{12} 1234^B *Chargements de M. de Baudry* (1772)

F^{12} 1300 *Petition*, 7 juillet 1773

F^{12} 1302 *Mémoire, traités: Forges de la Chaussade*, 13 juin 1761

F^{12} 1302 *Chaussade lettres* [to Baudry], 9, 16 avril 1764

F^{12} 1302 *Mémoire*, n.d. (c. 1770)

F^{12} 1302 *Chaussade à Trudaine*, 20 septembre 1770

F^{12} 1302 *Arrest du conseil d'état du roi*, 22 fevrier 1773

F^{12} 1302 *Sartine à Mr. le contrôleur général*, 3 fevrier 1775

F^{12} 1316 *Mémoire à Mr. le contrôleur général*, c. may 1760

F^{12} 1316 *Mémoire, Chaussade à Trudaine*, 22 may 1760

F^{12} 1316 *Lettre, Mrs. les Deputés du Commerce*, 1 juin 1760

F^{12} 1316 *Chaussade à Trudaine*, 20 juillet 1760

F^{12} 1316 *Circulaire*, 11 aout 1760

F^{12} 1316 *Chaussade à Trudaine*, 16 septembre 1760

F^{12} 1316 *Chaussade à Trudaine, La Rochelle*, 1 octobre 1760

F^{12} 1316 *Chaussade à contrôleur général*, 8 novembre 1760

F^{12} 1316 *Chaussade à Pellerin*, 8 decembre 1760

F^{12} 1316 *Chaussade lettre*, 15 decembre 1760

F¹² 1316 *Chaussade lettre,* 5 mars 1761
F¹² 1316 *Chaussade lettre,* 1 avril 1761
F¹² 1316 *Mémoire,* n.d. (pre-June) 1761
F¹² 1316 *Mémoire,* 14 aoust 1761
F¹² 1316 *Le Nain à Trudaine,* 10 octobre 1761
F¹² 1316 *Passeports,* 12 avril 1763, 4 novembre 1763
F¹² 1316 *Lettre, passeports, et état,* 6 decembre 1763
F¹² 1568 *Département de la Nièvre: Etat des usines à feu,* Nevers, 30 juin 1807
F¹⁴ 4436 Louise Rose la Chaussade, 8 Germinal an 2ᵉ; *Requisition,* 16 Germinal an 2ᵉ; Decision, 16 Prairial an 2ᵉ.
H¹ 159 (Administration Provinciale): *Procès verbal de visite de la rivière du Doubs faite par M. Masson,* septembre 1735 (58 pp. [67 articles], 22 pp. appendix, 44 maps, illus.; cf. B³ 379 Marine fols. 194–203)
K 2092 XI Montbéliard: *Ordres,* 26 janvier 1726, 15 juin 1736, and *Mémoire responsive aux observations,* 12 novembre 1736
K 2092 XI Montbéliard: *Etat général des arbres exploités dans le comté de Montbéliard par le Sieur Monzé* (surrogate of J. Babaud) (n.d.)
K 2092 XI Montbéliard: *Marché,* Tornaco [governor of the principality of Montbéliard for the duke of Würtemberg] et Sieur Jean Babaud, Paris, 20 octobre 1736; *ratifié,* Stuttgart, 11 novembre 1736
K 2092 XI Montbéliard: *Mémoire responsive aux observations sur le traité du 12 novembre 1736, par le Sieur Prieur* [Masson-Babaud surrogate]
K 2092 XI Montbéliard: *Lettre, Hertzog, Hatzel et al.* [forest officers], dtd Montbéliard, 31 janvier 1737
K 2092 XI Montbéliard: *Mémoire du directeur à M. le Conseiller Beuttel,* n.d.; and *Copie d'une lettre de M. Babaud,* Paris, 28 aoust 1737
K 2092 XI Montbéliard: *Etat des arbres qui doivent martelés,* 3 decembre 1738
K 2092 XI Montbéliard: *Remonstrance de Grand Forestier Sattler,* Stuttgart, 22 janvier 1738
K 2092 XI Montbéliard: *Babaud lettre,* 24 avril 1738
K 2092 XI Montbéliard: *Convention, Babaud et la Conseil de Montbéliard,* Paris, 15 octobre 1738, *signé* J. Babaud
K 2092 XI Montbéliard: *Lettre, signé De Lamprecht et De Rossel,* Montbéliard, 21 may 1739
K 2197 XI Montbéliard: [proposals for establishing navigation and *flottage* on the Doubs], 1730s
KK 1005ᴱ Lorraine: *Project d'arrest, [bois de] Lorraine et Barrois,* 1738
O¹* *(Lettres patentes, scellées) Minutes, octobre–decembre,* 1780
T *Papiers sequestrés,* Brossard, Lumière, Lezardière
V² 42 *Secrétaire du roy,* 12 mars 1743
V² 49, p. 132; V² 70, p. 631; V² 71, p. 700
Y 473 *Registre d'insinuations: Donation, Babaud de la Chaussade,* 1785

BIBLIOTHÈQUE NATIONALE

Fonds Fr. 20,700 *Chaussade à Mgr. l'Evêque d'Auxerre, signé* Chaussade
Fonds Fr. 20,700 *Copie du deprix entre M. l'Eveque et M. de la Chaussade,* 1780

Fonds Fr. 20,700 *De Calonne à Monsieur l'Eveque d'Auxerre*, (1784)

Fonds Fr. 20,701 *Observations particulières sur l'exploitation des Forges de la Chaussade* and *Supplement aux observations sur les Forges de Cosne, dites Forges de la Chaussade*, 1780

Fonds Fr. 29,594 *Marché (Babaud)*, 11 fevrier 1735

Fonds Fr. 29,594 *Arrest du Conseil d'Estat du Roy concernant le flotage* [sic] *des bois de marine sur la rivière Doubs*, 5 novembre 1737 (*imprimé*)

Fonds Fr. 30,279 Item 8: *Babauds, de Bellac et Confolens*

Fonds Fr. 30,297 D'Hozier

Paris Notaries

Chaussade and his business partners lodged or lived in many different parishes of the City of Paris, but they always established themselves in or near what might now be called the central district of modern Paris and normally used the services of notaries located in that area. Hence the historian has not far to go when the archives of the family's notaries are to be consulted.

It was standard practice when I first worked with these notarial papers for a researcher to visit the office of the living incumbent of each notarial post (*étude*) whose archives were known to be relevant to the subject under study in order to seek permission to consult the archives, though the papers themselves were usually on deposit in the Minutérie Central at the Archives Nationales. The researcher was expected to present the *notaire* with a description of the research project being undertaken and also with a list, compiled from the *répertoires* at the Archives Nationales, detailing the exact date and description of each act to be consulted. At some *études* several hundred acts passed by Chaussade and his partners and associates were included in the archive. The twentieth-century notaries with whom I dealt proved to be cooperative, helpful, and more interested than busy *hommes d'affaires* might be expected to be; they readily gave their permission.

The eighteenth-century predecessors of the Paris notaries were also helpful, in their way; they and their clerks wrote legibly, as did most family partners and their clerks. It was otherwise with many of the family's *prête-noms*, surrogates, and associates; worst of all were the papers of small-town and village notaries. Few of them had scribes or clerks, and their own penmanship was apt to be difficult to read. They and their clients were manifestly poorer in many ways than their Parisian contemporaries. Their fees must have been smaller. The paper they used must have been harder to come by and expensive for them since they often used (at least in the Nivernais) small sheets and wrote on both sides, in tiny scrawls using inadequate quill pens. They themselves must have been hard-pressed to decipher some of their own minuscule scribbles. *Hommage* to the patience and the skills of the archivists and their aides, and to the few historians who work extensively with the papers of provincial notaries, as I did not.

Listed below, in chronological sequence under the number and name of the eighteenth-century incumbent of the notarial post involved, are those acts cited in this study. Some acts include important supporting papers; a few (such as the *inventaires*) include substantial appendixes.

CII LINACIER

Constitution et quittance, Masson à C. de la Motte, 23 septembre 1721
Vente, Guillaume de Lange à Jacque Masson, 18 janvier 1724
Vente de bois, Marie de Berthier à Jacque Masson, 16 may 1724
Inventaire après decès de Marie Ann Duru, 23 may 1732
Société déposée and *Dissolution de société* (appendix), 1 octobre 1733
Mariage, Mlle. Masson et [Pierre] Babaud de la Chaussade, 4 mars 1734
Obligation, 6 aoust 1734
Transport, 31 janvier 1735
Société deposée, 14 fevrier 1735
Etat des mairains et rebuts de bois de construction, 14 fevrier 1735
Société déposée J. Babaud, J. Masson, Chaussade, 14 fevrier 1735
Convention, 14 fevrier 1735
Etats deposée, Jean et Pierre Babaud et Masson, 14 fevrier 1735
Compte, constitution et partage, 31 aoust 1735
Compte, Masson à P. Babaud, 4 fevrier 1736
Vente, procureur de Philibert du Bouchat à Masson, 14 juin 1736
Transaction, Masson et B. de la Chaussade, 25 septembre 1736
Quittance, Everat à MM. Masson et Babaud, 26 juillet 1737
Procurations, François de Blumenstein et Chaussade à Alexandre Baudry, 28 septembre 1737
Convention, J. Masson-de Guérigny et MM. Babaud, 6 may 1738
Déclaration par Jacques Masson, 9 aoust 1738
Convention ou société, Nicolas Mathieu et Jean Babaud, 9 aoust 1738
Dissolution de la société, 8 decembre 1738
Inventaire [après decès] de Jean Babaud, 10 janvier 1739
Société, P. Babaud et Marie Boesnier, 9 fevrier 1739
Transport, 11 aoust 1739
Association, Masson. Vve Boesnier et N. Doyen, 6 janvier 1740
Vente de terre, Claude Berger, Seigneur de Frasnay, à J. Masson, 4 juin 1741
Vente de terre, C. Berger à J. Masson, 4 juin 1741
Inventaire après decès de Jacques Masson, 23 juin 1741
Procuration, Chaussade à Pierre Goossens, 19 aoust 1741

XCVI D'Aoust

Procuration deposée, Jean Babaud à Jacques Masson, 4 decembre 1733
Convention et resiliation, Maurepas à Jean Babaud, 14 decembre 1733
Société, J. Arnaud et J. Masson et al., 7 aoust 1734
Procuration deposée, Arnaud à Chaussade, 20 avril 1735
Dissolution de société, Masson et al. et J. Arnaud, 24 mars 1736
Marché de marine pour les ancres, 19 novembre 1736
Marché de marine pour les bois de Montbéliard, 5 janvier 1737
Marché de marine pour la fourniture des bois dans les forts du Ponant, 26 juin
    1738
Marché de marine, 3 octobre 1748

VI Silvestre

Inventaire après decès de Marie Ann Duru, 23 may 1732
Vente, 19 fevrier 1738
Renonciations [Boesnier], 16 novembre 1741
Renonciations [Chaussade], 22 novembre 1741
Procuration, Chaussade à Sr. René Duval, 21 fevrier 1742
Société, 29 mars 1742
Procuration, Chaussade à M. Salmon, 22 juin 1742
Déclaration deposée, Chaussade, 24 septembre 1742
Liquidation des droits et abandonnement, 1 octobre 1742
Constitutions, 1, 8 fevrier 1743
Procurations, Chaussade à Jean Rivét, 28 juillet 1743, 14 avril 1744
Vente de forges et moulins, Chaussade à Boesnier, 5 novembre 1743
*Inventaire après decès de Dame Jacqueline Marie Ann Masson, épouse de Chaus-
    sade*, 18 juin 1744
Presentation, par Chaussade de Jean Juniat, Prestre, 13 juillet 1744
Bail et marché, Chaussade et J. L'Estang, 18 janvier 1745
Vente de moitié de forges, fenderies, et moulins, Boesnier à Chaussade, 21 avril
    1749
Vente de moitié de forge, 23 avril 1752

LXXXVI Magnier

Bail et rente, Mouchy à Chaussade, 30 decembre 1750
Vente de la terre de Richerand, Louis de Creuset à P. Babaud de la Chaussade,
    8 avril 1751
Devis et marché de forge, Ravot, 13 avril 1752 (Cosne)
Devis et marché de forge, Ravot, 13 avril 1752 (Villemenant)
Traité et transport, 23 avril 1752
Constitution, Chaussade à Marie Rouillé, 8 aoust 1752
Traité et convention, les associés, 5 septembre 1752
Procuration, Chaussade et Anne Rose Le Conte de Nonant à Mangin, 7 sep-
    tembre 1752

Quittance, Marie Boesnier à Pierrecourt, 13 fevrier 1753
Constitutions (rentes sur les postes), le Roy à Antoine Mangin, 16 fevrier 1753
Constitutions (rentes sur les postes), le Roy à Pierre Babaud de la Chaussade, 23 mai, 7 juin 1753
Transaction, procureur de Marie Boesnier et P. Babaud de la Chaussade, 7 septembre 1755
Procuration, 21 juin 1756
Traité d'office de conseiller, 28 janvier 1759
Présentation, curé de Guérigny, 29 aoust 1759
Bail à ferme, Cardinal Bernis à Ducatellier et declaration, 29 avril 1766
Remboursement, 5 janvier 1768
Procuration, Chaussade à J. F. Lucas, 3 septembre 1768
Procurations, 16 fevrier 1771
Cie. des Secrétaires du Roy à Chaussade, 11 mars 1772
Procuration, 21 avril 1773
Procuration, Chaussade à Martin Sionville, 17 fevrier 1778

CXV Doyen

Marché, Rouillé à Gabriel Michel et P. B. de la Chaussade, 5 juin 1750
Quittance, Goossens à Chaussade, 5 may 1751

LXXXVI Aleaume

Procuration, Chaussade à Deveaux, 7 septembre 1778
Procuration, Chaussade à M. Chanu, 30 juin 1779
Traité d'une chargé, Chaussade à Valleton de Boissière, 31 mars 1780
Constitutions, 1 novembre 1780
Vente des maisons auprès St Gervais, Berluc à Chaussade, 12 decembre 1780
Remboursements, Chaussade à divers, 1781
Quittance, Chaussade à Pierrecourt, 8 juin 1781
Transport de Bail, 6 octobre 1781
Procuration, Chaussade aux Srs. Grenot et Guay, 14 decembre 1781
Vente de terre, Guichy à Chaussade, 12 mars 1783
Vente de terre, prince de Soubise à Babaud de la Chaussade, 1 fevrier 1788
Bail à ferme, Chaussade à D. Delisle, 29 juillet 1785
Retrocession et transport, 13 juin 1787
Testament, Chaussade, 26 novembre 1787
Vente des maisons, Papillon d'Autroche à Chaussade, 13 janvier 1788
Foy et hommage, M. de Chaillon à M. de Chaussade, 13 janvier 1789
Consentement de mainlevée, 12 janvier 1792
Remboursement, l'etat à P. Babaud de la Chaussade, 23 mars 1792
Inventaire après decès de Mr. Babaud de la Chaussade, 5 mars 1793

Archives de la Marine: Paris

The historian's best general guide to this source, for both *fonds anciennes* (before 1789) and *fonds modernes,* is Etienne Taillemitte, *Les Archives de la Marine Conservées aux Archives Nationales* (Vincennes: Service Historique de la Marine, 1960). More detailed, of course, is that "*breviaire* of all maritime historians," Didier Neuville's *Etat sommaire des Archives de la Marine antérieures de la Révolution* (Paris, 1898). For anyone seeking to locate pertinent material scattered over a long span of years for a thematic or biographical study such as this, Taillemitte's chapter on Serie B, Service Général, offers useful orientation, providing data to supplement and update the old, still indispensable *Inventaire des Archives de la Marine: Série B, Service Général* (Paris, 1885–1913) in 9 volumes.

B¹   Travail du roi et travail du ministre

Vols. 66, 68–69, 71–75, 81, 83–85, 87–90, 92, 95, 99. Includes many extracts prepared for perusal by king or minister, with the minister's observations or decisions.

B²   Ordres du roi et depêches

Vols. 269, 279, 281, 283–84, 286–87, 289–90, 293, 295–96, 298, 300, 302, 304–5, 307–10, 313–14, 316–17, 319–20, 322, 325–26, 331–32, 335, 337, 339, 341, 343, 345, 350, 352–53, 355–56, 358–62, 364, 373, 375, 376, 381, 385, 387, 392, 394, 399, 401, 407, 409, 411, 413, 416–17, 419, 421–22, 425. Out-letter series, consisting of bound volumes of copies or summaries of letters sent; useful for this study until about 1770, when Chaussade began to make more extensive use of surrogates in timber exploitations and directors as well as *régisseurs* for managing his metallurgical enterprises.

B³   Correspondance reçue

Vols. 315, 321–22, 326, 335, 340–41, 348, 355, 361, 367, 371, 379, 382–85, 389, 392–94, 398–99, 402, 405, 409, 411–13, 420, 438, 448, 450, 486, 488, 494, 499, 514, 519, 591, 708. In-letter series, for the most part letters from the ports, *commissaires* on mission or special assignment, or from officials in other government agencies, with some letters from government contractors and private persons.

B⁷   Correspondance consulaire

Vol. 316.

C⁷ PERSONNEL INDIVIDUEL

C⁷ 316 *Dossier Tassin: Instruction* (when dispatched to duty in Berry, 10 Sept. 1722)
C⁷ 168 *Dossier La Rue de Francy*
C⁷ 14 *Dossier B. de la Chaussade*

D³ MATERIEL: BOIS

(Concerned with the general problem of obtaining timber and masts, but little on individual contractors; a few useful *mémoires* on particular problems.)
D³ 5 *Mémoire*, Truguet, 15 janvier 1759
D³ 6 and 8 *Mémoires* (miscellaneous)
D³ 30 *Mémoires* (on forges, anchors and irons)
D³ 31–34 Foundries, forges, and related matters
E205 *Dépenses par apperçu de l'année 1781*

Archives de la Marine: Ports

BREST

Vols. 1E 187, 1E 191, 1E 192, 1E 193, 1E 194, 1E 505, 1E 506, 1E 521, 1E 522, 1E 523

ROCHEFORT

Vols. 1E 145, 1E 148, 1E 210, 1E 215–16
5E² 18 *Mémoire de M. l'Intendant*, juin 1738
Facture d'une Cargaison, janvier 1740
5E² 19 *Mémoire de Sieur Michel*, septembre 1749
5E² 21 *Marché des fers*, 14 aoust 1774
5E² 22 *Marché*, 28 septembre 1776
5E² 23 *Marché*, 10 mars 1780
5E² 23 *Soumission*, 1 janvier 1779
5E² 23 *Prix accordées au . . . Chaussade*, 1780

LORIENT

Vols. E⁴ 55, E⁴ 65, E⁴ 67, E⁴ 68, E⁴ 70, E⁴ 73, E⁴ 74, E⁴ 78, E⁴ 81, E⁴ 83, E⁴ 86, E⁴ 91, E⁴ 101, E⁴ 103, E⁴ 108; 1P4

Archives Départementales

Meurthe-et-Moselle

B 168   *Régistre: Naturalité pour le Sieur Masson,* Lunéville, 20 novembre 1727
fols. 145–46
Jacques Masson, membre, conseil des finances, Lunéville, 20 octobre
1727
fols. 149–50
3F¹ 290   *Copie d'un ordre de Son Altesse Royale,* septembre 1728
Mémoire de Mrs. Paris sur le payement de neuf millions de dettes,
17 fevrier 1725
*Sur les mesures à concerter avec Mrs. Paris pour le payement des
debtes de l'état,* 7 octobre 1728
3F 296   *Etat sommaire des dettes de Son Altesse Royale* (Masson's *mémoire*),
may 1729
Observations sur le recueil des billets paiables aux porteurs, n.d.

Bas-Rhin

C 351   *Lettres de Jean Babaud,* 3 janvier 1732, 20 fevrier 1733
C 351 (6)   *Marché,* 22 aoust 1728
Lettre, Maurepas à M. de Bron, 21 aoust 1732
Observations sur la demande du Sieur Babaud, 1733
Mémoires de Jean Babaud, 15 et 25 mars 1733
Mémoire pour rendre compte, 25 mars 1733
Mémoire, signé François, 25 mars 1733
Lettres Babaud à Bron, 1733, 1734
Le comte de Hanau à M. le Comte de Maurepas, 24 novembre 1734
Mémoire du Sieur Babaud, Strasbourg, 11 mars 1738
Lettres, Babaud à de Bron, 12 juin 1739, and *Lettre à Babaud,*
24 juillet 1739
Passeports, 1740, 1741
Intendant Vanolles, exploitation de bois, 9 fevrier 1747
Passeport, 1748
Mémoire à Mgr. de Vanolles (Alsace) *de Du Pasquier* (Chaussade),
(1748)
Etat des arbres (Meukelbac), 1746–1748

Nièvre

For the history of Chaussade's enterprises, the archives of the Nièvre
are richer than any others. They include the papers of most of the notaries of the region. A very considerable portion of the papers of the
"Etablissement de Guérigny" (Ste-Lorraine des Aciéries de Rombas) have

been deposited there, along with other pertinent papers, including titles and tax series related to Chaussade's estates and the management of his metallurgical enterprises. The eighteenth-century history of the city and of the Nivernais itself is inseparable from that of the Forges de la Chaussade. The following citations of materials used in this departmental archive intermingle a classification and numbering system in use in the 1950s with some citations using the system now in use.

AO *Fonds de Guérigny, Catalogue des Domains*, Villemenant

AO *Fonds de Guérigny, Terrier de Guérigny* (no. 39), 3 mars 1740

AO *Fonds de Guérigny*, Forges (File no. 134) (*liasse*), *Marchés Forges de la Chaussade, Chartrier de Villement, Grosse du contrat d'acquisition*, 5 mars 1750

AO *Série de Villemenant* (description and drawing of properties), c. 1775

AO *Série de Richerand, serie de Demeurs* (accessions), 1773

A² *Forges de la Chaussade: pièces divers*
   Lettre, 19 mars 1743 (*signé* Chaussade)
   Extrait des registres du conseil de S.A.R. Mgr. le prince de Condé, 30 aoust 1764
   Litigation: Chaussade vs. Fougis (Berthier-Bizy), *Dossiers* in B² *Forges*, C⁴ *Forges*, D³–D⁴, E³–E⁴ (*Contestations*)
   Pièces 267, janvier et juin, 1764
   Chaussade à Bort, 20 fevrier 1768
   Notes, 14 aout 1766, 25 novembre 1771
   Jugements de Lieutenant Juge Bailly, 12 novembre 1760
   Ordonnance de police
   Reglemens de Jean François Rouelle (for Guérigny, Saint-Aubin, etc.)
   Relevé des amendes (*état*, prepared for Chaussade), 1769
   Etats des Dépenses (Guérigny), 11 janvier, 1 fevrier 1755
   Pièces divers (on estate management)
   Bourry papers, 14 aout 1766 (*signé* Babaud de la Chaussade)
   Result du mémoire envoyé par M. Goussot au sujet de directes, 1765–1766

C⁴ *Forges (Nièvre) Demeurs: Lettre de M. de la Chaussade*, 1756; *procedure* and *procès* vs. the bishop of Nevers, (1767–1768)

D¹ and D² *Forges de la Chaussade*
   Pièce 49, *Vente, Le Loup à Masson*, 1740
   Pièces 50, 51–62, 90 (*Extrait contre Chaussade*, 8 novembre 1760), 93 (*Extrait de l'arrest du conseil d'état du Roy*, 27 decembre 1729)

D³ and D⁴ *Forges (Nièvre) Guérigny: Liasse, anciens marchés*, including contract for sale to king

E⁴ and E⁵ *Forges (Nièvre) Frasnay: Inventaire des acquisitions; Actes confirmant . . . Sr. Dufaud*, 1773

3E 1-1461 *Notaire François Boury*, Nevers
   Marché de forgeron, Masson et J. Le Gendre, 11 may 1741
   Marché de forgeron, Masson et Claude Parene, 11 may 1741
   Marché, L'Etang, receveur, et Kiesard, forgeron, 28 octobre 1741

3E 1-1461 *Notaire François Morlé: Aveu et dénombrement, Chaussade à Mazarin Mancini*, 10 octobre 1775

F³ *Forges (Nièvre) La Vache,* 1777–1781
H⁴ *Forges (Nièvre) Quittance,* 31 octobre 1755
H⁵ *Forges (Nièvre) Narcy: Mémoire des syndics contre Chaussade,* 1759; *Exploits de M. de la Chaussade,* 1773, 1774

CHER

C 316 *Arrest du conseil,* 29 septembre 1729
       Marché, 4 fevrier 1751
       Marché (imprimé), 14 fevrier 1751
       Marché, Denis et Chaussade, 14 fevrier 1751
       Lettre, Chaussade à Charan, 12 juin 1752
       Lettre, Dodart à Chaussade, 17 juin 1752
       Etat des gens d'affaires de Sieur de la Chaussade, 1 septembre 1752
       Lettre, B. de la Chaussade, dtd Paris, 7 septembre 1752
       Marché, Sieur Claude Le Blanc (prête-nom Jacques Thoreau) de forges des Clavières, 30 novembre 1756
       Marché, 30 novembre 1756
       Machault à Dodart, 23 decembre 1756
       Lettre, Charan, 3 juin 1757
       Lettre, Charan, 8 juin 1757
       Mémoire (Chastignier), 1768
       Réponse (du Sieur Durrie), 1768
       Mémoire (Chaussade), 6 decembre 1768
       Lettres de La Charité, dtd 8, 13 Sept., 29 novembre 1783
       Enquête, 1783 (measures)
C 137 *Marché,* 17 juin 1756
       Etats des ouvriers, 3 octobre 1756, 23 janvier 1757
       De Sartine à De Bron, 13 avril 1777

LOIRE-ATLANTIQUE

C 768 *Mémoire, Babaud de la Chaussade,* 11 septembre 1760
       Directeurs du commerce à Trudaine, 4 novembre 1760
       Mémoire, n.d.
       Chaussade lettre, avec plan de l'opération de change, 14 aoust 1761

Bibliothèque Municipale: Rouen

Collection Martainville Nos. 2897, 2980, Y. 102: *Dossier Babaud, Note sur Franleux,* 17 may 1789.

Archives Municipales: Bellac

Unnumbered *régistres paroissiaux, XVIIIième siècle*

Doucet, R. *Les Institutions de la France au XVIe siècle.* 2 vols. Paris: Picard, 1948.

Flinn, M. W. *Men of Iron: The Crowleys in the Early Iron Industry.* Edinburgh: University Press, 1962.

Ford, Franklin. *Strasbourg in Transition, 1648–1789.* New York: Norton, 1966.

Forster, Robert. *Merchants, Landlords, Magistrates: The Depont Family in Eighteenth Century France.* Baltimore: Johns Hopkins University Press, 1980.

———. *The Nobility of Toulouse in the Eighteenth Century.* Baltimore: Johns Hopkins University Press, 1960.

Gale, W. K. V. *The British Iron and Steel Industry: A Technical History.* Newton Abbot: David and Charles, 1967.

Geiger, Reed. *The Anzin Coal Company, 1800–1833.* Newark: University of Delaware Press, 1974.

Gille, Bertrand. *Les Forges françaises en 1772.* Paris: Domat-Montchrestien, 1960.

———. *Les Origines de la grande industrie métallurgique en France.* Paris: Domat-Montchrestien, n.d.

———. *La Sidérurgie française au XIXe siècle.* Geneva: Droz, 1968.

Gillispie, Charles C. (ed.). *A Diderot Pictorial Encyclopedia of Trade and Industry.* 2 vols. New York: Dover Publications, 1959.

Gras, L. J. *Histoire économique de la métallurgie de la Loire.* Saint-Etienne: Imprimerie Theolier, 1908.

———. *Histoire économique générale des mines de la Loire.* 2 vols. Saint-Etienne: Imprimerie Theolier, 1922.

Guéneau, Louis. *L'Organisation du travail à Nevers aux XVIIe et XVIIIe siècles, 1660–1790.* Paris: 1919.

Gueneau, Victor. *Dictionnaire biographique des personnes nées en Nivernais.* Nevers: 1899.

Henderson, W. O. *Britain and Industrial Europe, 1750–1870: Studies in British Influence on the Industrial Revolution in Western Europe.* Liverpool: University Press, 1954.

Holt, Robert T., and John E. Turner. *The Political Basis of Economic Development: An Exploration in Comparative Political Analysis.* Princeton and Toronto: Van Nostrand, 1966.

Hyde, Charles K. *Technological Change and the British Iron Industry, 1700–1870.* Princeton, N.J.: Princeton University Press, 1977.

Jal, Auguste. *Glossaire nautique: répertoire polyglotte de termes de marine anciens et modernes.* Paris: Firmin Didot Frères, 1848.

Labrousse, Ernest and Fernand Braudel, eds. *Histoire économique et sociale de la France.* 5 vols. Paris: Presses Universitaires de France, 1970–1980.

Lacour-Gayet, G. *La Marine militaire de la France sous le règne de Louis XV.* Paris: Honoré Champion, 1910.

Landes, David S. *The Unbound Prometheus.* Cambridge, Mass.: Harvard University Press, 1969.

Le Bouedec, Gérard. "Nantes et la Compagnie des Indes." Unpublished thesis, no date.

Léon, Pierre. *La Naissance de la grande industrie en Dauphiné (fin du XVIIe–1869).* 2 vols. Paris: Presses Universitaires de France, 1954.

————. *Les Techniques métallurgiques dauphinoises au XVIIIe siècle.* Paris: Hermann, 1961.

Lespinasse, René de. *Depêches et mémoires du ministère de la Marine sur les forges et charbons du Nivernais pendant les guerres de Louis XIV.* Nevers: G. Vallière, 1895.

Lüthy, Herbert. *La Banque protestante en France de la Révocation de l'Edit de Nantes à la Révolution.* 2 vols. Paris: SEVPEN, 1959–1961.

Lyonnet, Jean. *Les Gens de métiers à Nevers à la fin de l'ancien régime.* Paris: Domat-Montchrestien, 1941.

Mackrell, J. Q. C. *The Attack on "Feudalism" in Eighteenth Century France.* Toronto: University of Toronto Press, 1973.

Maire, Claude. "Commerce et marché du fer à Paris d'environ 1740 à environ 1815." Ph.D. dissertation, McGill University, Montreal, 1986.

Mantoux, Paul. *The Industrial Revolution in the Eighteenth Century.* Preface by T. S. Ashton. New York: Harper, 1961.

Marion, Marcel. *Dictionnaire des institutions de la France aux XVIIe et XVIIIe siècles.* 2nd edition. Paris: Picard, 1968.

Martin, Gérard. *Le Mariage à Cosne au XVIIIe siècle (Mémoire de maîtrise).* Besançon: 1979–1980.

————. "La Vie municipale à Cosne au XVIIIe siècle." Thesis, Besançon, 1983.

Martin, Germain. *La Grande industrie en France sous le règne de Louis XIV (1660–1715).* Paris: A. Rousseau, 1899.

Massé, Alfred. *Monographies nivernaises: Canton de Pougues.* Nevers: Th. Ropiteau, 1912.

Matthews, George T. *The Royal General Farms in Eighteenth Century France.* New York: Columbia University Press, 1958.

Meyer, Jean. *L'Armement nantais dans la deuxième moitié du XVIIIe siècle.* Paris: SEVPEN, 1969.

————. *La Noblesse bretonne aux XVIIIe siècle.* 2 vols. Paris: SEVPEN, 1966.

Mirot, Albert. *Manuel de géographie historique de la France.* 2 vols. Paris: Picard, 1948, 1950.

Mousnier, Roland. *The Institutions of France Under the Absolute Monarchy, 1598–1789: Society and the State.* Trans. Brian Pearce. Chicago: University of Chicago Press, 1979.

Nef, John U. *The Rise of the British Coal Industry.* 2 vols. London: C. Routledge & Sons Ltd., 1932.

Ozanam, Denise. *Claude Baudart de St. James, trésorier général de la marine et brasseur d'affaires (1738–1787).* Geneva and Paris: Droz, 1969.

Parker, Harold T. *The Bureau of Commerce in 1781 and Its Policies with Respect to French Industry.* Durham, N.C.: Carolina Acadia, 1979.

Raistrick, Arthur. *Dynasty of Ironfounders: The Darbys and Coalbrookdale.* London and New York: Longmans Green, 1953.

————. *Quakers in Science and Industry.* Newton Abbot: David and Charles, 1968.

Reading, Douglas K. *The Anglo-Russian Commercial Treaty of 1734.* New Haven: Yale University Press, 1938.

Remond, André. *John Holker, manufacturier et grand fonctionnaire en France au XVIIIe siècle, 1719–1786.* Paris: Rivière, 1945.

Richard, Guy. *Noblesse d'affaires au XVIIIe siècle.* Paris: Colin, 1974.

Rouff, Marcel. *Les Mines de charbon en France au XVIIIe siècle (1744–1791).* Paris: Rieder et Cie, 1922.

Schmookler, Jacob. *Invention and Economic Growth.* Cambridge, Mass.: Harvard University Press, 1966.

Schubert, H. R. *History of the British Iron and Steel Industry.* London: Routledge, 1957.

See, Henri. *Les classes rurales en Bretagne du XVIe siècle à la Revolution.* Paris: V. Giard et E. Brière, 1906.

———. *Histoire économique de la France: le môyen âge et l'ancien régime.* Vol. I. Paris: Colin, 1948.

Thuillier, Guy. *Aspects de l'économie nivernaise au XIXe siècle.* Paris: Colin, 1966.

———. *Economie et société nivernaises au debut du XIXe siècle.* La Haye: Mouton, 1974.

———. *Georges Dufaud et les débuts du grand capitalisme dans la métallurgie, en Nivernais, au XIXe siècle.* Paris: SEVPEN, 1959.

Tramond, Joannes. *Manuel d'histoire maritime de la France des origines à 1815.* Paris: Société d'editions géographiques, maritimes et coloniales, 1947.

Vidalenc, Jean. *La Petite Métallurgie rurale en Haute Normandie sous l'ancien régime.* Paris: Domat-Montchrestien, 1946.

Woronoff, Denis. *L'Industrie sidérurgique en France pendant la révolution et l'empire.* Paris: Editions de l'Ecole des hautes études en sciences sociales, 1984.

ARTICLES, ESSAYS, AND PAMPHLETS

Bamford, P. W. "Entrepreneurship in Seventeenth and Eighteenth Century France: Some General Conditions and a Case Study." *Explorations in Entrepreneurial History* 9, 4 (1957): 204–13.

———. "French Shipping in Northern European Trade, 1660–1789." *Journal of Modern History* 26 (1954): 207–19.

Boëthius, B. "Swedish Iron and Steel, 1660–1955." *Scandinavian Economic History Review* 6, 2 (1958): 144–75.

Boissonnade, Prosper. "Trois Mémoires relatifs à l'amélioration des manufactures de France sous l'administration des Trudaine (1754)." *Revue d'Histoire Economique et Sociale* 7 (1914–1915): 56–86.

Bremner, Robert H. "Privilege and Labor." Unpublished.

Cahen, Léon. "Ce qu'enseigne un pèage du XVIIIe siècle: La Seine, entre Rouen et Paris, et les caractères de l'économie Parisienne." *Annales d'Histoire Economique et Sociale* 3 (1931): 487–517.

Chevalier, Jean. "La Mission de Gabriel Jars dans les mines et les usines britanniques, en 1764." *Transactions, Newcomen Society* 26 (1947–1949): 57–68.

Cole, Arthur H., and George B. Watts. "The Handicrafts of France as Recorded in the *Description des Arts et Métiers, 1761–1788.*" Kress Library Series. Cambridge, Mass.: Baker Library, Harvard University, 1952.

Corbier, C. "Les établissements impériaux de la marine française: Les forges de la Chaussade." *Revue Maritime* 1 (1869): 257–92, 709–20.

————. "Notice historique sur les forges impériales de la Chaussade." *Bulletin, Société Nivernaise des Sciences, Lettres et Arts* 4 (1870): 350–94, 427–60.

Crafts, N. F. R. "Industrial Revolution in England and France: Some Thoughts on the Question, 'Why Was England First?'" *Economic History Review* 30 (1977): 429–41.

Crouzet, François. "England and France in the Eighteenth Century: A Comparative Analysis of Two Economic Growths." In (ed.) Marc Ferro, *Social Historians in Contemporary France: Essays from* Annales, pp. 59–86. New York: Harper, 1972.

Daumas, Maurice. "Le Mythe de la révolution technique." *Revue d'Histoire des Sciences* no. 4 (1963): 291–302.

Drouillet, M. "Les Forges de Cosne en Nivernais et la fabrication des ancres de marine au XVIIIe siècle." *Revue d'Histoire Economique et Sociale* 25 (1939): 313–23.

Freudenberger, Herman, and Fritz Redlich. "The Industrial Development of Europe: Reality, Symbols, Images." *Kyklos* 17 (1964): 372–402.

Gaulejac, Bernard. "La Loire commerciale." *Annales des Pays Nivernais,* no. 20 (1978).

Gauthier, G. "Ancienne mesures du Nivernais comparées à celles du système métrique." Pamphlet. Paris, 1905.

Gille, Bertrand. "Les Archives de l'établissement de Guérigny (Société-Lorraine des Aciéries de Rombas)." In "Inventaires d'archives privées." Typescript, n.d.

————. "*L'Encyclopédie,* dictionnaire technique." *Revue d'Histoire des Sciences et de Leurs Applications* 5 [*numéro spéciale*] (1951–1952): 26–53.

————. "Lents progrès de la technique." *Revue de Synthèse* 32 (1953): 69–88.

————. "Un exemple de la formation de la grande industrie: les forges de la Chaussade." *Bulletin de la Société Nivernaise des Sciences, Lettres et Arts* 30 (1938–1942): 366.

Guichon de Grandpont. "Les intendants de la marine au port de Brest." *Bulletin de la Société Académique de Brest* 15 (1890).

Harris, John R. "Attempts to Transfer English Steel Techniques to France in the Eighteenth Century." In (ed.) Sheila Marriner, *Business and Businessmen,* pp. 199–233. Liverpool: University Press, 1978.

————. "Industry and Technology in the Eighteenth Century: Britain and France." Inaugural Lecture, University of Birmingham, 27 May 1971.

————. "The Rise of Coal Technology." *Scientific American* 231 (August 1974), pp. 92–97.

————. "Skills, Coal, and British Industry in the Eighteenth Century." 61 (1976): 167–82.

Hildebrand, K.-G. "Foreign Markets for Swedish Iron in the Eighteenth Century." *Scandinavian History Review* 6, 1 (1958): 1–52.

Huard, Georges. "Les Planches de l'*Encylopédie* et celles de la *Description des Arts et Metiers* de l'Académie des Sciences." *Revue d'Histoire des Sciences* 5 (1951–1952): 238–49.

Jenkins, Rhys. "The Reverberatory Furnace with Coal Fuel, 1612–1712." *Transactions, Newcomen Society* 14 (1933–1934): 67–81.

Léon, Pierre. "L'Industrialisation en France, en tant que facteur de croissance économique du début du XVIIIe siècle à nos jours." In *Première conference d'histoire économique internationale,* Stockholm, pp. 163–204. Paris and La Haye: Mouton & Co., 1960. Editors: *Ecole Pratique des Hautes Etudes.*

———. "Techniques et civilisations du fer dans l'Europe du XVIIIe siècle." *Annales de l'Est* 6 (1956): 227–64.

———. "Tradition et machinisme dans la France du XVIIIe siècle." *Information Historique* 17 (1955): 5–14.

Lespinasse, René de. "Question de droit féodal entre le roi et Champion de Cicé . . . à propos de la vente des forges de M. de La Chaussade à Cosne et Guérigny." *Bulletin, Société Nivernaise des Sciences, Lettres et Arts* 18 (1898): 84–108.

Levy-Leboyer, M. "Les Processus d'industrialisation: le case de l'Angleterre et de la France." *Revue Historique* 239, 281–98.

Locke, Robert R. "French Industrialization: The Roehl Thesis Reconsidered." *Explorations in Economic History* 18 (1981): 415–33.

Mackrell, John. "Criticism of Seigniorial Justice in Eighteenth-Century France." In (ed.) John F. Bosher, *French Government and Society, 1500–1850: Essays in Memory of Alfred Cobban,* pp. 123–44. London: Athlone Press, 1973.

Mott, R. A. "Abraham Darby (I and II) and the Coal-Iron Industry." *Transactions, Newcomen Society* 31 (1957–1958): 49–93.

Ozanam, Denise. "La Naissance du Creusot." *Revue d'Histoire de la Sidérurgie* 4 (1963): 103–18.

Roehl, Richard. "French Industrialization: A Reconsideration." *Explorations in Economic History* 13, 233–81.

Schmookler, Jacob. "Economic Sources of Inventive Activity." *Journal of Economic History* 22 (1962): 1–20.

Scoville, Warren C. "The Huguenots and the Diffusion of Technology." *Journal of Political Economy* 60 (1952): 294–311, 392–411.

Stowers, Arthur. "Watermills, c. 1500–c. 1850." In Charles Singer, E. J. Holmyard, et al. (eds.), *A History of Technology,* 4:199–213. Oxford: Clarendon Press, 1975.

———. "Observations on the History of Water Power." *Transactions, Newcomen Society* 30 (1955–1957): 239–56.

Index